Authority
and Challenge

Who are they?

"Messieurs de
Vendôme"

Chalais Conspiracy
1626

A PORTRAIT OF EUROPE
EDITORS: MARY R. PRICE AND DONALD LINDSAY

A Portrait of Europe 1300–1600

Authority
and Challenge

Donald Lindsay
and
Mary R. Price

Oxford University Press · 1975

Oxford University Press, Ely House, London W. 1

GLASGOW NEW YORK TORONTO MELBOURNE WELLINGTON
CAPE TOWN IBADAN NAIROBI DAR ES SALAAM LUSAKA ADDIS ABABA
DELHI BOMBAY CALCUTTA MADRAS KARACHI LAHORE DACCA
KUALA LUMPUR SINGAPORE HONG KONG TOKYO

Filmset by Oliver Burridge Filmsetting, Ltd, Crawley, Sussex
and printed in Great Britain at the University Press, Oxford
by Vivian Ridler, Printer to the University

Editors' Preface

Recently there have been marked changes in the methods of teaching history and in our conception of what it is possible for amateur historians to experience and enjoy. The changes are designed to encourage them to make use of sources very early, to penetrate as deeply as they can into historical topics, to enjoy discovering for themselves what life was like in the past, and to develop their own individual interests. All this has had a very stimulating, in many cases a re-vitalizing, effect upon our presentation of the subject, and not least upon our attitude to the kind of books we need. There must now be few places where students are provided with only a single book for a year's work. Instead they are introduced to a multiplicity of publications dealing with separate topics, movements, and personalities, and the study of history is much enriched for them.

In view of this trend it may be asked if there is any place today for a series of background books such as these. Are they not quite outmoded and useless, if not positively harmful? We do not think so, for we are convinced that, if historical knowledge at any level is to be of lasting value and interest, such knowledge must not be piecemeal, but in the end set in a firm framework. Thus, in addition to books dealing with separate topics, young historians need books which will help to create this framework. It is not sufficient to relate topics solely to the history of our own country; historians will want books about the larger units with which their own country is particularly and obviously linked, about Europe in the first place, and ultimately about the world. The need for as much knowledge about the history of Europe as possible in order to lead to better mutual understanding is today more important than ever before.

In these new Portrait books we have tried to avoid the superficiality of a brief chronological recital of events, and instead have chosen to highlight significant movements and people. Above all we have, wherever possible, introduced in the text and in the illustrations the sources of history, believing that this is one of the best ways to kindle the minds and imagination of the readers.

M.R.P.
D.D.L.

Contents

Acknowledgements

Black and white photographs are reproduced by kind permission of the following:

A.C.L., Brussels, page 127; Aerofilms, 144; William Anderson: *Castles of Europe* (Paul Elek Ltd., 1970), 147; Archives Photographiques, 114; *European Brasses* ed. A. C. Bouquet (B. T. Batsford Ltd., 1967), 167; Biblioteca Apostolica Vaticana, 31; Bibliotheque Nationale, Paris, 49, 57, 67, 124, 159, 211, 326; Bibliotheque Royale, Brussels, 161; Bodleian Library, Oxford, 52, 104, 334 (bottom); British Museum, 12, 15, 17, 21, 22, 41, 61, 64, 70, 73, 151, 334 (top); Brooklyn Museum, New York, 84; Dean and Chapter of Hereford Cathedral, 329; Department of the Environment (Crown copyright), 44, 45, 152, 153, 313; Earl of Leicester, 130; French Government Tourist Office, 198; Gemäldegalerie, Berlin, 117; Giraudon, 14, 54, 58, 76, 77, 78, 87, 115, 133, 154, 155, 188, 196 (centre), 201, 288; Sonia Halliday, 245, 247, 251, 252–53, 256, 258; Kunsthistorisches Museum, Vienna, 106, 197, 281; Kunstmuseum, Winterthur, 231; Leicester Museum, 38; Leipzig University Library, 342; Lutherhalle, Wittenberg, 221; Mansell Collection, 11, 26, 29, 32, 103, 156–57, 163, 172, 177, 179, 181, 184, 185, 186, 189, 194, 204, 217, 262, 273, 285, 338; Metropolitan Museum of Art, New York: Robert Lehman Collection, 113; The Cloisters Collection, 118–19; gift of J. Pierpont Morgan, 1900, 332; Musee Guimet, Paris, 283; Museo de America, Madrid, 299; Museo Naval, Madrid, 335; Museo del Prado, Madrid, 95, 99, 206, 293; Museu Nacional de Arte Antiga, Lisbon, 330; Museum Boymans van Beuningen, Rotterdam, 236; National Gallery of Art, Washington, 123; National Gallery, 190, 347; National Portrait Gallery, 69; National Trust, 134; Novosti Press, 263, 264, 265, 268, 274, 275; Oeffentliche Kunstsammlung, Basel, 225; Photographie Bulloz, 55, 303, 305; Remy, 165; Rijksmuseum, Amsterdam, 208; Royal Collection (Crown copyright), 196 (top); Royal Commission of Historical Monuments, 140, 164, 166; Science Museum (Crown copyright), 345; Staatliche Kunstsammlungen, Dresden, 227; Staatliche Museen, West Berlin, 214; Topkapi Palace Museum, Istanbul, 255; Victoria and Albert Museum, 309; Woburn Abbey, by kind permission of his Grace the Duke of Bedford, 321.

Colour plates are reproduced by kind permission of: William Anderson: *Castles of Europe* (Paul Elek Ltd., 1970), facing page 144; Metropolitan Museum of Art, New York, facing page 168 (bottom); National Gallery, facing page 169; National Gallery, Prague, facing page 168 (top); Scala Instituto Fotografico Editiorale, facing page 145.

List of maps

Bronze statue of Boniface VIII. He is wearing the high papal tiara, though not the elaborate one which he himself designed.

Prologue: The Holy Year

The year was 1300. In February, standing on the balcony of his new Lateran Palace in Rome, Pope Boniface VIII proclaimed the first Jubilee, or Holy Year, during which faithful Christians would celebrate the long life of the Church and also have the chance to earn a special reward. All foreign pilgrims who made the journey to Rome and there visited seven important churches thirteen times, where they would make their confession and receive the sacrament, were promised full pardon for their sins. Those living in or near Rome could receive their pardon after visiting these churches thirty times. Those unable to make the journey were given the same promise of forgiveness in return for paying the travelling expenses of a poor pilgrim. There are few, if any, rigid dividing lines in history, and 1300 by itself is not of great importance. It is, however, a useful date to mark the moment when Boniface VIII made a dramatic attempt to insist that the ancient, world-wide authority of the Church, whose laws no mere national frontiers could keep out, was far above that of all earthly rulers like kings and princes.

Boniface had become pope in 1294 at the age of 77. He had succeeded a saintly old man, Celestine V, who had lived most of his life as a hermit and who had little wish and no ability to rule the Church. In the Vatican, Celestine had wandered pathetically from room to room, munching a dry loaf and saying that it was the only food worth eating, an opinion not shared by the clergy and courtiers around him. After less than four months as pope he declared that in a dream he had heard a voice telling him that he should give up his great office and return to his hermit's cell. Rumour maintained that the 'voice' was in fact that of Boniface whispering through a speaking-tube. Whether that is true or not, Celestine was succeeded by Boniface, a worldly politician, famed for his skill as a lawyer and known as a first-rate organizer. He was a man of hot temper, which he could not control, insolent to those who disagreed with him, and determined to rule as an autocrat. His courage in pursuing his policy regardless of what opponents might say or do was grudgingly admitted by his many enemies, but it was also said that no pope before him had ever been so intent on using his position as a way of bringing wealth and fame to members of his own family.

Boniface VIII presiding over a meeting of the cardinals. The documents are papal decrees. Here Boniface is wearing the triple tiara.

Boniface would have been much more successful in achieving his aims if he had lived a hundred years earlier. What he was determined to do was to make the power of the pope far greater than it had been for many years, if possible even greater than it had been in the days of Innocent III (1198-1216), the most powerful pope of the Middle Ages. Unfortunately for Boniface, times were changing. Strong kings of new nation states, like Philip IV of France and Edward I of England, had no intention of allowing the pope to interfere with the way in which they ruled their countries. Yet this is what Boniface claimed as his right.

In St. Luke's account of the Last Supper mention is made of two swords taken by the disciples to the Garden of Gethsemane. St. Bernard of Clairvaux, the famous monk who lived in the first half of the twelfth century, developed the idea that as at least one of the two swords had been wielded in Gethsemane by St. Peter, they must now belong to the pope, who, as bishop of Rome, was

St. Peter's successor. One sword, said St. Bernard, represented the spiritual power of the pope, that is his right to rule over the Church; the other represented the duty of emperors and kings to defend the pope and the Christian faith. Thus the pope, it was said, was not only head of the Church but, as ruler over all mankind, was in the last resort supreme over all earthly rulers. Since the whole of western European society in the Middle Ages rested on an acceptance of the truth of Christianity, it was argued that the pope, as God's representative on earth, could not be challenged in any way.

Boniface, with the help of his lawyers, maintained this view to the full. As one man wrote: 'No one can in full justice hold a field or a vineyard from anyone at all except in submission to the Church and through the Church.' A little later a Spanish monk was to sum up all that Boniface stood for in these words: 'The pope governs all, rules all, disposes of all, decides all at his discretion. He may deprive anyone of his rights as he sees fit.' From the moment of his accession Boniface made it clear that he intended to exert the papal power to the uttermost.

Boniface loved pageantry and the stately ceremonies of the Church. His great chance to make plain his position came in 1300 when, surrounded by cardinals clad in the purple which had once been the Roman emperor's colour, he proclaimed the Jubilee, or Holy Year. In addition to the purple, he had given his cardinals the right to wear a red cloak to match the cardinal's hat, first bestowed in 1245, a colour supposed to show that a cardinal was always ready to be martyred for his faith; but to Boniface the purple mattered more than the red. A rising young artist from Florence, Giotto, was commissioned to perpetuate the scene by painting a fresco for the Lateran Palace; in this Boniface was shown addressing the excited crowd below his balcony. We know from chronicles that throughout the Holy Year Boniface several times appeared to the pilgrims dressed in imperial robes, with two swords borne before him. In front of the swords marched two heralds shouting 'I am Caesar! I am the Emperor!', which was a curious slogan for the head of the Christian Church.

Boniface also designed a new papal tiara, which was to be an ell in height (the standard measurement used by Noah when he built the Ark of Salvation) and round like the world over which the pope ruled. Apart from the splendid rubies, emeralds, sapphires, and pearls which adorned the tiara, two golden diadems encircled it. One, representing the spiritual power of the pope, had always been on the crown; the second was added by Boniface to show that he also possessed the temporal power, that is power over earthly rulers. It was a determined attempt to revive and increase the ancient claims of the papacy; but unfortunately for Boniface he made it at the very moment when new claims were being put forward by equally determined men bent on uniting and increasing the power of the countries over which they ruled. The inevitable clash had begun long before the Holy Year and Boniface cannot have been surprised that no ruler came to Rome in person to attend the celebrations, though most sent an ambassador or special agent to represent them.

★　★　★

There was nothing new in the idea of going on a pilgrimage. For centuries before the birth of Christ the Israelites had been accustomed to 'go up to Jerusalem' at the great Jewish festivals; and this custom was taken over by Christians from the second century onwards, when pious folk began to travel to Rome to pray at the tombs of St. Peter and St. Paul. There were many reasons why people went on pilgrimage: to show sorrow for sin; to seek a cure for sickness or disease; to fulfil the duty laid on them as a punishment by a priest; to pray for success in war or some private venture. To strengthen devotion to God in one way or another was the cause of every pilgrimage.

There were three main places to which pilgrims went. The Holy Land naturally ranked first on the list and those achieving this ambition were known as palmers, a name taken from the image of the palm leaf worn around their necks in memory of the waving palms with which Jesus Christ had been greeted as he rode into Jerusalem. Rome, the heart of Christendom, was the second great centre and pilgrims reaching Rome could wear the emblem of the vernicle (or veil) of St. Veronica. Chaucer's Pardoner in the *Canterbury Tales* was one of these:

> A vernicle had he sewn upon his cap,
> His wallet lay before him in his lap,
> Brimful of pardons, come from Rome all hot.

Above *A group of pilgrims, such as Chaucer might have known, returning from Canterbury.*

Left *Pilgrims returning from Compostella. Many of them have strings of cockleshells hanging around them. The picture comes from a fifteenth-century Book of Hours belonging to the Duchess of Burgundy.*

The third centre was Compostella in north-west Spain where, according to legend, St. James, first of the twelve apostles to be martyred, was burned. The 'Jacobites' or 'Jacquots', as those who had worshipped here were nicknamed, were distinguished by the string of cockle-shells worn around their hats.

Not everyone had the time or the opportunity to travel as far as one of these three cities. Fast travellers could cover the distance from Canterbury to Rome in fifty days in the early twelfth century, but the ordinary pilgrim took much longer. When a voyage was involved in going to the Holy Land and back, the journey might well mean an absence from home of up to three years. Every country had its own shrines and places of worship, which were almost as important as the Holy Land, Rome, and Compostella. In Normandy, Mont-Saint-Michel was the sanctuary of the archangel Michael; in England crowds came to Canterbury to the tomb of

15

Thomas à Becket 'the holy blisful martyr for to seke'; in Germany the cathedral at Cologne contained what was believed to be the tomb of the Three Wise Men; in Italy the most popular places of pilgrimage, apart from Rome, were Assisi and the other towns associated with St. Francis; at Bari it was possible to venerate the bones of St. Nicholas of Myra, a saint more familiar to us as Santa Claus.

The pilgrim routes had long been established by tradition, and after Eastertide, when the worst of the winter's mud would have begun to dry, the tracks and rough roads were thronged with travellers. Accurate figures are not easy to obtain, but it is thought that some half a million people visited Compostella every year. In 1064, even though Jerusalem was in Muslim hands and the journey therefore especially dangerous, no fewer than 7,000 pilgrims saw the holy places. More than two million pilgrims were said to have been in Rome in 1300, though it is possible that those responsible for organizing the Holy Year may have made a pardonably boastful exaggeration. For travellers able to read there were guide-books describing the towns through which the pilgrims would pass and a list of the cathedrals, churches, tombs of saints, and sacred relics which should not be missed. One of the most famous of these has survived. It is the *Guide du Pélerin* (The Pilgrim's Guide), thought to be written in 1140 by a monk from Poitou, Aimery Picaud, for the benefit of those travelling to Compostella. The information given must have been helpful, though sometimes daunting:

Then you must count on three tiring days to cross the Landes Bordelais [in south-west France]. It is a desolate country where all is lacking; there is neither bread, nor wine, nor meat, nor fish, nor water nor springs; villages are rare on this sandy plain which nevertheless abounds in honey, millet, panic [another sort of millet] and pigs. If by chance you cross the Landes in summer, make sure you protect your face from the enormous flies that proliferate there, and which they call wasps or horse-flies.

Picaud clearly thought little of Navarre either, where 'the whole household, servant and master, maid and mistress, eat all alike, out of the same stewpot, the food has been mixed together there, and that with their hands, without recourse to spoons, and they drink from the same goblet.'

Since few could afford the luxury of a horse or donkey, the great mass of men, women, and children travelled on foot, clad in the pilgrim's garb of a large hat with upturned brim, a leather hood, a heavy cloak marked with a scarlet cross, and a 'scrip', or wallet, hanging from a belt. In their hands they carried a 'bourdon', or crooked staff, which with the 'scrip' had been handed to them in church by a priest after he had said Mass and offered special prayers for their safety.

The first part of a route map from London to the Holy Land. The map begins at the bottom of the left-hand column where London is shown; then Rochester, Canterbury, and at the top Dover Castle. The next stage of the journey from Calais to Reims is on the right-hand side, again starting at the bottom of the page.

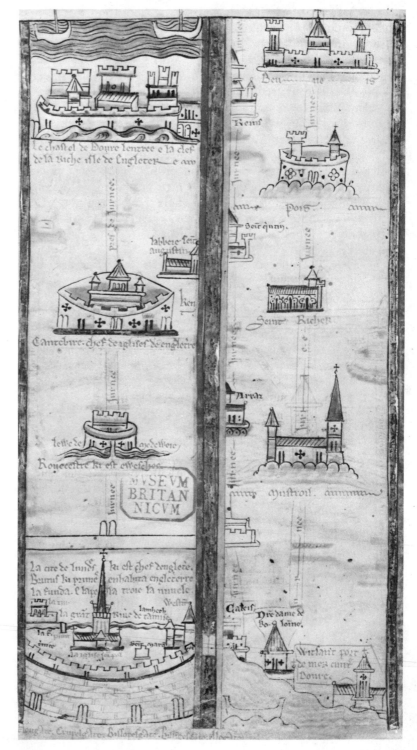

The hazards of bad weather and the dangers from thieves and robbers could not be avoided, but care was taken to make provision for the journey in other ways. English pilgrims could make currency arrangements for the next spring's journey when they visited Winchester Fair in September. At other fairs on the Continent it was possible, if your credit was good, to organize drafts on foreign merchants along the main routes. An even more impressive piece of pilgrim organization was the regular travel agencies, which existed as early as the fourteenth century to help pilgrims travelling to the Holy Land when they reached Venice, Genoa, or Marseilles. Venice did the biggest trade and had probably the most efficient organizers. We know about this from a fifteenth-century Dominican friar, Brother Felix Fabri, who twice made the journey to the Holy Land and who became an experienced traveller. On his second journey he describes the Venetian system for booking passages on the galleys:

In this square, before the great door of St. Mark's Church there stood two costly banners, raised aloft on tall spears, white and ensigned with a red cross . . . By these banners we understood that two galleys had been appointed for the transport of pilgrims; for when the lords of Venice beheld a number of pilgrims flocking together there, they chose two nobles from among their senators, and entrusted the care of the pilgrims to them. The names of these were, of the first, Master Peter de Lando, and the second, Master Augustine Contarini. The servants of these two noblemen stood beside the banners, and each invited the pilgrims to sail with their master, and they endeavoured to lead the pilgrims, the one party to the galley of Augustine, the other to that of Peter; the one party praised Augustine and abused Peter, the other did the reverse.

Unless they were very careful, pilgrims would find that their baggage had been seized and taken on board in the general hubbub and confusion. To entice them, Cretan wines and sweetmeats from Alexandria were displayed in the stern and were handed out by the captain as the bewildered pilgrims boarded the ship. Once committed to a particular captain, there was no guarantee of an immediate departure. Bad weather or danger from Turkish attack at sea might well mean quite long delays.

In 1300, by some means or another, more pilgrims than ever before came from all parts of Europe to Rome to celebrate the Holy Year and to take advantage of the offer which Boniface VIII had made. After all the strains and dangers of the journey, the sight of Rome must have been overwhelming to them as they gazed down from the top of Monte Mario on the wonders of churches and palaces, on countless houses, and on the vast ruins of the old imperial Rome spread out below them.

On arrival in Rome it was no easy matter to get a night's lodging unless a high price could be paid. This meant that the poorer pilgrims had to sleep outside the city, with the result that over

200,000 strangers poured into and out of Rome every day. A new bridge had to be built over the Tiber, and one-way traffic was enforced on all bridges leading to the city. With so many people jostling each other in the narrow streets it is surprising that there were not more accidents. We read that people occasionally got trampled under foot, but most chroniclers praise the way in which it was made possible for the pilgrims to reach the tombs of the apostles, many carrying children and some even with sick folk or aged parents on their shoulders.

Though accommodation was difficult to find, there was no lack of provisions. Harvests around Rome had been good and the organization of the market won high praise. Visitors could buy wine, meat, fish, and grain at fair prices. Once in the city, a pilgrim's first visit was always to St. Peter's, the oldest church in Rome but not yet the great cathedral which we know today, where stood the statue of St. Peter, whose big toe then as now was worn and shiny with being kissed by devout worshippers. This statue was the work of a fine sculptor called Arnolfo. It is to Boniface's credit that he loved works of art, and his reign was marked by much new building in Rome. He commissioned men like Arnolfo or Giotto to help in the task, and although much of their work in Rome has been destroyed, enough remains for us to see that in sculpture and in painting these two men were of the first importance.

Also in St. Peter's was the saint's tomb and, perhaps the most sacred relic of all, the veil of St. Veronica. The legend tells of how on his way to crucifixion Jesus Christ wiped the sweat from his face on this veil which Veronica gave him and of how the picture of his head, surrounded by a crown of thorns, at once was printed on the veil. Just outside the city walls lay the tomb of St. Paul and, in addition to many churches and other sacred places, there were the ruins of the Colosseum to be visited where in the days of the Roman empire so many Christians had been put to death. At the tombs pilgrims were expected to give as much money to the Church as they could afford. For some the long journey had taken all their savings, but most people were able to throw some offering on the flagstones in front of the altars. A chronicler visiting St. Paul's church saw two priests with rakes gathering up the money day and night, a story which has led many to believe that the chief purpose of the Holy Year was to make money for the Church. But when we think of what it must have cost to build new bridges, improve roads, and organize special protection for pilgrims as they travelled through Italy, it is unlikely that the final profit was high. In a normal year about 30,000 florins in gifts from pilgrims were received by the main churches in Rome; in 1300 the sum reached 50,000 florins, which is not as big an increase as might have been expected. Boniface certainly loved wealth but he did not gain greatly from the Jubilee.

What in fact was there to show at Christmas 1300 when the Holy Year ended? In one sense very little. The Church certainly gained something from the gifts of the pilgrims; innkeepers and tradesmen would have gained very much more. In many people religious faith would have been strengthened, and belief that the pope had power to set free men and women from the punishments which they might expect in another world for their sins in this world was also renewed—a fact of much importance later at the time of the Reformation. The real significance of the Holy Year is much clearer to us, viewing it from a distance, than it was to those living at the time. Despite all the fervour of humble pilgrims, the old ideas about the power of the papacy and about the unity of Christendom under the pope were being questioned. However much simple folk might be dazzled by the pomp and pageantry of Boniface's Jubilee, real power was passing from the pope to the rulers of the developing nation states and also to the towns. The Jubilee failed to do what Boniface intended, because by 1300 it was already too late to try to put back the clock.

Among the crowds in Rome that year was a Florentine, Dante Alighieri, born in 1265 and chosen in 1300 to be one of the six Priors, or rulers, of his native city. Long before this, in fact a month before his ninth birthday, Dante had fallen passionately in love with a girl a year younger than himself, Beatrice Portinari, whom he met at a May-Day party. This proved to be no passing example of calf-love but the most enduring influence on his life. Describing this first meeting in his *Vita Nuova* ('The New Life'), a book of love poems inspired by Beatrice, with a running commentary in prose, he wrote: 'Behold a god stronger than I that is come to bear rule over me.' It was a strange story. Dante did not again speak to Beatrice until he was 18 and he was destined never to marry her. She was married to a banker in 1287 and three years later was dead, but despite his own marriage some six years afterwards Dante was never to forget her.

Fortunately for the future of Italian literature, Dante's experience of Florentine politics was brief. It was an age of constant fighting both between the great Italian cities and often within the cities themselves, so Dante, like most young Florentines, was no stranger to warfare. In 1302 a political upheaval in Florence led to his banishment and the threat of death by burning should he ever return. Released from political battles, Dante was free to devote himself to his writing and his philosophy and to become one of the great poets of the world.

No man hated Boniface more than Dante, for he had no sympathy with the pope's claims, and in a Latin treatise, *De Monarchia* (1311), he looked not to the pope but to the emperor to be the universal sovereign without whose rule peace was impossible. He argued that the Roman empire had been the divinely appointed instrument of

On the left-hand side of the picture Dante is being expelled from Florence. He is writing his poetry on the opposite side.

government on earth because Christ had been born at a time of universal peace in the reign of Augustus, the first emperor; so to Dante it was the Roman emperor who was God's representative on earth, in no way subject to the pope. Dante's dream was as out of date as that of Boniface. Frederick II, who had died in 1250, was the last emperor to be supreme in Italy for any length of time. In central Europe another two centuries were to pass before a Holy Roman Emperor could show his potential strength.

Dante's greatest work, the *Divina Commedia*, written between 1314 and 1321 and called a comedy partly because of its happy ending, dealt with both politics and religion. The city which had banished him was inevitably held up to ridicule:

> Florence, rejoice because thy soaring fame
> Beats its broad wings across both land and sea
> And all the deep of Hell rings with thy name!
> Five of thy noble townsmen did I see
> Among the thieves; which makes me blush anew
> And mighty little honour it does to thee.

Dante also had his revenge on Boniface, with whom his disagreement was not just one of ideas, for the pope had played a part in bringing about his exile. Dante prophesied that Boniface would be placed firmly in Hell, head first in a hole, to pay the penalty for his crimes.

21

There are plenty of references in *The Divine Comedy* to political figures of the day, but it is really a religious poem. It tells of Dante's imaginary journey first through Hell, then Purgatory, and finally to Paradise. In the first two parts Dante is accompanied by the Roman poet, Virgil; in Paradise his guide is Beatrice. *The Divine Comedy* is an allegory which can be read as a story in its own right or for the meaning behind it, and Dante's purpose was in this way to describe the journeyings of a man's soul in his search for God. As an allegory it marks one of the highest points reached by medieval thought and poetry, but in its political and personal attacks it is a sign of changing times.

In another way, too, Dante looked to the future by making it respectable to write in one's native language rather than in Latin, which was the accepted literary language for all Europe. In about 1305 he wrote *De Vulgari Eloquentia* ('On Common Speech') which, although unfinished, defended the use of Italian and attempted to collect examples of particular regional dialects. Dante explained that *The Divine Comedy* was written in Italian 'in which even women

An early fifteenth century illustration of Dante's Divine Comedy. *The Roman poet Virgil is guiding Dante (in the hood) through Purgatory. On the left they meet Pope Adrian V, in the centre Hugh Capet, and on the right the poet Statius.*

can exchange ideas'. He wanted everyone to be able to read his work and he knew that not everyone, especially not women, had received an education full enough to enable them to read Latin. Furthermore, by writing in Italian Dante was also challenging the Church, for the use of Latin as a universal language was one of the ways in which the power of the Church over Western Europe was maintained.

Boniface believed that the supreme power in western Europe—in Christendom—should be the pope, Dante thought it should be the emperor, others that the two should jointly share authority. All through the fourteenth century the idea of a Christendom united through a supreme ruler or rulers remained the ideal for many men, but it became less and less of a practical reality. The dream of a united Christian Europe was to give way before the ambitions of national rulers and fiercely independent towns. Throughout the three centuries covered by this book we shall be watching the ways in which the old authorities like the papacy and the empire, which regarded themselves as above upstart nations, were challenged and largely defeated by the new authorities, who were determined to be masters in their own house and to reject the claims of any universal pope or emperor to interfere in what they increasingly insisted was their own business and nobody else's.

Chapter 1
The Church under Attack 1300–1450

The quarrel between the popes and national rulers was nothing new: the story of Henry II and Becket in England, which ended with Becket's death in 1170, is one proof of that. By the time of Boniface VIII, kings had become even more certain of their powers and when necessary were fully prepared to use them. When Boniface claimed that Edward I of England had no right to tax the English clergy, Edward retaliated with a threat to seize Church lands. When Boniface then claimed the right of 'provision', that is the right of appointing men to bishoprics before the existing holder of the office died or resigned, Edward argued in 1299 that this infringed his royal rights of patronage: 'Even if the King should submit or permit it to pass, the magnates of his realm, who are bound by homage and fealty to defend his dignity and his crown, would not allow his rights thus to perish.' Boniface gave way.

In France the struggle between king and pope was much fiercer because powerful lawyers at the court of Philip IV, 'the Fair', were busily engaged in putting forward a theory of French nationalism and of the French king's independence of the pope. One royal advocate in Normandy wrote boldly that 'it is a peculiar merit of the French to have a surer judgement than other nations, not to act without consideration, nor place themselves in opposition to right reason': that, in fact, the French knew their own business and did not need the pope to interfere. Philip IV, in urgent need of money for fighting the English, was involved in the quarrel on a more practical level. When he demanded a tenth of clergy incomes in taxation, the French clergy appealed for help to the pope, who in 1296 issued the bull *Clericis laicos*. A bull was a papal pronouncement, known by its opening Latin words and sealed at its foot by a number of *bullae*, or seals. 'The laity, such is the witness of antiquity, have ever been hostile to the clergy' were the opening words of this bull, which went on to assert that all countries were subject to the pope and that no lay ruler had any power over the persons or property of the Church. Philip at once prohibited papal messengers from coming into France and he did his utmost to stop money going out of France to Rome. By 1300 the attitudes on both sides had hardened and a year later Boniface issued another bull setting out his full claims: 'We would have you know that you are subject to us in spiritualities and in temporalities.' Philip's answer delighted the States General, which was a kind of parliament divided into three 'Estates', the clergy, the nobility, and the commons, and which had been summoned in 1302 to give the king advice in dealing with Boniface. 'Philip, by the grace of God king of the Franks, to Boniface, who gives himself out for Supreme Pontiff, little or no greeting. Let your great fatuousness know that in temporalities we are subject to none.' Bonifice issued yet another bull in 1302, *Unam sanctam*, in which he repeated his claims and stated that 'the Church has only one body and one head. It is not a monster with two heads, the Pope and the King of France. Its one head is the Vicar of Christ.' His hatred of France and its king grew more and more intense and he swore that he would rather be an ass or a dog than a Frenchman. Philip continued to stand his ground in face of the storm and again rejected Boniface's claims. 'Before the clergy existed the King of France had custody of his own kingdom', was Philip's reply.

Boniface had one weapon left—excommunication—and he prepared to use it. News of this reached Philip, who sent his adviser, Nogaret, to Italy to deal with the pope, or, in official language, 'to secure the peace and unity of the Church'. With a force of armed men Nogaret planned to seize Boniface at his summer residence at Anagni, then to take him to France as a captive, where it was hoped that a specially summoned General Council of the Church would depose him. Boniface was duly captured but did not long remain a prisoner. His own personal courage in the face of danger, Italian hatred of the French, and a general feeling that an outrage had been committed, all combined to force the French troops to leave Anagni hurriedly and to free Boniface, who died from the shock of his capture a month later (October 1303). The bull of excommunication was never issued. Nevertheless, for a French king to have tried to summon a pope to appear before a General Council on a charge of heresy showed that the whole structure and importance of the Church was being called in question. Since the idea of the summons had come from a body of lawyers, it was clear that a new class of educated laymen would have to be reckoned with, men more than ready to express their own views on Church matters. If the Church were to regain its old power it would have to undergo a complete transformation of its whole way of life.

'He crept in like a fox, reigned like a lion and died like a dog', said contemporaries about Boniface VIII; and few dared to wish good luck to his successor, Benedict XI, a poor shadow of a pope, who feared to live in a Rome which was torn by fighting between rival families. Benedict was so completely under the control of Philip IV that he was forced to acquit Philip publicly of any share in the events at Anagni, and before a year of his reign had passed he fled from

Rome to Perugia, where he died suddenly in 1304, whether from poison or exhaustion has never been determined.

For nearly a year feuds between Italian and French cardinals prevented the choice of a new pope. From France came open threats of what would happen if the cardinals dared to choose another man like Boniface; the Italian cardinals had no intention of allowing the French cardinals to control the election. Eventually the two sides agreed on an 'outsider', a man not yet a cardinal, who as archbishop of Bordeaux was a subject of the king of England and might be more independent than some other candidates. But Clement V, as the new pope called himself, disappointed these hopes, for he was a Gascon by birth and, more important, was so hopelessly irresolute that he quickly came under the influence of Philip IV, who persuaded him to be crowned at Lyons. Unfortunately during the coronation ceremony a wall fell in, slightly injuring the pope and knocking off the papal crown from which the precious carbuncle was lost—an ill omen! Clement had plenty of excuses for not hurrying to Rome: it was a dangerous city to live in with its street fighting; he was very anxious to stay in France until he had settled the quarrel over Aquitaine between Philip IV and Edward I; he himself loved France, as did the ten new Gascon cardinals whom he created. (It was Clement who altered the whole balance in the College of Cardinals in favour of France. In the nine years of his reign, twenty-three of the twenty-four new cardinals created by him were born within the frontiers of modern France and the Italians were for a long while in a minority.) After wandering around France for a time Clement decided to settle at Avignon.

There was nothing new in a pope not living in Rome. In the 204 years between 1100 and 1304 the popes had spent only eighty-two in Rome. At first the decision to stay at Avignon was a temporary measure and not until the reign of Benedict XII (1334–42) did a pope make it clear by his vast building programme that he had deliberately decided to make Avignon the new headquarters of the papacy. If Avignon were to become the capital of Christendom it was a good choice to make. It was a middle-sized town of about five or six thousand inhabitants, calm and peaceful and very ready to welcome the curia, the papal court, as likely to bring money from increased trade. After the break away of the Eastern Empire and the conquests of Islam, Avignon was much more at the heart of western Christendom than was Rome. The Rhône valley in which it stood was one of the main lines of communication between southern and northern Europe, and much east-to-west traffic moved through Avignon and crossed its famous bridge, the southernmost of the only four bridges across the river. In one sense the town was politically neutral because it was not part of France but belonged to Naples until bought by the papacy in 1348. But although there

A statue of Pope Benedict XII carved by a sculptor from Siena. Note the key, a symbol of authority, held in his left hand.

was nothing outwardly new in Clement's refusal to go to Italy, it was the first time that a pope had so obviously made another city and another palace take the place of Rome and the Vatican. What the poet Petrarch was to call 'the Babylonish Captivity'—a Biblical reference to the captivity of the Israelites by the kings of Babylon—had begun and it was to last for seventy years. Under Clement V, a well-intentioned but lamentably weak man, the papacy at Avignon got off to a decidedly bad start.

Philip IV had threatened to organize a 'trial' of the dead Boniface VIII in order to expose to the world all the scandals—true or false it mattered not—which he said were rife in the papal court. To avoid this, Clement paid the price of stating that the bulls *Clericis laicos* and *Unam sanctam* did not apply in France. Clement was also forced to support Philip's attack on the Knights Templars, one of the military Orders which dated from the time of the Crusades. The Templars were rich and in the twelfth century their headquarters in Paris had been the centre of the European money market. However, they were not prepared to lend money to Philip as quickly and as often as he wanted to borrow it and this led to their downfall. In 1307 all Templars in France were arrested on trumped-up charges of heresy and vice; in 1312 the entire Order was officially suppressed. Then again Clement inevitably found himself in conflict with national rulers when he introduced annates, the payment to the pope of the first year's revenue of every benefice conferred by the pope. He was driven to this because for some time no money had come from the pope's Italian dominions to Avignon; it soon proved very lucrative. Unfortunately for Clement's reputation, more than half of his treasure went to his relatives and he was too weak to insist upon the honest administration of the curia by his officials. When Clement died in 1314, the cardinals, as so often, began to look for a very different man as the next pope.

John XXII (1316–34), only chosen after a long interval, was indeed the very opposite in every way of Clement V. Although 72 years old, he was a man of vast energy, clear-headed, and utterly relentless. Where Clement had been easygoing, wasteful, and a lover of luxury, John was stern, a more efficient organizer and a man of simple habits. He knew exactly what he intended to do: to keep the papacy independent of any secular ruler and to make the organization of the Church efficient by bringing as much of its work as possible under the pope's direct control. In both aims his insistence on getting his own way aroused great opposition and in the end made the papacy more unpopular than had Clement's slackness.

If the pope were to be truly independent he must be strong enough to hold a balance not only between rival states in Italy but also between the chief rulers of western Europe. To be powerful in Italy was bound to mean living in Italy, not at Avignon; but no return was possible until the Italian possessions of the papacy, a considerable belt of territory across the centre of the country, had been reconquered, and for this John must equip an army. He did not shrink from this but found that to act like any Italian prince at once brought him into conflict with other rulers, especially the emperor in Germany, who were also interested in Italy. In the bull *Unam sanctam* Boniface, quoting St. Paul's epistle to the Corinthians, had declared: 'He that is spiritual judgeth all things, yet he himself is judged of none.' It became very difficult to accept this when the pope acted like one of the national rulers whom he regarded as his inferiors. Yet John was well intentioned and the ways in which he kept power in his own hands were genuinely meant to improve the Church. There was something to be said for a strong, centralized system when it came to running the Church, but it did not work if the pope were not himself an efficient administrator, like John, or was a less virtuous man who intended to use this great organization for his own ends. This soon became apparent.

Benedict XII (1334–42) was virtuous but not a competent organizer. No born aristocrat like John, but of humble birth, Benedict was a Cistercian monk, who went on wearing his monk's habit even after he became pope. He was naturally anxious to improve the condition of the religious Orders but he was so narrow-minded and rigid about small details that he gained little support for his reforms. The real trouble about the papacy at Avignon was that it had by now become a vast machine, which could only be run by a high-powered businessman, and such a man as pope was most unlikely to be seriously concerned with reforming the evils in the Church. What was needed was a thorough reform of the whole method of papal government, and this not even those popes most anxious for the ending of abuses ever contemplated. Benedict's chief importance in this story was his realization that an immediate return to Rome was not possible. It was he who set about building the gigantic palace-fortress which dominates Avignon to this day; by erecting what in its early stages was a rather monastic-looking building, Benedict made plain that Avignon had become the normal and not the temporary home of the papacy.

No man showed better what could happen to the reputation of the papacy when the machine fell into unworthy hands than Clement VI (1342–52). The cardinals were tired of being governed by a monk and so, in complete contrast, they unanimously elected the most outstanding French bishop of his day, brilliantly clever, eloquent and friendly, brave, and a skilled diplomatist. At the same time his private morals were notorious and his love of splendid living, learned at the French court, nearly bankrupted the papal treasury. 'My predecessors did not know how to be popes' was his reply when accused of gross extravagance. He gave away benefices on the

A modern photograph of the papal palace at Avignon, with the cathedral on the left.

principle that a pope 'should make his subjects happy'. 'No one', he said, 'should leave the prince's presence dissatisfied.' Announcing that a return to Rome was impossible, Clement VI decided that Avignon must be made a worthy new capital. His court became the social centre of Christendom and, with the rapid growth in the number of those engaged in the business of the curia, a new and grander palace became a necessity. The outside continued to look like a fortress but within its walls there was nothing monastic or austere. Enormous rooms were decorated with frescoes, and the audience chamber and the great chapel were built on a scale worthy of a pope who had temporarily made himself leader of the world.

Clement's private life and the dazzling splendour of Avignon did not help to make the papacy more popular. When the Black Death came to Europe in 1347, it was widely believed that this was God's punishment on a sinful Church. This plague and the ravages of the Hundred Years War led to a revival of genuine religious life, especially among ordinary folk. Here was a wonderful chance for the pope to encourage this spirit, but Clement and the whole organization at Avignon were hopelessly incapable of understanding what was happening. The spirit of this religious revival was best expressed by two women, St. Brigitta of Sweden, daughter of a wealthy landowner, and by St. Catherine of Siena, daughter of a working man. Their writings are full of devotion to the Virgin Mary and of the importance of a life of prayer, but they also contain bitter attacks on Clement and pleas that he should do God's will. 'Poor miserable creature that I am,' wrote St. Catherine, 'I cannot wait longer; life, to me, is worse than death, when I look and see what outrages are committed against God!'

In 1348 Clement bought Avignon from Queen Joanna of Sicily for 80,000 florins, and two years later, partly to quieten those who demanded that as St. Peter's successor the pope ought to live in Rome, partly to raise much-needed money, he proclaimed another Jubilee year. Once again crowds flocked to Rome and many pilgrims came as an act of thanksgiving for having escaped the Black Death. If it had ever entered Clement's head that he might return to Rome, all such thoughts would have been banished by the contrast between Avignon where he could live in pomp and luxury and the lawless conditions in Rome. Even his legate was not safe there and narrowly escaped assassination when he was making a personal pilgrimage to the main churches. But if ever peace came again to southern Italy it would be difficult for a pope to find convincing reasons for not returning to the city of which he was bishop.

The three successors of Clement VI—Innocent VI (1352-62), Urban V (1362-70), and Gregory XI (1370-8)—were all men of good character, anxious to rule honestly and to try to control the

The coronation of Pope Clement VI.

worst abuses in the curia. But by this time it was not enough for a pope to be an honourable man, it was the whole system of papal government which was being criticized. During the second half of the fourteenth century the position of the pope was affected in three ways, each of which increased the strength of the attack upon the Church.

First, the power of the cardinals grew greatly from the time of Clement VI and, with honourable exceptions, they were not men of worth or quality. It was the luxury in which they lived which scandalized so many people. In 1316 one cardinal needed thirty-one houses, or parts of houses, for his retinue and possessions, and in 1321 another cardinal required fifty houses. In addition to lavish presents from those wanting to curry favour, they obtained possession of the richest benefices and were said to own half the income of the Church. Banquets were on an enormous scale. When Clement VI was entertained by one of his cardinals he sat down to a meal of nine courses, each with three dishes. Describing the twenty-seven items on the menu the chronicler records: 'After the fifth course they brought in a fountain surmounted by a tree and a pillar,

31

flowing with five kinds of wine. The margins of the fountain were decked with peacocks, pheasants, partridges, crows, and other birds.' The cardinals lived and behaved like the Italian princes of their day and were prepared, subject to a handsome bribe, to further the interests of any secular ruler who wanted papal support for his foreign policy. In their choice of a pope they favoured a weak man rather than one who might actively reform the curia at their expense. When Urban VI looked like controlling the power of the cardinals, one of them said openly to him: 'Holy Father, you do not treat the cardinals with that honour which you owe to them, as your predecessors did; you are diminishing our honour, and I tell you in all truth that we shall do our best to diminish yours.' Their power is also seen from the fact that even virtuous popes felt it necessary to grant them vast sums as 'gifts' after their election. Innocent VI, for instance, paid out 75,000 florins in this way.

Secondly, if the popes were under pressure from their cardinals, they were even more at odds with secular rulers. Both popes and kings desperately wanted money and it could only come from the same source. The wars of the fourteenth century, especially the Hundred Years War, and the economic distress which followed the Black Death made these secular rulers cast greedy eyes upon the wealth of the Church in their countries and they tried their hardest to bring the Church under their control. 'In my land', said Duke Rudolf IV of Austria in 1364, 'I will be pope, archbishop, bishop,

HIC IACET·VRBANVS·VI · PONT·OPT·MAX

Pope Urban VI receives the keys from St. Peter. The carving comes from the pope's tomb. The popes have always claimed that St. Peter, who died about A.D. 64, was the first bishop of Rome and that they receive their authority in direct descent from him.

archdeacon, dean.' But at the same time the pope was equally in need of money to run the papacy at Avignon and also to wage his personal war in Italy for the recovery of the Papal States. It was this increasing demand for money and the uses to which it was put that was everywhere the cause of bitter criticism, much more than the desertion of Rome for Avignon. Papal revenue came from many sources—the most lucrative being appointments to bishoprics and benefices and the heavy charges made by papal lawyers when hearing disputes between rival claimants. In addition there was open taxation of clergy to the extent of a tenth of their incomes, and failure to pay up was punished as if it were a sin. On one day in 1328, five archbishops, thirty bishops, and forty-six abbots were excommunicated for not having paid their debts to the papacy. There was also a vast amount of profitable business in the Church courts, which dealt not only with Church affairs but in many other matters, like those concerning a man's will, which today are the work of the ordinary courts of law. Many men were able to go to a Church court, where they expected more lenient treatment, rather than to the royal courts, on the plea that they were clergy. 'Benefit of clergy', as it was called, was open to all who could claim to be in any kind of Orders, and this meant not just priests and monks but anyone with a university degree, or, sometimes, a man who was merely able to read. In England the traditional test for 'Benefit of clergy' was the ability to read the first verse of Psalm 51, 'the neck-verse', as it was nicknamed. It is not surprising that the Avignon popes tried very hard to control as many appointments in the Church as possible so that much-needed money would continue to flow into their treasury. It is equally obvious that secular rulers did their utmost to stop money from leaving their countries when they wanted it to come to themselves. As yet they made no direct attack on the pope because they often wanted his support, but it was becoming clear that the amount of power which a pope had in any particular country depended on how much the ruler of that country was prepared to allow.

Thirdly, the popes were affected by the lawlessness and disorder all over western Europe during the Hundred Years War, which will be described in a later chapter. In 1364 Urban V had to borrow large sums of money to repair and extend the walls and battlements around Avignon itself, as the city was in danger of attack from roving bands of discharged soldiers. At the same time the feuds between the great families and their followers were still making Rome unsafe for its citizens. There was urgent need for the pope to restore order in southern Italy by winning back papal lands from those who had seized them while the popes were away. Innocent VI found the right man for the job in the Spanish cardinal Albornoz, who was an experienced soldier as well as being the head of the

Church in Spain. He was surprisingly successful and between 1353 and 1363 he reconquered the Papal States, which, of course, created more enemies for the pope. Rome was now safe enough for the pope to return: he could no longer plead that Avignon was safer.

It was Gregory XI who ultimately ended the 'Captivity'. A nephew of Clement VI, a cardinal at the age of 19, it might seem as if he would prove as worldly as his uncle. But he knew Italy well and loved the arts and literature, so that, with his genuine piety, he was the man to bring the papacy back to Rome. His journey was postponed for six years, thanks to an empty treasury and the extreme reluctance of the French cardinals to leave the comforts of Avignon. They did everything possible to delay the return: they tried to persuade Gregory that his first task was to end the Hundred Years War, which would be easier to do from Avignon, and they echoed the opinion of the French king who wanted to keep the pope near at hand, that 'Rome is wherever the pope happens to be'. But nothing could deter Gregory, who left Avignon in the autumn of 1376. He had to leave behind a well-staffed section of the administration as well as the great papal library, which had been built up during the exile, for in days of poor transport it was too hard a task to move the entire papal machinery back to Rome at once. One reluctant bishop wrote a description in verse of the trials which he endured: 'Dear God! If only the mountains would move and stop our journey!' The final stages were made in stormy seas and in January 1377 Gregory sailed up the Tiber and entered Rome. Much of the city had been destroyed by fire and fighting, and although some of the ruins were hidden beneath gay carpets, nothing could disguise the swamp which flanked the route of the procession. In the late afternoon the pope reached St. Peter's to be welcomed by the light of 18,000 lamps, almost one for each remaining inhabitant. The 'Captivity' was over but not the troubles of the Church.

*   *   *

Just over a year after his return to Rome, Gregory XI, always a frail man, died from exhaustion at the age of only 48. Almost at once the rivalry between Italians and Frenchmen showed itself in a way which was to do much more damage to the papacy than had the 'Captivity' at Avignon. 'We want a Roman pope, or at least an Italian,' shouted the crowds outside the Vatican as the election of the new pope was being debated. The cardinals' choice fell on the Italian archbishop of Bari, who took the title of Urban VI (1378–89) and who proved to be a good man, anxious for reform but rude and tactless when he did not easily get his way. As a measure of reform, he began to reduce the privileges of the cardinals, even ordering them to restrict themselves to one course at meals. Within two months, urged on by King Charles V of France, thirteen rebellious

French cardinals left Rome for Anagni where they proceeded to elect a rival pope, a cruel but successful warrior-cardinal, Clement VII (1378–94), and tried to justify their action by claiming that the election of Urban VI had been due to popular pressure and was not a free vote. Clement settled at Avignon; Urban remained in Rome. 'They don't know me well,' said the unworried Urban, 'if they pointed a thousand swords at my neck I still would not give up.' And in this spirit he created twenty-eight new cardinals.

In this way began the Great Schism, which was to last until 1417 and which split the Church into two opposing camps. The real question at issue was purely political and had nothing to do with religion. The Italians wanted the papacy for Italy; the French intended that the pope, whether he lived at Rome or Avignon, should continue to be closely allied to French interests. Nobody bothered to consider fairly the rival claims of Urban VI and Clement VII; it was sufficient that Urban was the Italian and Clement the French candidate. National passions and political alliances decided which nations would recognize which pope. France, Scotland, Savoy, and, later, Spain, supported Clement; England, Bohemia, Hungary, and, later, Portugal, supported the Italians in their wish to have Urban as pope.

The Schism unhappily outlasted both popes. When Urban VI died from falling off his donkey, the Italian faction at once elected a successor, Boniface IX (1389–1404). He gave away lands to his followers so lavishly that there was a danger of the Papal States breaking up into a series of tiny principalities. There was a faint hope that on his death the Schism might end and that both Italian and French factions might recognize Benedict XIII (1394–1423), Clement's successor at Avignon, as the one lawful pope. It was not to be, and two 'Italian' popes were to succeed Boniface IX.

Nothing did more than the Great Schism to strengthen the cause of those who said that the reform of the Church was urgent. The spectacle of two and, for a time, three popes in conflict shocked devout Christians everywhere and encouraged men like the spokesman for the university of Paris to say: 'Little does it matter how many popes there are, two or three or ten or a dozen; each kingdom might as well have its own.' Nothing shows better the loss of prestige of the papacy than this suggestion that Europe could get on perfectly well without it. As has been said, this was an age of religious fervour and two men above all others urged the need for drastic reform of the curia before it was too late—the Englishman, John Wyclif and John Huss from Bohemia.

Little is known of John Wyclif's life. He was born in Yorkshire about 1329, taught in Oxford, where he became a famous figure and

for a time Master of Balliol College, was expelled in 1382 because of his views, and returned to his parish of Lutterworth in Leicestershire, where he died two years later. That his opinions became so widely known is partly due to his fame in Oxford, then the freest and most powerful university in Europe, and partly to the band of poor preachers, called Lollards, who carried his message in simple terms all over the country. Wyclif believed that both preaching and the Bible should be available to all in their mother tongue and not in Latin. For, as he wrote: 'Cristen men and wymmen, olde and yonge, shulden studie fast in the Newe Testament, for it is of ful autorite, and opyn to understonding of simple men, as to the poyntis that be most needful to salvacioun.' It was under his influence that the English Bible which bears his name was translated by some of his followers. He attacked the way that the wealth of the Church was misused, the giving of English benefices to Italians who never came near them, the heavy papal taxation, which drained money from the country, and he claimed for the English kings powers which would have fully satisfied Henry VIII a century and a half later. In much of this teaching, with its almost patriotic note, he found ready listeners. As his ideas developed, he attacked the bishops for being statesmen rather than shepherds of their people, and monks and friars for so often failing to live up to their vows. He went on to assert that no priest, bishop, or even pope had any authority unless he himself were a worthy man. In the end he reached the point where he denied the doctrine of Transubstantiation, which stated that through the operation of the priest at Mass, the consecrated bread and wine became the body and blood of Christ. Even Luther, who a century later was to be the leading force in the German Reformation, could not have gone further in his attack on the Church.

Wyclif's teachings might well have remained a purely English concern had it not been for the interest which they aroused in Bohemia. The university of Prague had been founded in 1348 and had close ties with Oxford. Thirty years later friendship between the two countries was strengthened by the marriage of Richard II with Princess Anne of Bohemia. Thus it is not surprising that the views of one of Oxford's leading figures should be studied in Prague and taught there.

One of these teachers was John Huss, a Czech priest of humble origin, born in 1369. He was a fine man, scholarly, intensely patriotic (he hated Germans), a preacher of great eloquence, who in his sermons steadily attacked the corruption in the Bohemian Church. To Huss the final test of faith was Scripture, and he maintained that the pope should only be obeyed in so far as he acted in accordance with Scripture. He strongly condemned the sale of Indulgences, which were documents sold by the pope's authority and purporting to remit some of the punishment which the buyer might expect in the next world for his sins in this. Huss constantly asserted that he could be no heretic for he based all his teaching on the very words of Christ in the gospels, but his enemies were determined to silence him. In 1415 he was enticed by a false promise of a safe conduct to appear before the General Council of the Church, then in session at Constance. Here he was condemned as a heretic and burned at the stake. His death marked the start of the first of the long series of religious wars, which in one country after another were to last for over two centuries, and which finally destroyed the idea of a united Christendom. From 1419 to 1431 Bohemia was torn by bitter fighting between the followers of Huss led by the brilliant general Ziska, and the forces which supported the old ways. By their passionate belief in Huss's teaching and their fervent national pride, the Czechs in 1436 won recognition from the pope of the kind of church which Huss and Wyclif had each wanted for his own country—a largely national church, purified of abuses, with its authority based on Scripture, but still part of the universal Church in obedience to Rome.

The universities of Oxford and Prague were not the only centres of learning where leading teachers found themselves involved in conflict with the Church on a scale originally quite unexpected. The Great Schism brought to the fore two well-known figures in the university of Paris, John Gerson and Peter D'Ailly, both gravely concerned with the scandal which rival popes and the abuses within the Church were causing. Preaching before King Charles VI of France in June 1391, Gerson urged that if the Schism could not be ended by the resignation of both popes there was no alternative to the calling of a General Council of the Church, which was held to be superior to the pope. Such a Council could not only end the Schism but might well become the divine instrument for a thorough reform of the Church. But who should summon it?

Neither of the two 'Italian' popes who succeeded Boniface IX would resign or even submit his claim to arbitration. In 1407 it was hoped that pope and antipope might be persuaded at least to meet, but, when the two men were forty miles apart in their journey to the agreed meeting-place, each refused to go further for fear of losing face. At this the cardinals lost patience and themselves called a General Council of the Church to meet at Pisa in 1409; but, when it met, not only was the Schism not ended but worse confusion followed from the election of yet another pope, Alexander V. There were now three rival popes—Gregory XII, Benedict XIII, and Alexander V—competing for support. Alexander's death within a year was no help, for he was at once replaced by the notorious Cardinal Cossa, who took the title of John XXIII. (Since a recent pope took the same title, it was made clear that the Roman Church does not recognize this fifteenth-century cardinal as a true pope.) More at home in a soldiers' camp than in the Vatican and described by one writer as 'a malevolent and calculating scoundrel beyond

even the usual Italian standard', John XXIII was a disgraceful choice. Nevertheless, he received some support from the emperor Sigismund, who persuaded him to call another General Council at Constance in 1414 in the firm belief that as emperor he would be able to dominate its meetings and decisions.

Constance was one of the many free Imperial cities of Germany. It was not a large town; it took less than ten minutes to walk from one end of it to the other. Into this city in 1414 came the prelates from all over Europe—29 cardinals, 3 patriarchs, 33 archbishops, 150 bishops, and 100 abbots, as well as a host of less important clerics. This was not, as at Pisa, only a meeting of clergy, for the laity attended in strength. One hundred dukes and earls, 2,400 knights, and 116 envoys of the cities came to Constance, and the Emperor attended the Council in person. With the notables came the usual hangers-on, comedians and gamblers, tumblers and flute-players, and 1,500 prostitutes.

The first purpose of the Council of Constance was to end the Schism, and business opened with a demand for the resignation of all three popes. John, finding no supporters anywhere, fled from Constance disguised as a groom and was deposed as 'unworthy, useless, and harmful'. Gregory agreed to resign, but Benedict refused, ending his days at the age of 94, still defiant but largely forgotten, on a rocky peninsula in Spain. With the election of a completely new pope, the Italian Martin V (1417–31), the Schism was over.

But when the Council turned to the question of reform, little was achieved. It is true that right at the start it had been made abundantly clear that a General Council of the Church was superior even to the pope, but it was not difficult for a wily politician like Martin V to play off the rival factions, especially the Italians and French with their supporters, against each other and to emerge with little or no loss of power. It is also important to understand that most members of the Council had not come to Constance intent on making drastic changes in the Church. They believed that if they could once end the Schism and return to the old days all would be well. They saw no point in kicking the pope when he was down; they thought that their task was to put the right pope on his feet again. Furthermore, the Council was always worried lest the kind of fighting which was happening in Bohemia would spread to other countries. Huss was burned, in spite of his safe conduct, to show the world that the Council had no intention of supporting violent reform. The tragedy of the papacy was that the Council of Constance and later Councils had given it the last chance to put its house in order of its own accord. Martin V and his successors were clever enough to outmanoeuvre what came to be called the Conciliar Movement but not clever enough to see that the only hope of averting the attacks of the reformers was to encourage and direct the new religious fervour which was everywhere arising within the Church.

With Martin V as pope the Italians were once more in control of the papacy, and he heads the long line of Italian popes for whom the Papal States mattered more than anything else. Martin, it was said, put the papacy before the Church, Italy before Europe, and his own relations before everything else. His successors were cast in the same mould, for we are reaching the age of the Renaissance popes. For the moment the attack on the fortress of papal power had been beaten off, but few would then have guessed that within fifty years after the last Council had broken up, the unity of the Roman Church would have been destroyed for ever.

Chapter 2
A Hundred Years of Fighting

(i) How men fought

In the Middle Ages society was organized for war. Popes protested frequently against the evil of a war between two Christian rulers; kings and their subjects regularly paid lip-service to the blessings of peace; yet fighting remained supremely honourable. This was true not only for the great nobles but also for ordinary folk; even a common criminal could win pardon for his crimes by his prowess in battle. No better proof of this attitude to war can be found than by reading Froissart's Chronicle. In spite of all the horrors which he recounts, there is again and again in his history almost a joy in war. For war appealed to the spirit of adventure in men and it had its rewards: it was an escape from boredom and it also brought booty, ransoms, promotion, and renown. Froissart cannot have been the only man alive to the beauty of war's pageantry, though few knights could have expressed their feelings as he did. He loved 'the fresh, shining armour, the banners waving in the wind, the companies in good order, riding a soft pace.' His heart was stirred at the sight of a famous knight, like the English Sir John Chandos, 'with his banner before him and his company about him, with his coat of arms on him, great and large, beaten with his arms.' Although war in reality was harsh and grim, the adventure and excitement were sufficiently appealing to ensure that enough men were ready to go on a campaign when 'the king went forth to Normandy'. As a French knight, Bertrand de Born, wrote frankly: 'I tell you I find no such savour in food, or wine, or sleep as in hearing the shout "On! On!" from both sides . . . and the cries of "Help! Help!" as men go down in the grass . . . in seeing at last the dead with stumps of lances still in their sides.'

Soldiers in the Middle Ages were seldom moved to fight by loyalty to king or country. The sense of belonging to a particular country developed very slowly, though it was helped by war. War was a business, and the profit motive was accepted by all concerned. It was frequently laid down how much of the spoils of war, whether from pillage or ransoms, were to go to the king, how much to the soldier's superior, and how much he might keep for himself. Enormous sums of money came from ransoms, much of which had to be used to look after and feed the prisoner until his ransom money had been agreed and paid, a task which sometimes took several years. The booty obtained from the capture of a castle or the sack of a

A picture which shows the various methods of fighting. Long-bows and cross-bows as well as hand guns and cannon can be seen. Those in the ship, with its specially built after-castle, are joining in the attack.

town was considerable, and Froissart tells of how, after the merciless sacking of Caen in 1346, the English ships took home jewels, clothes, and vessels of silver and gold.

Nor was it only the soldiers who found war a profitable business. Conquered territory meant that men would be needed to rule it in the king's name, and grants of houses, lands, and estates were made to Englishmen, especially in Normandy. Merchants and traders found new customers among both the military and civilian population in France. Even the clergy, who existed in such numbers that the supply of livings in England was insufficient, got what they wanted abroad; while foreign clerics like Peter Cauchon, Bishop of Beauvais, found it highly profitable to meet the wishes of the new English rulers when, for example, it came to deciding the fate of Joan of Arc.

It would, however, be very misleading to depict warfare in the Middle Ages simply as a highly coloured pageant. Daily living even for the nobly born was hard and uncomfortable. Human life counted for little and hideous cruelties were accepted without much protest. Nevertheless, attempts were made to curb men's passions and to soften the worst practices. The first task was to try to limit actual fighting, and the Church had taken a lead in this since the eleventh century, when local quarrels between rival barons were regular occurrences leading to fighting between their followers, destruction of villages, and devastation of the countryside. By what was called the Truce of God men were urged not to engage in private war between the start of Advent and Epiphany, nor from the start of Lent until Ascension Day. They were also to refrain from pursuing their personal rivalries in any week from Wednesday evening till Monday morning—the days associated with Christ's Passion. The Truce, whether observed or not, shows how much fighting went on in the early Middle Ages. However, it is not with private warfare but with national wars that this chapter is concerned.

Before the reign of Edward III, the English army, like the French, was raised on a feudal basis, was unpaid, and existed primarily to repel invasion. By the thirteenth century the system was working very badly. For example, in 1277 only one in every eighteen English knights obeyed the royal summons to serve in the field. This lack of discipline was due partly to loyalty to an immediate overlord rather than to the commander of the army, but even more to the shortness of the customary forty days which was all that a man was obliged to fight for his feudal lord. The consequent difficulty of campaigning abroad showed that changes were much needed. The French continued for a long while to rely on traditional tactics and methods of recruitment, but Edward I was the man who first realized that the way to bring discipline and organization to the disorderly feudal host was to introduce a regular system of pay. By the time of the Hundred Years War it had become the accepted custom for members of the English nobility to be appointed to recruit a certain number of soldiers to serve for a given period of time (usually for not more than a year) at agreed rates of pay. A typical example of an indenture, as this kind of agreement was called, is that signed between the king and Thomas Holland, Earl of Kent on 30 September 1360. The earl contracts to serve the king 'at the accustomed wages of war' for a quarter of a year; the money due is to be paid by the king in advance so that the earl may have sufficient money to equip his men. He is to provide sixty men-at-arms, of whom one was to be a banneret, a rank superior to a knight and so called from the rectangular banner which he carried, and ten are to be knights; also 120 archers, all of whom are to be provided with horses. At first these indentures were verbal agreements but they soon became written documents. The principle of paid service applied to high and low alike and even the Black Prince did not scorn to draw his pay at the rate of 20 shillings a day. In this way the English king came to rely upon a professional, short-service army, ready to fight as effectively in France as at home. Although the greater part of the army was raised by indenture, it was usually necessary to recruit the rank and file both by insisting upon the ancient obligation of the shires and boroughs to enrol men for national defence and by voluntary enlistment.

In the army of Edward III the troops fell into four main categories —knights, men-at-arms, archers, and foot-soldiers. The commanding officers were chosen from the leading nobles, though men of rather lower social rank might win command if they had gained renown in battle. All were knights, but it is clear from their different titles and rates of pay that all knights were not of equal rank. Dukes and earls were ancient titles and beneath them came the bannerets and then the knight-bachelor. It was their arms, armour, and the weight of their war-horses which distinguished the knightly class in battle and which put knighthood beyond the reach of poor men. Most knights needed to own three or four war-horses, which in battle were entrusted to pages, who also had the task of looking after and cleaning their master's armour. The names of some of the more famous of these horses have come down to us—Bayard Dieu, Morel de Francia, Bauzan de Burgh; in each case the first word denotes the horse's colour, bay, black, and piebald. They might cost £100 each (perhaps £1,000 in today's money), and Edward III had agents buying war-horses for him as far away as Spain and Sicily. In battle they were encased in armour like their masters.

A knight was armed with lance, sword, and a short narrow-bladed dagger which was used for slipping between the plates of armour or through vizor-holes. Our knowledge of armour comes mainly from church brasses or from the sculptured effigies on the tops of tombs; it also comes from illustrations in rare books or from stained glass windows. The main fact is that the period of the Hundred Years War saw the gradual change from mail to plate, made necessary by the deadly fire of longbowmen and made possible by the developing skill of armourers. In the early days of the war a knight would begin by clothing himself in a quilted tunic and thick stockings before proceeding to put on his armour. He covered the main part of his body with a hauberk, or short tunic of mail, on top of which he fixed a metal breastplate. His arms, shoulders, and legs were protected by plate and on his hands he wore iron gauntlets. Special metal shoes protected his feet, over which his spurs were strapped. Over all of this he wore his surcoat on which, for purposes of recognition, was painted his coat of arms, both before and behind. A sword belt was around his waist and on his head was a heavy, conical helmet of plate, closed by a vizor. As the armour grew heavier and more efficient so the shield became unnecessary in battle. By the middle of the fifteenth century armourers had become so skilled that the armour not only became more closely fitted to the shape of the body but it varied in thickness according to the likelihood of attack at certain points and by various devices the blow from an enemy lance could often be deflected. The 'all-white' armour, which is the name given to the complete suits of armour at the end of the Hundred Years War and later, could well weigh over sixty pounds. They were extremely beautiful examples of craftsmanship, and wealthy English or French knights would buy their armour from Milan or Nuremberg, which were known throughout Europe as the homes of famous families of armourers. Nevertheless, as a means of defence against attack, armour ultimately became useless because it afforded little protection against firearms and hence its excessive weight became an unnecessary burden. As early as Agincourt, Edward of York died from heart failure without receiving any wound, and in 1452 at the forgotten battle of Dendermonde, fought on a sultry day, knights were seen supported by their pages lest they should lose their footing and be unable to rise again.

The second category of troops were the men-at-arms. These are difficult to describe because the word had two different meanings. Sometimes it refers to all who rode into battle, even though they actually fought on foot. On other occasions the word is used to describe light troopers, inferior in status to the knights, who were especially valuable for purposes of reconnoitring and harassing the enemy. These were originally known as 'hobelars', a name derived from a word for an Irish pony, and they proved their worth in the Scottish wars. As the Hundred Years War progressed, their importance grew steadily less and their place was taken by the mounted archer. The hobelar was much more lightly armed than the knight and, apart from his thickly padded tunic, he only wore a light coat of mail, a helmet, and iron gloves. He carried into battle a sword, a knife, and a lance. His status can be measured by his pay: he received 6*d*. a day in comparison with the 2*s*. paid to a knight bachelor, 4*s*. to a banneret, and 13*s*. 4*d*. to a duke. By contrast the humblest foot-soldier received 2*d*.

If a Frenchman who knew of Crécy, Poitiers, and Agincourt—battles which could have fallen within a single lifetime—had been asked what his countrymen dreaded most in fighting the English,

I

1. *A mail hood c. 1350.*
2. *A mail shirt and aventail (the helmet's mouthpiece) c. 1280 from Germany.*
3. *A bassinet (helmet) with visor and aventail from North Italy.*
4. *A suit of plate armour from North Italy—c. 1480.*
5. *A shoe of plate armour.*
6. *A rowel spur made of bronze —c. 1370.*

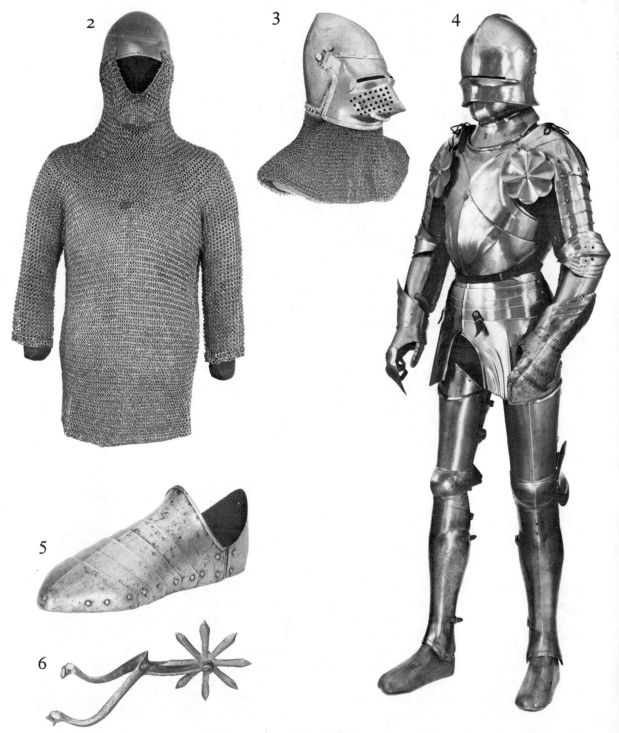

2

3

4

5

6

the answer would probably have been the longbowmen. Archers had formed part of the English army since Norman times, but at first their weapon was comparatively small and the string was drawn back only to the chest and not to the ear. The long-bow originally came from Wales and in early days was probably not more effective than the cross-bow. It proved capable, however, of much greater development once Edward I had ruled that archery should become a national sport, learned and constantly practised on the village green. By the time of Edward III, bows of yew, maple, or oak were six feet tall, and a skilled archer, standing sideways to the enemy so that aiming and loading were almost one operation, could fire ten or twelve arrows a minute. His maximum range was not far short of 400 yards and the iron tip of the arrow could penetrate chain mail. By contrast the cross-bow, on which the French depended, though firing a more powerful bolt, was less accurate, had a shorter range, and, most important of all, could only be fired twice a minute.

At first all archers were infantrymen and it was never possible to fire a long-bow unless a man stood on firm ground. However, the need to move quickly when taking up new positions or pursuing an enemy led increasingly to the use of mounted archers, and they came to combine the work of both archer and hobelar. In addition to his bow and one or two sheaves of arrows, the archer took with him a short sword and a knife. His armour consisted solely of a light coat of mail, but his arm was protected by a bracer, or guard, to catch the bow-string after the arrow had been fired.

The lowest ranking men in the English army were the foot-soldiers, of whom a large proportion were Welsh, distinguished by their white and green uniforms. Although they might sometimes be despised by the knights, they could give a good account of themselves with their knives and daggers as they came round the flanks of the main body of troops and fell upon an enemy which had first been devastated by the rain of arrows—'shot with such force and quickness,' said Froissart writing about Crécy, 'that it seemed as if it had snowed'—and then halted by the line of lances held by the dismounted knights.

It was a long time before the French fully understood why so often their army was no match for the English invaders. Chivalry had a disastrous influence on French ways of fighting in the first half of the Hundred Years War and even longer. The flower of the French army was the cavalry, but when it came to a battle there was almost no discipline at all in their ranks. The sole aim of the French knights was to charge bravely but wildly against the enemy in the hope of driving them from the field of battle. They were commanded by their feudal lords, who had little idea of tactics or of obedience, and whose followers often went off home when their forty-day term of feudal service was over. They were unlikely to win a battle unless fighting against an enemy who had the same idea of warfare and unless the battle took place on the kind of ground suitable for a gigantic tournament.

When the Hundred Years War began, most of King Philip VI's infantry were foreign mercenaries from Italy or Switzerland or Spain, hired as need arose and with little interest in the cause for which they were paid to fight. They were armed with the rather cumbersome cross-bow, which, as has been said, was no match for the long-bow. Worse still, the French knight, true to the ideals of chivalry, despised the man who merely fought on foot, with the result that there was little or no co-operation between cavalry and infantry.

Until the early fifteenth century it was always easier to defend than to attack a walled town or a castle. The strength of the walls enabled the defender to hold out at least as long as food and water lasted. Often the attackers knew that the only way to capture a stronghold was to starve it into surrender, a lengthy task. It was the coming of gunpowder which ended reliance upon stone walls as a protection against the enemy and also made armour useless. Nobody knows who first invented gunpowder, though it is believed to have come from western Europe, not from China or India. The first man to record the composition of gunpowder was the English Franciscan friar, Roger Bacon. He set down the formula in a cipher of his own in 1249, making clear the reasons for his secrecy: 'The common herd is unable to digest scientific facts, which it scorns and misuses to the detriment of the wise. Let not pearls be cast, then, before swine . . . It is madness to commit a secret to writing unless it be done so that it is unintelligible to the ignorant and just barely intelligible even to the most educated and wise.' However, all Roger Bacon's care could not prevent men from learning the secret of gunpowder.

Nevertheless, it was more than sixty years before the first cannon appeared. The first-known drawing of a cannon is to be found in an English manuscript of 1326 and the first known reference to a cannon was made in the same year in a decree issued by the Council of Florence. The drawing, which is in the library of Christ Church, Oxford, shows a strange weapon looking rather like a fat-bodied, narrow-necked vase, resting on its side on a four-legged wooden bench. It was loaded with a cross-bow bolt and fired by a man who, in the picture, is rather gingerly applying a light to a hole in the fat part of the gun. It must have been about three feet long and was known to the French as a *pot-de-feu*. From about the middle of the fourteenth century cannon became cylindrical and much more like the modern shape. They could be carried by hand and then mounted on wheeled carriages or fitted in ships. They were only able to fire a seven-ounce projectile at the start of the Hundred Years War, but

47

by 1377 we know from Froissart's account of an attack near St. Omer that stone and iron projectiles weighing 200 pounds could be fired.

It is uncertain when cannon were first used in battle. They were being made in increasing numbers from about 1330, and there is good evidence that Edward III had some with him at Crécy. How effective they were at this date is doubtful, though they may have been terrifying to the enemy because of their noise rather than the actual damage inflicted. They were mostly used for siege warfare, and Edward III had them with him when he besieged Calais. There was steady development in the design of cannon and primitive fire-arms throughout the fourteenth century, and Charles V of France did much to strengthen the artillery in his army reforms. 'Portable guns' about 9 inches long were used by the French at Liège in 1382 and by the end of the century they were in fairly general use.

Firearms seem to have been unpopular at first, especially with the knights. They were noisy, unreliable, and, above all, unchivalrous, for guns gave a new advantage to the infantryman and soon made him as valuable in war as the feudal knight, his master. In his *Henry IV, Pt. I* Shakespeare makes Hotspur express this point of view—though it must be admitted that the words are spoken in jest:

> And that it was great pity, so it was,
> That villainous saltpetre should be digg'd
> Out of the bowels of the harmless earth,
> Which many a good tall fellow had destroy'd
> So cowardly; and but for these vile guns,
> He would himself have been a soldier.

Hotspur's speech was doubtless a caricature of an effeminate coward, but according to an anecdote related in a book called *The Courtier*, written early in the sixteenth century and about which more will be said later, even ladies had little more use for the old knight-errant:

A lady asked a man to dance with her, and was told that such frivolities were not his business. And when at length the lady asked what his business was, he answered with a scowl 'Fighting'. 'Well, then,' the lady retorted, 'I should think that since you aren't at war at the moment and you are not engaged in fighting, it would be a good thing if you were to have yourself well greased and stowed away in a cupboard, so that you avoid getting rustier than you are already.'

With the coming of firearms and cannon in large numbers, the days of chivalry were over. The era of modern warfare had begun.

Philip VI presiding over a meeting of his lawyers.

(ii) French and English 1328–1380

When Philip VI became king of France in 1328, his country was the most powerful and prosperous in Europe. For many hundreds of years French kings had been gradually increasing the lands over which they ruled and, although Philip VI was not master of the whole of what today we call France, his kingdom was bigger than that of his ancestors and he was certainly regarded as the strongest European ruler. The royal house of Capet had through marriages given rulers to England, Hungary, Naples, and Sicily, and, as we have seen, even the papacy was for a time French. King John of Bohemia, later to die at Crécy, thought no place in the world could be compared with Paris, and most people would have agreed with a French missionary who had written to Avignon from India some ten years before Philip VI's accession: 'I believe that the king of France could conquer the world for himself and the Christian faith without the help of an ally.'

In other ways France was the leading nation. The revival of monastic life had begun in France: it was in France that the idea of a Crusade had first been preached. All over the land superb cathedrals and parish churches had been built, over 600 churches in the thirteenth century alone. English and German and Italian builders might alter French ideas to suit their own needs, but there never was any doubt that France was the country to whose 'Gothic' architecture they turned naturally for inspiration. To the great university of Paris came scholars from all over Europe; while from Provence came the troubadours, the minstrel-poets of the twelfth century, out of whose songs grew the ideas of chivalry.

There were, however, three serious weaknesses in the position of the French monarchy, of which only the third was immediately obvious.

First, France was cursed with a feudal nobility, who cared little for their country if their own interests were likely to suffer. They fought among themselves regardless of any danger to the State; they oppressed their villeins on whose labour the country's wealth largely depended; they were so stupid and arrogant in war, as we have just seen, that it took France a century to learn the need for a disciplined national army. Second, not until the French Revolution in 1789 did the French people, for all their genius, learn to pay their way as a nation. France should have been wealthy and able to meet her expenses from a full treasury, but no French king ever discovered what was a good tax, nor even how to raise enough money from the bad taxes which he did impose. Taxes were farmed out to greedy tax-collectors, who wrung from the wretched taxpayers far more money than ever found its way into the royal coffers. Merchants were hampered not only by heavy taxes on all that they tried to sell, but also by the large number of duties which were levied on goods as they were transported through France. Several kings tried to make money quickly by debasing the coinage, that is by issuing coins which were not as valuable as the stamp on the coin stated. There was no secret about this: it was accepted as an easy way to raise money without taxation. When it came to direct taxes none was more hated than the *gabelle*, a tax on salt, which was an essential commodity for preserving meat in winter. This was first levied by Philip VI in 1343. To crown all, wealthy and faithful supporters or royal favourites were rewarded by being let off from paying any taxes at all.

In spite of these two deep-seated weaknesses the supremacy of France might have continued for much longer if the incredible luck of the House of Capet in regularly producing a male heir to the throne had not suddenly run out. When Charles IV died in 1328, he left behind him only daughters, and the third great weakness of France became clear, the old Salic Law of France by which no woman could inherit the crown. In the minds of the French nobles and leading churchmen there was no doubt that the crown ought to pass to Philip of Valois, cousin of the late king; but could a woman, although she could never herself rule France, pass on her claim to her son? If this were permitted, then, as the family tree shows, the crown of France would be inherited by Edward III of England, then For the moment Edward did not press his claim and Philip of Valois became king of France as Philip VI.

Philip's father, Charles of Valois, had always hoped that his son might one day become king of France and he had ordered a special

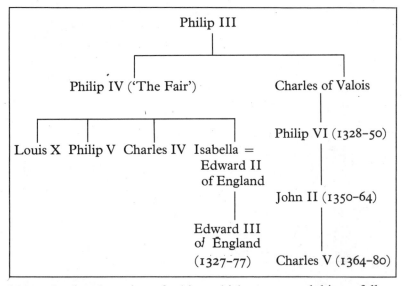

history book to be written for him, which was to teach him to follow the example of the Jews, Greeks, Romans, and Trojans. Unfortunately for France, Philip's head was much more full of chivalry than of history. His upbringing had led him to think that the day-to-day business of good government was beneath him and he unwisely left most of the work to clerks to whom he had not the sense to give real authority. He was a typical French noble, who later happened to become king, and he had all the interests and failings of the French nobility. He was pious, liking to discuss points of doctrine with the pope, but not very intelligent. He spent far too much time dreaming about a crusade instead of looking after the real interests of France, and when it came to war he could not see that the day for new ways of fighting had come.

War between France and England was inevitable so long as an English king held large parts of south-west France. From the days of Henry II of England, Guienne and Gascony were ruled by the king of England, as a vassal of the French king. Guienne in the Middle Ages was vital to England for the wine and other supplies which were shipped from Bordeaux and which made it rather like a British colony of a later date. The 'tonnage' of a ship originally meant the number of tuns, or barrels, of Bordeaux wine which could be loaded into the ship's hold. Not only were later English kings determined to keep control of this valuable part of France but they also hoped to get back Poitou, which had been lost to France in 1224. Edward III's decision in October 1337 to assert his right to be the true king of France only sparked off the fighting.

Lesser causes of quarrel abounded. War might have come at any time from the constant fights between French and English sailors

The wool trade—a typical scene at a port.

in the Channel, or in retaliation for the help steadily given by France to England's ancient enemy, the Scots. Philip VI equally hated the close ties which existed between English wool merchants and Flemish cloth workers, who were the subjects of Philip's vassal, Count Louis of Flanders. In 1336, acting on orders from Philip, Count Louis arrested all Englishmen living or travelling in Flanders. Edward at once stopped the export of English wool to Flanders, which led to an uprising among the merchants against Count Louis, who was left in no doubt that the Flemings were not going to have their trade ruined to please the king of France.

The course of the Hundred Years War has been compared to a clock whose pendulum twice made a double swing backwards and forwards; backwards to the depth of misery and misfortune for France and then forward to better times and recovery. The first backward swing began with the opening of the war in 1337 and continued until the death of King John of France in 1364. The slow recovery of France lasted till the early years of the next century. The second backward swing was caused by the meteoric career of Henry V of England; the final forward swing came with the revival of French fighting spirit under Joan of Arc and the creation of a French army ready to fight in new ways. At the start it was much more of a civil war than a war between two nations, for Frenchmen and Englishmen did not think of themselves as such much before the time of Joan of Arc. By then the cruelties of the English soldiers, the strange language spoken by the 'Goddams', as the hard-swearing English soldiers were nicknamed, and the inspiration which Joan herself gave to the troops made most Englishmen seem enemies and foreigners to most Frenchmen. But this came very slowly, and in the fourteenth century whenever Frenchmen were in revolt against their king or the nobles, they were quite prepared to accept help from English soldiers in their neighbourhood.

★   ★   ★

The war opened slowly and little action took place until 1340. In January of that year, to mark the full alliance between the English and the Flemings, Edward III chose the prosperous Flemish town of Bruges as the city from which to lay formal claim to the French throne. He then added the arms of France to those of England and had a new surcoat made on which the French fleur-de-lys were sewn alongside the English leopards. He went back to England to raise an army for an invasion of France. To prevent this army from landing, Philip VI collected over 200 French, Spanish, and Genoese ships— 'their masts,' said an eye witness, 'seemed to be like a great wood'— and drew them up across the estuary at Sluys, chained together in four lines so that they were like the walls of a castle. On Midsummer Day, with wind and tide behind them, the English fleet steered straight at the French. There was then little difference between a sea and a land battle, and for the first, but not the last, time the French faced the combined power of the long-bow and dismounted men-at-arms. The French fleet was largely destroyed and its admiral was hanged in disgrace at the mast-head. But little came of the victory; the fighting in France was indecisive and both Edward and Philip agreed to the pope's request for a truce, which lasted till 1345, when war flared up again in Guienne. Here the main interest lay in the Earl of Derby's *chevauchée*, the name given to a merciless march of an army through enemy territory during which the countryside was devastated and the inhabitants put to the sword.

In 1346 Edward landed in Normandy with apparently no very clear plan in mind. A dash for Paris would have been too dangerous, for in the fourteenth century defence was always easier than attack and in Paris Philip had an army three times the size of the English force. Moving at a leisurely pace—on some days he only marched three or four miles—Edward advanced from La Hogue to Caen and onwards to the Seine, which he crossed at Poissy. As he turned north-eastward toward Calais he found himself in a very dangerous position. Ahead of him lay the Somme with its bridges deliberately broken and behind him Philip was giving chase. At this moment he had a stroke of luck, for a peasant betrayed the position of a ford which enabled the English to cross the river before the tide rose. Two days later Edward chose an excellent site and awaited the French attack. Well before midnight on 26 August Philip's army was annihilated at Crécy. A new force—the English army—had entered European politics.

Edward used his victory to attack Calais, the home of French privateers, which if captured would provide a permanent doorway into France. To house his troops during the winter siege, he built a town of·wooden huts, with a market where local produce could be sold, and by August 1347 Calais was in his hands. Any plans which

The battle of Crécy. Notice the French cross-bowmen and the English long-bowmen in the front of the battle. The pictures comes from an illustrated copy of Froissart's Chronicle.

Philip and Edward may have had for the next season's fighting were completely destroyed by the Black Death (see p. 160), which prevented any chance of continuing the war for the next two or three years, and before it could be resumed Philip had died. In the last year of his life Philip had acquired for the French Crown the valuable district of Dauphiné in the south-east corner of France, so named because the reigning family bore a dolphin (*dauphin*) on its coat of arms. The ruler himself was known as the dauphin, a title which from March 1349 passed to the eldest son of the French king.

John II (1350–64), known as 'le Bon', the genial, was even less able than his father but equally devoted to chivalry. He was slow-witted, very obstinate, and dangerously headstrong, qualities which destroyed all confidence in him, though his personal courage and sense of honour must not be forgotten. Thanks to an empty treasury, a heavy debasement of the coinage, and a total failure to drive away the English against whom fighting had begun again in 1354, John's government was very unpopular. The third Estate, the 'Commons' of the States General (as distinct from the clergy and the nobility), under the leadership of Étienne Marcel, a wealthy cloth merchant,

In the top half of the picture John II is receiving the dukes of Lancaster and Brunswick. Below he is presiding at a feast of the Order of the Star, one of the orders of chivalry.

55

refused to vote any taxes for the war until they had secured some kind of control over the way in which the taxes were collected and also over the troops for whose pay the taxes were being raised. When in the end the new armies appeared they were no more successful against the English, especially in Languedoc where Edward III's son the Black Prince had conducted a terrible *chevauchée* in the autumn of 1355, ruining over 500 towns and villages. The next year the Black Prince marched north on another plundering raid, intending to join up with a second English army near the river Loire. To prevent this, John, at the head of a large force, drove the Black Prince back until, despairing of saving either his troops or his booty, the Prince turned at bay near Poitiers. In spite of his overwhelming strength, John threw away every advantage. Confusion worse than at Crécy set in among the heavily armoured knights, who got bogged down in the mud like small tanks. Fighting bravely but stupidly to the last, John was captured and sent a prisoner to England, there to await the collection from his wretched subjects of the largest ransom ever demanded.

The situation facing the Dauphin (the future Charles V), who acted as regent, was desperate. Étienne Marcel and the States General might demand reforms in return for helping to raise money for John's ransom, but long before any reforms could have been put into force the country had drifted into anarchy. The first horror was the hordes of disbanded mercenaries—the 'Free Companies'—who with no prospect of employment had been turned loose upon the countryside after Poitiers. As Froissart wrote: 'They saw a good town or castle, a day or two's journey away; and then they gathered twenty or thirty brigands together and journeyed night and day by hidden ways until they entered this town and castle . . . exactly at break of day and set fire to a house. And the people of the town thought it was a thousand men in armour come to burn the town and so they fled as best they could and these brigands broke into houses, chests and coffers.' In one area the brigands dug a vast moat in which a great fire was kept burning day and night, which they called 'Hell' and into 'Hell' they threw everybody who refused to surrender their goods and money. Jean de Venette, another chronicler, wrote of the year 1358:

In this year numerous unfortified villages transformed their churches into fortresses, surrounding them with deep ditches, arming the towers with machines of war . . . and carrying up great stones to resist the brigands. . . . Children kept guard in watch boxes at the top of the tower. If they saw the enemy coming afar off, they blew horns or set the bells in motion, the country people ran to take shelter in the church. On the banks of the Loire they were seen taking refuge with their families and beasts, in the islands of the river or in boats moored along its course.

The Jacquerie. From the indifference shown by the ladies on the left it would appear that the nobles have gained the upper hand. It is an interesting picture because it also clearly shows what town buildings looked like. It comes from Froissart's Chronicle.

As if this were not bad enough, the peasants now rose against their lords, blaming them for all the disasters and misery which had fallen on the country since Poitiers. This rising, called the 'Jacquerie' from the nickname for a French peasant, 'Jacques Bonhomme', lasted little more than a month (May–June 1358). At first the nobles were terrified and powerless, but once they had recovered from their panic they dealt out savage vengeance. The leader of the rising was captured and killed by being 'crowned' with a tripod of red-hot iron and in the next three weeks over 20,000 peasants were cruelly slaughtered.

With the country in such a terrible state it may seem surprising that some kind of 'parliamentary' government was not tried as in England, where parliaments of a sort had existed for nearly a hundred years. But France was a country in which each district,

Charles V of France. Part of a statue made at the time of the king's funeral.

almost each town, prided itself on its own liberties and privileges, often given in times past by former kings, and which they would not give up. The only force which could possibly bind France together into a united country was the monarchy, and that is why people thought that John must be ransomed. By the Treaty of Brétigny in 1360 John surrendered to Edward Aquitaine and Poitou in the south-west and Calais and the district of Ponthieu in the north-east; for none of these lands had Edward to pay homage. Once back in France, John quickly discovered that he had no hope of raising the three million crowns due to his conqueror, and true to his extraordinary ideals of chivalry he decided that in honour bound he must return to London. Here he did such ample justice to English food and drink that he died in captivity in 1364. A contemporary French poet wrote: 'The English were very angry at his death.' Well might they be angry for the new reign was to see a very different king, under whom the pendulum of the clock of France's fortune was to move forward at last.

★   ★   ★

'There has never been a king of France who has armed himself less, and never one who has given me more trouble.' Such was Edward III's opinion of Charles V (1364–80), and he was right. Curiously enough the recovery of France was not the work of a great soldier, for Charles had none of his father's passion for chivalry in warfare and after his experiences at Poitiers he never took part in another battle. Instead he preferred good books and talking with scholars and artists, men who 'spoke fine Latin and were argumentative', rather than with feudal barons, who usually could neither read nor write. He was determined to make Paris a civilized and cultured city and he ruled over a brilliant court with great strictness. We are told that he did not allow 'a man of his court, however noble and powerful, to wear too short clothes, or shoes with too outrageous a turn upwards, nor women to be sewn up too tightly in their clothes, or to wear too large collars.' Charles suffered much from feverish headaches and a partly useless right hand, as well as from the doctors and apothecaries who tried to cure him, but underneath his gentle and scholarly appearance lay a will of iron. He was intelligent, shrewd, and a penetrating judge of men, and it was he, not the fighting noblemen, who saw how to drive the English out of France.

Charles set himself to unite all his countrymen by showing them that the only way to preserve their lives and their possessions was by being loyal to him. He knew that a long war and an extravagant court cost money and that therefore everything turned on a full royal treasury. So during his reign the States General were regularly summoned; but whenever they were persuaded to vote money for the war Charles did his utmost to turn a temporary grant of money into a permanent tax. For example, a new tax on every hearth, the *fouage*, originally levied to raise money for King John's ransom, went on being collected. Since even the poorest household had a hearth, this was the easiest way of taxing the whole population; the only alternative was a poll-tax, a tax on each 'head' of the population. Meanwhile the hated *gabelle* became a permanent tax from 1360. The royal domain was now run much more efficiently and far fewer of the great nobles were let off having to pay their taxes. Charles certainly gave his people better government and comparative peace, but they had to pay for it. He himself never lost the affection and gratitude of his subjects, but when he died his successor inherited not only a reserve of seventeen million *livres* but also a legacy of bitter discontent.

Because he was no chivalrous knight-errant himself, Charles V found it easier than his commanders to see why French armies were so often badly beaten by the English. He insisted that pitched battles must be avoided until there was a French army trained in new methods of fighting. If the enemy were given no army to destroy, they were going to find it hard to feed and look after their troops indefinitely while far from home. So he gained a breathing-space in which to create a new French army and, in particular, he made his artillery much more efficient for siege warfare. By contrast, since it was harder for the English to maintain their siege-train in another country, Charles found money to strengthen the fortifications of many towns and castles so that they could withstand attack for much longer. He can also claim to have been the first French king to give his people some understanding of sea-power: he encouraged the building of ships so as to challenge the English mastery of the Channel.

The most obvious sign of changed times was the rise to supreme command in the army of Bertrand du Guesclin, the younger son of a Breton squire and very different from the kind of nobleman who had commanded French armies in the past. Strong, squat, and hideously ugly, du Guesclin had been born about 1330, had quickly made his mark in the army and soon proved to be exactly the man that Charles wanted to carry out his new policy. He was a fine professional soldier—probably the best on either side in the whole war—who had nothing but contempt for men who took part in serious fighting as if they were in a tournament, and by 1370 he had become the hero of France and commander-in-chief of its armies. Like his master, du Guesclin saw that the immediate need was to rid French soil of the Free Companies. A civil war in Spain, in which the Black Prince supported the ruler of Castile, Don Pedro, against his bastard half-brother, provided the answer. For three years du Guesclin fought on behalf of the Bastard, thereby not only making sure that a great many men in the Free Companies died in battle or

The Black Prince receives from his father, Edward III, the document giving him the right to rule the Duchy of Aquitaine.

from disease but also exhausting the Black Prince, who since 1363 had been governor of Aquitaine. Eventually the Black Prince struggled back to Bordeaux, ruined in health and carrying only a store of jewels in place of the fortune which Don Pedro had promised him. Du Guesclin returned victorious, leaving those in the Free Companies who survived the war to seek a living in Spain or to be dealt with very sternly by Charles if they came back to France.

61

It is still much too early to speak of national resistance to England by the French, but at least the south-west of France no longer preferred English to French rule. No man was more responsible for this than the Black Prince. To the hatred which his *chevauchées* had aroused ten years earlier was now added hatred at the crushing taxation which he imposed in Aquitaine to pay for his useless Spanish expedition. On being told that 'right or wrong his vassals should do his bidding' two leading nobles, after protesting in vain against the tax, appealed for help to Charles V—a sign of changed times, indeed. This was the moment for which Charles had worked. With great diplomatic skill he had already thwarted Edward III's hopes of help from Spain and Italy, and even from Flanders; his reform both of the French army and of French finances was almost complete. Knowing that hundreds of the Black Prince's subjects were eager for an excuse to turn against him, Charles in January 1369 formally summoned the Prince, as a peer of France, to appear before him in Paris. 'We shall willingly attend on the appointed day at Paris since the king of France sends for us,' replied the Black Prince, 'but it will be with helmet on head and with sixty thousand men at our back.' Brave words! But the day was over when they could be backed by brave deeds.

Throughout Aquitaine Frenchmen banded together, encouraged by the sermons of their clergy, and within a few weeks over 900 towns and castles had thrown over their allegiance to the English king. Large areas were regained without a fight, and Charles now felt strong enough to declare that the lands surrendered at Brétigny to Edward III once more belonged to the French Crown. The English king tried by making *chevauchées* in the old style to provoke du Guesclin to the pitched battle which he brilliantly avoided as more lands in the south-west were recaptured for France. In August 1370 the city of Limoges declared for Charles, an action which the Black Prince was determined to avenge. Too ill to walk, the Prince from his litter directed a night attack on the city and the hideous sack which followed. This savage revenge only made the English cause more bitterly hated, and in November the Black Prince returned home a dying and defeated man.

Everything now went in favour of France not only on land but also at sea. In 1372 an English fleet trying to relieve La Rochelle was driven off and English towns on the south coast were at the mercy of French raids. By 1374 all that remained of English territory in France was Calais and a thin coastal strip between Bordeaux and Bayonne. Two years later the Black Prince died, to be followed to the grave in June 1377 by his father, now a pathetic, half-crazed figure with a long white beard, deserted by his servants and plundered of money and jewels by his mistress. Before Edward's body could be buried in Westminster Abbey the French had landed at Rye.

France in the fourteenth and fifteenth centuries.

62

Bruges

Calais

FLANDERS

Brussels

Liège

Agincourt

Crécy

Arras

PONTIEU

Somme

Péronne

Meuse

Compiègne

Harfleur

Rouen

Reims

CHAMPAGNE

La Hogue

Caen

Seine

Meaux

NORMANDY

Poissy

Paris

Nancy

Vernevil

Montlhéry

Brétigny

MONTEREAU

Troyes

BRITTANY

Patay

Fontainebleau

Domrémy

MAINE

Orléans

Loire

Yonne

Beaugency

Jargeau

Blois

Chambord

Plessis-les-Tours

Tours

Chenonceaux

Dijon

Azay-le-Rideau

Chinon

Bourges

BURGUNDY

Poitiers

B E R R Y

POITOU

La Rochelle

Limoges

DAUPHINE

GUIENNE

Castillon

Rhône

Bordeaux

AQUITAINE

Garonne

Avignon

ARMAGNAC

LANGUEDOC

Bayonne

GASCONY

| 0 | 50 | 100 | 150 | 200 km |

| 0 | 50 | 100 | 150 miles |

The death of Bertrand du Guesclin in 1380. He had arranged the siege of Chateauneuf-Random, held by brigands and discharged soldiers against Charles V. The place was about to surrender when the great soldier died. It is said that those who had been besieged laid the keys of the fortress on his coffin.

It looked as if the war were almost over and the triumph of France complete, especially as the new English king, Richard II, the Black Prince's son, was a mere boy of 10. Yet, by a cruel stroke of fortune, only three years later France lost Charles V and also du Guesclin, who both died in 1830. The partnership which could have achieved the overthrow of England had ended just too soon, and France had another seventy years of misery and fighting to endure before the English were finally driven back across the Channel.

(iii) French, English, and Burgundians 1380–1461

For the time being, however, France could enjoy a breathing-space before the next crisis of the Hundred Years War broke on her. The situations in France and England were curiously similar. Edward III was succeeded by his ten-year-old grandson, Richard II; while the new French king, Charles VI, was a boy of 12; both kings were controlled by royal uncles who were mainly interested in pursuing their own selfish interests. In both countries widespread misery among the peasants led to open rebellion; the Peasant's Revolt in England in 1381 was matched by even more serious troubles in France. As both countries urgently needed peace, there was no difficulty in arranging a series of truces, which were not due to end until 1413, and to cement this uneasy peace Richard II was married by proxy in 1396 to the seven-year-old daughter of Charles VI. But at this point the fortunes of England and France diverged. Richard II was deposed in 1397 and murdered two years later, but his cold-blooded and unattractive rival, who became Henry IV, handed on to his son, Henry V, a strong and united nation. By contrast France was torn apart by civil war and lay wide open to a conqueror.

The long reign of Charles VI (1380–1422) was one of the most wretched periods in the history of France. We have seen how his father had remained popular in spite of all the taxes which he had imposed, but on Charles VI fell all the discontent which had been growing during the last years of Charles V's reign. In 1382 a rising in protest against new taxation began in Rouen and more serious trouble followed in Paris, where the mob broke into the Town Hall, seized the iron mallets which they found in the arsenal and took control of the city. Jews, tax-collectors, and lawyers were beaten or murdered, prisons were thrown open, and wine-cellars plundered. At the same time much of the south of France was in the hands of brigands, while open rebellion in Flanders against the most powerful of the royal uncles, Philip, Duke of Burgundy, forced Charles to send an army to restore order.

In 1388 Charles came of age and took over the government from his uncles. He had none of his father's ability, and the strict economy, which his country so sorely needed, was the last thing to be expected of either the king or his brother, Louis, Duke of Orleans, and for three years they lived in a riot of ceremonies, spectacles, balls, banquets, and tournaments. Suddenly in August 1392, at the head of an army which he was leading into Brittany, Charles went violently mad. Although he recovered after a few days, the attacks of madness went on throughout his life, becoming more frequent and more serious. Nothing could have been more disastrous for a country in which the only hope of unity was a strong king. In effect, until Charles died in 1422, France had no king and, in place of peace and unity, came thirty years of rivalry between the two great houses of Burgundy and Orleans, ruled over by Charles's uncle and his brother.

To understand the power of these two royal princes it is necessary to go back a little into French history. From quite early times French kings had created great blocks of territory within France, known as apanages, for princes of the blood royal. The purpose was to make sure that these areas were governed more strictly than was then possible for the king to do from Paris. So long as the king was strong, such princes could be easily controlled; but if the king were weak or, like Charles VI, incapable of governing, the result could be very dangerous for the monarchy. Most powerful and splendid of these apanages was the dukedom of Burgundy.

King John had made his younger son, Philip, known for his bravery at Poitiers as 'the Bold', Duke of Burgundy in 1363. With its capital at Dijon, Burgundy contained the area of France then, as now, renowned for its wine and cookery. But Philip was not content with this magnificent fief and set about extending his power by three very important marriages. He himself married the heiress to the Count of Flanders, while two of his children married into the Bavarian royal house, which then ruled most of what is now Holland. Charles V was strong enough not to be much worried at his younger brother's marriage policy and indeed hoped that it might mean the control of the rich Flemish cities by the French king. In fact exactly the opposite happened. When in 1384 Philip succeeded to the county of Flanders, he and his successors found that their new lands were much more important and far richer than Burgundy, and Brussels soon seemed a much more exciting capital than Dijon. More important for France was the fact that through their lands in the Netherlands the rulers of Burgundy became princes of the Empire and therefore subject for that part of their territory to the Emperor and not to the king of France. In addition, the cloth trade on which the Flemish wealth so much depended meant that friendship with England mattered more to the Flemings than support of a French king against his old enemy. So as the years went by, the dukes of Burgundy became less and less French in outlook and more Flemish; they behaved less like subjects of the French king and more like ambitious rulers of a rival state, which lay like a buffer between France and the Empire. Charles VI was quite incapable of dealing with such a situation.

The position of Charles's brother, Louis, Duke of Orleans, was rather different. He had only gained his dukedom shortly before his brother first went mad but he quickly set about increasing his lands in France until in size, but not in wealth, they were nearly as great as those of the Duke of Burgundy. They were, however, more scattered than Duke Philip's lands and so, while valuable in any civil war against the king, they were less likely to be useful to a foreign enemy seeking an alliance. For example, Burgundy was always more useful to England than was Orleans. At the turn of the century Louis was only 28, while Duke Philip was nearing 60. He was witty and eloquent, a lover of sports and festivals, an expert on jewellery, and a wearer of sumptuous and strange clothing. He was less wealthy than Philip and so seized more of the royal income for himself. Charles VI liked his brother and disliked his uncle, so that, generally speaking, in the periods when the king was sane the Duke of Orleans was the more powerful; when the king was mad the Duke of Burgundy was the real ruler of France.

The rivalry between the two houses did not become serious for France until after Duke Philip's death in 1404, when he was suc-

The funeral procession of Charles VI.

ceeded by his son, John the Fearless, a man only a year older than Louis. Small in stature, with a big head and bulging frog's eyes, Duke John had little charm but a great deal of intelligence. He always feared an attack on himself and therefore, according to a contemporary, 'he always wore armour under his robe and had his sword girt and made himself redoubted and feared above all others'. Despite this and a difficult stammer, he was popular with his subjects. On every important matter he was in bitter dispute with Duke Louis. During the Great Schism they supported rival popes; towards England, Duke John was friendly, while Duke Louis did everything possible to provoke the old enemy, even offering to fight Henry IV in a duel; each did his utmost to get more money than the other from the royal coffers.

In his periods of madness Charles VI was disgracefully neglected, left to roam his apartments with hair unwashed and long, uncut nails, while his queen, Isabel, lived a life of luxury and immorality which shocked even those used to living at court. Duke John did not interfere in the government until Queen Isabel and Duke Louis debased the coinage and imposed new taxes. Then in the summer of 1405, announcing that these taxes would never be paid in his dominions, he marched on Paris and took charge. The rivalry between the two dukes grew increasingly bitter until on the night of 24 November 1407, as Duke Louis was returning to his house in Paris, he was set upon and murdered. Although the murderers escaped, there was no doubt who was behind the murder, and before long Duke John confessed that 'through the suggestion of the devil' he had been responsible. Not only did Duke Louis's death remove the one man who, in the absence of the king, might perhaps have led the country against the English, but the mortal hatreds created by the murder were to plunge France into civil war at the very moment that fighting with England was likely to flare up again.

Duke Louis was succeeded by his son Charles, a youth of 16, who three years later married the daughter of a great Gascon noble, Count Bernard d'Armagnac, whose family had for over a century been bitterly hostile to England. The Count's influence was great and Orleanists soon became known as Armagnacs, wearing as their badge a white cross or scarf to distinguish themselves from those wearing the red cross of Burgundy. Fighting between Burgundians and Armagnacs began in 1411 with the armies of both sides a terror to the countryside, and the fact that in 1413 Henry V came to the English throne did not stop these selfish nobles from fighting among themselves even though an English invasion was likely to come soon. The third phase of the Hundred Years War was about to open.

Henry V, now 25 years old, had when Prince of Wales been hardened in battle against his father's enemies in Scotland, at Shrewsbury, and for some years along the Welsh Marches. He was a brilliant soldier, who believed that in war skill was much more important than numbers. He had a genius for ruling other men and in Wales he had learned how important it was to rule efficiently. Tall and athletic, he was able to run so fast that with the help of one or two friends he could run down a deer in the open. Henry had great charm and also was a sincerely religious man, who, from the moment of his coronation, dedicated himself to his tasks as a king. Shakespeare's portrait of the hero-king was not far from the truth. With a united nation behind him, Henry was all set to achieve his great ambition of ending once and for all the age-long quarrel with France by uniting both countries under his rule. As a descendant of William the Conqueror, he was convinced that Normandy was his by right and he was equally convinced, after studying all the legal documents, that he should revive the claim of his great-grandfather, Edward III, to the French throne. Until the very last moment the French never took Henry or his claims very seriously; to them the quarrel with England had always been a feudal quarrel between a Gascon vassal and his royal overlord. Henry, more modern in outlook, was

Henry V. Portrait by an unknown artist. The short-cropped hair was then fashionable.

determined to stand on what he regarded as his legal 'rights' and he saw that the condition of France gave him a wonderful chance of imposing a final settlement.

Two courses were open to Henry: what was then called 'the way of justice', which meant long and complicated negotiations, and, if these failed, 'the way of force'. The House of Commons, thinking anxiously of the cost of yet more fighting, urged Henry to make every effort to pursue 'the way of justice' before going to war. It is not easy to be sure how sincere Henry was in his bargaining with

Preparations for war at the Tower of London. London Bridge is seen in the background, the White Tower in the foreground.

the French. Those walking near the Tower of London in 1414 and hearing the noise of hammering from the wharves must have been convinced that Henry was bent on war at all costs. However, the negotiations dragged on until the summer of 1415 when any hope of a peaceful settlement was ended by the assertion of the French envoys that Henry was not even the rightful king of England and that it was with the descendants of the murdered Richard II that they should be talking. Henry's conscience at once assured him that 'the way of force' was now both inevitable and just.

Henry's first invasion of France nearly ended in disaster. He was extremely lucky to capture Harfleur in September because his army was suffering severely from dysentery, contracted partly from a virus rife in the neighbouring salt-marshes and partly from the effects of too much local fruit and wine. The twenty surgeons who appear in the lists of his expedition for the first time could do nothing to check the disease from which many died. Henry, who on arrival had proclaimed that he had 'come into his own land, his own country, his own kingdom', sent home messages to persuade people to come over and settle in Harfleur.

On 8 October, with seriously reduced forces, Henry set out for Calais on what he hoped would be an eight-day march. Thus his troops were only given a week's rations; all baggage was carried on pack animals; and the sole transport provided was for a six-inch-long portion of the True Cross. The well-disciplined force, forbidden even to swear, reached the Somme four days later. Here trouble began, for not until 19 October were the English safely across the river and by this time substantial French forces had come up and were marching on a parallel course, neither army knowing where the other was. When contact was made on 24 October, Henry found an overwhelming French army barring the road to Calais. So dangerous was his position that Henry offered to surrender the lands conquered in Normandy in return for a safe passage to Calais. The French, who were said to have brought with them a specially painted cart in which Henry was to be paraded through the Paris streets, refused. There was nothing left for the English but to prepare their weapons for battle and themselves for certain defeat and probable death.

Agincourt (25 October) was one of the most complete victories ever inflicted by a small, tired, and hungry army on vastly superior forces. It was Poitiers all over again: for many Frenchmen died, not of wounds, but of suffocation as the great heap of French armour grew when those behind pressed rashly forward on those in the van unable to move across the sodden fields. After arranging about the prisoners, Henry returned to England as winter was coming on and there would be no more fighting. On 23 November all London was gaily decorated, and cheering crowds, choirs dressed as angels, and priests greeted the serious-faced king as he rode to Westminster Abbey to give thanks for his victory. In Henry's mind gratitude must surely have mingled with relief at the narrowness of his escape.

Agincourt made England once again an important force in Europe. The battle had come at a moment when the emperor Sigismund was trying to get both England and France to support the same pope and he decided to come to each country in turn in the hope of acting as a peacemaker between them. The visit to Paris in the spring of 1416 was a complete failure. So many of the leading Armagnacs had either been killed or taken prisoner at Agincourt that Count Bernard himself had become the leading figure in the government. He was a hot-headed, boastful, and brutal man, who had no intention of making peace with England at least until Harfleur had been recaptured. Sigismund's meanness and undisguised immorality did not help his cause. He had no difficulty in finding money for a private dinner-party given to 600 ladies, but he could only offer half a franc to Notre-Dame Cathedral in gratitude for a special display of relics. So in May he moved on to England, where he was warmly welcomed by Henry V and created a Knight of the Garter, perhaps in return for a present of what he assured his host was the heart of St. George. By mid-August the Treaty of Canterbury was signed between Sigismund and Henry, and the two rulers decided to isolate France completely by bringing Burgundy into their alliance. When all three men met at Calais, Duke John promised support to Henry when he next invaded France but he refused to sign any written agreement.

In August 1417 Henry landed in France and in the next six months had regained Lower Normandy (the country west of the Seine) and had advanced against Rouen, capital of Upper Normandy, which only surrendered after a desperate resistance in January 1419. The Armagnacs had done practically nothing to meet the English invasion, and Duke John decided that the time had come for him to act. He now allied himself with Queen Isabel who, in return for being set up in a new court at Troyes, appointed the Duke as governor of France, and Burgundian forces broke into Paris. Wild disorder followed, and many Armagnacs, including Count Bernard himself, were murdered. With both the Queen and the capital in his hands, Duke John felt that the time had come to forget his promises to Henry and to pose as defender of France against the invaders.

Henry knew that great difficulties lay ahead of him, for he had had to leave so many of his soldiers behind him as garrisons in the towns which he had captured. So in May 1419 he formally met Charles VI, Queen Isabel, and Duke John; he also met for the first time Charles's daughter, Catherine, whom he had always professed that he wished to marry when he became king of France. Henry cannot have set much store by these negotiations, for he knew that the slippery Duke John was at the same time in touch with the Dauphin (the future Charles VII), who had been kept firmly in Armagnac hands. The Dauphin was an out-at-elbows youth of 15, detested by his mother, who denied that the king was his father, but he was a valuable pawn on the Armagnac side. Henry cannot have been very surprised when in July the Dauphin and Duke John promised eternal friendship and he returned to 'the way of force' with the prospect of a long struggle against an apparently united France.

Suddenly the entire picture changed. On 10 September the Dauphin and Duke John met at Montereau, where the Seine and the Yonne join. As the Duke entered the specially fenced enclosure on the bridge over the river, he was felled by an Armagnac axe. It is extremely unlikely that the Dauphin knew of the plot, but once again, as in 1404 after the murder of Duke Louis of Orleans, the bitter hatred of Burgundian for Armagnac split France in two and delivered her over to the English invader, as both Burgundians and

The marriage of Henry V and Catherine, daughter of Charles VI, who is on the left of the picture. The wedding took place in the cathedral of Troyes.

Queen Isabel appealed to Henry for help. Duke Philip, the new duke of Burgundy, wanted vengeance for his father; the Queen wanted her daughter Catherine, whom she loved, to sit on the French throne even if it meant being Henry's wife—anything rather than see her hated son become king on his father's death. Negotiations were complicated and lengthy, and Henry continued his steady advance towards Paris while they were in progress. Eventually in May 1420 a treaty of peace between England and France, to which Duke Philip assented, was signed at Troyes. By the Treaty of Troyes Henry was recognized as Charles VI's heir and as regent of France while Charles still lived. As a pledge of the union of the two crowns Henry was to marry Catherine and, in alliance with Burgundy, he promised to recover all the French territory which still recognized 'the so-called Dauphin' as heir to the throne. On 2 June Henry and Catherine were married at Troyes and after a one-day honeymoon Henry was off to the wars again.

So long as Henry was personally in command all went well, but when early in 1421 he had to return home to reassure his Council and parliament that England had not been submerged in France by the Treaty of Troyes, a force of Dauphinists, greatly aided by troops from Scotland, inflicted a serious defeat on the English at Bauge, near Tours. Henry hurried back to France, and the Dauphin's army quickly retreated behind the Loire, leaving Henry free to besiege Meaux, a Dauphinist stronghold some miles north-east of Paris. It was probably here that during the long winter siege Henry contracted dysentery from which on 31 August 1422 he died, leaving as his heir a son of less than ten months old.

Had Henry lived but another two months he would have achieved his ambition of wearing the crowns of both England and France, for in October Charles VI's tragic life ended. The only prince to accompany the mad king's body to burial at Saint Denis was the Duke of Bedford, brother of Henry V and regent for the infant Henry VI. At the end of the funeral service the cry rang out through the ancient church: 'God grant long life to Henry, by the grace of God King of France and England, our sovereign lord'. Such was the result of the forty-two years of Charles VI's miserable reign, but it was a result which could not last for long.

$$\star \quad \star \quad \star$$

The death of Henry V did not mean that everything immediately went well for the French. The Duke of Bedford did his utmost to rule France on behalf of the infant king wisely and sympathetically. But he had a hard task, for the uncrowned Dauphin, Charles, remained in control of much of the centre and south of the country and it was as clear to Bedford as it had been to Henry V that there was no hope of beating the Dauphin and making sure of uniting England and France under one English king without the help of Burgundy.

The Dauphin—he was not known as Charles VII until after his coronation in 1429—was a pathetic creature. Born in 1403, by 1422 he looked, moved, and lived like an old man. He spent his days in his various castles in the Loire valley, a terrified man and totally under the influence of favourites whom he did not even choose himself, but who were forced on him by court intrigues. He was ill-fed, shabbily dressed, with patched clothes and worn-out boots, always chronically short of money and hopelessly in debt to nobles, who shamelessly lent him his own money which they had diverted from the royal treasury to their own pockets. Uncertain whether he was truly son of Charles VI, he lacked all self-confidence and his moods alternated between long bouts of apathy and short spurts of activity. Cowardly but intelligent, he preferred diplomacy to fighting and recognized the importance of Burgundy. His court was filled with quarrelsome nobles, who, when there were no English to fight, had nothing better to do than carry on their own private wars against each other, some even hiring English mercenaries to help them.

So it was not very surprising that when the Dauphin could scrape together enough money to raise an army, it was far less well equipped and disciplined than Bedford's troops and he was forced to rely much on his Scottish ally, always ready to discomfit the English when the chance arose.

There is no clear pattern in the military history of the years following Henry V's death. It was mostly a dreary story of sudden raids and sieges of castles, which were captured and recaptured as the fortunes of war changed. The one exception to this was Bedford's overwhelming victory in the summer of 1424 over a large army of French, Scots, Spaniards, and Lombards at Verneuil in Normandy, a battle which French writers have called 'un autre Agincourt'. The Scots were virtually wiped out, which gave great pleasure in London, where with boastful exaggeration it was claimed that 17,000 'of these proude Scottes went to Dog-wash the same day'. However, shortage of troops and the need to return to England prevented Bedford from following up his victory, but he was back in France in 1427. Here he found the Earl of Salisbury, his ablest general, determined to make an all-out attack on Orleans, to which, with some misgiving, he agreed.

The siege did not begin until October 1428, and after a week a piece of sheer ill-luck led to Salisbury's death. Hearing a chance cannon-ball coming in his direction, Salisbury ducked down to avoid it, but the ball hit the lintel of a window in the tower where he stood and dislodged an iron bar, which removed half of his face. Thereafter the siege was never prosecuted with much determination and long before the town was captured a relieving force was near at hand with the dauntless Joan of Arc at its head.

Joan was born at Domrémy, a village on the Meuse, in 1412, the daughter of a prosperous farmer. Somewhere about 1425 she became convinced that she was hearing the 'Voices' of St. Michael and St. Catherine and St. Margaret, who repeatedly told her that the English must be driven from France but that this could not happen until the Dauphin had proved himself the true king by being crowned and anointed in Rheims Cathedral. Joan, who had been brought up on the farm, had gained the reputation of being a quiet and very religious girl, able to tell fortunes and cure diseases. Even the Duke of Lorraine had invited her to Nancy to consult her about his health and fortunes.

In 1428 Joan persuaded Robert de Baudricourt, the principal officer in the district, to send her to the Dauphin at Chinon, where she arrived in March 1429. She was at first received with suspicion and sent on to Poitiers, where for three weeks theologians questioned her without reaching any convincing result. Ultimately the Dauphin, perhaps to keep her quiet, allowed her to join the force which was

mustering for the relief of Orleans, though she was never given any position of command.

In full armour Joan rode at the head of the relieving army, which reached Orleans on 29 April and by 4 May was inside the town. Three days later the English abandoned the siege and were allowed to move off unmolested. Joan had shown great personal courage in the fighting, and her presence in the attack on one of the forts led the English to assume that she must be a witch. Against her they hurled the kind of language which accurately described the women who normally followed in the rear of any French army. Their failure to capture Orleans proved to be the turning-point in the war, for although there were still to be periods of English success, the story of the years 1429 to 1453 is the story of the slow but sure expulsion of the English from France.

With her usual impetuous haste, Joan now urged the Dauphin to travel to Rheims for his coronation. Those at court who disliked Joan and were jealous of her—and there were many—persuaded Charles not to heed her, and for the moment she had to be content with being allowed to remain with the troops, whose task was to clear the English out of the Loire valley. Jargeau and Beaugency were recaptured and at Patay an English force under Talbot was defeated. The Dauphin now agreed to go to Rheims, where on 17 July 1429 in the great cathedral he was crowned and anointed as Charles VII. Immediately after the coronation Charles made a demonstration march through Champagne and in September agreed to what proved

Joan of Arc meets the Dauphin and persuades him to let her attack Troyes. Contemporaries praised her figure rather more than her face.

Joan directs the attack on Paris. This was the occasion on which she was wounded, perhaps because of her lack of armour. The bundles of faggots carried by two soldiers will probably be used to burn down a gateway.

an ill-advised attack on Paris, in which Joan was wounded. Shortly afterwards his army was disbanded for the winter as the money had run out.

In the spring of 1430 the Duke of Burgundy decided to join the English in the siege of Compiègne. Largely on her own initiative, Joan led some troops to the aid of the town. On 24 May, while taking part in a sortie outside the walls, Joan was captured by a Burgundian archer. Duke Philip was 'more delighted than if a king had fallen into his hands' and, after some negotiation, sold Joan to his allies for £80,000. The English were determined to show that their recent defeats were solely due to sorcery and so from December 1430 until the following March Joan was tried as a heretic and sorceress by the Inquisition. She was condemned, handed over to the English for execution, and on 30 May in the market-place at Rouen faced death by burning with a serenity born of her unshakeable faith.

Joan had been no general. She might, according to contemporaries, have had some skill in placing guns, but she was far too impetuous ever to have been given any position of command. Her gift to France was far greater than a knowledge of tactics. She had rekindled the long-dead offensive spirit in the French army and had taught dispirited troops and half-hearted commanders that what appeared as miracles could be achieved by courage, speed, determination, and a passionate belief in the justice of their cause. The English were triumphant at her death, for they believed that, with the removal of the witch, all would again go well for them. Their treatment of Joan,

Joan of Arc at the stake. A monk holds a crucifix so that she can see it and receive strength to meet her death.

while cruel to us, was understandable at the time. Far less excusable was the conduct of Charles VII, who never lifted a finger to save the girl who had done so much for him. He even went so far as to declare that her capture was due to her own self-will and that he had received a successor in the person of a young shepherd boy from the south of France who seemed to be just as good.

Joan, perhaps without fully understanding it, was another of those leading figures—we have already seen something of the same spirit in Wyclif and Huss—who saw the future in terms of the nation rather than of a universal rule. In his play *Saint Joan* Bernard Shaw puts into the mouth of Cauchon, Bishop of Beauvais, words which he could not have spoken but which in fact sum up the challenge of the new authority towards the old:

When she threatens to drive the English from the soil of France she is undoubtedly thinking of the whole extent of country in which French is spoken. To her the French-speaking people are what the Holy Scriptures describe as a nation. Call this side of her heresy Nationalism if you will: I can find you no better name for it. I can only tell you that it is essentially anti-Catholic and anti-Christian; for the Catholic Church knows only one realm, and that is the realm of Christ's Kingdom. Divide that kingdom into nations, and you dethrone Christ. Dethrone Christ, and who will stand between our throats and the sword? The world will perish in a welter of war.

Cauchon was not entirely wrong, as the later chapters of this book will show.

English hopes ran high, but there was never again any real chance of an English victory in the war. As ever, the key to victory by either side lay in securing the support of Burgundy, and there were increasing signs that Duke Philip was contemplating making his peace with Charles VII without, if possible, breaking his oath to the English that he would uphold the Treaty of Troyes. Duke Philip the Good—a strange title to be given to one who had not only inherited his father's skill in crooked diplomacy but who also openly acknowledged twenty-four mistresses—tried to achieve this impossible feat at the Congress of Arras in 1435, called originally to arrange peace between France and Burgundy but at which Philip had insisted that his English allies should be present. When during the negotiations the familiar deadlock was reached over rival claims to the French throne, Philip announced his intention of supporting a French king for France, and in fury the English representatives left Arras faced with the now hopeless task of continuing the war against both France and Burgundy.

Plots and rivalries at Charles's court prevented him from giving his full attention to the war and not until 1441 did he finally get the better of those nobles who had tried to depose him in favour of his singularly unpleasant, yet clever, son, the Dauphin Louis. In 1445 a great effort was made to end the war when a marriage was arranged between Henry VI and Margaret of Anjou, as a price for which the English surrendered Maine. By 1450 Normandy had been lost to England, and for the next three years the French steadily reconquered Guienne. In July 1453 the battle of Castillon led to the capture of Bordeaux and this is usually regarded as the end of the long struggle. No final peace treaty was ever signed and for another 350 years the English continued to incorporate the fleur-de-lys in their national flag.

A postscript must be added. Three years after the English had been driven out of all their former French possessions save for Calais, a special commission re-examined the story of Joan of Arc and declared that all that had been said at her trial in 1431 was false and that, far from being a witch, she had been inspired by God. This is not a question on which historians can pass a final judgement, though five centuries later in 1920 the Roman Catholic Church was to declare her a saint. Both in 1431 and in 1456 the judges 'proved' what was required of them at the time. What is certain is that Joan was no witch and that from the moment of her arrival at Orleans the flame of French patriotism was kindled. Charles, known somewhat flatteringly as Charles the Victorious, lived on until 1461, and in a later chapter we shall see what he did to make France stronger and more united. An inglorious monarch, he had through the commission paid his debt to the girl who had been the first to make his reign so much more glorious than himself.

Chapter 3
The King's Majesty

The Hundred Years War greatly strengthened the feeling among Frenchmen and Englishmen of belonging to separate nations. This spirit, as we have seen, was quite contrary to the old medieval belief that Christendom should be united under the pope, who was supreme in all spiritual matters, and the emperor, who was the chief earthly ruler. The 300 years covered by this book witnessed the challenge to this belief by national kings and its overthrow. During this period the challenge came from new nation states of which France and England were the first to develop, to be followed in the sixteenth century by the Dutch republic. There were three empires which upheld the old ways: the Papacy, which survived the challenge of the Reformation; the Hapsburg empire in Germany, a shadow of the old Holy Roman Empire; and the Ottoman empire, a version of many races under the conquering Turks and bound together by a belief in the religion of Islam. Spain, a nation of the utmost importance in these centuries, grew strong under two rulers, Ferdinand and Isabella, who strove to create a feeling of unity under the crown, but ended its days of greatness when Philip II in the last half of the sixteenth century tried to revive the old ideas of empire under his rule. The Scandinavian countries and countries like Poland and Bohemia followed slowly in the path which western monarchs had made.

In this section of the book we shall be studying the ways that kings made their countries strong by being united and, by contrast, how weak and defenceless were disunited lands like Italy or the countries which had to face the Turkish attacks in eastern Europe. The growing power of the king is the factor which really matters, for, in whatever country strong central government existed in our period, it was the king who had brought it about. Before turning to the story of some of the countries in detail it is important to understand how kings set about their task.

Geography mattered a great deal. It was much easier to make an island, like England, into a united country than to unite France, where on the east there are no clear frontiers, or Spain, which is rigidly divided up by mountain ranges. Italy, which looks a unity on a map, was so divided politically that it did not become a nation in the real sense of the word until the nineteenth century. However, even when geography appeared to help, there were always wild and remote parts of a country where the word of a king meant little or nothing. It was in areas like the north of England or the Massif Central in France, or in countries like Scotland or Norway and Sweden, that the power of the nobles was greatest and hardest to overcome.

Broadly speaking, a king faced two great rivals—the Church and the feudal nobility. If he was to be supreme in his country he had either to crush these rivals or enter into partnership with them. Different kings adopted different tactics. Yet in all European countries where the monarch was steadily gaining power, there were three developments which greatly helped him. First, there were important changes in the royal council—kings had always had their advisers but in earlier days these had been their chief vassals, who felt that they had a right to be consulted. Gradually they began to be replaced by humbler men, chosen because they were skilled in finance or in domestic affairs; above all, men skilled in managing others. They might be created nobles as a reward for their work, but by the end of the fourteenth century in England and France, which set a pattern for other lands to follow, a councillor was a paid adviser, sworn to serve his royal master loyally. A royal council, as its business grew, often set up smaller bodies to deal with special matters, and this gave a king the chance to extend his power. This was one of the reasons for the success of Ferdinand and Isabella in Spain.

Secondly, these royal councils needed secretaries. Some would move about with the king as he went on his travels, but more and more they remained in Paris or in London to transact the royal business in the king's name. By the end of our period these secretaries are developing into something akin to a modern minister, though completely dependent on the will of the king and not part of parliament. Thirdly, we see in these centuries the gradual emergence of a new type of diplomacy. While heralds and trumpets would still greet the arrival of a special embassy from a foreign court, the king came more and more to rely for his information on his ambassadors, men who lived abroad, grew to know the country and to speak its language.

From all these developments the king gained greatly. The business of government was growing increasingly complicated and could no longer be transacted by illiterate barons or even by legally trained churchmen. Kings relied more and more on experts and saw the advantage of having them totally dependent on them.

Nothing was more important to royal power than a full treasury. War could not be waged without it; in domestic affairs no king was master in his own house if he was totally dependent for money on his nobles. It was in France that the king's power most markedly grew from his control over finance. The ransom demanded for King John after 1356 made the poor French people accustomed to taxes. At first they were levied and then later approved by the States General. A century later we find the king explaining that he had levied the taxes without discussing them with the States General so as to save his loyal subjects the expense of travelling to a meeting. Soon in matters of finance the French kings commanded a more certain source of revenue than other monarchs. At the same time the importance of the States General dwindled. This did not happen in England where the king never had the same control over taxation. French kings ignored the States General, English kings, if they were wise, learned to achieve their ends through parliament. It was the gradual understanding that the king had to have money and could only get it through parliament which by the seventeenth century gave the English parliament the whiphand over the Stuarts. The importance of finance in the rivalry of the various European nations cannot be exaggerated. In France because of financial control the kings became absolute rulers; in England in the last resort the kings depended on parliament and their power was limited.

We must now turn to the detailed story of some of the European countries.

(i) France

'He, with his kingdom all desolate, vexed, and destroyed, like a ship dismantled and demolished on all sides, ruined in its foundations, and in all its beauty and magnificence brought to ruin; without labour, without inhabitants, merchandise or justice, without rule or order, full of thieves and brigands . . . with even its royal throne lying low, overthrown, a footstool for men's feet, for the English to trample on and plunderers to wipe their feet upon, he, with great labour, restored it to freedom and prosperity.' Thus a Flemish chronicler wrote in praise of Charles VII, who, with his son Louis XI after him, rebuilt the greatness of France after the Hundred Years War. It is a strange fact that Charles VII, timid, uncouth, and despised in his youth, developed an interest in warfare as he grew older and became with remarkable speed not only a powerful French king but one of Europe's leading sovereigns. 'He is the king of kings,' wrote the Doge of Venice, 'nothing is possible without him.'

Long before the war with England ended, Charles had set about creating a regular, paid, royal army, able to be used to stop the scandal of private wars among the nobles or to be turned against the English. In 1445 all captains and their 'companies' were ordered to appear before the Constable of France, who took into the royal service such men as he chose, while the remainder were sent home, or, if foreigners, escorted to the nearest frontier. The flower of this army was the new *compagnies d'ordonnance* consisting of some 10,000 cavalry, commanded by officers chosen and dismissed by the king, and they were paid from the royal treasury. In addition, between 1445 and 1451 the 'Free Archers', who were crossbowmen, were enlisted from villages throughout France. Every fifth household had to furnish one archer, who was required to practise regularly every Sunday, to keep his equipment in good condition, and to fight when summoned. Once in the field they were paid by the king and in peace time they were free (hence their name) from all taxation, which was a very handsome privilege. Perhaps most important of all was the great development of artillery under the two brothers Jean and Gaspard Bureau, who not only built the guns but often directed them in battle. Since gunpowder was the unanswerable reply to any rebellious noble who defied the king from behind stone walls, this branch of the army belonged solely to the king.

A strong ruler needed not only soldiers but money. As Charles VII became more powerful, taxes granted for a particular purpose often became permanent and it was the royal council, not the States General, which decided how much should be demanded. But it was one thing to levy a tax, quite another thing to extract the money from an impoverished people. So, side by side with a reorganization of the tax system went a determined effort to restore the prosperity of the nation.

In this uphill task Charles was greatly helped by a remarkable man, Jacques Coeur, a merchant born at Bourges about 1395, who built up a gigantic fortune in the Levant trade. It was said at this time that there could no longer be seen 'in the eastern [Mediterranean] sea any mast which did not bear the fleur-de-lys', and this meant prosperity for many more people than just Jacques Coeur. He was very much the sign of a new age, for although he was no aristocrat, by 1436 he had become Master of the Mint in Paris, three years later the controller of the king's finances and court banker, and in 1442 a member of the king's Council. As he grew ever more powerful, he was employed by Charles on diplomatic missions and he kept in touch with his 'agents' all over Europe by means of an elaborate pigeon post, an idea which he probably learned from the Arabs. The superb house which he built for himself still stands in Bourges, and it is easy to see the holes in the attic roofs through which the carrier pigeons flew. It was probably inevitable that this wealthy and important upstart should arouse great jealousy, and in 1451 he fell from power on a trumped-up charge of being involved in poisoning Agnes Sorel, Charles's mistress. After two years in prison he entered papal service and died in 1456 on the island of Chios, while taking part in an expedition against the Turks. What really matters about Jacques Coeur in French history is not his private wealth but his readiness to devote his energies and great financial skill to the restoration of French prosperity. He was a new type of self-made man, who was at the same time a patriot and a good servant of the state.

The most serious problem facing Charles was his own family, those near relations, the 'sires of the fleur-de-lys', or princes of royal blood—the dukes of Burgundy, Anjou, Bourbon, Brittany, and others. Of these, as we have seen, Burgundy presented by far the greatest threat to France. At Brussels and at Dijon were courts at which French art and culture were richer than in Paris. In 1429 the Duke of Burgundy had founded the Order of the Golden Fleece, which came to be regarded as the most noble order of chivalry in Europe and thus the most prized by its members. The danger to the French monarchy was that the dukes of Burgundy might by their marriage policies revive the old 'middle' kingdom between France and Germany, which dated from the break-up of Charlemagne's empire. The most dangerous moment for Charles VII came in 1440 when the princes of the blood rebelled and were joined by the Dauphin, the future Louis XI. The rebellion was crushed, but at the end of it Louis fled to Burgundy for protection. 'My cousin of Burgundy knows not what he does', said Charles on hearing of his son's disloyalty. 'He is suckling the fox who will eat his hens.' It proved a very accurate prophecy.

Readers of Sir Walter Scott's novel *Quentin Durward* will remember Louis XI, the leading character, whom Scott depicts as a ruthless

Louis XI. This portrait has made no attempt to make the ugly king better looking than he was.

and sinister figure; and though this portrait is exaggerated and over-dramatic, it is by no means wholly untrue. We owe our real knowledge of Louis XI not to a nineteenth-century novelist but to Philippe de Commines, the last of the great medieval chroniclers and the first modern French historian. Commines had been brought up in the Burgundian court, but in 1472 was persuaded to desert Duke Charles the Bold for the service of the French king. The memoirs which he wrote were very different from the gay chronicles of Froissart, with their love of chivalry and medieval pageantry. Commines wrote with the express purpose of compiling a guide to politics for rulers and their advisers. So he was always at great pains to get to the bottom of every intrigue, to discover the causes of wars, and to discern the truth behind the peace treaties; hence the great value of his book to us.

Louis XI (1461–83) was one of the least attractive characters in French history, but also one of the chief creators of the French kingdom. Ugly, fat in body but spindle-shanked, there was nothing knightly or chivalrous about this strange, abnormal man, with his over-large head, who neither kept his word nor trusted others to do so. He hated royal state and preferred to dress in coarse and shoddy clothes, to choose his advisers and friends from the lower ranks of society, to haunt the Paris taverns at night, where he would drink, elbows on table, with boon companions and there gain valuable information. Deeply devout by nature, he became increasingly superstitious as he grew older and developed a morbid fear of death. (He used to pay 10,000 crowns a month to his doctor to keep him alive.) He wore on his greasy, black felt hat little leaden figures of saints 'which, on every occasion when good news reached him, he kissed, falling on his knees, wherever he happened to be, so suddenly that sometimes he seemed stupid rather than a wise man'. Yet there is no doubt of his acute intelligence, his skill in diplomatic intrigues, nor, somewhat strangely, of his personal courage and ability to command loyalty. Commines overrated Louis's ability as a statesman, for his achievements, as we shall see, were often the result of remarkable luck. But in his contempt for chivalry, his love of absolute authority, in his reliance on lower-class officials and counsellors—men like the one-time executioner, Tristan the Hermit, described by an Englishman, Robert Neville, as having 'the most diligent, quick and subtle mind in the kingdom'; or the royal valet and barber, Oliver the Bad, ennobled and renamed Olivier le Daim—and in his own considerable administrative ability, Louis is no longer a medieval king but a ruler on the threshold of the modern world.

'When he was resting, his mind was at work. . . . When he had war, he wanted peace; when he had peace or a truce, he was scarcely able to endure it. But that was his nature and thus he lived,' wrote Commines. In peace time Louis continued his father's work of restoring the prosperity of France, not least so that its people could bear the 'great and awful taxes'. In the fifteenth century the hope of immediate royal gain usually prevented any long-term policy, but Louis set out actively to encourage trade and industry. He was the first king to introduce commercial clauses into all treaties with foreign powers. His ambassadors were expected to take part in trade missions as well as in diplomacy, and in 1470 we find him trying to organize an exhibition of French products in London so 'that the inhabitants of the aforesaid kingdom should know that the French merchants were able to provide for them, like the other nations'. Thanks to Louis XI, Lyons became the principal market for silk in Europe, and it was he who in 1464 created a postal service in France, whereby every four leagues along the main roads there were relays of horses ready to carry the mail on its next stage. He welcomed the new art of printing at the Sorbonne in 1470 and set up or reorganized universities and schools. He examined laws and customs, reforming them when necessary, and set them out more clearly.

Despite all this commercial and enlightened activity, Louis's main task was the extension of the royal domain and the removal of all rivals. 'In my opinion.' wrote Commines, 'the trouble which he had in his youth, when he was a fugitive from his father under the Duke of Burgundy . . . benefited him very greatly, for he was forced to make himself agreeable to those of whom he had need and this advantage—which is no small one—adversity taught him.' It was perhaps rough justice that Louis, who had once joined discontented nobles against his father, should find himself in 1465 faced by much the same selfish princes of the blood. They had banded together under the name of the League of the Public Weal, claiming that they intended to put an end to 'the exactions, oppressions, wrongs and other countless ills done to Churches and nobles as well as to poor and lowly folk'. The League was officially headed by Louis's brother, the Duke of Berry, a weak lad of 18, but the support of the dukes of Burgundy and Brittany made it seem alarmingly powerful. However, the League failed to get much help from the lesser nobility, the clergy, or the towns for it was obvious that, in spite of its high-sounding name, it had been formed to break the power of the Crown and existed almost solely for the benefit of the great nobles. In July the Burgundians tried by force to bar Louis's path to Paris, but a battle at Montlhéry was too indecisive to check him and, by shrewd grants of territory and promises which he had no intention of keeping for long, the king broke up the League.

Two years later Philip the Good died and was succeeded as duke of Burgundy by his son, Charles the Bold, a wildly reckless and arrogant man. The new duke was determined to create a strong state from the Channel to the Alps which, apart from other difficulties, meant that he must conquer Lorraine from Louis. At first it seemed

Louis XI decides on war against the Duke of Burgundy.

possible that Charles might succeed. After Montlhéry Louis had been forced to give back a number of fortresses on the river Somme to Burgundy and in 1468 for a short while the king was dangerously in the power of his rival. Louis had demanded an interview with Charles at Péronne to discuss terms for a permanent peace, but while negotiations were proceeding Charles learned that the citizens of Liège, aided and abetted by Louis, had revolted against him. Louis only escaped with his life by temporarily making most degrading concessions.

Yet in the long run Charles was no match for the wily king and, though he might for the moment overrun Lorraine, he did not trouble to maintain the traditional English alliance and Louis was able to pay Edward IV handsomely to remain inactive. Louis was further able to form an alliance with the Swiss and certain German princes, all of whom were alarmed at Charles's ambitions. In 1476 Charles proceeded to deal with the Swiss, to teach these 'Alpine cowherds' a lesson; but the cowherds first checked his advance and then utterly defeated him. In January 1477 Charles was killed outside the walls of Nancy, which he was blockading before making it his new capital. The wily king had caught and, with a fair amount of good luck, removed his prey. In the end Louis's diplomacy and unyielding pursuit of his aims were too much for a man who a contemporary admirer admitted 'brewed more enterprises than several men's lives would have been sufficient to fulfil'.

Charles the Bold's death meant a great gain for the French monarchy because as he had died without male heirs the duchy of Burgundy reverted to the Crown. It is possible that Louis might have acquired the whole Burgundian inheritance, but his schemes failed, and the lands which were subject to the Emperor were never destined to become part of France. But if he did not gain all that he desired, the danger of a rival kingdom along his eastern frontier had gone. Other provinces came to Louis in his last years. Maine and Anjou passed to him when their rulers died and he made sure that one day Franche-Comté would also belong to the Crown. So by 1483 the only part of the kingdom to enjoy feudal independence was Brittany. Thus 'did he gather in his basket the fruits which had ripened in his garden'.

Louis spent the last years of his life in his castle of Plessis-les-Tours, a grim fortress 'closed with great iron bars in the form of gratings, and, at the four corners of the house, four bastions of iron, good, big and thick. . . . And he placed ten bowmen . . . to draw on those who approached before the door was opened.' From the branches of the surrounding trees, in 'King Louis's orchard', swung the corpses of those whom he had ordered to be hanged. He took apparent delight in visiting the Fillettes du Roi (the King's Little Girls), as the iron cages in which his enemies rotted away were nicknamed. As his own death approached, he turned to relics for comfort; these had been sent to him not only by the pope, but also by the Sultan of Turkey. France owed much to this king, for with all his faults, his cruelty, and his trickery, he was one of the founders of her greatness.

Charles VIII (1483–98), of whom we shall hear much more in Chapter 7, was Louis's only son and a boy of 13 when his father died. Until he came of age his sister was regent, and right at the start of her brother's reign she had to face an attempt by some of the nobles to revive the League of the Public Weal. That she had the support of most of the country, which was heartily tired of feudal lords and their senseless fighting, is shown by the fact that the brief war in which the

League was completely crushed was nicknamed 'The Senseless War'. Strong government by the Crown seemed to most people to be what France needed most. Three weeks after his defeat of the League, the Duke of Brittany, a leading figure among the princes, died and was succeeded by his daughter, Anne. The emperor Maximilian I proposed himself as a suitable husband for the new duchess, and at once the danger arose that France might find herself encircled by a likely enemy. The Regent immediately put forward her brother as a rival suitor, backing his claim with an army of 40,000 men—a form of courtship which proved irresistible. In December 1491 Charles VIII and Anne of Brittany were married and another vital part of France came under the Crown. At the same time Charles decided to rule the country himself, with what results we shall see.

(ii) The British Isles

English kings were not so well placed as French kings when it came to raising money. An English king could usually make ends meet so long as he did not go in for expensive wars. As we have seen, an efficient army in the fourteenth century was a regularly paid army and the cost of the wars in France often forced the king to ask for extra money. The nobles were asked to contribute either privately or as members of the Great Council; the clergy voted their share through their own Convocations of Canterbury and York; towns might be asked to make a special gift from their funds; and, of steadily growing importance, there was parliament. It was during the fourteenth century that parliament began to take a more formal shape; in the previous century it had been little more than an enlarged Great Council called together for a special purpose. After 1327 we find that the Commons are always summoned to join the 'lords', those who attended by right to give the king advice. The Commons consisted of two knights from each shire and two burgesses from a steadily lengthening list of towns, and from 1376 onwards they elected their own Speaker. Parliament could be both a check on the king's power and a valuable ally. When in 1362 Edward III tried to tap the one great source of wealth in the country, the wool trade, he was forced to agree that any such grant must first be approved by parliament. In this way the Commons began to discover the value of not agreeing to royal requests for more money until their own wishes and grievances had been considered. On the other hand, if discreetly managed, parliament could help the king greatly not merely in levying taxes but in sorting out the mass of petitions which poured in and also in making known the king's wishes when the Commons returned to their homes.

One peculiarly English institution, the Justice of the Peace, dated from 1361, when the title was first used, though country gentry had helped in local affairs before then. They were essential partners in maintaining the King's Peace in their districts, and we find that more and more statutes rely on the Justice for their enforcement. By the end of the fourteenth century there were usually eight Justices to each county and they swiftly proved themselves to be invaluable, unpaid representatives of the Crown, especially in parts of the country where otherwise law and order would scarcely exist.

When the king was abroad or on his travels in his own country—and the court was never in one place for long at a time—much business was transacted in his name by his officials. Nevertheless, throughout the fourteenth and fifteenth centuries a king was hard put to it to survive unless he was very clearly in charge of affairs. The reigns of Edward II, Richard II, and Henry VI prove this. At such times parliament might appear to become more powerful. When Richard II abdicated in 1399, the news was formally given to parliament by his triumphant rival, Henry Bolingbroke; and, when Bolingbroke claimed the throne as Henry IV, he did so before parliament. But the more frequent summoning of parliament in the next fifty years—sometimes known as the 'Lancastrian experiment' —is not really a sign that parliamentary power was increasing. Parliament was no more able than a weak king to control unruly nobles. The long minority of Henry VI, the failures of the French wars, and the violence of the Wars of the Roses made many English people realize the value of a strong king. But it was not enough for a king to be strong. Kings like Edward IV and, even more, Henry VII understood that to be truly master in his own house an English king could not afford the luxury of foreign wars. Furthermore, both Henry VII and Henry VIII found that parliament could be a method of achieving their ends. Parliament was only too ready to pass laws for Henry VII against the barons and their retainers. When Henry VIII entered on his quarrel with the pope over his intended divorce of Catherine of Aragon, he found in parliament a willing agent in stopping payments to Rome.

★   ★   ★

Scotland for most of the period of this book was in effect two lands —the English-speaking Lowlands and the east coast were quite apart from the wild Celtic Highlands. Because the Scottish army was unpaid, the king could usually manage to live on his ordinary revenue, but he could do little to improve the machinery of government. Scottish history for the most part is a story of turbulent nobles and kings who were never fully in control. It is an interesting sign of the times that James I (1406-37) and James VI (1488-1513) both tried to introduce some of the methods which their fellow monarchs in other countries practised successfully and both met with even more resistance than was usually shown to a ruler. James IV was especially unpopular because he began to rely on officials of humble birth. He it was whose marriage to Margaret Tudor gave Scotland and England the same man as king in 1603. One other sign of far distant union was the fact that in the fifteenth century men were beginning to speak of Great Britain.

In Ireland, which unlike Scotland was part of the English Crown, the king had his representatives and there was some attempt at setting up a system of lawcourts and financial control. However, little was achieved, for the country was in a state of almost continuous war. Such power as could be exercised was in the hands of the Norman-Irish nobles and those descendants of the ancient kings of Ireland who still survived.

(iii) Spain

'The only country in the world where twice two did not make four.' That was the Duke of Wellington's comment on Spain some three centuries later, and it expressed vividly the age-old conviction that Spain was very different from the rest of Europe. 'The China of Western Europe' is a more modern description of a country isolated and remote behind the great wall of the Pyrenees. Fifteenth-century Spain was a barren and poor country with 10 per cent of its soil bare rock, a further 35 per cent laboriously difficult to cultivate, and a mere 10 per cent rich and fertile. The mountain ranges which lie east to west across the peninsula made travel difficult and isolated the various areas of population from each other. This lack of unity imposed by geography was made worse by the early history of Spain, which had resulted in the existence within Spain of three separate races and three religions—Christians, Muslims, and Jews.

Yet in the last thirty years of the fifteenth century and the early years of the sixteenth all these apparently hopeless disadvantages, which largely accounted for Spain's backwardness compared to other European nations, seemed to be suddenly and almost miraculously overcome. For much of the sixteenth century Spain was the greatest power on earth, the master of most of Europe, and the possessor of the largest and most widespread empire which the world had ever known. Why this suddenly happened and why a century and a half later Spain began to sink back into her old unimportance are questions to which historians still can give no final answer.

In 711 the Arabs, or Moors as they are generally called in Spanish history, crossed over from Morocco into Spain and in seven years conquered the greater part of the Iberian peninsula. It took 700 years to win back what had been so quickly lost, and the story of the Reconquest is the main fact in the history of medieval Spain. The pattern of the Reconquest varied greatly in different parts of the peninsula, but by the thirteenth century the three main divisions

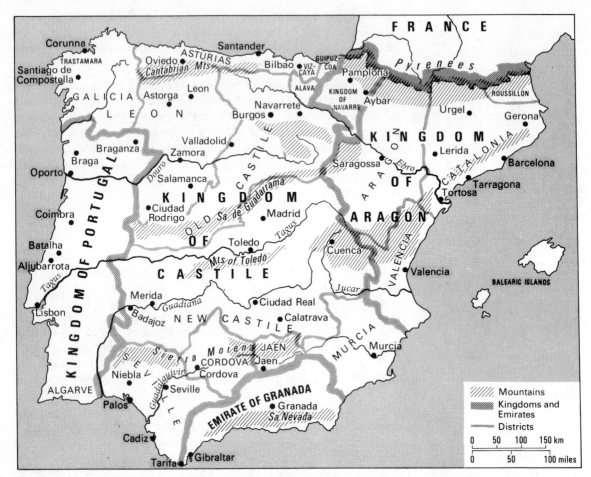

were fixed—Castile, Portugal, and Aragon. There was nothing inevitable in all this: Spain and Portugal might well have remained
united as they had been when part of the Roman empire; there was
certainly nothing inevitable in the later union of Castile and Aragon,
for the Castilians and Aragonese, although ruled over by two branches of the same Castilian family, disliked each other greatly. It was
much more likely that Castile and Portugal would unite.

But things worked out differently. During the fourteenth century
Portugal began to look westward to the Atlantic and encouraged her
sailors in their voyages of discovery. Castile, because of quarrels
within the royal family and revolts among her nobles, was forced for
a time to be concerned mainly with her own domestic affairs. On the
other hand, Aragon, having completed her share of the Reconquest,
was busily engaged in founding a commercial empire in the eastern
Mediterranean, with its headquarters at Barcelona. Aragonese and
Catalan merchants—the two states had been united since 1137—
were to be found all over the Levant and in the North African ports;

The Iberian Peninsula
thirteenth to fifteenth centuries.

they traded in Alexandria and also in the Low Countries. They were successful rivals to the Venetians and the Genoese in the spice trade and they opened up markets for Catalan iron and textiles in Sicily, Africa, and in other parts of Spain and Portugal. Furthermore, the powerful Aragonese merchant classes were able to hammer out with the Crown a curiously modern form of government based on the idea that both ruler and ruled had not only rights but duties. Thus King Martin I of Aragon could say to the *cortes*, or parliament, in 1406: 'What people is there in the world enjoying so many freedoms and exemptions as you; and what people so generous?' The reverse side of the coin could be seen, even more bluntly expressed, in the famous oath of allegiance which the Aragonese took to a new king: 'We, who are as good as you, swear to you, who are no better than we, to accept you as our king and sovereign lord, provided you observe all our liberties and laws: but if not, not.'

Because of its wealth, for most of the thirteenth and fourteenth centuries Aragon was far more important and powerful than its much larger neighbour, Castile. But this was not to last. During the fifteenth century the positions were slowly reversed for a number of reasons. Aragon had been very severely hit by the Black Death and by continuing outbreaks of plague, which, as in other European countries, led to labour troubles, aggravated, in the case of Aragon, by the failure of several private banks in Barcelona in the 1380s. More important was the failure of the Aragonese to keep control of the Mediterranean spice and cloth trades with the result that they were cut out by the Genoese, who also began to set up as traders in Cordoba, Seville, and Cadiz whence they exported the now famous Castilian wool. Since so much of Castile was barren, sheep farming offered a much better prospect of making money than arable and it was the introduction into their country from North Africa of the merino sheep early in the fourteenth century that laid the foundations of later Castilian wealth. So by the middle of the fifteenth century the prosperity of Aragon, based on trade in the Mediterranean, was declining, while that of Castile, based largely on sheep farming, was increasing steadily.

With this change in their fortunes the Aragonese saw the advantage of trying to make a close alliance with Castile, and King John II of Aragon (1458–79) worked hard to bring this about. His chance came in the autumn of 1468 when Henry IV of Castile had, after much hesitation, declared that his heiress should be his half-sister Isabella and not his daughter Juana, who was said to be illegitimate. John II was determined that his son and heir, Ferdinand, should marry Isabella and in this way unite the Crowns of Aragon and Castile. But it was not all plain sailing. Ferdinand had two rivals, Charles of Valois, son of Charles VII of France, and King Alfonso V of Portugal. In this situation Isabella proved herself to be a young woman of great determination, who had no intention of being given away by her half-brother to the highest bidder; she meant to make her own choice. Fear of French ambitions meant that a French marriage would have been very unpopular; Alfonso was an elderly and unattractive widower; Ferdinand, a year younger than Isabella, who was 18, was both attractive and shrewd and was not in a position to haggle long over the marriage contract. Ferdinand seemed the obvious choice.

But there were powerful forces anxious to prevent this marriage if possible, not least Henry IV, who threatened to arrest his daughter Isabella. She was rescued from the king's hands by the Archbishop of Toledo at the head of a body of horsemen and hurried away to safety among friends at Valladolid. Ferdinand, with a few attendants, all disguised as merchants, set out to join her. It was a hazardous journey, for his disguise was not sufficient to prevent a stone being hurled at him from the top of a battlement and he was nearly crushed. However, he got safely to Valladolid, where he saw his bride for the first time four days before the wedding. Both bride and bridegroom had to borrow money for the ceremony, and since they were blood relations it was necessary to get the pope's consent before they could be married. To avoid delay, John II, the Archbishop of Toledo, and Ferdinand hastily forged the necessary document. On 19 October 1469 Ferdinand, King of Sicily and heir to the throne of Aragon, was married to Isabella, heiress to the throne of Castile, in a private house in Valladolid. Isabella's choice of a husband was momentous in the history of Spain.

They were a remarkable pair, both wholly Spanish and both utterly devoted to their peoples. Isabella, with her open, honest face, and her greenish-blue eyes, could have been mistaken for a villager or the inhabitant of a small country town. Castilians came to adore her, for they thought of her as one of themselves. Ferdinand, on the other hand, had nothing of the villager about him. Except for a total lack of cruelty in his nature, he had most of the qualities of a typical Renaissance prince. He was charming, with straight black hair and laughing eyes, one of the best horsemen of his day, and as astute and crafty as any ruler in Europe. Louis XII of France once complained that on two occasions Ferdinand had deceived him. 'He lies,' was Ferdinand's comment, 'I have deceived him not twice but ten times!' Strangely, there was no formal alliance between the fathers of the bride and bridegroom, only a marriage contract in which it was made abundantly clear that Ferdinand might have secured his bride but he was never to rule Castile as king. When they eventually succeeded to their thrones, each was sovereign in his country alone; they were never joint rulers of a united kingdom. Nevertheless, Spanish greatness in the sixteenth century dates from this marriage.

Ferdinand and Isabella knew that if Spain were to avoid becoming, like Italy, a prey to stronger nations, she could not afford to remain

Ferdinand and Isabella. The painting dates from 1490 and the unknown artist has been anxious to show how devout the 'Catholic Kings' were. On the extreme right is Torquemada, the Inquisitor-General.

so disunited. They never succeeded in uniting the whole of what is now Spain, but, by concentrating on Castile, destined to become the richest and most powerful of the Spanish Crowns, they laid the foundations for the much fuller unity which came under their grandson, Charles V. No wonder that Philip II, the king of Spain who sent the Armada against England, once stopped before a portrait of Ferdinand and remarked: 'To him we owe it all.' They had the

95

advantage of already existing foundations on which to build. Royal officials had for some years been a sign of the growing power of the king, and in Castile the *cortes* could only be summoned when the king wished and was usually prepared to meet the king's wishes. A start had been made towards an organized system of taxation and there had been a steady development of royal justice in the lawcourts. Nevertheless, Spain was still a land of separate kingdoms, and if greater unity were to be achieved it would only come by showing that in Castile efficient government meant a more peaceful and prosperous life for everyone.

The first task, as in France and in England, was to bring the nobles to heel and to put a stop to private fighting. In doing this, Ferdinand and Isabella could rely on the support of most of their subjects, especially the townsfolk of Castile, whose trade was suffering from the chronic lack of law and order in the countryside. Private warfare and the building of new castles were forbidden; like the Tudors in England, Ferdinand and Isabella worked through the *cortes*, which in 1476 was persuaded to revive the old medieval league of towns, which had existed to rid the roads and countryside of brigands. Once again every hundred hearths had to provide a mounted archer to chase criminals, and soon squadrons of these archers patrolled Castile with power to inflict mutilation or death on their captives. About the same time Ferdinand managed to get the Grand Masterships of the three great Orders of Knighthood away from the nobles and into his own hands, which gave him not only power but considerable wealth, which was essential if the king were to be powerful. The nobles also found themselves, as in France, replaced in the royal councils by legally trained officials of humble birth, and, with the help of the *cortes*, Ferdinand and Isabella got back from many nobles large areas of land, which once had belonged to the Crown. They had no hostility to the nobility as such—in fact the number of people with titles actually increased during their reign—but they were determined to see that all Castilian nobles were obedient to the Crown, and everything possible was done to encourage them to become decorative figures at court instead of robber barons.

Having successfully controlled the nobles, thanks to the help of the *cortes* and the support of the towns, Ferdinand and Isabella decided that the next step was to control these allies, whose help was now no longer needed. The *cortes* of Castile presented no problem: it simply was not summoned between 1483 and 1497. Town government had for long been very corrupt, and this gave the excuse for the steady removal of municipal liberties. In each important town a *corregidor*, a royal official who watched over royal interests, was appointed.

So far we have been considering what Ferdinand and Isabella would have regarded as the less important part of their joint task. What mattered most to them was the Catholic Faith, and their passionate devotion to it had been rewarded by Pope Alexander VI, who gave them the right to call themselves 'the Catholic Kings'. The good government of the Church was even more important than the good government of the State to these two rulers; and to them good government meant unity under the Crown. So it was that a policy intended to strengthen the Catholic Faith happened at the same time to strengthen the hold of the Catholic Kings over their two countries.

The Church in Spain was both enormously powerful and fabulously rich. The Archbishop of Toledo, Primate of Spain and second only to the king in importance, with a personal income of 80,000 ducats a year, was the wealthiest prelate in Christendom after the pope. To control the Church in Spain meant securing the right of appointment to all the leading positions, and, as other kings had discovered, to win this right meant a long struggle with the papacy. In their struggle Ferdinand and Isabella held one trump card, which was the urgent need of successive popes to hire Spanish troops to fight on their behalf in Italy. This was a good start, but soon an even better way of securing what they wanted arose. The conquest of the kingdom of Granada, the last stronghold of the Moors in southern Spain, was nearly complete and new Catholic churches would be soon needed. Should not the pope reward the crusading work of the Catholic Kings with something better than an honourable title? Should he not grant to Ferdinand and Isabella complete control when the Church was again supreme in Granada? Sorely in need of military help, Innocent VIII granted this right in 1486; it was the vital first step which led inevitably to the king being in control of the Spanish Church not only within his Spanish dominions but in his empire in the New World.

To Ferdinand and Isabella unity under the Crown must mean religious uniformity; it was impossible to accept the idea that any of their subjects did not share their own Catholic faith. Spain had once been the most tolerant country in Europe, but this was now to end. Muslims and Jews must be converted or expelled from Spain. Muslims were mostly living in Granada, but the Jews were everywhere, holding key positions in the business world, in politics, and in medicine; some even became royal advisers and physicians. But the fourteenth century was a time of plague and bad trade, and many impoverished Spaniards became bitterly jealous of the Jews, who still seemed somehow able to make money. The chronicle of the curate of Los Palacios in Andalusia shows some of the extraordinary ideas which began to be held about the Jews: 'This accursed race were either unwilling to bring their children to baptism, or, if they did, they washed away the stain on returning home. They dressed their stews and other dishes with oil instead of lard; abstained from pork; kept the passover; and sent oil to replenish the lamps in their synagogues ... they were exceedingly politic and ambitious people, engrossing the most lucrative municipal offices; and preferred to gain their livelihood by traffic, in which they made exorbitant gains, rather than by manual labour or mechanical arts.' Jealousy brought mob violence and in 1391 terrible massacres of the Jews took place.

To save their lives and fortunes over 100,000 Jews professed themselves ready to be baptized and to become *conversos*, or New Christians. However, it was not long before many Spaniards began to question the sincerity of these mass conversions. During the middle years of the fifteenth century when New Christians were again successful in trade and politics and also, as official Christians, had even won positions in the Church, anger began again to mount against them. Suspicion was aroused when a man was seen to wear better clothes or cleaner linen on the day of the Jewish sabbath than on other days; if he had no fire in his house the preceding evening; if he washed a corpse in warm water, or, when dying, turned his face to the wall. Jealousy again brought riots and violence, followed in Toledo in 1449 by a sinister decree insisting that 'purity of blood' was essential for anybody holding any official post in the city. Great pressure was exerted at court to bring toleration to an end, for more and more believed it was that these so-called New Christians endangered the very existence of both Church and State.

Thus it was that Ferdinand and Isabella asked Pope Sixtus IV for permission to set up the Inquisition in Castile to deal with the Jews. In his negotiations with the pope, Ferdinand insisted that in his territory the Inquisition must be entirely under his authority. Sixtus agreed with reluctance, and the Holy Office—the official name of the Inquisition—was set up in 1478. Although originally intended solely for Castile, Ferdinand soon forced it on Aragon, appointing the grimly pious and implacable Torquemada as Inquisitor-General for both kingdoms. Later the Inquisition was set up in Sicily, Sardinia, and Spain's American colonies. No other institution had such power over all Ferdinand's dominions, with the result that, although its purpose was religious, the Inquisition played a big part in creating a united Spain.

Historians have differed greatly in their accounts of the Spanish Inquisition. To some no language is too harsh to condemn its cruelties; later historians remind us that, judged by the standards of its times, it was neither cruel nor unjust. What was terrifying about the Inquisition was its secrecy. Suspects were arrested in the dead of night, were not allowed to communicate with their relatives, and were often never heard of again. Since it was men's thoughts rather than their actions with which the Inquisition was concerned, the only satisfactory form of evidence was a confession by the accused. To force this, torture was employed, though usually only as a last resort. The rack, the pulley, and the water-torture were the most commonly used, but these were no invention of the Inquisition.

The two naked men on the right have been condemned to death by the Inquisition and the sentence is carried out at an auto da fé. The officials of the Inquisition watch but laymen have the task of putting the condemned men to death.

Statements were all too often accepted from discreditable witnesses, and one proof of conversion, inevitably demanded if the accused were to be pardoned, was the furnishing of a list of the accused's friends, guilty of the same beliefs. Apart from the absence of 'brainwashing', there is a curiously unpleasant similarity between the methods used by the Spanish Inquisition and those employed in a modern political trial in a totalitarian state. Moreover the Inquisition moved equally slowly and remorselessly: five years might easily elapse between an arrest and the end of a trial. It is true that the accused had a lawyer to help him, but he was also given a confessor, whose duty it was to urge a plea of guilty and repentance. Nor could the accused prepare his defence until the prosecution was ready to proceed, for during all this time he was kept in ignorance of the charges against him. In proportion to the number of trials the death penalty was rare. Flogging, the confiscation of all property, and the dreaded galleys were the usual punishments. Those who persisted in their beliefs were burned alive. The sentence was not carried out by the Inquisition but by the civil authorities, after an elaborate public ceremony known as an *auto da fé* (act of faith) in which the Day of Judgement was supposed to be represented.

1492 must have seemed an *annus mirabilis* to patriotic Spaniards. On 6 January the Catholic Kings made their victorious entry into the city of Granada, though ten years of bitter fighting lay ahead before the Moors finally capitulated and the Reconquest was over. On 30 March, in the full flush of religious zeal, Ferdinand and Isabella issued an edict which gave all Jews in Spain four months in which to choose between becoming Christians or leaving the country. Of the 200,000 Jews, about 150,000 chose to leave their homes. On 17 April, at Santa Fé, six miles outside Granada, agreement was reached on the terms under which the Genoese Christopher Columbus would set out on 3 August in search of a new route to the Indies. Spain, so long backward and of little account, had suddenly appeared like a new comet in the European sky.

Although the Moors were at first reasonably treated, from 1502 they were given the same choice as the Jews: conversion or expulsion. Since most Moors had nowhere else to go, they became officially 'Christians'. Expulsion was to come later.

Between them, Ferdinand and Isabella had greatly increased the power of the Crown and had prepared the way for the full unity of Spain, which was to come later. Moreover, the fame of the Spanish soldiers was quickly spreading through Europe. It was in the mountains of Granada that the Spanish infantry, created by Gonzalo de Cordoba, learned to endure extremes of heat and cold and to fight with invincible faith. But time was to show that unity had been bought at a heavy price. The average Castilian not only despised hard work but had an incapacity for economic affairs which was almost inspired. Religious zeal was driving out of Spain those on whom the prosperity of the nation rested.

(iv) Italy

'I think verily that in one region of the world again are not half so many strangers as in Italy: specially of gentlemen whose resort thither is principally under pretence of study.' So wrote an English traveller in 1549. Italy, then as now, was a lure to all who loved art and beauty and blue skies. But it was a sad fact that the country which had once been the heart of the Roman empire and which had taught men the importance of law and order and good government had now no unity of any kind and little feeling of being one nation. As Machiavelli, the sixteenth-century political writer, declared: 'The Church being on the one hand too weak to grasp the whole of Italy, and on the other too jealous to allow another power to do so, has prevented our union beneath one head and has kept us under scattered lords and princes.'

In medieval times two powers, the Church and the emperor, had claimed universal obedience and for a while the northern part of Italy was imperial territory. But soon after 1300 both pope and emperor gave up any serious attempt to control Italian affairs. The years at Avignon and the Schism had left the papacy in often doubtful control of a mere band of territory, the Papal States, running diagonally across the peninsula. As for the emperor, until the age of Charles V, he was little more than a shadowy figure living north of the Alps who, at the start of his reign, agreed to accept coronation with the Iron Crown of Lombardy—said to be a nail from the True Cross beaten into a thin ring—at the hands of the pope. In place of government by pope or emperor, Italy was now divided into a number of states. After the Papal States the most important were the duchy of Milan, the republics of Florence and Venice, and the kingdom of Naples. There were also much smaller states like the kingdom of Savoy, which guarded the north-western route into Italy and which centuries hence would provide a royal family for a united Italy. In addition there were scores of lesser cities and towns, with varying degrees of independence, but mostly looking to one of the bigger states for some protection.

Florence, birthplace of the Italian Renaissance, officially a republic but usually controlled by the great banking house of Medici, will feature largely in chapter 6 and needs no further description at this moment. The city of Milan was about twice as large as Florence and its 200,000 inhabitants delighted in well-paved streets, beautiful fountains, richly stocked shops, and many grand palaces. The wealth of Milan came from its cloth and silk weaving and also from

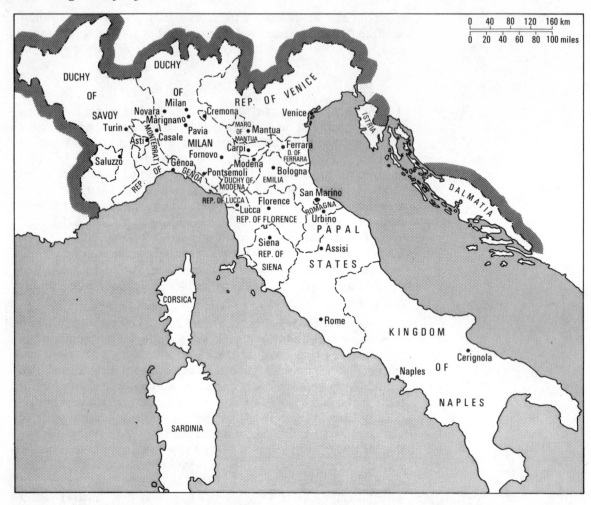

Italy in the fifteenth and early sixteenth centuries.

the making of some of the best armour in Europe and the breeding of fine war-horses. After a long struggle for power between nobles and rich merchants, the Visconti family had emerged as rulers of Milan at the start of the fourteenth century. Fifty years later through a marriage with Francesco Sforza, an adopted surname meaning 'force', the Visconti-Sforza family greatly extended their wealth and power through offers of military aid in return for splendid titles, such as a dukedom for the head of the family. In time this enabled their legitimate children to marry into royal houses, and their illegitimate daughters were often given as wives to valuable allies like the *condottieri*, the soldiers of fortune.

These *condottieri* (the name comes from an Italian word for a contract and shows that they were hired mercenaries) played a big part in the story of Italy and did much to prevent any chance of unity. In the fourteenth century they were men of many nationalities, redundant

102

Sir John Hawkwood. This picture is painted on a wall in the cathedral at Florence.

soldiers when the Hundred Years War died down. One of the most famous of these was an Englishman, Sir John Hawkwood, whose White Company—so called from the brilliant polish which his men gave to their armour—was formed in the years after the Peace of Brétigny and who served the pope before settling for life in Italy. By the time that Hawkwood died in 1394 foreigners were rare and most *condottieri* were Italians, who came from all parts of the country but especially from the Romagna, a poor area where it was hard to earn a living. They were men of very different social background; some were younger sons of good but impoverished families, others, like Francesco Sforza, were sons of peasants. They were also very different in character: some, like Federigo of Urbino, a passionate lover of art and culture, ruled over a court famed for its encouragement of learning; there were others like Malatesta or the nicknamed Gattamelata ('the Honeyed Cat') who were cruel and ruthless men,

103

infamous for their depraved behaviour. In fulfilling their contracts they might be said to resemble modern professional footballers. They were highly skilled in their job; they were loyal to the state or town which hired them, but were always ready to transfer to another master for a higher fee, with the result that colleagues in battle one day might be the foes of tomorrow. Machiavelli maintained that since the *condottieri* earned their living by fighting they took care not to be killed and that the battles were often bloodless. This is untrue, though most *condottieri* took care not to go into battle until they and their quite large armies had been paid. Their importance and fame

Venice. The Lion of St. Mark can be seen on the pillar to the left of the central bridge. Two galleys and two smaller vessels are in the foreground. On the right some Venetians seem to be doubtful about how many the rowing boat will take. The picture comes from a book telling about the voyages of Marco Polo.

is shown by the fact that the two finest equestrian statues of the Renaissance were erected in honour of *condottieri*—Donatello's statue of Gattamelata and Verrocchio's statue of Bartolomeo Colleoni. Both these men made their fortunes in the service of Venice.

Venice, protected from sudden land attack by her lagoons, looked towards the sea and the east for the enormous wealth which came to her through trade. At the head of the republic was the doge, chosen by an incredibly complicated system of lot and election, but real power lay with the Council of Ten. Genoa was her great trade rival but her wealth and aloofness excited jealousy throughout Italy. Her famous Arsenal, which in 1500 consisted of sixty acres of docks, sheds, and store-houses, enabled her to build and maintain a powerful war fleet capable of facing even the might of the Turkish navies.

At the southern end of the peninsula lay the kingdom of Naples, ruled in the fourteenth century by a branch of the French Angevin house; close at hand was Sicily under Aragonese rule. Both kingdoms were poor and backward and for long provided an excuse for France and Spain to fight out their rival claims on Italian soil. Wealthy and divided, Italy was the perfect prey for strong and united neighbours.

(v) Germany

If Italy was hopelessly divided, her disunity was as nothing compared with that of Germany, which, it was said with slight exaggeration, comprised more states than there were days in the year. In theory Germany was united because all German lands lay within the boundaries of the Holy Roman Empire—'Holy' because of its supposed co-operation with the pope, who crowned the emperor; 'Roman' because it claimed to be the heir of the old Roman empire; and 'Empire' because of the extent of its territory. In reality there was no substance to these shadowy claims and the great days of the Empire were over. On the other hand the emperor himself could be a powerful prince in his own right if the seven Electors (for the position of emperor depended on election not on heredity) happened to choose a man with important family possessions. Indeed, ever since 1436 the choice of the Electors had fallen on the head of the House of Hapsburg, a family with vast territorial ambitions. The original Hapsburg lands lay near the upper Rhine, close to Switzerland; to these were added a group of states to the east, the lands which are today Austria; finally by the marriage of the emperor Maximilian I to Mary of Burgundy in 1477 the seventeen provinces out of which modern Holland and Belgium have grown came under Hapsburg control. It looked as if the Hapsburg claim that it was the right of Austria to rule over the whole world might come true: the vowels A.E.I.O.U. were said to stand in Latin for this right, 'Austriae est imperare orbi universae'. The same motto can be devised in German. Thus a Hapsburg emperor was bound to be a powerful ruler but not

powerful because he ruled over a united empire, or even a united Germany, for there was no hope whatever of such unity. Germans, whether nobles, churchmen, or townsmen, kept alive some sense of belonging to the same empire but they had no intention of being closely united under a powerful emperor.

Broadly speaking, the appallingly complicated tangle of independent states fell into three main groups: the great princes, both ecclesiastical and secular; the imperial cities; and the lesser nobility, or imperial knights.

The most powerful princes were the seven Electors on whom fell the task of choosing a new emperor. Of these, the prince-bishops of Mainz, Trier, and Cologne were at the same time both leading churchmen and men who governed their states like any lay ruler. Nearly one-sixth of Germany was occupied by ecclesiastical states, but the geographical position of the lands of these three Electors meant that their rulers were inevitably drawn into any contest between Germany and France. By the sixteenth century even

The emperor Maximilian and his family. The Hapsburg jaw is very pronounced both in the emperor and in the young man in the middle of the picture.

greater power was in the hands of the secular princes, and the other four Electors, the rulers of Bohemia, Saxony, Brandenburg, and the Palatinate of the Rhine played a vital part in German affairs. The so-called imperial cities, some eighty-five in number, accepted the vague authority of the emperor over them but were fiercely jealous of their independence. Most of them were extremely wealthy and some, like Nuremberg, owned considerable territory outside their walls. Both princes and cities strove hard to keep their independence and also to extend their lands, with the result that the imperial knights, the name given to the lesser nobles who ruled their tiny possessions from romantic but uncomfortably grim and draughty castles, often found it hard to make ends meet. Those who could not prey on the countryside were often forced, like the *condottieri*, to enter the service of one of the great princes and so lost much of their independence. Occasionally the knights banded together, as did the Swabian League in the south-west of Germany, and became at times a force in German politics, though for the most part they did little more than add to the general confusion.

There did exist one institution, the Diet, which was supposed to deal with the affairs of the whole Empire. It was completely ineffective, for nobody had ever decided exactly what its powers should be. The Golden Bull of 1356 had carefully laid down the dress and privileges of the seven Electors but had omitted to define how the Diet, with its three chambers, should conduct its business. Maximilian I, an attractive and hopelessly unrealistic dreamer, tried at the start of the sixteenth century to make the government of the Empire more efficient, but he achieved little in face of the determination of all German rulers, great or small, to remain independent at all costs.

Political chaos did not prevent Germany from enjoying great prosperity. It is true that this prosperity lay mainly in the towns, for the peasants were poor and foreign travellers noted the dirt and meanness of their houses and farms. Town wealth came mostly from trade: in the north the Hanseatic League controlled the Baltic and North Sea commerce; while in the south thriving towns along the upper Rhine and the Danube grew rich on the trade across the Alps with Italy and on that between France and Burgundy and eastern Europe. All this prosperity made it possible to develop natural resources as never before, and Germany became the centre of the mining industry, which meant being also a centre for metal and armament manufacture. From the city of Augsburg the two famous rival banking houses of Fugger and Welser stretched their tentacles all over Europe, even doing business in the Spanish New World colonies. Not only were German towns prosperous, they were also intellectually alive. There was a great demand for lay education, and many universities were being founded. Above all, the fifteenth and sixteenth centuries were an age of great artists and craftsmen, none more distinguished than Albrecht Dürer (1471–1528) of Nuremberg, the son of a master-goldsmith, who became one of the greatest engravers and woodcut illustrators, as well as a painter, able to stand comparison with the famed Italian artists.

As we shall see, the failure of the emperor to impose any form of unity on Germany was to be one of the reasons why Luther's Reformation spread so swiftly; the seething unrest beneath the prosperous surface was to prove equally important.

(v) Central Europe

Between Germany and Russia there lies a vast area of land, the geographical heart of Europe. Here during the Middle Ages three main kingdoms had developed: Poland, Bohemia, and Hungary. Since 1386 Poland and Lithuania had been united under the rule of the Jagiello family, which meant that Polish kings ruled over not only the old kingdom of Poland and the grand duchy of Lithuania but also the Ukraine. Nevertheless, these three realms felt themselves to be in every way part of Europe and they looked far more readily to the west than to the east. The great universities of Cracow in Poland and Prague in Bohemia were famous throughout Europe; the Church in each kingdom had taken part in the work of the General Councils.

If only these three kingdoms could have been united into one, or had even been prepared to remain friendly allies against a common danger, the history of Europe would have been very different. Differences in race, language, and, later, in religion, made any lasting unity almost impossible; with the result that any ambitious German or Russian ruler has always been tempted to extend his empire at the expense of these countries. This happened in the fifteenth and sixteenth centuries when the growing powers of Russia and the immediately far more dangerous threat in the southeast from the Turks turned the three kingdoms into frontier outposts. Had there been a strong kingdom in central Europe instead of three internally weak and frequently warring states, the Turkish advance might have been halted much further to the east.

Although closely linked in tradition, culture, and religion with western Europe, there were important differences which distinguished the central kingdoms from what was happening in the west. Chief of these was the power still wielded by the nobles. The struggle of the king with his nobles was familiar in all European states, but on the eastern frontiers the king was far less successful. This was due partly to economic, partly to political, factors. The great eastern plains were the best corn-growing land in Europe and were ideal for the rearing of cattle and pigs. As the population of western Europe increased, so did the demand for grain and meat from Poland, Bohemia, and Hungary. Only large-scale farming could meet this demand successfully and big farms could only be financed by the aristocracy and farmed by peasants. So it was that in the three kingdoms the power of the nobles grew rather than decreased and at the same time the peasants lost their liberty and became serfs. Furthermore, when the military threat from the east developed, it was the nobles who alone could meet it, and all along the frontiers, especially in Hungary, we find nobles ruling large districts, with their own private armies, and virtually independent of the Crown.

However strong a king might be, his position was seriously undermined by the fact that he was king not by hereditary right but by election; in all three kingdoms there was an elective monarchy. So when a king died there was every likelihood of serious trouble between rival candidates supported by rival bodies of nobles. Since the kings of the other two countries often saw the chance of being elected to the vacant throne themselves, especially if their claim could be backed up by sufficient force, the periods of peace and stability in central Europe were short. The various Diets, or assemblies, through which both national and local government were supposed to operate, only reflected the general chaos. They were dominated by the nobles who usually succeeded in frustrating any attempt by the king to bring law and order to his country.

The fortunes of the three kingdoms fluctuated greatly in our period. Poland, in spite of some brave attempts by able kings to assert their authority, slid more and more deeply into anarchy. Hungary, as we shall see in Chapter 9, was left to bear the full brunt of the Turkish attack, and was largely overrun. Bohemia was more fortunate. This was partly due to the existence of a merchant class in a few important towns which could exercise some opposition to the landowners. It was also a country in which, as elsewhere in western Europe, a feeling of patriotism grew up. This, as we saw in Chapter 1, was a marked feature of the religious revolt led by John Huss, a revolt which was also a protest against the power of the nobles. Downtrodden peasants were encouraged by the wilder Hussite preachers: 'You will no longer pay rent to your lords or serve under them, but their estates, fish ponds, meadows, woods and all their lordship are to be free to you.' However, Czech patriotism, shown in a fierce hatred of Germans, did not prevent Bohemia in the sixteenth century from becoming part of the Hapsburg dominions.

Chapter 4
Living and Working

(i) In the town

Pilgrims on their way to Rome, Jerusalem, Compostella, or other places of special sanctity like the great gold-covered shrine of Thomas à Becket at Canterbury, were among the most constant travellers on the roads of Europe all through the Middle Ages. But they were not by any means the only ones, and indeed people travelled much more than we might think possible without the swift modern transport now taken for granted, and traffic steadily increased. Among the travellers commonly to be met were, for instance, the retinues of great men journeying to war or to visit their estates, with their long baggage trains and men-at-arms, and, at the other end of the scale, professional wanderers, singly or in groups— pedlars, acrobats, minstrels, beggars, and vagabonds—as well as local people of the countryside trudging to market or doing carting service for their lord. There were churchmen of many sorts, lordly bishops, papal legates, humble priests and friars, and other less respectable persons in holy orders who lived by hawking pardons and relics to the ignorant and credulous. Above all there were merchants, the men who spread trade all over Europe, banded into companies for safety, their loaded packhorses and mules strongly guarded.

Whoever they were and wherever they went, travellers generally found the roads bad—in the fourteenth century they were often 'broken and noyous' according to the English poet Geoffrey Chaucer (1340?-1400), who described many travellers in his *Canterbury Tales*, and 200 years after him they were still 'very foul and full of holes' and certainly nothing like as good as the direct well-made Roman roads which had once marched from end to end of Europe. Though some of these were still in use, the art of making them with their five layers of carefully graded stones and gravel had been quite lost and most traffic went on rough tracks winding through the countryside, deep in mud when the weather was bad, thick in dust when it was fine. No wonder the nickname 'pieds poudrés' was given to those who travelled far on foot, and in England the law-courts which judged cases concerning long-distance travellers were often called 'pie-powder' courts by people who could not get their tongues round French words. Only humble travellers went on foot, others rode on horseback, and the sick, the old, and women travelled in carts or litters. A man seldom travelled in a cart unless compelled by age or illness or because he was a prisoner.

The months from April to October brought better weather, longer hours of daylight, and a great increase of traffic. Not only was this the main season for pilgrimage, but military campaigns were planned for spring and summer and the frequent outbreaks of fighting sent armed men hurrying along the roads to the discomfort and peril of other travellers. Also the great fairs like those at Paris, Antwerp, Messines, Bruges, London, Troyes, and Winchester were held in the summer months, and fairs of any kind, wherever they were, were like magnets, drawing to them travellers of every sort from far and near. At Bruges, for instance, merchants from over thirty nations were registered.

The countryside through which they passed was, of course, immensely varied, as any modern traveller in Europe knows, varied in climate, scenery, and the look of towns and villages, and at the end of the Middle Ages much of it was also wild and untamed, still almost as nature had made it, in spite of all men's efforts to change it. In places, driven by hunger for land, men had cut into the forests and sown crops and grazed their beasts in the clearings; in some parts the wastes and grass lands had been ploughed and cultivated; but in many more there were still impenetrable woods and 'wyde places, waste and desolate' empty of humans and habitations. Along the courses of many rivers lay swamps and marshes which were more or less permanent, since drainage and flood control were hardly yet attempted. Only slowly, and in limited areas such as Holland, parts of France, the fenland of East Anglia, and the valley of the great river Po in Italy were dikes and drains and watercourses planned and constructed on any scale.

Europe was dotted over with villages and towns, and long-distance travellers worked their way between town and town according to their business, or their souls' health, or their need of safety and shelter at night. In many parts there were enough hazards by daylight without adding the perils of darkness too. No one wanted, for instance, to fall into the clutches of the notorious tramps of France and be forced to drink a dark cup laced with a mysterious powder which made a man 'slepe agaynz his wille' or to meet wolves like those which in 1350 could be seen killing dogs in the streets of Rome itself. The wise traveller stopped in good time to find a lodging for the night.

In 1331 John de Middleton, journeying from Merton College, Oxford to Avignon, a distance of about 540 miles, stayed in twenty-two different places, usually small towns, on the way there. He was thirty-four days on the journey, carried his own bedding, and, being a shrewd man, lost only sevenpence in false coins and wrong change. The fact that he took more than a month to get to the south of France would be no surprise to him. People expected to move at a leisurely pace, and only messengers on urgent business, who could change a tired horse for a fresh one whenever necessary, moved about Europe as swiftly as the royal courier of 1394 who covered the 400 miles from Paris to Avignon in four days. However, conditions improved gradually. By the beginning of the sixteenth century the Dutch scholar Erasmus, who moved restlessly from one centre of learning to another, found that, provided travellers kept to the main routes and avoided areas of war, travelling, though still slow, was reasonably safe and not too uncomfortable. Inns in France were said to be excellent, in Germany shocking, but one great advantage was that it was never difficult to make oneself understood, for Latin was still everywhere the common language for educated people.

Towns varied greatly in size and appearance—as illustrated opposite and facing page 169—but they had certain things in common. They were all rather small places as we now judge size. It is difficult to get accurate figures of population for the three centuries 1300-1600 for there were no regular census returns, no official registration of births and deaths. Evidence of numbers can be found in manorial records, tax returns, lists of men liable for military service, and parish registers, but these are scanty and were not kept regularly. Probably London in 1300 had about 35,000 and was by far the biggest town in England. Except for York (11,000), Bristol (10,000), Coventry and Plymouth (about 7,000 each), there were no other places with more than 6,000 people, not much more than what we should think of as large villages. Across the Channel there were bigger towns. Paris, for instance, had 70,000 in the early fourteenth century, Bruges had 35,000, Antwerp 18,000, and some Italian towns were larger still. But it is important to realize that, small though towns might be in 1300, they continued to grow in spite of all setbacks and disasters, such as the famine which in 1316 killed one in every ten of the population of Ypres. By 1500 five cities, Paris, Naples, Milan, Venice, and Constantinople, had more than 100,000 inhabitants. By 1600 Paris had doubled, London had climbed to 100,000. The discovery of America depressed some places on older trade routes and seaways, but brought numbers up in others. Antwerp, Madrid, and Lisbon, for instance, grew rapidly and Bristol, also looking westward towards the New World, reached 15,000 in 1602 and was to increase still faster.

Another common characteristic of the towns was the closeness of their links with the country. There were always gardens, orchards, and sizeable bits of pasture to be found among the houses, and outside the fields and woods lay close up to the walls. Nearly all contemporary pictures show this, and there are many echoes of the country in the names of streets which still exist today. In the old centre of Bristol is one called Broad Mead; a main thoroughfare in

A view of Paris in the middle of the fifteenth century from a miniature painted by Jean Fouquet called 'The Descent of the Holy Spirit'. This accounts for the beam of light coming from the sky and the flight of departing devils. Paris was then a city of 70,000–80,000 people and was encircled by walls. The fields come close up to the walls, and farmers can be seen working in them.

Ghent is the Veldstraat, to mention only two. It was quite normal for townsmen of every degree to be actively engaged in the life of the country as well as the town, whether in work or pleasure. In 1592 Thomas Stowe wrote in his *Survey of London*, 'On May Day in the morning every man, except impediment, would walke into the swete meadowes and greene woods, there to rejoyse their speretes with the beauty and savour of swete floures and with the harmonie of birds', and in Italy Federigo da Montefeltro, Duke of Urbino (1444–82) rode out from the city every morning before breakfast, and fresh food came daily to the palace from his nearby farms. There were wealthy townsmen all over Europe who made a point of owning

113

estates in the neighbouring countryside; for land, though no longer the only source of wealth, was still a very important one and it could still give a family more prestige than anything else. Many nobles like Duke Federigo who lived in towns kept close links with the country; many merchants like the Frenchman Jacques Coeur of Bourges who built himself the splendid town house shown on page 115 were careful to invest their profits in land.

Towns were still essentially strongholds, 'burghs' (citizens were often called burghers or burgesses), and, in spite of the open spaces in them, the houses lay closely contained within defensive walls. Gradually as times became more peaceful they spread outside, but it was long—often centuries—before walls were allowed to fall into ruins and their stones carted away for other buildings. There were indeed parts of Europe where, for special reasons, towns did not outgrow their medieval walls until the nineteenth century. In France and Germany, plagued so long by the Wars of Religion and the Thirty Years War, some even shrank or hardly increased at all so that they were little bigger and far less thriving in 1600 than they

Aigues Mortes in Provence. An example of a medieval city lying off the main streams of trade and travel which has hardly grown since its walls were built between 1267-75. It was founded by Louis IX of France as a port of embarkation for his crusades.

The house of the rich merchant Jacques Coeur of Bourges. In one of its towers (not shown here) there are specially made holes through which carrier pigeons entered bringing news of business enterprises to the master of the house. The house was begun in 1443 and took eight years to complete.

had been in Roman times. These were places which lay in the path of armies, or had never recovered from the effects of the Black Death, or which had no particular attractions for industry and trade. Usually there was a market-place near the centre of the town where, week by week, tradesmen set up their stalls and merchants did their business and country people came to sell their surplus eggs, cheese, and chickens. From this point the streets ran out towards the walls and to the gates which pierced them. These were closed every night with a good deal of clanking and noisy warnings. The houses, built of the materials most easily available in the locality, stone or brick, or wood and lathe and plaster, varied in size and shape. Many were narrow and tall, perhaps two or three storeys high, the upper floors often overhanging the street below and almost touching the opposite house. Spacious houses were few, and for one citizen with a house like Jacques Coeur there were hundreds who lived crowded together into dark tenements and stinking hovels, 'dark dens for adulterers, thieves, murderers and every mischief worker', as a London man described them in 1592.

115

At street level the work of the town went on either in ground-floor rooms or outside in the shelter of the overhanging upper storey which protected workers to some extent from rain and from rubbish thrown out from above into the street. Often the symbol of a trade hung over the door, a gilded boot, a giant key, an axe, or a bunch of fresh ivy-leaves at a tavern to advertise a new brew of ale. Goods for sale were hung round the doorway or displayed on movable wooden counters and their merits were shouted aloud to the passers-by.

In the workshop the master of the house reigned supreme. According to his status and the size of his business, he had a number of apprentices and day-workers—in England called journey-men from the French word *journée*, a day—working with him. His apprentices were bound to him for a period of years which varied according to the complexity of the trade—four years for a rope-maker, but eight for a silversmith or a fisherman—and he was pledged to teach them all the secrets of the trade. They were in his care and lived in his house, getting free board and lodging, shoes, hose, and one new suit a year, but no wages. Apprenticeship could be very hard on a spirited lad, for he was bound to obey his master in every-thing and do him no injury; not to waste or lend his goods, not to frequent taverns and alehouses, not to play unlawful games or brawl in the streets, and not to marry. When his apprenticeship was over he was entitled to submit a masterpiece, a sample of his best work, to the senior masters in the industry. If they approved it and he could raise the necessary entrance fee, he became a full member of his craft-guild, a master craftsmen entitled to train apprentices himself; otherwise he joined the guild as a journeyman. At this point his master was obliged by their contract to give him at least one new suit and certain essential tools. An English mason, for instance, would depart with a pickaxe, a brick-axe, a hammer, and a trowel. Henceforth his future depended largely on himself and his own skill. He might, as many did, remain humble and poor; he might become a master craftsman in a small way; he might prosper and become a rich man, not only working for local customers but selling his goods far afield. In that case he would enlarge his premises and, even if not as wealthy as Jacques Coeur or the Datini family of Florence, or the Celys of London, he would certainly need an office or counting-house as well as work-rooms and stores. One successful cloth merchant in Italy made an inventory of the contents of his counting-house in 1348. It contained several desks, some with book-compartments, large tables for measuring cloth, shelves along the wall, a case on the wall with pigeon-holes for letters, a strong cash box, a heavy steel-yard, ink-wells, and a couch (perhaps for an occasional nap!). Though not listed, there would have been at least one abacus, the wooden frame with beads of different colours strung on wires used in the Middle Ages for calculations much as adding

George Gisze, merchant of the Steelyard in London, the headquarters in England of the hated Hanseatic League. He is surrounded by the paraphernalia of his business—letters, pens, inkpots, seals and sealing tape (in the elaborate chased basket to his left) and account books.

machines are today. Evidently there was a steady demand among merchants for books about business methods, and in one of these, produced in Naples in 1458, the author urged his readers to be methodical over accounts and letters.

I warn, and encourage every merchant [he wrote] to take pleasure in knowing how to keep his books well and methodically. And whoever does not know how to do this let him get instruction or let him keep an expert young book-keeper. Otherwise your commerce will be chaos and a confusion of Babel, of which you must beware if you cherish your honour and your substance. You must keep your writing desk in order and note on all letters you receive where they come from, of what year and of what day. And then each month you shall make a bundle of those letters and put each bundle into the drawer in your writing desk.

The careful merchant who followed this advice, kept his accounts, filed his letters, and tidied his desk could become exceedingly prosperous and powerful, especially if he looked beyond the limited horizon of his own town and its local trade and ventured into international business, dealing perhaps with other merchants from the Baltic coast to the Mediterranean, from the thriving wool towns of Flanders to the proud cities of Italy, even handling the costly merchandise which came from the East—silk, spices, sugar, cotton, drugs, and perfume—for which since the Crusades demand among the wealthy had steadily grown.

Such men, bold, self-reliant, and industrious, made their fortunes through their own enterprise and energy, and that energy naturally spilled over into other sides of life. Although in the centuries 1300–1600 most merchants, like the rest of society, took for granted the social superiority of princes and noblemen, this did not prevent them from taking a leading part in the long struggle of townsmen to escape from their domination, for they knew well that their own existence and way of life depended on wringing certain basic concessions from the lords, whether princes, nobles, knights, bishops, or abbots.

The first of these concessions was personal freedom. A town community was at first linked to a lord or lords in exactly the same way as a rural one, and the lord could demand services and dues from townsmen just as he did from his tenants on the manor. But it was obviously impossible for a man to carry on trade or industry successfully while remaining servile and unfree, obliged to give service and dues to some lord or lords, unable to travel or move or marry without permission or payment of a fine or to dispose of any property at will. Personal freedom was essential.

Next to their personal freedom townsmen desired the right to be judged in a single court, not in a multitude of different ones which led to endless delay and confusion but which was quite possible when a town was under the authority of several lords.

Detail from an altarpiece by Robert Campin, the master of Fermaille. The painter has made it appear as if we were looking through a window into a street of tall narrow houses in a Flemish town. The ground floors contain shops and work-rooms, one house has a cellar door leading to a store-house.

The third basic concession sought by townsmen everywhere was the right to what was often called a 'peace' of the town, that is a set of laws made by themselves by which they could judge and punish all who threatened its security or order, corrupted its trade, fouled its streets, or damaged its good name in any way. 'Let no man lay out any muck at his door', ordered the Mayor of Leicester in 1467 by the advice and consent of all the commons of the town, 'neither stocks nor stones, timber nor clay', and the order went on to declare that all able-bodied citizens must be ready to turn out in 'all affrays', and to forbid ducks 'to be abroad in any street on pain of forfeiture of a halfpenny for every duck to be levied for the use of the town'.

Gradually all over Europe concessions were won from feudal lords and written into town charters. Sometimes this happened peaceably but often only after bloody affrays like the tumult at Laon in France where the townspeople rose in a body and murdered the bishop because, having once granted them self-government, he had changed his mind and withdrawn it. The grip of the feudal system of holding land was weakening and nowhere more rapidly than in towns. Feudal lords were shaken out of their old habits and they became accustomed to accept money rents instead of services and dues, even though they might often despise townsmen and merchants as 'common people—folk who ought rather to burrow into caves than make demands of their betters''. By degrees every vestige of serfdom or villeinage disappeared from towns; townsmen gained the control over many of their own affairs, and gradually won the right to elect their own officials, to punish malefactors, to repair and guard their walls, to raise money for their own purposes and in their own way. At first it was the most powerful citizens, in France called 'grands bourgeois', who benefited most from these things—this, of course, was why they fought for them—yet, in the long run, some benefits filtered down to the grass roots of town society, and the humblest journeyman, though he might be exploited and bitterly poor, knew the truth of the German proverb 'Town air makes a man free'.

Struggles for freedom and rights brought townsmen together and taught them to co-operate. They also learnt this by organizing themselves in trade associations whose names varied from place to place, craft guilds, *corps de métiers*, *arti*, or *Hanses*. The first guild in a town was usually the guild merchant formed by men who were engaged in general and wholesale trade. Besides being the most enterprising and the richest, they were also often exclusive and snobbish, deliberately keeping out of the guild the poorer men, small shopkeepers, and hand-workers, by the heavy entrance fees and expensive feasts, and expelling any man who disgraced himself by going bankrupt. Often, too, only members of certain powerful families were admitted, and the guild merchant sometimes monopolized all power so that its members became tyrants as greedy and haughty as any feudal lord, 'oppressing their neighbours and subjecting them to violence'.

As towns grew, so did the number of guilds formed by separate crafts or trades. In Florence in the middle of the fifteenth century there were twenty-one; in Leicester in 1430 there were thirty, and they included bankers, notaries, goldsmiths, physicians and apothecaries, butchers, bakers, stonemasons, carpenters, tanners, oil-, salt-, and cheesemongers, tool-makers and tinkers, and the various subdivisions of the wool trade, such as weavers, fullers, dyers, and so on. The most ancient of these craft guilds were the butchers and bakers. Every craftsman, master and journeyman alike, belonged to the guild; there was no division between the employer and the men who worked for him, and to become a master you simply had to prove the quality of your work by presenting a masterpiece, prove your good character by getting other craftsmen to speak for you (not difficult in a small community where a man was known by all his neighbours), and prove that you had some substance by producing the entrance fee. The main objects of a guild were to keep up the standard of work and charge a fair price for it, and to keep out 'foreign' competitors. A foreigner was any craftsman not a resident of the town. He might come from another country or from another town only twenty miles away, it was all the same, he could not set up a workshop unless first admitted to the appropriate guild, and this was not made easy. Standards were kept high by the system of apprenticeship, by presentation of masterpieces, and by 'searchers', men who were appointed to inspect work, test weights and measures, and report cases of dishonesty. The craft guilds also fixed wages, usually so that a journeyman earned about one-third less than a master, a woman about two-thirds less. Their rules were harshly enforced, but they also had a generous and sociable side. If a member fell on evil days, he and his family were helped; if he died leaving a widow badly off, she was supported and his sons apprenticed without charge. From their funds the guilds made generous gifts to churches, providing stained glass windows, like those in Chartres Cathedral, and building chantry chapels where Masses were said for the souls of departed members. And at least once a year the entire guild sat down to a rich and lengthy feast, in England roasted beef, veal, and pork, 'grene geese, and spyce cake'—a most welcome change for many of the poorer guildsmen from their simple rather coarse everyday food of bread and cheese, soup, beans, peas, and bacon, and they were usually content with 'good bere and ale' and did not hanker for the fine wines provided for the high officers of the guild.

The advantages of the guilds, even though some of them were often 'not as good and honest as they ought to be', were obvious, the most important being the high quality of workmanship, which was greatly to the advantage of customers, the protection of members from unfair competition, and the habits of self-government they taught to generations of townsmen. But they had bad effects too. The very rules and regulations which made it difficult for members to do shoddy work without being caught and punished became so minute and rigid that in the end they destroyed initiative and strangled new ideas, since no man was permitted to introduce any improved methods by which he could produce goods more cheaply and quickly, in case some backward members of the guild might be harmed. And even though master and man belonged to the same guild, which in theory sounds excellent and democratic, yet journeymen often had a hard time of it and a bad master could be an oppressive and remorseless tyrant. Journeymen worked literally from morning till night, from dawn to sunset, and, like the poor man in the country, had no reserves. If disaster struck the town or the trade, they were the first to suffer, to be turned out of work and come face to face with starvation. It is no wonder that some of them were always discontented, did as little as possible, and were much given to 'conspirations, murmurings, and desire to increase the price of their work, and other villainies'.

On the other hand, everywhere the class of 'grand bourgeois' tended to become steadily richer and more solid and important and to develop a life and standards of its own. One such citizen living in Paris in 1392–4 and using a nom de plume 'le ménagier de Paris' (the goodman of Paris) wrote a book for his young wife on how to manage her household, and it is obvious that it was a large one and that he was a wealthy man. He kept a house steward and a house-keeper and a bailiff (reeve) to look after his farm, for, like the duke Federigo, he had close links with the country. He had three classes of servants: domestic servants living in the house; day workers, such as reapers, carriers, and coopers, for special jobs; and piece-workers such as shoemakers and bakers. He warned his wife that day workers were commonly lazy and rough and given to answering back and arguing about their wages. But his employees were well treated. The indoor servants had two hearty meals with meat each day and were allowed to warm themselves by the fire in winter, though as soon as they began to argue or lean their elbows on the table and tell stories they were to be made to go off to work again or, if it was evening, to take their candles and go to bed.

The ménagier of Paris could well afford comforts, and he relished them. He expected his wife always to give him good food and drink, clean white sheets and fur coverings on his bed, and was insistent that there must be no fleas. When he got back after a long hard day she must see that there was a warm fire, hot water for his feet, and dry shoes and stockings. Unfortunately he does not reveal what his trade was, but he evidently was accustomed to be much occupied with 'the care of outside affairs . . . to go and come and journey hither and thither in rain and wind, in snow and hail, now drenched, now dry'. He also expected when travelling on business to be 'ill-fed, ill-lodged, ill-warmed and ill-bedded', but the rewards were high: wealth and servants, a large comfortable home, an accomplished and well-behaved wife, a status in society high enough for him to dine with bishops and members of the king's Council and himself to give fine feasts to his fellow burgesses, feasts of venison and beef, sausages and special pottages, round sea fish and flat sea fish, pies, pastries, blancmange, and 'sugar meats' and custards.

The ménagier must have been well known in the Paris of his day as a solid prosperous citizen, and he may well have left sons who carried on the family business for a time, but he was not in the top class of merchants nor, as far as we know, was his name widely known in Europe. There were by the end of the fourteenth century other men who did business on a far grander scale, who had international reputations, and who rivalled noblemen, princes, and kings in their wealth and their splendid style of living. Some of them like the Bardi, the Peruzzi, and the Medici of Florence and the Fuggers of Augsburg were so enormously rich that they were able to finance needy sovereigns with huge loans, thereby adding hugely to their profits and influence, but also, as we shall see, running great risks.

It was the Italians who led the way in building up international business and who were capitalists in the sense that they invested money in joint enterprises. They had all the shrewdness, the drive, and the readiness to take risks of their forerunners in trade of earlier times, but their methods were very different. Unlike the ménagier who expected 'to go and come and journey hither and thither' on his business, the big merchants of the fifteenth and sixteenth centuries conducted their affairs from their desks in their counting-houses, working from a centre and employing agents to travel for them and open or manage branches in distant places. Some combined a form of banking with buying and selling goods, and here too the Italians were pioneers. They took money on deposit and paid interest on it; they lent money to customers and charged them interest; they financed individual merchants who needed capital for their trading. They were the first to invent the efficient 'double-entry' method of keeping accounts which is still used today. The example on page ooo shows how the method works and how easy it is to see at a glance from it whether a customer is in debt to the company or has a credit balance.

Italian cities all had their great families engaged in trade, whose ventures might reach round the Mediterranean and the Black Sea and to the Far East, like those of the merchants of Venice and Genoa, or chiefly over the land mass of Europe, like those of Pisa, Milan, Siena, and Florence. In Florence there were powerful clans

Two methods of book-keeping. The first, the older method, meant that a man had to read through the whole of the transactions before he could see how the account stood. By the double-entry method, invented by the Italian merchants, he could tell by a glance at the bottom of the page what his client owed or was owed.

1340   CARCASSONE

Riquet, wife of Adam of Rovenay, in the city of Carcassone, owes s.10 for 2 palms of vermillion and for 1½ palms of white cloth which was for hose with edging for her, which she took on Wednesday, Oct. 4. Also she owes d.1. Also she owes d.1. Also she owes d.1. Paid s.3 d.11. Remains (to be paid) s.6 d.5.

1396   MILAN

Alberico of Medea, maker of spurs, must give :		*Alberico must have :*	
Item on March 6 for money paid to him	£9	Item for 6 doz. fine jewelled spurs at £14 s.10 per doz.	£27
Item on March 11 for money paid to Filippo his (Alberico's) brother	£15	Item for 6 doz. small fine jewelled spurs at s.54 per doz.	£16 s.4
Item on March 24 for money to be given to Alberico	£18	Item for 4 doz. spurs with a prick at s.26 per doz.	£5 s.4
Item for money paid on Alberico's account to Pietrino Bazuello	£10	Item for 4 doz. quality spurs at s.26 per doz.	£4 s.12
Item for the balance on Jan. 3 1397	£15	Item for 4 doz. medium quality spurs at s.20 per doz.	£4
	£57 s.0		£57 s.0

Terra-cotta bust of Lorenzo di Medici (il Magnifico) by Verrocchio (1435–88). The powerful grim face is in marked contrast to the portrait of Lorenzo as a gay young aristocrat shown in Gozzoli's painting facing page 145.

who gained fame and fortune through trade. Their huge stone palaces, grim as fortresses from the outside, dominated many of the narrow streets of the city; their furious rivalries stainéd those streets with blood. Sometimes they rose to dazzling heights of wealth, sometimes they were reduced to bankruptcy by a gamble which did not come off or a loan which was not repaid, like the one for £125,000 made to Edward III of England in 1358 towards the cost of his wars in France, which brought the Bardi and the Peruzzi families to the verge of ruin. The greatest of all Florentine families, of course, was the Medici, all-powerful in the city from 1378 to 1494. In the middle of the fifteenth century they controlled four companies in Florence itself, two engaged in the wool trade, one in silk manufacture, and one in banking, and eight others engaged in general trade in Venice, Rome, Pisa, Milan, Geneva, Avignon, Bruges, and London. The London company was formed in 1456 by Piero and Giovanni de'Medici, sons of Lorenzo the Magnificent, their cousin Piero Francesco, and two friends. Each of them put £1,000 (£10,000 in modern money) into the business and agreed to trade together for four years, but none of them went to the London branch which was run by a manager, Simone Nori. The partners kept their agents and managers under strict control, and Simone had to promise not to do any business on his own but only for the company, not to hire any workmen without permission from Florence, not to gamble with cards or dice, and to send his accounts on 24 March each year to be examined in Florence.

The Fuggers of Augsburg in Germany were another family with an international reputation as businessmen in the fifteenth and

sixteenth centuries. They started humbly enough. A certain Hans
Fugger was a weaver in Augsburg in the 1360s; he was an excellent
craftsman and very thrifty and he left a tidy sum of money to his sons
to continue in the cloth trade. The business flourished and was soon
dealing with many other kinds of merchandise besides wool and
cloth. It was strictly confined to the family, and all male descendants
of Hans the first were bound by an undertaking to invest their money
only in the Fugger company so that more and more capital was
constantly available for expansion. At the height of their power the

*Jacob Fugger, head of the great
banking family in his office at
Augsburg. He is not shown here
as the impressive figure in the
Golden Room who received
impecunious clients from all
over Europe, but as a busy man
dictating to a secretary. The
labels on the drawers or filing-
cabinets give a good idea of the
wide range of the firm's
business—Rome, Lisbon,
Cracow, Antwerp etc.*

Fuggers formed one of the greatest financial companies in Europe. In 1511 Jacob Fugger became head of the company, by that time so wealthy that it was banker to half a dozen rulers in Europe. Charles V borrowed half a million florins for the expenses of the imperial election, and without Jacob Fugger's help he would not have become emperor. In another emergency, when Charles and his household were actually short of food, this descendant of the thrifty weaver once again came to the rescue of an emperor. To call on the Fuggers for financial aid became a habit with the needy, and all sorts and conditions of men visited Jacob Fugger in his richly panelled room in 'the Golden Counting House' as the head office of the family in Augsburg was called. From the arrogant but impecunious aristocrat to the plain hard-working merchant in need of extra capital for an enterprise, they came face to face with the big stately man sitting in a heavily carved armchair covered in red flowered velvet behind a great desk inlaid with gold and mother-of-pearl, his feet on the lion's skin. His eyes, under heavy brows, were set in a deeply lined face, and he looked just what he was, a very formidable person well aware of his own importance, well able to sum up his clients, ready to accept from his royal debtors titles of nobility and a splendid coat of arms for the family, but never deflected from the purpose of his business, which was to make money. Yet the Fuggers, though they could be ruthless, nevertheless had consciences. In Augsburg they built six streets of houses to let to their work people for modest rents, and set aside a proportion of them for pensioners too old to work, and in this way provided some of the benefits of the modern welfare state.

Business companies like those of the Medici, the Fuggers, and others not on such a big scale increased in the fifteenth and sixteenth centuries, and their area of trading widened far beyond the boundaries of their own city or country, especially if they ventured to the newly discovered lands. Some of them, as we have seen, were powerful enough to influence the wars and politics of Europe. Yet there were still merchants who continued to trade on their own, though even the boldest individuals tended to form groups for protection against violence and robbery and hazards of travel. One such group was the Merchant Adventurers of London. Each adventurer provided his own capital, bore his own losses, and raked in his individual profits, but the company gained useful privileges for its members, as, for instance, in 1407 when they were granted the monopoly in exporting English cloth by Henry IV. Another English company, known as the Eastland Company, was a group of merchants who traded in Germany and Scandinavia; they certainly needed to act together, for they were in opposition to the formidable Hanseatic League, known as the Easterlings. These German merchants traded as individuals chiefly in wool, timber, furs, wax, copper, and grain, but they were strongly organized for protection and for the extraction of valuable trade privileges, such as freedom from customs and taxation in the countries where they operated. The tentacles of the Easterlings spread out from Lübeck on the Baltic where their headquarters were until they had 130 depots in other European cities and four major establishments in Novgorod, Bergen, Bruges, and London. Compared with those of the Italians, the business methods of the Hanseatic League were old-fashioned and inefficient; they did not use double-entry book-keeping or make up accounts annually. But what they lacked in up-to-date methods they made up by force. Hanseatic agents sometimes behaved with brutal arrogance and a total disregard for any claims except their own, especially in weaker towns. In Bergen their depot occupied one whole side of the harbour, and they dominated the town. Until the Germans had taken their pick of newly arrived goods, no local trader could buy anything. In London they never behaved with this insolence and they were careful not to offend the city authorities or the royal customs officials. Even so their depot, known as the Steelyard, where they worked and lived, was heavily fortified. It was frequently attacked by London mobs, so hated were the Germans, and none of them dared to walk abroad after dark. In the end its own arrogance and its rigid outlook ruined the Hanseatic League. Its members did not move with the times; they did not pioneer in the vast new fields for trade which opened in the east and the west after the discovery of the sea route to India and the discovery of the New World; and because they confined themselves too much to Europe, their trade and their power declined, so that it was possible for an English merchant in 1608 to write cheerfully about the Hanseatic merchants 'most of their teeth have fallen out, and the rest sit but loosely in their heads'.

The life of a thriving town was a busy one, whether on the warm plains of Italy or the bleaker shores of the Baltic. The citizens themselves watched its boundary and defended its walls. They kept the peace in its streets, took charge of its common property, and managed the spending of its money. They strove and sweated for a living, but they enjoyed a good deal of gaiety, feasts of various sorts, the mystery plays which were performed by the guilds at certain Christian festivals, and all the travelling minstrels, jugglers, pipers, and acrobats who entertained them in the streets. There were processions at frequent intervals, either to mark a saint's day or an event of special importance, or to celebrate the visit of some illustrious person. Then the whole town assembled, each dressed in his best according to his rank, and walked through the streets to the sound of trumpets, pipes, and drums 'all loudly and noisily blown or beaten'. Over all would be the sound of church bells, an inescapable part of the background noise in a medieval town and so familiar to the citizens that their very

A procession on a Holy Day, by P. Bruegel the Younger (1559– 1637). Church festivals and saints days were occasions for recreation, enjoyed by people in town and country.

notes were recognized and in England they were given homely names like Great Tom and Big Ben. The single common bell rung in the tower of the parish church announced to everyone alike the arrival of a courier, the opening of the market, the start of the guild plays, the death of a fellow townsman, or a common danger; the whole peal ringing out meant some joyous event. But whatever the message might be, all citizens would feel that it concerned them, for they had a strong sense of community in spite of differences in rank and work and fortune.

127

These differences increased and the gulf between rich and poor, between master and man, tended everywhere to deepen. Life in the town might offer opportunities to the vigorous and the ambitious which life in the village did not and enable some men to better their condition, others to achieve great wealth, but the majority did not succeed even in reaching a little prosperity. At least half the population of the towns and cities of Europe in the sixteenth century lived in poverty as bitter as any countryman. Bad harvests occurred all too often, and with them came high prices for bread and near starvation for those who could not pay them. Bread riots were common occurrences in many towns, for violence lay always just below the surface, and when hunger was linked with some other powerful force, as it was with religious fanaticism in Paris on the night of St. Bartholomew's Day in 1572, the hungry mobs of the towns could be savage and terrible indeed.

(ii) In the country

Life in the towns attracted a growing number of people who looked to find freedom, safety, and work there; yet even at the end of the sixteenth century only about one out of every ten Europeans was a townsman. The other nine lived in the country, most of them peasants working on the land and occupied with growing crops, raising livestock, and the countless other jobs connected with farming. First and foremost these country people produced the basic necessities of life, the bread crops (wheat, oats, barley, and rye), the meat and milk, and then other foods which varied according to climate, soil, and local eating habits. In the more northern parts of Europe these were such things as cheese, bacon, lard, peas, and beans; in the more southerly lands oil, wine, fruit, peas, and beans. Vegetables of rather poor quality such as cabbages, leeks, and onions were grown in small amounts, but it was not until the sixteenth century that the potato began to appear in garden plots and to form part of a peasant's diet. People living in the country also produced the raw materials for clothing and coverings, the wool, hides, flax, and hemp out of which cloth, leather, and linen were made.

Tools and methods of farming varied in different parts of Europe, so did crops and livestock. In some places they remained very primitive—as in some they still do—and every process consumed an immense amount of human sweat and toil. But in other parts there was slow progress, and this showed itself in better tools and harness, in better breeds of animals—though all were distinctly poor specimens by modern standards—in better ways of fertilizing the soil. Books on 'husbandry', as farming was called in England, began to appear in the thirteenth and fourteenth centuries: one famous one by the Englishman Walter of Henley, another in French by an anonymous author, and much later, in 1573, *Five hundred pointes of*

128

Good Husbandrie by Thomas Tusser. Such books were only useful to people who could read, still a mere handful compared with those who could not, but the advice they gave would be passed on by word of mouth to those without learning and added to their store of ancient knowledge. Walter of Henley was very vigorous about using manure to improve crops: 'Don't sell your stubble', he says, 'strew it in wet places, your sheep house and folds and then before March comes gather it all together and put it on the land.' Walter was obviously an up-to-date as well as an economical person, and his remarks about the weekly cost of feeding and shoeing horses (12s. 6d. each) compared with oxen (3s. 1d. each) are interesting, for they show that more horses were coming into use on the land. For centuries they had been too scarce and too costly; oxen were cheaper to buy and feed and did not have to be shod; alive they gave years of slow plodding work and dead they provided meat, leather, and horn for cups and lanthorns. But by the middle of the fifteenth century heavy horses were no longer monopolized by the knightly class for pounding about in plate armour at tournaments and in war, and so were found more often working on the land as you can see in the picture on page 130. Yet there were always some men who could not afford them and went on using oxen, and even now, in parts of Europe, oxen still pull ploughs and carts.

The variations in crops and livestock, in weather and geography, meant variations also in the way men lived and worked in the country. The people of the high uplands in Switzerland or Scotland, far from towns and markets, had little in common with their fellow country-men living in warm fertile lowlands; and conditions in the hot valley of the river Po were utterly different from those on the cold clay round the Thames. Some of these variations are illustrated in the picture on page 144. The luxuriant rows of vines in the valley would never flourish on the alpine meadows on the mountain side, but the lush grass which grows up there even in the hottest summer gives excellent fodder for cattle.

There was, however, one pattern of living and working which was still common in many parts of Europe and that was the manorial or open-field system. In modern English or French the word 'manor' or 'manoir' usually means a single large house, but it can also mean an estate, and in the Middle Ages the manor was a small unit of society, a group of houses, a barn or two, probably a church and a mill, and round about three or four great fields stretching sometimes as far as you could see. Beyond the fields were woods or waste land.

One of the houses, bigger and better built than the others, was the manor-house itself, the dwelling of the lord, the landowner, who might be a layman great or small from the king to a simple knight, or a churchman, bishop or abbot or other head of a religious community. One lord might live permanently in the manor-house, or at

least stay there once or twice a year, another might never come near the place but leave it to his steward or bailiff to manage his properties. But in any case he expected to get his living, his wealth, from the land of the manor which was divided into two parts, one often called the demesne, cultivated entirely for him, the other divided among his tenants who lived in the other houses. His wealth was of two kinds: first he received the direct yield of the demesne, the wheat, grapes, cheese, eggs, meat, and so on, which he either consumed on the spot or had carted to him wherever he might be. This was produced by the unpaid labour of his tenants. Secondly, over and above such produce and labour, he expected to receive dues from the tenants in money or in kind. Some of these were demanded at certain times each year, for instance, 'on St. John's day 5 sous', 'at Christmas a fowl fine and good', 'on Palm Sunday the sheep due', and these were regular and inescapable. Also inescapable but demanded only on special occasions were dues like mortmain which was levied on a dead tenant's goods or merchet which he had to pay when his daughter married.

In the fields of the manor, which were open and unfenced, the land was divided into strips by narrow lines of unploughed ground, and every tenant held a number of strips. The number varied but on average each man was supposed to have enough land to support himself and his family. They did not lie all together as in most modern villages but scattered in each of the fields, and though this was a rough and ready method of sharing out good and bad soil, it was obviously very wasteful in ways which are easy to discover. Sometimes the demesne land was also scattered in strips, but more often it was conveniently collected together.

Every tenant on the manor had a right to his strips of land; to his house, such as it was; to a small croft round the house where he could grow a few extra crops, some herbs and vegetables, and keep his bees; and to the right of pasture for a certain number of cows, sheep, pigs, and geese in the fields after the crops had been lifted. For these rights, by which alone he could get his living, he paid heavily. When the manorial system was at its height in Europe from the tenth to the twelfth century, the peasant or villein had to work for his lord at least three days a week. This week-work might be almost anything concerned with farming: ploughing, sowing, harvesting, threshing, pruning, picking grapes, putting up temporary fences to keep beasts out of growing crops, in fact anything that was needed. He was also obliged to do extra at certain busy times or on demand, and this was called boon-work. His wife and family were also bound to do week-work and boon-work 'at the will of the lord'. In addition, there were the dues already mentioned, and when all this is added up, it is easy to understand the determination of townsmen to escape such demands on their time and energy and

easy to grasp the harsh truth of a verse from a poem written in
medieval French which said:

> Terres arer, noirrer aumailles
> Sor le vilain est la bataille
> Guar chevalier et clerc sans faille
> Vivent de ce qu'il travaille.

'To plough the field and feed the beasts is the struggle for the villein,
for the knight and the priest live on his work.'

Five centuries before, Alfred the Great had written of the three-
fold division of society and of the peasants as 'the men who worked'
and by their work supported 'the men who fought' and 'the men who
prayed'; this was still largely true in the fourteenth century. They
have left so few traces behind them that it is difficult to know what
kind of men and women they were. They could not write; their
homes, usually built of perishable materials, have long ago succumbed
to wind and weather, fire, or neglect; their few household goods and
chattels have disappeared except for an occasional tool or broken pot
accidentally preserved. But a picture of them and their daily lives can
be built up bit by bit from various sources. There are manorial
records, chiefly those kept for church lands because there was always
someone in a monastery who could write them, and these reveal a
good deal about their arduous lives and their relationships with their
lords. For instance, in the documents of Gloucester abbey there
appears the name of a woman who held land on one of the abbey
manors at the beginning of the fourteenth century. She is simply
called 'Margery the Widow', and this must mean that the village
was so small that everyone knew their neighbours well and surnames
were not necessary. Margery held 24 acres of land. For this she paid
a rent of 3s. a year, but she also owed a long list of week-work on the
abbey demesne. On three days of every week she had to plough, sow,
weed, mow, lift hay, and do 'other manual services' according to the
time of year. Every fourth day from the Feast of St. John the Baptist
till the end of August she had to 'carry on her back to Gloucester or
elsewhere at the bailiff's will'. This was only the week-work—she
also owed the harvest boon 'fed by the lord', but with what kind of
food is not stated, and eight more boon-works in the autumn,
apparently not fed by the lord. There were also chickens to be found
at Christmas 'at will', and no doubt the will was not hers but the
bailiff's. One can easily imagine the bowed figure of Margery toiling
along the road to Gloucester in the hot weeks of July and August and
thinking resentfully of her own little crop of hay or corn waiting to
be gathered.

Another document, this time from France, tells of a certain
'Richard son of Jehan' living on one of the manors of the monastery
of Rouen. His land was about the same as Margery's, but his manual
service was much lighter and he was always fed by the monastery

Winter in the Country from the Très Riches Heures of the Duc de Berry, painted by Pol de Limburg, c. 1411. The artist has given the impression of bitter cold and stagnation of farm-work. He has cut away part of the side of the house, and the simple stark interior is in marked contrast to the hall of the duke shown on page 155.

with 'bread and stew once a day' or 'bread three times a day when seated and a pennyworth of cheese and a loaf in the evening". Richard also did carrying service, but not on his back. He used a horse, and the monastery supplied a boy to lead it. But he had to give a great deal in money and in kind, eggs, hens, three day-old chicks, wheat, and oats, and he had to bring all timber wanted by the monastery from the Seine or 'as far as he can, so he can go home in the evening'.

Then there are poems like Chaucer's *Canterbury Tales*, and the *Vision of Piers Plowman*, which was written in 1362 by another Englishman, John Langland, both full of country characters and conditions. But the clearest pictures of all are in the beautiful calendars and books of hours, the personal prayer books made for rich patrons by the artists like Pol de Limburg or Simon Bening who

133

specialized in illuminations and who filled sections of their pages with brilliant little scenes of country life and people. Other artists, too, noticed the peasant and his doings with sharp enough eyes to put them in their picture, painters like Pieter Bruegel (1525–69) known as 'Peasant Bruegel' because he so often depicted the peasants of his native Flanders. These are precious sources of history, for here we see the ordinary country people working, eating, drinking, merry-

The Vision of the Shepherds from a Book of Hours illustrated by Simon Bening, a Flemish painter, about 1450. He has made no attempt to romanticize the shepherds who appear as clumsy figures in coarse ragged clothes and broken boots.

making, or in exhausted slumber. We see their clumsy bodies, their faces moon-like or gaunt, vacant or cunning, their torn and shabby clothes. 'As he trod the soil his toes peered out of his worn shoes' wrote Langland about a ploughman, and exactly the same was clearly true of the shepherds that Simon Bening observed. Many, probably most, peasants lived short lives of poverty and exacting toil, working from first light to dusk and going back at the end of the day to eat and sleep in a dark, smoky, smelly hut: dark because the windows were very small, unglazed, and closed by shutters of lattice or leather; smoky because chimneys were rare and fire smoke found its way out through a hole in the roof; smelly because most people were dirty, drains rudimentary, and animals often shared the house with humans. In his cottage the peasant and his family sat on home-made wooden stools and benches; they hung their belongings on pegs or kept them in wooden chests; they slept on the floor or a low wooden bedstead on straw-filled mattresses.

But as well as poverty, hard work, and inescapable demands for services and dues, there was another side of the manorial system which nearly everywhere oppressed the peasants of Europe and was bitterly resented. When it was in full force they were little better than serfs or slaves, bound to the land, as much the property of the lord as the cattle on the demesne. At the worst a man could not move from the manor, change his job, choose a wife, or leave his goods as he liked when he died, and his sons and daughters were equally bound. Only if their lord had no further need of a family on his manor would he set them free and then by a special writ of manumission like this one granted in 1449: 'I, Richard, by divine permission Abbot of the monastery of Peterborough, declare that we have manumitted and caused to be free William Clopton our bondman with all his brood, begotten and to be begotten, with all his goods and chattels'.

Gradually, however, the whole hated pattern of serfdom, or villeinage, with its forced labour and lack of freedom weakened and changed, and by the end of the fifteenth century it had all but disappeared in many parts of Europe except Russia. The heaviest week-work was converted into money rent and only the lighter boonwork remained, and personal freedom was everywhere common. There were various reasons for the change. It began when the population of Europe increased, as it did steadily until the fourteenth century, when famine and plague and war reduced it again. There was a limit to the number of villeins needed on a manor and the number of stomachs that could be filled from the crops, and when this limit was reached, the lords were no longer so particular about the bonds which bound men to them and so these began to loosen. A younger son would be allowed to go to the wars, of which there was never a shortage, then a whole family drift away to the nearest town, and not be chased and brought back. It was, of course, more than likely that in the town too they would still be very poor, but at least they would be reckoned as free to come and go as they willed, and even possibly, by hard work, they might rise a little in the world.

Another reason for the change was the growing need for hard cash, and no one felt this more than the lords. Lay lords wanted money to buy up-to-date armour and weapons, for the cost of hunting, fighting, for generally keeping up with their neighbours at court, for finer clothes, softer living, bigger households. Ecclesiastical lords also found their expenses rising and many of these too liked to live softly. Both had to meet demands for taxes from king and pope, which were always increasing and had to be paid in money, not settled with homely dues like '8 hams and a bucket of beer'. So landowners became eager to take money rents for land instead of service. It paid them better to let out even the demesne itself for rent, and if necessary hire men to work for wages, rather than rely on services often reluctantly and slackly performed. Money rents became more and more common and, as week-work disappeared and boon-work diminished, so did the other bonds which had bound men so tightly to the lords and the land. This did not happen everywhere at once. For a long time there were black spots where men were still unfree and the property of the lord, and this was specially true on ecclesiastical estates. In 1358 the Abbot of Selby in Yorkshire gave away one of his villeins, 'with all his brood' as usual, as he might have given a cow or a set of harness; and about the same time two brothers living near Bordeaux admitted that if they ever left the manor 'to go and live in another place, city, town, castle new or old ... within or without a sanctuary' their lord—again an abbot—had the right to take them and deliver them back to the manor. It is quite clear that many landowners did not entirely renounce their rights to men's bodies and work, and even those who found it convenient to let those rights slip still liked to feel that they could go back to the old ways if necessary. When they found it very difficult to hire labourers, as they did after the Black Death, many of them tried to assert their rights again and met with bitter resistance. The Black Death came long after the beginning of the movement to change from service to money rents as payment for land. It did not cause the change but speeded it up and hardened the determination of country workers to escape from servitude. In the short space of three years (1347–50) the plague swept away one out of every three people working on the land, and those who were left were in a strong position to extract at least some of the things they wanted from their masters. Those lords who refused to commute services or free their tenants from dues and restrictions, who tried to hold on to their old rights, were likely to wake up one day to find tenants gone, leaving empty cottages and untended fields. These scarce persons had slipped away to seek more enlightened masters, and those that were left grumbled and slacked and stubbornly demanded wages for work.

Even personal freedom and escape from heavy burdens of service did not of themselves bring peace and contentment or well-filled stomachs to everyone. It is true that there were many who prospered as the result of the social changes after the Black Death, but many did not. Enterprising men took advantage of the fact that there was much land to be rented from owners who could not get labour to cultivate it, either because the plague had hit the locality very hard or because they were not ready to face changes, and who were only too glad to parcel out their land for money rent and be quit of some of their problems. It was therefore not difficult to rent a sizeable compact holding and, having enclosed it by fence or wall, farm it much more profitably than was possible with scattered strips. Men who did this worked very hard—so did their families—and some of them employed their less prosperous neighbours too. Often they built themselves solid farm-houses, furnished them with heavy carved wooden tables and chairs, warm feather beds, and pewter plates and mugs, and they lived well on plentiful country food and drink. Such men, known in England as yeomen farmers, were a new class of countrymen, who raised themselves above their poorer fellows and stood between them and the landed gentry, just as solid merchants and rising master craftsmen stood between the great men of the towns and the humble journeymen.

The less fortunate and the less energetic who could not afford to rent more than the old small customary holdings of land were in a much less favourable position. They might be free of irksome dues and services, but their land barely gave them a living and they were no longer secure in their claim to it. As long as a landlord needed labour he was not likely to disturb them, but if he wanted to let more and more of his estate to rising yeomen intent on increasing their farms, or if he decided to turn his arable fields into pastures and go in for highly profitable sheep farming which needed fewer workmen, then he did not hesitate to discard ancient rights and customs, to pull down cottages and turn adrift unwanted families. It was always the poor and the unthrifty who were the sufferers as changes came, and they were the first, too, to be hit by rising prices and food shortage. As inequality in wealth increased and because of the hardship and frustrations which resulted, there grew up more widespread bitterness and hostility between landowners and peasants than ever before; it sometimes smouldered as deep resentment and sometimes broke into open revolt. All manner of events sparked off trouble: the disasters described in Chapter 5, the irritating unfairness of freedom and serfdom existing side by side; the royal taxes which were now pressing downward in society till they hit even the pockets of the poor—'Tax hath tenet us alle', as a doggerel poem in English said.

There were many small upheavals in the fourteenth century and three major ones. The first of these was in Flanders from 1323 to 1328. It lasted so long because the peasants, who were the first to revolt, were later joined by discontented townsmen, but in the end it was cruelly suppressed by French troops. Then, as we saw on p. 57 in the summer of 1358 came the short violent eruption in France of the 'Jacquerie'. Maddened by the pillaging armies and the greed of landlords, the peasants surged through northern France, savage and inarticulate, burning castles and murdering the inmates, until the nobles, recovering from their stunned surprise, organized themselves and crushed the revolt. Then 20,000 peasants were slaughtered and the rest sank back into silence.

In England, where the Peasants' Revolt broke out in 1381 (according to Froissart, 'a great mischief and rebellion and movement of the common people'), the rebels were not inarticulate and they were led by able men: Wat Tyler, 'a cunning man endowed with much sense if he had decided to apply his intelligence to good purposes', the gallant William Grindcombe who had been 'educated, nourished and maintained' in the monastery of St. Alban, and others. There were eloquent speakers, too, ready to express in words the deep feelings of the unlearned peasants about the wrongs done to them, men like John Ball the priest who used as text for one of his fiery sermons the ancient rhyme,

> When Adam delved and Eve span
> Who was then the gentleman?

John was certainly no ignorant clodhopper, or he could not have written his famous rhyming letters beginning: 'John Ball greeteth you well all and doth you to understand that he hath rongen your bell. Now right and might, will and skill, Now God haste you in every dele.'

The English peasants' demands were quite clear. They wanted personal freedom, land for a rent of 4*d.* an acre instead of for service, and an end to the detested poll-taxes of 1*s.* a head on all persons over 15, which had been levied in 1377 and 1380. These taxes were said by the king and his council to be for 'various needs, as well for the safety of the realm as for the keeping of the sea'—in other words, to pay for wars. The revolt reached its peak at Mile End outside London with the stabbing of Wat Tyler by the Lord Mayor of London, a single act of pure courage by the young king Richard II, and the issue of royal charters of pardon and freedom. After that it collapsed and the rebels went home deceived into thinking their demands had been met. But the king was prevented by parliament— mainly lords—from keeping his word, many of the men who had joined in the revolt paid with their lives for a few months of turmoil, and bloodshed and broken promises seemed to be the end of it all.

Nevertheless the gradual change from serfdom and service to letting land for rent to men who were free could not be stopped and it moved steadily on until, by the end of the fifteenth century, English peasants were nearly all free men. In this, England was well ahead of other European countries, for there were serfs in France until the French Revolution in 1789 and in Russia until the nineteenth century.

Gradually between 1300 and 1600 standards of living rose in many parts of Europe, though progress was uneven and there were black spots where country life was rough and hard almost beyond description. In England in the reign of Elizabeth I (1558–1603) old countrymen spoke of 'a great amendment of lodging', by which they meant not only that houses had glass in the windows, chimneys instead of holes in the roof, but also better beds, bedding, and other furniture. Wooden plates gave way to pewter and decorated earthenware, wooden spoons to iron and tin, forks were to be seen in use instead of fingers. The roughest wooden furniture was replaced by heavy carved chests, stools, and bedsteads; and sometimes in more prosperous homes the walls were plastered and brightly painted, or hung with painted cloths. Windows were glazed with thick greenish glass, and, though this was not clear, there was more light and certainly fewer draughts, and at night candles or rushlights could be used without too much guttering. But always it is important to remember that there were wide differences of living standards even in one and the same country. One French farmer in the fifteenth century gave his daughter on her wedding 50 *livres* in money, a chest, two sets of bedding, and a robe trimmed with fur; while another at the same time could only scrape together a coverlet and two pieces of homespun cloth, and there must have been hundreds like him.

The same was true of food. Plenty of families still went hungry in winter and ate the coarsest of food at all times. Black bread and milk and water was a common meal in Germany. But on the whole food was becoming more plentiful and varied, and in some places white bread could be seen in cottages, though 'barley and rye browne brede' was preferred by many country people as 'abiding longest in the stomach'. In wine-producing countries there was plenty of cheap rough 'vin du pays'; in most northern parts of Europe the commonest drinks, for men, women, and children alike, were ale and beer. Meat was still a luxury for many, but even so beef, mutton, pork, rabbits, geese, hens, wild-fowl, fish, and fallow deer were eaten—the wild-fowl and fallow deer probably poached from the lord's land and disguised in a savoury stew. To everyone, eating and drinking were major pleasures, especially when the food was fresh, or made particularly appetizing, like 'a dish of mutton cooked in parsley, onions, vinegar, pepper, cinnamon, salt and saffron', which must certainly have smothered the bad taste of the meat if it was 'high'.

Cruck cottage, Didbrook, Gloucestershire. Originally this medieval cottage would have been supported by crucks, massive beams meeting at the top, at each end. The roof would be of thatch, the walls of wattle and daub. Here the roof porch, dormer window and stonework are later improvements.

There were a good many opportunities for feasting, dancing, and country sports of one kind or another. Even the poorest and most oppressed did not work incessantly, and at least up to the Reformation there were many holy days in the Church calendar when no one did a full day's work, and these, together with Sundays, gave most people at least one day off each week, with longer spells at the great festivals of Christmas, Easter, and Whitsuntide. Feast days and rest days were chiefly associated with the seasons and saints of the Christian Church, though some, like May Day when people greeted the return of spring with dancing and feasting and decked their houses with fresh green branches, were survivals from their ancient pagan past.

But there were other things besides holidays and festivals by which people were closely linked to the Church, and indeed it was still deeply embedded in their lives. Perhaps the image of the Church at the time was not edifying, but in spite of all resentments, questionings, and criticisms, in spite of all the mad and bad priests that could be pointed at, and the spectacular abuses everywhere commonly to be seen, there must have been plenty of villages where the old ways of worship still satisfied people and anti-clerical feelings hardly existed. Between the extremes of lordly abbots stubbornly exacting labour and submission from their tenants and John Ball passionately crying for freedom there were scores of country parsons who led their people in quieter ways and served them with their whole hearts. Chaucer described one of them: 'a poore persoun' (parson) who was 'a lerned man that Christes gospel trewely woulde he preche', a man benign and patient and close to the life of the country, who would visit the farthest cottage in his parish, help the poor out of his own slender resources, and give to all men 'this noble ensample, that first he wroghte and afterwards he taughte'. No doubt there were many like him, priests, curés, pastors, who, though they attracted no publicity, impressed all who knew them by their simple goodness, to whom their flock would turn at every crisis of life for help and comfort. Such men still drew people to the village church on Sundays, and to confession twice a year— even those obstinate sinners whom Chaucer's parson 'woulde snibben sharply' for their misdeeds. In their parishes the people paid the tithes of corn, hay, calves, lambs, eggs, chickens, and so forth, on which the parson lived without too much grumbling, and forked out their pennies for the repair of the church nave and for the holy bread and their light silver for candles to burn round a corpse before burial with reasonably good grace.

(iii) Castle, palace, manor-house

Castles are not uncommon sights in Europe today, and in most places there is usually one to be found within reach and worth a visit. They vary greatly in size, shape, and situation. The castles of Dover, Edinburgh, and the Tower of London, are still used as official buildings; others are museums; there are a few which are actually lived in by the descendants of the men who built them. But the majority are likely to be empty shells, dilapidated or in ruins, though, because they were so strongly built in the first place, they take a long time to decay.

In the Middle Ages when fighting was the chief occupation of large numbers of men and warfare hardly ever ceased, castles were essential. First and foremost they were strongholds for defence against enemy attacks and places of refuge for non-combatants, but each one was also a centre of power from which the owners kept a sharp eye and a tight hold over the neighbourhood—often largely his own estates—and either subdued or protected the inhabitants— often his own tenants. For instance, the knights of the military Teutonic Order, which held vast lands in Germany in the fourteenth century, gave succour to 1,000 villages from their stronghold of Ordensland, making sure, of course, that they were well rewarded for doing so. Besides being strongholds, refuges, and centres of power, castles were also the homes of the families who built them, and though by our standards they might seem uncomfortable, inconvenient, and often isolated, they were accepted as quite normal dwelling-places.

They ranged from straggling wind-swept erections like Hohen-salzburg in Austria to neater more compact places like Aigle (p. 145) in Switzerland or small squat towers as at Lydford, Devon. They were sometimes permanently occupied by the owner, sometimes left entirely or for long periods in charge of a knight—called the constable—and a garrison of suitable size. Their builders intended them to be impregnable and awe-inspiring, and even those which now have only empty roofless rooms and broken walls are still very impressive. Their splendour is often emphasized by the spectacular places where they are built, always chosen for sound military reasons, perhaps perched on a towering crag which commanded an immense view of the surrounding country, or frowning over a town, a road, or a river, or standing square on the wide floor of a valley where other valleys converge, down which hostile armies might march. They were always costly to build in money and labour, and, as methods of fighting changed, they were frequently in need of adaptation to keep them up to date. Hohensalzburg, for instance, was first built in 1077, but it was continually altered and added to until the seventeenth century, when it really was no longer in line with military needs. In time many castles became so hopelessly out of date that they were abandoned; in time, too, the expenses of building and upkeep made them far too expensive for any but the most wealthy and powerful to contemplate.

The earliest castles were simple towers, commonly made of wood like the prefabricated one which William the Norman shipped over to England in 1066 and which is shown in the Bayeux tapestry being erected on its motte or mound. Later these towers were built of stone to avoid the hazard of fire. Stone towers had two other advantages. They could safely be made taller than wooden ones and they could be built with rounded edges, so doing away with square corners which were easily bashed down or undermined by an enemy with good battering equipment.

A tall stone tower in an enclosure (bailey) circled by a pallisade or a wall could be a useful refuge in certain conditions and could be defended by quite a small garrison as long as food, water, and missiles, such as 'huge boulders to be thrown down if the castle is strongly besieged', lasted. But it was essentially passive, unless the garrison could sally forth and fight, and, moreover, if the enemy was prepared to settle down outside for a long siege, or if he had the means to knock it down, it was clearly less satisfactory. Gradually, therefore, the design of castles changed so as to make them more aggressive and better able to cope with larger armies rather than local raiding parties. They were given higher and more formidable walls with battlemented walks on top and passages in the thickness of the stonework so that the defenders were able to move quickly and safely to wherever they were wanted. Towers were built at intervals along these curtain walls, particularly at corners, so that the garrison could get a good view in two directions and a good angle for aiming missiles at attackers at the base of the wall. Massive and elaborate gatehouses or barbicans were put at the most vulnerable entrances with all sorts of intricate devices for repelling invaders, great iron portcullises, hidden places for archers, and holes through which boiling tar etc. could be poured. All these changes had the effect of making the defenders more active, and of keeping attackers guessing. If an entrance was forced at any point, and part of the castle was taken, this did not mean the end of resistance, for the defenders could retreat along or within the walls, fighting as they went, and hold out in another part. The aerial view of Caernarvon, built by Edward I between 1282 and 1287 when he was subduing Wales, gives a good idea of these larger castles of irregular shape with their many strong points instead of only one central keep or tower. Obviously such places were very costly. Beaumaris, another of Edward's castles, though not nearly as large as Caernarvon, is a perfect example of elaborate concentric design; its building took three years, employed 400 stonemasons, 30 smiths and carpenters,

Above *Aerial view of Caernarvon castle. The irregular lay-out allowed the defending force to be moved about as necessary rather than remain concentrated and perhaps trapped in a central tower. Notice the strategic position at the mouth of the river. The wall of the town is just visible. Edward I began the building of Caernarvon in 1285. It took thirty-seven years to complete.*

Left *Sir Edward Dalyngrigge's castle of Bodiam built in 1383 is perfectly symmetrical, but also flexible in the same way as Caernarvon.*

Right *The Castle of Aigle, Switzerland* (see caption overleaf).

and 1,000 labourers, and cost money, roughly equivalent to a quarter of a million now. Costs continued to rise, and by the end of the fourteenth century few men of moderate wealth could build castles, only the king and enormously rich nobles could pay the bills, or someone like the owner of Bodiam in Sussex, Sir Edward Dalyngrigge, who made a lot of money out of the ransoms of his French prisoners and in 1385 built himself a castle as a boast in stone of his wealth.

Castles, particularly early ones, must have been barbarous places to live in: dark and sombre even in summer time, freezing cold and clammy in the winter. There was little comfort and little privacy, though, as time went on, the lord and his family ceased to live cheek by jowl with the whole of the household and were able to withdraw to separate quarters, the privy chamber for the lord, the well-guarded solar for the women. Here a little softness began to appear, so that a writer of the fourteenth century, perhaps a castle-owner himself, wrote:

> And sooth to sayn my chambre was
> Ful wel depeynted, and with glas
> Were al the windowes wel y-glased
> Ful clere and not a hole y-crased [broken].

His 'chambre' must have been quite a contrast to stark stone walls and open arrow slits. But even when some privacy for the privileged was possible, all eating, drinking, and social life went on in public, chiefly in the great stone hall with its wide hearth, at first open in the middle of the floor but later moved to the side and given a huge hooded mantel to draw the smoke up and out through the wall. Here everyone slept, except the lord and his family, lying among the rushes on the floor unless they preferred the warmer stink of the kitchen below. Here the entire household, in strict order according to their rank, sat down to meals at trestle tables and on wooden benches, and ardently hoped that the steward had good stocks of 'wheat, haunches, bacon, sausages, entrails, meat puddings, mutton, pork, beef and vegetables', that the castle spring was flowing continuously, and the ale was not yet sour with keeping.

For many centuries life and work in the castle was entirely centred on the two main occupations of men of the landed class, fighting and hunting. The two were closely connected and both required special training in the use and care of arms, horses, dogs, and hawks as well as in the code of conduct suitable for a knight. This could all be summed up in the single word 'chivalry', meaning literally 'horsiness', and from this it is clear that it only applied to the highly born and comparatively rich, who could afford horses and armour, both expensive things. It had nothing to do with humble folk who went on foot. The oldest image of a knight—the man who fought, as distinct from the priest who prayed and the peasant who worked—

145

was of a rough pugnacious character who performed mighty deeds of hardihood without paying any attention to ideas of courtesy and mercy and not much to religion. He was a person who loved 'the bloody battle, the glory and the loot'. His feats of arms, his courage and endurance, his loyalty to his lord were all that mattered, and these alone earned him honour and high place in society, and later, so he believed, a seat in paradise. Life was hard and merciless and so was he, with no tender feeling toward anyone, not even women. However, as time went on, there grew up the more complicated ideal, carefully fostered by the Church as a means of checking the worst brutality and bloodshed, of the Christian knight, a man just as brave, loyal, and enduring, but much more graceful and courteous, inspired by higher ideals such as the service of God, the love of a virtuous lady, and the protection of the weak. Minstrels did much to popularize this code of chivalry. In castle and court they sang of the joy of adventure, the glory of unselfish love, the courtesy and grace of the true knight and his championship of the weak, particularly of women. Fighting, looting, and often senseless adventuring could still go on side by side with elegance, good manners, and unselfish love, and people saw no contradiction between the two. The Black Prince, regarded as a shining example of chivalry, could wait with the most courteous deference at table on his captured enemy King John but could also be responsible for the horrors of the sack of Limoges. To be fashionable and accomplished under this code of chivalry required more elaborate preparation than in the old days and the long training began very early. A boy of good birth left his family at the age of 7 and went to the castle of another lord, sometimes not far off but sometimes in another land. Here he was first a page, and in a strange household he had to make his way. He was educated as an immature man of his rank, untroubled by books but instructed in the first rudiments of fighting, in all branches of hunting, and in courtly behaviour. It was not a soft life; he lived in the hurly-burly of a rough household, sleeping with other pages, squires, and knights on the floor of the hall with the dogs and men-at-arms. Although he knew that as a potential knight he was superior in every way to other men of lesser rank, he had to learn to take blows and buffets from his equals when they were older than he. In early days a knight was 'dubbed' by being given a light but painful blow across the face and had to take this unmoved, without a wince.

At 14 the page became a squire. He was now always in close attendance on his lord, serving him at table and in his chamber, following him to war or to the tournaments where knights played out the game of war according to strict rules and elaborate ceremonial and with a proud display of arms, armour, and coats of arms. The squire had to gain 'a fair and full knowledge' of horses and horsemanship, of the arming of a knight, of the arts of hunting. He had to be

The great hall at Bunratty castle, Ireland. The lord would sit at the high table raised above his household. The brazier marks the original position of the fire; the smoke would find its way out through a hole in the roof. Although the hall, built c. 1460, has a large window instead of an arrow-slit and some hangings it gives an impression of coldness.

able to carve and serve at table, to amuse the womenfolk by singing, dancing, and games of various sorts, chess and skittles, for instance. He looked forward ardently to the day when he himself was dubbed a knight, and this usually came when he was about 21, sometimes on the stark field of battle if he had done some deed of signal bravery. In peace time it was an occasion for stately ceremony and took place on some suitable day, perhaps one of the great feasts of the Christian year, when many people would be gathered together and could witness his first appearance as a knight. The day before the ceremony the candidate for knighthood confessed his sins to a priest and attended Mass. During the night he kept vigil alone in the church. In the morning he was given a ritual bath, his hair and beard were trimmed, and he was dressed in special new clothes by attendant squires junior to him and certain other knights: a white linen tunic, a scarlet coat, a black surcoat, and white sword belt but with no sword, spurs, or armour. The climax came when, kneeling before his lord, he promised to be true to the laws of chivalry and was then invested piece by piece with the different parts of a knight's armour, last of all receiving his sword, the symbol of truth and knightly valour, from his lord's own hands. Often a priest took part in the ceremony by saying the noble prayer 'Most Holy Lord, Almighty Father, thou who on earth hast permitted the use of the sword to repress the malice of the wicked and defend justice, who for the protection of thy people hast thought fit to institute the order of chivalry, cause this thy servant here before thee by disposing his heart towards goodness never to use his sword to injure anyone unjustly but let him use it always to defend the just and right'.

'To defend the just and the right.' It was a splendid ideal but difficult to put into practice, and so also were the additional duties which, for those knights who could read, were spelled out in *The Boke of the Ordre of Chyvalry* by the Spaniard Ramon Lull (1235–1314). 'He should incline to works of mercy and pity', wrote Lull, 'and defend women, widows, orphans and all men who are diseased and not powerful and strong.' Lull knew well what the temptations of knights would be, and went on sternly, 'They should understand that destroying cities and towns, burning houses, hewing down trees, slaying beasts, and robbing in the highways are contrary to chivalry... Nor should a man be a knight if he is vainglorious ... Let him hear the word of God and matters of chivalry, but not troubadours and story-tellers for a knight ought to be sober, not giddy.'

Whether he had read *The Boke of Chyvalry* or not, a new knight was keen to observe all the rituals of his knighting. He rode out and showed himself to the people 'that all men may see and know that he is newly made knight and that he is bound to defend the high honour of chivalry'. He gave a feast and presented gifts to the Church, to his lord, and to those who had brought him up, or from whom he hoped one day to gain honour and a chance to fight. If he was a landless man he could only hope for a fief through his lord's generosity or from the spoils of war.

All this could mean an active and exciting life for a man, a life entirely centred on his interests and occupations. Even when he was not actually taking part in war he could fill his days with various kinds of violent exercise and war games, practising feats of arms, attending tournaments, giving hospitality to other knights, hunting and hawking—these last two sometimes not only for sport but to increase the food supply. For most women it was very different, and to us it seems that their life in the castle or great house must often have been tedious and boring in the extreme. They had their children to bring up, the girls till they married or went into a convent, or left home to become a waiting woman in a greater household; the boys till they were 7 and started on their training for manhood. Children were treated much more severely than they are now. Their parents were harsher and colder towards them and on the whole spent little time playing with them or even talking to them. The rules were strict and children had to submit absolutely to their parents and treat them with such respect and awe that there was not much chance of warmth and love. A book of instruction for children written in the sixteenth century stresses that reverence towards your parents is one of the first lessons to be learnt:

> Reverence to thy parents deare, so duety dothe thee bynde,
> Agaynst thy parentes multiplye no words but be demure.

Another book of 'Wysdome for all maner of children' is even more definite about behaviour 'when that thy parents come in sight thou shalt knele adowne'. The proper way to begin a letter to one's mother was: 'Right reverend and worshipful mother I recommend me to you as humbly as I can think'.

Sometimes parents were really cruel to children. Agnes, who married William Paston, the head of the well-to-do Norfolk family, in 1420, used to beat her high-spirited daughter Elizabeth regularly, and sometimes twice a day, even when she was 20 and old enough to marry, because she refused the man that her family had chosen for her—a battered widower more than twice her age.

Many women supervised the upbringing of their children in a business-like way, without much kindness or particular care, and they were also business-like over their names. The death-rate among young children was very high—plague and smallpox, colic and fever, neglect and ignorance took heavy toll, as indeed they did among adults too—and this is reflected in the habit of giving the same name to more than one child if you wanted to be sure of passing it on. Sir John Paston, eldest son of Agnes, had two of his sons christened John; and three Johns in a family, though it seems inconvenient to us, was thought a wise precaution to prevent the name from dying out.

Women in castles or great houses probably gave more time to the supervision of the household than to the care of their children. The greatest families of course had stewards and their minions to take most of the burden off the lady, which left her with long hours of idleness, but in many cases she occupied herself with providing for the needs of her household, and when that household lived far from a market or town, this was more than a full-time job. Spinning and weaving and making up the cloth into clothes kept the serving women busy all the year round, and every girl had to learn these practical arts. Even the most high-born lady would know how to use the distaff and the spinning wheel. They must also become wise in the making of butter and cheese, the preserving of meat, and the preparation of simple medicines.

Every palace, castle, and manor had its bakehouse, brewhouse, and dairy. Bread and ale were consumed at almost every meal and in every family. In the Earl of Northumberland's house, Lady Margaret and Master Ingeram Percy, though still in 'the nursery', had 'a manchet [small loaf] and a quarte of Bere for braikfast' while 'my ladis gentyllwoman' had 'a loofe of brede and a potell of bere'.

Everything possible was grown or made on the estate. Other goods had to come long distances. Dried and salted fish, for instance, was eaten in huge quantities during Lent, and supplies must be ordered in good time. 'As for herring I have bought a horse-load for 4/6,' wrote one thrifty English housewife, 'I can get no eels yet.' Salt for preserving fish and meat was something that every housewife, rich or poor, needed, and rich ones were also interested in imported products—pepper, cloves, ginger, cinnamon—and in luxuries such as almonds, rice, 'raysonys', and of course the conical spires of hard sugar, 'sugar loaves' as they were called, from which lumps were chipped as necessary.

For women who were not too high in the social scale to be allowed to occupy themselves in all this practical side of house-keeping there must have been plenty to do. Indeed, it must have been a relief sometimes to sit at leisure, even if they did continue their sewing or spinning, and gossip with their women, or listen while the domestic chaplain read aloud. Custom allowed women to hunt, and not only on a pillion. They rode on journeys, they rode round their lord's land overseeing his affairs when he was away; some on side-saddles, but some astride, like Chaucer's Wife of Bath who had 'on her feete a paire of spores sharpe'. Yet for many women there must have been long hours of boredom to be got through, especially in winter when endless chit-chat or stitching had to satisfy them. Not all ladies were supplied with such comfortable solars as Isabel of Bavaria, who is

Elizabeth of Bavaria, wife of Charles VI of France (1380–1442). She is shown here with her ladies in a comfortable chamber, hung with tapestry and well-carpeted. The window is a glazed lattice. The contrast with Bunratty is marked.

shown among her gentlewomen on page 000, nor would many have been taught to read or be able to get books, but the faces of Isabel and her ladies show a marked lack of animation or interest, and there must have been many like them to be found in castle, palace, and manor-house.

By the fifteenth century great changes had taken place not only in the pattern of dwelling-houses for the wealthy but also in the habits of those who occupied them. There were always parts of Europe where the castle remained a military necessity either for fear of invasion, or because of private warfare, or in border districts where peace was always fragile; but on the whole life became more peaceful and there was less need for fortified strongholds. Warfare itself of course had changed. Armies were larger—18,000 men fought at Crécy, 11,000 at Agincourt—and few castles could hold out for long against their numbers. Gunpowder and firearms had replaced battering-rams and bows and arrows, and the most massive walls were not proof for long against explosives and cannon-balls. The

number of walled towns had increased, and non-combatants pre-ferred to seek safety in these instead of in isolated fortresses. Gradu-ally the castle ceased to be the chief type of residence for the ruling classes, especially as the most powerful men were not always those entirely dedicated to war, but included among them other types, such as merchant princes and great lawyers whose wealth did not depend on vast estates but on merchandise or professional fees.

For all these reasons, the wealthy and the important turned their attention to building residences of a different sort, less military, less spartan, from which they still dominated the neighbourhood but in a different way. These residences varied greatly in size and style, as some of the illustrations show, ranging from a vast edifice to a com-pact house. Sometimes they were adapted from an original castle but so altered and added to that their military character almost disap-

The old stronghold of Tretower in Wales became out of date and was abandoned by the owners in the fourteenth century. They then built a much less military home. Even so it was provided with a

strongly fortified gate-house in case of need. The right hand part of the house with large windows was the latest to be built. The windows of the earlier parts all looked inward onto the courtyard.

peared and they appeared as fanciful and extravagant as a fairy palace. Sometimes, as at Cowdray in Sussex, the owner simply added a modern wing to an old stronghold, its large graceful windows in marked contrast to the original arrow slits. Others again, like the Vaughans of Tretower in Wales, built themselves completely new houses and left the old stone keep, in which the family had lived since the twelfth century, to crumble away in the farmyard.

From the fourteenth century onwards, increasing comfort, even luxury, could be found in castle dwellings. Not only were the walls 'ful wel depaynted' but there were rich hangings, carved chimney-pieces, cupboards, and chairs, soft draught-proof beds, and side-boards laden with silver—all marks of a rising standard of living and a change in outlook. A royal castle like Saumur, which became one of the most luxurious dwellings in Europe, 'could shine with gold leaf

on metal work, sparkle with windows of clear and stained glass, have its chambers panelled, hung with tapestries or painted with strange and beautiful devices'. When the castle of Urbino was rebuilt in 1450 it was furnished, according to Baldassare Castiglione, 'not only with what was customary such as silver vases, wall hangings of the richest cloth of gold, silk, and other like things, but for ornaments he [Duke Federigo] added statues of marble and bronze and rare paintings'.

Saumur. The vast pile of the castle, one of the homes of the Duc de Berry. From the Très Riches Heures, by Pol de Limburg.

The Duc de Berry dines in warmth and luxury supported by the labour of his tenants, seen at work on the opposite page. From the Très Riches Heures.

Refinement of living came more slowly in England than in Italy, but when the wealthy knight Sir John Falstaf died in 1459 leaving Caister castle to his kinsman John Paston, it contained a wide assortment of tapestries, one made in Arras and called 'the Shepherd's cloth' showing the Adoration of the child Christ by the shepherds. His bedroom furniture included a feather bed and a mattress 'of fine blue', two pairs of sheets, four blankets, three

155

curtains, one set of Arras hangings for the bed, six white cushions, one long chair, one green chair, one hanging candlestick, and two little bells.

The owner and master of the castle and the great house was also changing, for the ideal man was no longer seen as a knight in armour. For a time attempts were made to match that armour to modern methods of fighting, until it was entirely composed of plates of metal of such weight that the man inside the armour was practically immobilized, and a point was reached where he had to be hoisted up by a pulley and dropped into the saddle and could not possibly get to his feet without help if he fell off his horse. Such a cumbersome iron-clad as this became a liability in war rather than an asset. Some knights continued to enjoy dressing up and thundering to jousts and tournaments, but such expensive war-games gradually lost their appeal. The tournaments at the Field of Cloth of Gold when Henry VIII met Francis I of France in 1520 were the last where such official splendour and extravagance were displayed, though as late as 1617 Henry, Prince of Wales, jousted almost every day.

The Boke of the Order of Chivalry remained popular long after Ramon Lull wrote it. In 1484 William Caxton the master printer of London reprinted it, and he would not have done so unless he expected it to sell readily. Even so, the preface is significant. After a snobbish sentence saying 'This boke is not for every common man to have but only for noble men', he went on to give as one of the reasons for reprinting it that 'now in England you sleep, take ease, go to baths and dice and are all disordered from chyvalrie'. In other words, Caxton obviously thought that 'things were not what they used to be', and he may also have believed that the younger generation of noblemen would benefit from a little strenuous training in arms and that a few sharp dubs would stiffen them up, yet nothing could revive the past. Lull's 'Boke' might still be popular enough to reprint at the end of the fifteenth century, but it was soon to be replaced by a more up-to-date best seller, *The Courtier* by Baldassare Castiglione who for twenty years lived in the household of Duke Federigo of Urbino and of his son. Nothing shows more clearly than this book the extent to which the old code of knightly conduct and training had become outmoded. The place of the unlearned fighting knight as the symbol of all manly perfection was taken by other types of men who might be skilful soldiers and military leaders in time of war but who had other accomplishments than the practice of arms and other qualities besides courage and endurance, whose interests were far more varied than fighting and hunting. Duke Federigo of Urbino, with whose life Castiglione was familiar and whom he greatly admired, was something much more than a military man. He lived in elegant style in a remodelled castle which was certainly not simply a stronghold. It might be guarded by men-at-arms, but it was

filled with a witty and intelligent company of men and women who enjoyed feasting and merriment to the full but would also sit up all night in serious conversation until, as dawn broke, 'every man rose to his feet . . . and not one of them felt any heaviness of sleep. Then taking their leave with reverence of the Duchess, they departed without torch towards their lodging the light of day sufficing.' Duke Federigo was painted as a knight in full armour, but he is shown with a book in his hand and he made and filled the great library at Urbino, which was, according to Castiglione, 'the finest library since ancient times'. In England, too, the gallant and chivalrous Sir Philip Sidney (1554–86) was a man of learning and wit; a poet as well as a soldier; the writer of a famous series of sonnets known as 'Astrophel and Stella' and of the poem which begins 'My true love hath my heart and I have his'.

Before such changes came, and when the cult of chivalry was at its height, there were many Orders of Knighthood in Europe, the Order of Knights Hospitallers, of the Knights of Malta, of the Knights of the Golden Fleece, for example. A few of them have survived, reminders of an ancient code of life which was rapidly coming to an end by 1600. In England two still remain; one is the Order of the Bath, a reminder of the ritual purification of a knight before his dubbing; the other is the 'Most Noble Order of the Garter'. Even now, on St. George's Day each year, this most exclusive Order of knights—there are never more than twenty-five—move in a stately procession through the courtyard of Windsor Castle to the Chapel of St. George for a solemn service. They still wear the robes of blue and gold, the colours of France, which their founder Edward III arrogantly chose in 1348 for his new Order of chivalry.

Federigo da Montefeltro, Duke of Urbino. Although he is dressed in full armour he is shown absorbed in a book. Painted by Piero della Francesco, c. 1472.

Chapter 5
'Timor mortis conturbat me'

'The fear of death disquiets me': these words come from a poem by a Scotsman, William Dunbar (1465?–1530?), in which he laments the loss of some of his friends, and they are repeated over and over again, an uneasy mournful refrain at the end of each verse. They illustrate something which was characteristic of people in the Middle Ages, particularly towards the end, the constant thought and fear of death, which haunted the minds of men and women more than at any time before or since. This was not surprising. Certainly anyone who lived during the latter part of the fourteenth century and through the fifteenth century must often have felt that it was a period of disaster and known that his life was threatened from many sides. The hazards of hunger and disease, of war and violence are always present in the world, as we know well, but there are times when, reaching terrible proportions, they become greater disasters than usual, and this was certainly true in the fourteenth and fifteenth centuries when famine, plague, and war took a terrible toll of human life, and death was never far away from any man at any moment.

There are not many parts of Europe now where large numbers of people are chronically short of food and have no possible reserves, but in the Middle Ages this was common. All but the well-to-do and their households and those who lived in communities such as monasteries felt the pangs of hunger at least in the long dark winter and early spring. Even after a good harvest, stocks of food could fall very low between Christmas and Easter before the new young grass sprang up for the livestock, and fresh foods, such as milk, butter, eggs, and cheese, began to be available to the human beings who longed for them.

By 1300 the population of Europe had increased to the point where it had really outgrown the amount of food that could then be produced, and many people lived so near the hunger line that after one bad harvest they crossed it into starvation. Other things, too, brought the spectre of famine nearer to this time. There seems to have been a general worsening of the weather from about 1309 onwards, and the harvests, never very good by our standards, were often poorer than usual, so that 'bred-corne' and therefore bread were scarce and expensive. Then from 1315 to 1317 for three years running there were three exceptionally wet cold summers and three very bad harvests, one after another. Corn and bread became even

The Dead man and his Judge. Miniature from the Grandes Heures de Rohan, fifteenth century. The dead man has commended his soul to God and it is on its way to Heaven. Angels are defeating an attempt by the devil to intercept it.

scarcer in France, Germany, Italy, Flanders, Scandinavia, and Britain, and prices rose sharply. In England, for instance, a quarter of corn cost 5s. in 1313, but by 1316 it had gone up to 28s. 8d. and many families went hungry. At the same time there was a shortage of meat because numbers of cattle died from diseases brought on by wet and cold, and more than usual had been killed for food, so that breeding stocks of cattle and sheep dwindled. The result was that in the years 1309–17, and especially in the last three, poor families in many parts of Europe faced the winter with stocks of food even more meagre than usual and ended it weak and undernourished, perhaps with only 'a little barley boiled with bracken and acorns' to fill their stomachs. Scores and hundreds died of hunger in town and country, as in Bruges in 1316 with its death rate of 1 in 20, and Ypres, where 1 in 10 died. When people are weakened by hunger, disease is always liable to break out, and after these lean years it did. Famine was followed by outbreaks of plague of which the most terrible was the Black Death (1347–50), a name which after more than 600 years still has a ring of menace about it.

Plague, like hunger, was nothing new in the Middle Ages, and the Black Death was only one of a number of bad outbreaks. There were others in 1361, 1368, 1371, 1375, 1390, and 1405, and the great plague of London in 1665 was the same disease. But the Black Death spread so fast and killed so swiftly that the memory of it bit deep into men's minds, and stories of its horror were passed on from father to son long after 1347. In that year an unusual number of black rats, hosts to the fleas that are hosts to plague germs, swarmed westward from Asia and the coasts of the Black Sea, driven on apparently by some natural disaster such as a serious flood. They were carried to Europe in ships, and in August 1347 the first cases of plague appeared in sailors, bitten and infected by the fleas, who landed at Messina in Sicily 'the sickness clinging to their very bones'. The rat-infested ships were hurriedly sent out to sea again, but the harm was done, and plague spread through the hot smelly streets of the port. The people of Messina fled by scores into the country round. This instinct to escape was entirely natural and everyone must have felt it, but it had obvious dangers and was one of the reasons why the plague spread with such horrifying speed. It was said that 'men sickened by thousands in a day' and there was no known cure. Even doctors shrank from visiting the sick, especially as 'the malady set at nought entirely both the art of the physician and the virtue of physic'.

There are many blood-curdling descriptions of those dreadful years, of the deadly infectiousness of the disease, the sinister black boils which gave it its name, the suddenness of death, the grim scenes by torchlight when the dead were buried in huge pits. In the end, the loss of life was enormous; probably one out of every three people in Europe died before the epidemic spent itself. Town and country

'Bring out your dead' was the grim cry that echoed in many European towns and villages during years of plague. Here, during the Black Death, the dead of Tournai are being buried in a common grave.

were equally hard hit, for if the plague arrived in any place it killed. In Florence the population fell from 90,000 to 45,000; Hamburg lost 18 out of its 40 master butchers and 12 of the best bakers. On one small manor in England, Oakington which belonged to the Abbey of Crowland, 15 out of 50 people died, almost one in three; and when you realize that the plague did not spare the strong and healthy, you can imagine the toll of bread-winners in that little community. The total population of England in 1348 before the plague first lapped at the Channel ports and then struck inland was $4\frac{1}{2}$ million, and of those more than 1 million died. No wonder that 'after the pestilence many buildings both great and small . . . fell into total ruin for lack of inhabitants . . . many small villages and hamlets became desolate for all those that dwelt in them were dead'.

Recovery from two such calamities of famine and plague was bound to take a long time, and it was made more difficult by the third, war. Again this was nothing new, but in the fourteenth century and the first half of the fifteenth century war in Europe was more continuous than it had been for the whole of the two centuries before. When it was quenched in one place it flared up in another and even then—600 years ago—it was terribly destructive. 'There can be no war without fire and blood' and of course this was true for non-combatants as well as soldiers, especially as the armies which marched and fought over so much of Europe were quite indifferent

161

to the sufferings of civilians. It is true that campaigns were short and only fought in the summer, but summer was the time when crops were ripening and livestock were out in the fields, and an easy way of doing extra harm to your enemy was to burn his crops and drive off his cattle. When the English were fighting in France, they made a point of cutting fruit trees down to the ground in order to ruin the country as completely as possible. The country people suffered more than townsfolk who could retreat from danger inside their walls, and though they might save their lives and their animals by taking to the woods and wastes when fighting came near, when it had passed on and they crept out again it was to find burning homes, ruined crops, and to face instant hunger. Corn indeed could soon be sown again and harvested the next year, but vines, for instance, take several years to bear, olive-trees even longer, and cows and sheep can only slowly be replaced. The havoc of war could last a long time.

Besides, when fighting stopped, the hired mercenaries who made up a large part of the armies did not disappear, but became an even greater menace, if that was possible. Their pay stopped, there were no more prisoners to ransom, and they had somehow to live till the next campaign began and employed them. You can imagine how easily they could support themselves by roving through the land and living by robbery and violence. Sir John Froissart (1337–1410), in his famous chronicle, described a certain Amerigot Marcel, leader of one of these marauding bands in Auvergne, as a man 'who was wont to search daily for new pillages'. One day, talking over some former exploits, he said to his companions, 'Sirs, what joy when we rode forth at adventure! Daily we got new money, wheat-meal and bread, oats for our horses, beef, fat mutton, and poultry. When we rode forth all the country trembled for fear.' It must indeed have trembled and, considering what Amerigot and his human wolves reckoned to devour, it is not surprising that people in their path were 'sore abashed', as Froissart puts it. In the end Amerigot was brought to justice and executed in Paris, but this was small comfort to his many victims.

Since death could come so easily from famine or plague or at the hands of some brutal mercenary like Amerigot or perhaps the Italian Bartolomeo Colleoni whose terrifying countenance is opposite, it is not strange that the thought of it was constantly in people's minds, or that it became for many a positive obsession. The Church continually reminded them of it and urged them to repent and save their souls, poets like Dunbar and the tragic disreputable Frenchman François Villon echoed it in verse and song, and it filled the imaginations of artists and sculptors. Villon was always aware of the passing of time, and of mortal life which disappeared as quickly as the snow melts. 'Où sont les neiges d'antan?' he wrote, 'Where are

The terrifying face of a ruthless mercenary soldier. Detail from the mounted statue of Bartolomeo Colleoni by Verrocchio, 1435–88.

the snows of former times?', and other men constantly asked themselves those ancient questions which they have always asked: 'What happens after death? Where are all those gone who once were alive and full of warmth and beauty?' At that time no one openly doubted that there was a life after death, and so the answer was that the dead were either carried away to the joys of paradise or snatched below to the torments of hell. The hope of one and the fear of the other still burn in many medieval works of art. In the picture on page 159 the man who has died with the words of Christ on his lips is clearly destined for paradise even though St. Michael, poised in space, is having a sharp little battle with the devil for the departing soul, but there were plenty of other reminders in stained glass windows and the wall-paintings in many churches of the less pleasant fate of those destined for the 'howling hopelessness of hell'.

163

Besides their dread of death and their anxiety for the safety of their souls, people also had a grisly interest in all the details of physical decay, and these were often shown in paintings and sculpture in a horribly realistic way. On the top of the beautiful tomb of Alice, Duchess of Suffolk in Ewelme church near Oxford, which her son had built in 1475, she is shown as she was in life, a great lady at the height of her wealth and power, graceful and richly dressed, wearing a coronet and the Order of the Garter. Underneath, to illustrate the swift passing of such mortal grandeur and earthly fortune, is an effigy of her wasted body wrapped in its shroud.

Bones and skulls, skeletons and shrunken bodies frequently appear in painting and sculpture and their message is always the same: 'memento mori', 'remember death'. Sometimes the skeletons, grinning unpleasantly, are shown leading their victims, men and women, priests, kings, and soldiers, in a horrible dance—the Dance of Death, an image which first appeared in France and gripped people's imaginations so strongly that it was used in verse, plays, and court-pageants as well as in pictures and carvings. The fashion soon

*Detail from the tomb of
Philippe le Hardi, Duke of
Burgundy (1304–1404).*

spread to other countries and became extremely popular because it coincided with the invention of the art of the woodcut. Woodcuts could be produced quickly and cheaply by the printing presses, and for this reason reached a multitude of people who could never have owned a painting or ordered an elaborate tomb but who could afford to buy a book illustrated with woodcuts and feast their eyes on these vivid black-and-white pictures and mull over the prospect of death and judgement and the thought that in the end 'that strange tyrant' whose 'awful strak no man may flee' respected no man for wealth, power, or strength.

If 'Remember death' was the chief message which the artist was trying to express when he made the tomb of Duchess Alice, there was also another one: 'Remember the person who lies buried here'. Indeed, it was a period when everybody who could possibly afford it wanted to leave some solid memorial behind, usually in a church. These varied from superb and elaborate tombs like that of Philippe le Hardi, Duke of Burgundy, now in the museum at Dijon, to much simpler affairs like the brasses of knights, clerics, and merchants and

165

The brass memorial to Thomas Busshe, Woolman, and his wife in Northleach church, Gloucestershire, c. 1525.

Right Sir Maertin de Visch, 1452 (memorial in the Cathedral of Bruges). The fish device is a pun on his name, the border is of horses' bits.

ladies which lie among the stone slabs of floors in many English and Continental churches and incidentally tell us so much about contemporary armour and dress. The important thing about these memorials whether of stone or brass was not only that they were very durable but they were also personal and individual, not like the almost uniform gravestones to be seen now in churchyards. Often they were planned and designed long before the death of the person they commemorate, for the uncertainty of life made men look ahead to death. Philippe le Hardi died in 1405, but he had his tomb built twenty years before; you can be sure that Sir Maertin de Visch had left very clear instructions about the armour in which he was to appear on his memorial; and Master Thomas Busshe had also made certain that he was to be shown in his best fur-trimmed gown with the symbols of the wool trade—a sheep and a sack of wool—at the feet of himself and his wife.

It might have been expected that the fear of death, and the belief that if they hoped to reach heaven men must repent and follow the example of Christ would have a powerful effect on their attitudes to each other and make them shun cruelty and violence and try to live in peace with their neighbours, but this was not generally so. It was a time when people behaved in extraordinarily contradictory

166

ways, swinging suddenly from one extreme to another, from floods of tears to coarse uproarious mirth, from rough pity to most revolting cruelty. It was common to see whole crowds of men and women weeping copiously in the streets at the sight of a passing funeral but hurrying off to gaze with relish on some horrible spectacle like a man burning at the stake or a woman publicly tortured because she was suspected of being a witch. Life was lived in violent extremes, with great gusts of energy, but without much sympathy or pity; with greedy enjoyment of the moment, but always with foreboding about its end.

Cruelty occurs when people are afraid. Because so many men and women felt quite helpless in the face of disasters like plague and famine, which they did not understand and could not prevent, they often worked off their fears by putting much of the blame for all their troubles on Jews, or witches, whom they could safely attack as they were already hated. Terrible cruelties were inflicted upon the Jews, who were widely believed to kill Christian children and then to drink their blood. They were savagely beaten in the streets and began to be confined to special quarters of town known as ghettos. In Spain they were actually driven out of the land. Even more frightening was the belief in witches.

There was nothing new in believing that certain women had magic powers to help or harm their village neighbours. It was quite useful to have a love potion made up, or to get an ointment which was supposed to cure fever or lock-jaw. In days when medical skill was almost non-existent it did not do much harm to know what herbs should be gathered 'on one's knees, facing the East, and saying the Lord's Prayer'. It certainly made no difference to the patient's chance of recovery. But it was also firmly believed that witches could cast spells to blight crops, or to spread disease among cattle, or even to make women unable to bear children. A mother who had given birth to a deformed child was easily persuaded that the local witch had cast an evil eye on her. Witches also claimed the power to kill. One method was discovered in a famous witch trial in Lancashire in 1612: 'The speediest way to take a man's life away by witchcraft is to make a clay model, in the shape of the person who they mean to kill, and dry it thoroughly. And when you wish them to be ill in any one place more than another, then take a thorn or pin, and prick it in that part of the model you wish to be ill. And when you wish any part of the body to wither away, then take that part of the model and burn it. And so by that means the body shall die.'

In a village full of ignorant folk, to whom the Devil was every bit as real a person as God, it was only too easy to believe that anybody at all unusual or who behaved strangely possessed these special powers. Witches might be beautiful young women quite as often as ugly old crones mumbling to themselves or their cats.

'Timor mortis conturbat me'

They were feared because it was difficult to tell for certain who really was a witch; unlike the Jews they wore no special dress. They were hated because they often banded together in a kind of secret society and at their night-time meetings they practised strange rites. It was not all imagination. Witchcraft was practised, though no doubt it did little harm to anyone. What most witches were doing was to perform remnants of bloodthirsty pieces of ritual which still survived from the darkness of earliest times.

It was in 1484 that Pope Innocent VIII published a bull instructing the Inquisition to deal with witches as they would with any other heretic. Three years later two Dominican friars wrote a book in Latin called *Malleus Maleficarum* ('Hammer of the Witches') in which, to help all inquisitors, the habits of the witches and the ways they might be recognized were carefully listed. From then on witch-hunting took place all over Europe. While some victims had probably tried to harm their neighbours, most of those who appeared before the Inquisition, or before special courts in countries where no Inquisition existed, were harmless. The penalty was usually death, and in the two centuries which followed the publication of *Malleus Maleficarum* the number of executions for witchcraft in Europe is thought to have reached the appalling figure of 100,000.

However, except in the matter of witch-trials, which lasted into the eighteenth century, by 1600 the whole outlook of Europe was beginning to change. Instead of being obsessed with ideas of death and doom, men were becoming aware of new worlds and tremendous new possibilities, and were looking forward with new hope to the prospect of changes ahead and to the enjoyment of what those changes would bring. As an understanding of science slowly spread, so the fears and superstitions which had for so long affected people in all walks of life began to be dispelled.

Two country scenes painted by P. Bruegel the Elder (1510–69). Both show his keen observation of people, tools, and crops. Haymaking and gathering vegetables and fruit are in full swing in the top picture. In the bottom the hot August day makes dinner and a nap very welcome. It is possible to follow the whole process of harvesting, scything the corn, gathering it and binding it into stooks, carrying these by hand down to the point where the wagon is loaded and driven along a grass track to the farm.

Chapter 6
Renaissance in Italy

'Renaissance' is a French word meaning 'rebirth' or 'revival'. In this sense the word was first used by an Italian about the year 1550, though the idea of such a rebirth had been discussed in Italy ever since the days of the painter Giotto, who had been in Rome in 1300 for the Holy Year. From this time onwards, whenever anybody wanted to praise an artist or a writer, the highest compliment they could pay was to say that his work was as good as that of the ancient Greeks or Romans. Since the Roman empire had long ago been destroyed by barbarians, Italians naturally tended to look back with pride to a now dead classical age but at the same time to look forward hopefully to a rebirth or revival in scholarship and poetry, in architecture, painting, and sculpture, which would make Italy great again. Throughout Italy, and especially in Rome, ruins of temples, triumphal arches, palaces, or market-places were a reminder of past greatness and of the desolation wrought by invaders. So it was that the fourteenth-century Italian regarded the years between the classical age and his own day as grim 'middle ages', and such art as was then produced he denounced as merely barbaric, or 'Gothic'. Living as we do seven centuries after the birth of Giotto, we are able to see that these ideas were much too simple. We know that about 700 years separated the Goths, who sacked Rome, from the art which we call 'Gothic'. We also know that Gothic art was far from being barbaric and that the revival of art after the confusion of the Dark Ages was much more gradual than the Italians of the fourteenth and fifteenth centuries believed. But in one important respect the Italians of Giotto's day and later were right.

'Now, indeed, may every thoughtful spirit thank God that it has been permitted to him to be born in this new age, so full of hope and promise, which already rejoices in a greater army of nobly-gifted souls than the world has seen in the thousand years that have preceded it.' So wrote an Italian early in the fifteenth century when describing the pride of civic life. Such people were convinced that they were living in an exciting new era in which it was their task not just to revive the glories of classical times but, much more important, to proclaim new ideas in scholarship and education, in morals, and in the arts, and then to express them in new ways. People living in the Middle Ages did not call themselves medieval people because historians did not speak of 'the Middle Ages' much before

169

the start of the seventeenth century. On the other hand, the people of the Renaissance were very much aware of being born into times which were to be marked by even greater literary and artistic triumphs than in the past. The revival of the past made possible, in their view, an exciting future. Nor were these feelings confined to Italians. Erasmus, the great Dutch scholar, who felt at home in all countries of western Europe, cried: 'Immortal God, would that I were young again in this new age that I see dawning!'

It might be supposed that for a country like Italy to produce great works of art and scholarship long years of peace were necessary. Nothing is further from the truth: the achievement of the Italian Renaissance took place in a world of violence and war. War between the rulers of states or between towns was frequent and bred a fierce local patriotism. It also led to the citizens despairing of ever finding peace unless they put their government into the hands of one strong man—the prince. It was an age of brilliant men and women, who found that they could not live the cultured life which they so greatly enjoyed so long as they were involved in endless tumults and petty wars. A strong ruler made these less of a burden to his subjects.

Thus, at the peak of Renaissance society was the prince. Although the term 'prince' was used for men who ruled the new nation states, it was often better applied to men like Federigo da Montefeltro, who from his brilliant court at Urbino ruled over only a small duchy measuring forty miles by forty with some 150,000 people. It was not size but the social and cultural influence which such rulers exerted that mattered. As times changed and war became more professional, so it was found better to rely on mercenary troops, and thus the prince needed to be a skilled politician and financier rather than a fighter, and the fame of his court increasingly turned upon its works of art, its library, and the richness of its social life. It was all very costly and, indeed, Renaissance society was designed for rich men, rich cities, and rich popes. With money a peacock world could be purchased, and rich men pursued beauty as if it were a drug. Gold, silver, and bronze ornaments, exquisite majolica ware, and sumptuous clothes and hangings of silks, satins, and damasks were to be found in the palaces of the prince and also in the homes of the new merchant classes, who by 1400 could easily afford to surround themselves with painting and sculpture once only possessed by the aristocracy.

We owe much of our knowledge about the prince and his court to two remarkable books written early in the sixteenth century, though published some years later: *The Courtier* (1528) by Baldassare Castiglione, which has already been briefly mentioned, and *The Prince* (1532) by Niccolo Machiavelli.

Castiglione based his book about court life on his four years spent at Urbino with Duke Federigo and his son Guidobaldo, where he could enjoy what was probably the finest library in Europe. It gives a dazzling picture of a cultured court filled with men who were both masters of all manly sports and accomplished linguists, musicians, and poets; and of women, preferably good-looking, 'for much is lacking to a woman who lacks beauty', who must be charming, gracious, musical, and generally well-educated. With Castiglione, to be a courtier was almost a new profession in itself, and such a man was required to be the cream of civilized society, proved by the way in which he exercised his many accomplishments with effortless ease. From this book we learn about the kind of subjects discussed in the evenings—the relation between painting and sculpture, for example, or questions about classical scholarship—there are descriptions of the games which were played and the dances which were popular, as well as the retelling of the jokes which amused the court. No book shows better the determination of the leading Renaissance men to banish the rough and crude behaviour of the past and to create a civilized life instead.

Very different, but even more important, was *The Prince*. Machiavelli (1469–1527) was a Florentine who entered the service of the state, becoming one of the secretaries who dealt with foreign affairs. Until he fell from power in 1512, he was employed on diplomatic missions within Italy and also was sent on behalf of Florence to Germany and to France. He thus saw at first hand a great deal of how various princes ruled their states. When he lost favour he used his time in writing a short but brilliant study of the art of government. To do this at all was something quite new and shows how men of the Renaissance were increasingly interested in politics and statecraft. No book has been more misjudged than this; for in describing what he had seen of the Renaissance prince with his lack of political morality, his trickery, his belief that it was more important to be feared than to be loved, his readiness to lie for the good of his state, Machiavelli was accused of saying that this was how a prince *ought* to govern, when he was in fact describing what had become the way to rule successfully. 'The manner in which men now live is so different from the manner in which they should live that he who deviates from the common course of practice and endeavours to act as duty dictates, necessarily ensures his own destruction.' The real purpose in writing *The Prince* was to teach Italians to be strong and united in face of the invading armies of French and Spanish, who were despoiling their land. It was a wicked world and princes could not afford to be kind, or honourable, or easy-going. They would be judged only by results. What most shocked contemporaries was Machiavelli's insistence that politics was a science of its own, unaffected by religion; what a man believed was his own concern; how he ruled and whether he was successful was what mattered to his subjects.

171

There can be no exact starting date for an era such as the Renaissance, but at least in literature and the visual arts there can be a starting-place—Florence. The republic of Florence had had to withstand attacks from rival states, especially Milan, and the successful defence of their city had made the Florentines intensely patriotic and supremely confident in themselves. They were justly proud of their city and wanted to express their pride in fine buildings and to spend their wealth on works of art. As in all cities, there was always a number of leading citizens, perhaps a trifle uneasy at the wealth which they had accumulated in quick business deals and in money lending, who thought it wise to put some of their money into churches and chapels where prayers would be regularly said for their souls after their death. Fortunately, there was in Florence between about 1380 and 1440 a number of rich, intelligent men anxious to become patrons both of scholars bent on 'recovering' the ancient world and, even more, of artists and architects determined to paint and build

The cathedral at Florence with its great dome built by Brunelleschi. Giotto's campanile is on the right.

in new ways. 'Florence', wrote Leonardo Bruni, one of the great Chancellors of the republic, 'harbours the greatest minds: whatever they undertake they easily surpass all other men, whether they apply themselves to military or political affairs, to study or philosophy, or to merchandise.' This was not really an exaggeration, and at the end of the fifteenth century Marsiglio Ficino, the famous Florentine scholar, summed up the city's achievement: 'It is undoubtedly a golden age, which has restored to light the liberal arts that had almost been destroyed: grammar, poetry, eloquence, painting, sculpture, architecture, music. And all that in Florence!'

But the fact that Florence became the home of the Renaissance was very largely due to the Medici, the fabulously wealthy banking family, which dominated the city for nearly three centuries, and whose early members were responsible for gathering within the city the band of men who, it can be said, created the Renaissance. Of all the 'princely' families none was more brilliant, for their influence extended throughout Europe, first through their banking and trading interests (for a time they were the pope's bankers) and then through the use to which they put their vast wealth. Cosimo de' Medici (1389-1464), justly acclaimed as 'Pater patriae' ('Father of his country') by a grateful city, manipulated the government of Florence in such a way that he appeared to have maintained the old republican traditions. It was not all plain sailing: three times the Medici were expelled and each time they returned to increasing power; in the end the ruler of Florence was to be acknowledged as Duke. But if the Medici took power from the Florentines, they gave back in return their money, their skill in diplomacy, and their love of art. Nearly four million pounds came from the Medici fortune, to encourage and buy the works of great artists and also to found places of learning. When in 1439 the General Council of the Church met in Florence to try to heal the breach between Rome and Constantinople, Cosimo de' Medici was himself the host to all the rulers and delegates, from the pope and the emperor downwards, who spent five months in his city. He delighted in the company of scholars and it was he who understood the greatness of Plato and encouraged the translation of his Greek writings into Latin. Medici methods of making a fortune were not always very scrupulous, and Cosimo 'was wont to say that to God he had never given so much as to find Him on his books as a debtor'. He could treat his enemies savagely, and many a Florentine family must have been kept loyal through the hold which Cosimo had over them as their banker. His great palace, a model for similar buildings throughout Italy, shows the nature of Medici rule. The ground floor is strong and grim, almost prison-like, as if Cosimo feared attack from the citizens; the upper storeys are light and elegant, while within were the latest works of art which he had commissioned.

Cosimo's rule was strong enough to survive the weaker control of his son, Piero, a martyr to gout, who had not his father's ability, though he inherited his love of art. It was Cosimo's grandson, Lorenzo the Magnificent (1449–92), who increased the power of the Medici by taking an active part in European politics. Lorenzo became head of the state at the age of 20. 'Considering that the burden and danger were great, I consented to it unwillingly'. He accepted the task 'in order to protect our friends and property for it fared ill in Florence with any who possessed wealth without any share in the government.' He was openly more of an autocrat than his grandfather, but, as Guiccardini, the historian of Florence, maintained, 'if Florence was to have a tyrant, she could never have found a better or more pleasant one'. According to a contemporary, 'he spoke sparingly and walked with dignity: he loved able and distinguished men in every art; it was, however, noticed that he was somewhat vindictive and envious. . . . He was tall and of noble presence; he had an ugly face, short sight, dark skin and hair, sallow cheeks and an extraordinarily large mouth. . . . His gait was princely; he dressed richly and enjoyed writing verses in the common tongue and wrote them beautifully.' Like so many Renaissance men, he had a remarkable range of abilities—a financier, a diplomat, a scholar, an attractive poet, and a musician. His patronage of the arts ate heavily into the Medici fortune, and in his time less trouble was taken to build them up. However, he looked upon himself as one who should spend his wealth on behalf of Florence: 'Some would perhaps think it more desirable to have a part of it in their purse, but I conceive it to have been spent to the great advantage of the public and am therefore perfectly satisfied.' Lorenzo was a strange and complicated character: grossly immoral, relying on an army of spies, ruthlessly efficient, he nevertheless presided over the most cultured court in Italy, perhaps even in Europe. His determination to enter fully into European affairs did not always help Florence but ensured that the Medici became a great Italian, instead of just a great Florentine, family in the next century.

During the Middle Ages the official teaching of the Church had been that man was a sinful being, living in a wicked world. The surest pathway to heaven was said to be found by renouncing the world and living in a monastery. This view of man was largely overthrown by a study of classical writings. The Greeks had always believed that the active life, that of the politician and the good citizen, was superior to any other. Greek and Roman writers had always emphasized the dignity and importance of man in a way that the medieval Church most certainly had not. For instance, a Roman playwright, Terence, makes one of his characters say: 'Homo sum: humani nil a me alienum puto' (I am a man; I consider nothing human foreign to me). It was not that at the Renaissance men ceased to be Christian; it was that they saw man no longer as a hope-lessly sinful being, cumbered with a sinful body, but as the greatest of God's creations. To the men of the Renaissance the way to obey God's law was to serve one's family and the community in which one lived. To be rich was not to be wicked, for it enabled a man to make life more gracious and comfortable for his fellow human beings and also to glorify God through the creation of great works of art. Of course, it took time for these new ideas to take root, for the teachings of St. Francis of Assisi on the virtues of poverty were still a strong in-fluence in 1400. But steadily the belief grew that to take part in the affairs of the world was quite as virtuous as to shut out the world from inside a monastery.

This new view affected all sides of life. It is very wrong to confine the meaning of the word 'Renaissance' to a revival of literature and art in Italy. A Frenchman living in the sixteenth century was really describing the Renaissance when he wrote in praise of his times: 'The world sailed round, the largest of earth's continents discovered, the compass invented, the printing press sowing knowledge, gun-powder revolutionizing the art of war, ancient manuscripts rescued and the restoration of scholarship, all witness to the triumph of our New Age.'

In its beginning the Renaissance was entirely a matter of books. The starting-point of all that was to develop in such splendour later was the labours of a small band of dedicated scholars who devoted their lives to rediscovering the literary heritage of Greece and Rome, and then made it available to all. The great Latin writers—Virgil, Ovid, and Horace—had never been completely forgotten during the Middle Ages, for schoolmasters had never ceased to flog some knowledge of their poetry into their pupils and Latin had always been the language of the Church. But these Latin classics had sur-vived only in corrupt and often incomplete texts, and so the first task of scholars was to correct the Latin texts which they already possessed and then to ransack the libraries of cathedrals and mona-steries for manuscripts which had lain there forgotten for centuries. It is difficult for us to whom printed books are a normal part of life to realize the excitement of finding a new manuscript. Poggio de-scribes his discovery of the unique, complete copy of a work of Quintilian in a monastery when it was lying 'in a sort of dungeon, foul and dark, at the bottom of a tower'. He said that the manuscript seemed to be stretching out its hands to him, begging to be rescued.

After Latin came Greek, a language practically unknown in the West much before 1400. So Greek had first to be learned before it could be translated into Latin. The number of Greek manuscripts available to scholars increased from the start of the fifteenth century, as the advance of Turkish armies forced learned men in Asia Minor and Greece to fly to Italy for refuge, carrying their precious manuscripts with them. Much of a scholar's life was spent in travelling from city to city to read the basic texts, for before the invention of printing the cheapest way to acquire a book was to copy out the text for oneself. It is impossible to exaggerate the importance of the revolution which printing caused. The spread of knowledge at once became possible and, as we shall see when we come to Martin Luther, a man's thoughts could be read and discussed all over western Europe in a comparatively short time. The discovery of how to print books with movable type came from Germany, where, in Mainz, Johann Gutenberg produced the first book to be printed in this way about 1450. In Italy the first press was set up at Subiaco in 1465, two years before the press at Rome. Before the end of the century, printing presses were everywhere at work.

But books and manuscripts were not solely an end in themselves to Florentines: learning had to be put to use and was the means whereby the youth of the city could be trained to serve the State. A study of the 'humanities'—grammar, rhetoric, literature and literary style, moral philosophy, and history—was regarded as the right education for those destined to play their part as good citizens. Thus it was that those concerned with this work were known as humanists. The word was at first used to describe those who taught the humanities, but it quickly came to be applied to all who sympathized with the aims of these educators. The humanities, wrote Leonardo Bruni, 'are the best and most excellent of studies and the most appropriate to mankind. . . . They took root in Italy after originating in our city [Florence].' To this day the university of Oxford still names its school of classical studies *Literae Humaniores*.

Florence was remarkably fortunate in having as citizens three men who led the way in their respective arts: Dante, the poet (see p. 20); Petrarch (1304-74), who was both scholar and poet; and Giotto (?1266-1337), with whom a new chapter in the history of painting opened.

Petrarch as a young man had fallen in love with Latin and he was very conscious of living on the threshold of a new age when the writings of Latin and Greek authors would be recovered. 'This slumber of forgetfulness will not last for ever. After the darkness has been dispelled our grandsons will be able to walk back into the pure radiance of the past.' So he wrote in 1338. Petrarch never mastered Greek, but not long after his death there were courses of study available in Florence and other cities. His greatest love was Cicero, and he was overjoyed when he himself found Cicero's letters to Atticus in the Chapter library at Verona. His love for Cicero even made Petrarch ill, for each time he entered his study his ankle bumped against a volume of Cicero's writings, which in time led to a festering but much appreciated wound. In one sense Petrarch

St. Francis preaching to the birds. One of the many frescoes illustrating the life of St. Francis, painted by Giotto on the walls of the Basilica of St. Francis at Assisi.

might be described as the first modern man, for he had a passionate interest in studying himself. 'I thought how, between one dip of the pen and the next, time goes on; and I hurry, drive myself and speed towards death. We are always dying. I while I write, you while you read and others while they listen or stop their ears, they are all dying.' This awareness of the mystery and marvel of everyday experience was something quite new. Modern man had begun to think for himself, to meditate on his place in the world, to find his own answers to the riddle of his existence.

* * *

It is much easier to create a lifelike figure in stone or marble than to make a painting look real. A statue stands in real space and in real light; in certain positions you can walk right round it. A picture, on the other hand, is an illusion, and the artist has to give a sense of distance and of space between his figures, which must not look as if they had been cut out of cardboard. To make a painting 'true to life' a painter must understand the laws of perspective, of how to use light and shade so as to give an illusion of depth. The ancient Greeks had known something of this, but their skill had largely been forgotten for a thousand years. It was the architects and sculptors of the great Gothic cathedrals who were the important people in medieval art, not the painters. Giotto was the genius who broke through the old ways of painting to give the same lifelike quality to his pictures that a sculptor gave to his statue.

Giotto was found as a boy on a hillside drawing sheep on a stone, and was taken to the studio of an artist and given his chance. His greatest work was done at Assisi when he painted scenes from the life of St. Francis on the walls of the church. Not only did Giotto rediscover the art of giving an illusion of depth on a flat surface more than a century before the laws of perspective were scientifically worked out, but he altered the whole sense of what a painting should be like. He set out to show those who looked at his work what it must have been like if they had been actual eyewitnesses of the events which he was portraying. In a way quite new to painting, he showed in his pictures the whole range of human emotions and it was largely due to him that artists, instead of being nameless like the unknown sculptor who carved the figures on Chartres Cathedral, became famous men of their day.

The Florentines had begun to build their cathedral—to which Giotto was later to add a beautiful campanile, or bell tower—in 1296. They had encased its walls in green and white and red marble, but over a century later it was still unfinished, for nobody knew how to build the huge dome which the citizens had decided was the only way to crown their work. A competition to solve this problem was announced, and perhaps the most ingenious suggestion made was to fill the cathedral with earth and coins to serve as a safe base for the dome. Once the dome was in place, then the Florentines could clear away the earth, keeping the coins which they found as a reward. Eventually the task was given to a Florentine architect, Filippo Brunelleschi (1377-1446), who had already studied the temples and palaces in Rome, not only to be able to copy them, but to use the old forms of classical architecture as the starting-point of a new style. Brunelleschi had an uphill task; before he could see his dream come true he had endless arguments with cathedral officials and with his builders, for whom he used to bring in canteens of food and wine to keep them at work for long hours, and on one occasion he had even to break a strike. The dome was almost finished when he died. Brunelleschi has every right to be considered as the first great Renaissance architect, and for 500 years architects in Europe and later in America followed in his footsteps, especially when designing public buildings. Even the shape of doors and windows on ordinary buildings remained unaltered until modern methods of construction and new materials enabled twentieth-century architects to revolt against the classical tradition, just as Brunelleschi had revolted against the past in his day. He was a supremely great artist who also began to work out the laws of perspective.

Not only did fifteenth-century Florence produce a pioneer architect but it was also fortunate enough to possess a pioneer painter and a pioneer sculptor. In his short life Masaccio (1401-28) completely mastered the tricks of perspective painting, which must have made his work very exciting to people who had never looked at anything except 'flat' pictures. Like the great artist he was, Masaccio never used these 'tricks' as ends in themselves; he used them to make his pictures powerful and compelling in quite a new way. Donatello (1386-1466) had received a long training in stone cutting and he was also a skilled goldsmith. Like Brunelleschi, as a young man he had visited Rome to study the remains of classical statues, but the work which he created was utterly different. One of his earliest works was a statue of Saint George. How different was this vigorous and defiant figure from the rather pious figures of the saints in a medieval cathedral! The change was even more marked in his famous statue of David. It had been the tradition to portray David as a bearded old man with a crown on his head; Donatello's David is a young Greek hero, intensely alive and human; it shows how close a study of human anatomy Renaissance sculptors now began to make.

The spirit of artistic adventure which marks the work of the great Florentine pioneers was catching, and it was this spirit which marks the real break with the traditions of the Middle Ages. In another way times were changing rapidly in art. In the Middle Ages there was little fundamental difference in art or scholarship, in politics or in chivalry, between one European country and another. This ended

Donatello's statue of St. George. It was commissioned by the guild of armourers whose patron saint was St. George. If you compare this with the work of medieval sculptors on the fronts of Gothic cathedrals you will see how great a break has been made with the past.

179

with the rise of towns. Intense local patriotism led to many towns in Italy, Flanders, and Germany having a school of painting of their own. The word 'school' does not here mean an art school such as today exists to train artists. A boy who showed promise would be apprenticed to a local painter or sculptor and would live with the artist's family. In return for board and lodging, he would run errands, mix the colours, and in time be allowed to paint some tiny part of the master's picture. Gradually he would be entrusted with the painting of draperies or, perhaps, the background, until he was finally good enough to set up on his own. This is how the various 'schools' of Italian painting grew up and why it does not take a great knowledge of painting to say which picture comes from Florence and why it is quite different from one painted, say, in Siena or Bologna or Venice. Yet, in spite of local patriotism, the lure of Rome was very strong and certainly by the sixteenth century artists looked to Rome for their most lucrative and exciting work, commissioned by men whom we can rightly call the 'Renaissance popes'.

'Since God has given us the Papacy, let us enjoy it,' said Leo X, who was a Medici, after his election. In differing ways the Renaissance popes 'enjoyed' the papacy to the benefit of themselves and their families but in so doing fatally lowered the office in the eyes of Europe. As their power and prestige as popes declined, they made up for it by becoming Italian princes, indistinguishable in their policies and methods from any other Renaissance prince, but forced to act more quickly, and therefore more unscrupulously, because the papacy was not hereditary. If the pope decided to become a prince, then most of his cardinals were happy to become courtiers; in the conclave of 1458 they even demanded that each should have an annual income of at least 4,000 gold florins in return for a life of ease and luxury, spiced with political intrigue.

As many of the leading cardinals hoped in their turn to become pope, the lengths to which they were prepared to go in the papal conclave to get elected became increasingly crooked and sordid. Pius II, a gifted and scurrilous writer, with at least one indecent novel to his name when younger, has left a highly entertaining account of the conclave of 1458 at which he was elected. After the first inconclusive vote had been taken, the cardinals 'adjourned for luncheon and then there were many private conferences. The richer and more influential members of the college [of cardinals] summoned the rest and sought to gain the papacy for themselves or their friends. They begged, promised, threatened and some, shamelessly casting aside all decency, pleaded their own causes and claimed the papacy as their right. . . . Many cardinals met in the privies as being a secluded and retired place. Here they agreed as to how they might elect Guillaume [Cardinal of Rouen] pope and they bound themselves by written pledges and by oath. Guillaume trusted them and was

This is one of a series of frescoes showing the life of Pope Pius II. It was painted in Siena by Pinturrichio and shows the entry of Pius II into the basilica of St. John Lateran in 1502. It is also a good example of the technique of perspective rediscovered during the Renaissance.

presently promising benefices and preferment and dividing provinces among them. A fit place for such a pope to be elected! For where could one more appropriately enter into a foul covenant than in the privies?' In the end Pius proved the better bargainer.

Three sixteenth-century popes stand out as typical of their age—Alexander VI (1492-1503), Julius II (1503-13), and Leo X (1513-21). There was nothing new or surprising in men who worked to promote their family fortunes at all costs, or who had little belief in the Christianity they professed, or who were vicious and wicked. What is extraordinary is that such men should be accepted as head of the Christian Church. Alexander VI, a Spaniard of the Borgia family, has become a legend for the scandals attributed to his reign. Many of these have never been proved, but enough remains in the life of this most disputed character to justify regarding him as the worst of the Renaissance popes. As a young cardinal of 29 he earned from Pius II, not, as we have just seen, a man of blameless life, a strong letter of rebuke in 1460: 'We leave it to you whether it is becoming to your dignity to court young women, and to send those whom you love fruits and wine, and during the whole day to give no thought to anything but sensual pleasures.' His teacher, Gaspare da Verona, later wrote of him that 'he has an amazing gift for attracting the affection of women, who are drawn to him as by a magnet'. But he was also a very gifted and brilliant administrator, who, in the opinion of one of his cardinals, 'would have been a great prince . . . had his natural gifts been allowed to develop and not been overlaid with so many vices'. His love for his evil son, Cesare, and his beautiful daughter, Lucrezia, and his determination to advance their interests largely directed his policy. To gain his ends he had no scruples in removing his enemies by poison or by less artistic means, so that, whatever the truth may be of the more lurid stories told against him, Alexander represents more brilliantly than any other pope the new position of the papacy as a secular power in Italian politics.

Julius II and Leo X were less evil but equally worldly. Julius, the warrior pope, occasionally took part in person in the wars which he promoted on behalf of the Papal States. More important was his patronage of Raphael and Michelangelo and his decision to rebuild St. Peter's in Rome. Leo, son of Lorenzo the Magnificent, like a true Medici, was a connoisseur of art, a pagan philosopher to whom Christ seemed so much less important than Plato. He rewarded Henry VIII of England with the title of *Fidei Defensor* in return for Henry's book against Luther, but he never appreciated the challenge to the papacy thrown down by this apparently obscure German monk.

The fantastic wealth of works of art of all kinds created in fifteenth- and sixteenth-century Italy makes it impossible to do more than point out the chief figures. The second generation of artists were

mainly concerned with developing the new discoveries and techniques, though often their patrons were not ready to accept what
appeared strange to them. Nor were all artists as advanced as some
of the pioneers. Thus a mixture of old and new can often be seen in
fifteenth-century work: it was the triumph of what is called the High
Renaissance to fuse the two. If a typical figure of the fifteenth-century
artist had to be chosen, the Venetian architect Leone Alberti (1404–
72) would be a good choice. He had the extraordinary breadth of interests of all great Renaissance characters—architect, poet, painter,
philosopher, and musician. His musical interests led him to study the
work of the Greek Pythagoras, who had worked out the mathematics
of the various musical intervals on a stringed instrument, and Alberti
believed that the same rules of proportion should apply to the design
of buildings. No Renaissance artist believed more passionately in
the dignity of man, for, as he said, 'A man can do all things if he will'.
Of the painters two men are examples of the half-way house between
old and new. In the exquisitely simple work of Fra Angelico (1387–
1455) we see a medieval view of religion expressed, thanks to new
devices, with a greater truth to life. Greatest of all in maintaining the
beauty of line and movement with medieval feeling but modern skill
was Sandro Botticelli (1446–1510). If you look at two of his greatest
paintings, *Birth of Venus* and *Spring*, you will see the beauty of
his flowing line. Here is still something which reminds us of the
Middle Ages, but it is coupled with a truly Renaissance interest in
the classics and in the beauty of the human figure.

Alberti's saying that there is nothing that man cannot do was
realised for a few years at the start of the sixteenth century in the
work of the three men who dominated the High Renaissance. Great
intelligence allied to heroic determination enabled man for a brief
span of years to reach heights which he was seldom again to attain.

Leonardo (1452–1519) was such a many-sided genius that we
must not think of him solely as the painter of the *Mona Lisa* or of
The Last Supper. All his gifts were dominated by an over-mastering
curiosity, which makes it appropriate to consider him both here as
an artist and in the last chapter of this book as a scientist. By 1472 he
had set up on his own in Florence after the usual apprenticeship;
later he worked in Milan and then was lured to Rome; he ended his
long life as court painter to Francis I of France. Despite a large
number of admirers, who have left accounts of his physical beauty,
his many gifts, his hatred of cruelty which led him to buy the caged
birds on sale in the Florence market and to release them, he was
essentially a lonely man, whose entire life was devoted to finding
answers to questions about man and his body, man and his relation
to the world around him, and, above all, to scientific studies of all
forms of movement.

Only some half-dozen paintings of his survive, but they are among the great paintings of the world. It was a tragic result of Leonardo's restless curiosity that he decided to experiment in a new method of fresco painting when working on *The Last Supper*, with the result that today it is a sorry ruin, worked over by later restorers. Its familiarity should not make us forget the original power of the picture, which was painted on the end wall of a monastery refectory in such a way that, as they ate their meals, the monks had the sensation of sharing the Supper with Christ and his disciples. Ever since she was painted, the smile of the Mona Lisa has haunted men; but the

Botticelli's painting of the Annunciation. The way that Mary is standing represents her submission to the angel's message, 'Behold the handmaid of the Lord'. One of the very attractive parts of many Italian paintings is the view of the countryside as seen through a window or doorway. From this landscape painting was later to develop.

Leonardo da Vinci's Mona Lisa.

background is almost as fascinating. Look at it carefully: the two lines of the horizon do not join; the weird landscape tells of Leonardo's interest in geology. Today in the Louvre in Paris the picture appears to have been painted in a sea-green light, but this is because the colours have faded, especially from the face. But the puzzle, the questions which one wants to ask, remain for ever.

Michelangelo Buonarotti (1475–1565) was born near Florence and trained as a painter, though his lifelong passion was for sculpture. He quickly attracted the attention of Lorenzo de' Medici, who encouraged him to study classical sculpture which did not for long

Michelangelo's statue of Moses, carved from a great block of Carrara marble in 1508, as part of the unfinished plan for the tomb of Pope Julius II. Vasari, who wrote the life of Michelangelo, said of this statue '. . . there was no other work to be seen, whether ancient or modern, which could rival it'.

satisfy him. On Lorenzo's death in 1492, he was able to give full reign to his obsession with the principles of anatomy both by drawing the human body in every conceivable posture and by secretly at night dissecting corpses in the mortuary of a Florentine priory. In 1496 he went to Rome where he carved the exquisite Pietà, now in St. Peter's; but five years later he was back in Florence working on a vast block of marble from which he carved the eighteen-foot-high statue of David, justly given pride of place in the centre of their city by the Florentines. At this moment into Michelangelo's life erupted the stormy figure of Pope Julius II, who had decided to have built for himself a bigger tomb than had ever been built before and that only Michelangelo could do it. Julius was a terrible taskmaster, for he was always altering his plans, and when Michelangelo had done no more than carve the vast figure of Moses, Julius decided that the rebuilding of St. Peter's according to the grandiose ideas of his architect, Bramante, was more important than the tomb. A long and violent quarrel resulted between pope and sculptor and when Michelangelo eventually agreed to serve Julius once more, he found that his commission had been changed from carving the tomb to painting the ceiling of the Sistine Chapel in the Vatican, so called because it had been built by Pope Sixtus IV. Michelangelo was forced to grit his teeth and obey. For four years, lying for much of the time on his back on the top of the high scaffolding, Michelangelo painted a series of frescoes on the theme of the Creation. On 31 October 1512 the scaffolding was finally removed to reveal one of the wonders of the world's artistic history. Michelangelo was only 37 and had another fifty-two years to live.

In the last half of his life some of his greatest works were created, not least the design of the dome for the new St. Peter's. All his work, both in youth and age, bears the signs of titanic struggle. His friend and pupil, Vasari, whose *The Lives of the Painters* is an important source, describes the way that he worked: 'I have seen Michelangelo at the age of sixty . . . make more chips of marble fly apart in a quarter of an hour than three of the strongest sculptors would do in an hour. . . . He went to work with such impetuosity and fury of manner that I feared almost every moment to see the block split in pieces. It would seem as if, inflamed by the great idea which inspired him, this great man attacked with a species of fury the marble in which his statue lay concealed.' Michelangelo belongs to the very small band of artists and poets whose supreme greatness has never been questioned. Throughout his long life he had one unvarying aim: to use the beauty of the human body to show its relation to God the Creator and thus to proclaim the high destiny of man.

Very different in character and temperament was Raphael (1483–1520). He was born at Urbino but in 1504 came to Florence to study at a time when Lorenzo and Michelangelo were reaching heights

Left *Raphael's portrait of his friend Count Baldassare Castiglione, who wrote* The Courtier.

hitherto unattained in art. In no way dismayed by the challenge, Raphael set out to achieve greatness in his own way and this sweet-tempered and charming young man was far more acceptable to wealthy patrons than his two turbulent rivals. Probably it is as a painter of lovely Madonnas that most people think of Raphael. The familiarity and beauty of his work look effortless, but behind every painting lay deep thought, planning, and insight. In 1508 Julius II gave him the task of decorating the walls of his private study and library in the Vatican. The *Stanze*, the name given to these paintings because the word is the Italian for 'rooms', were designed to show the unity of man's efforts to reach the truth, and he painted what he regarded as the four paths of this understanding: Theology, Philosophy, Poetry, and Law. Raphael died from overwork on his thirty-seventh birthday at the very moment when the unity in which he and the other High Renaissance artists believed was being shattered by the challenge of Luther and the Reformation.

Above *Bellini's painting of a religious procession passing through the Piazza San Marco in Venice. In the centre is St. Mark's Cathedral.*

The Renaissance came late to Venice, shut off behind her lagoons and more concerned with trade from the East than ideas from the West. As the danger from Turkish advances grew, so Venice became less separated, and once the artistic revival began, Venice rapidly became second only to Florence in importance. Venice could attract artists to work there because she had a strong and stable government and many rich patrons; the brilliance of the light and the beauty of the city were added attractions. Some people claim that true painting began in Venice rather than in Florence. By this they mean that the Florentines were basically concerned with the laws of perspective and composition; only after they had achieved this in the drawing was colour added. To the Venetians colour was the most important feature of the picture, and in the work of Giovanni Bellini (?1431–1516) we first see the glorious colouring of the Venetian school—azure and scarlet, pale silver, blue and rosy red and golden brown, offset by white and deep green. Correggio (?1489–1534) revelled in

189

new techniques of oil painting and he was mainly concerned with the ways in which light can be painted and also how it can be used in a picture to direct attention to the most important parts.

The greatest of all the Venetians was Titian (?1480–1576), whose fame was only a little less than that of Michelangelo. He broke all the accepted rules of composition and relied upon his brilliant colouring to give his pictures a unity. Titian was one of the greatest of all portrait painters and his lesser success in religious subjects is historically interesting. In a painting like his *Bacchus and Ariadne* in the National Gallery in London there is a riot of life and movement which is completely pagan; the artist is no longer primarily interested in religion. Finally, in his use of light and darkness, in his brooding on the secrets of the grave and the trials of old age, Titian is foreshadowing the work of Rembrandt in the next century.

To compress an account of the Renaissance into a single chapter of a small book is an impossibility and later chapters will deal with other aspects. Even so it is impossible to do justice to such a vast subject, and all that can be hoped is that those who read this book will want to find out more for themselves. The best way to learn about sculpture and paintings is to look at them, if possible in an art gallery, but, failing that, in one of the many wonderfully illustrated books which are available nowadays. Another way is to read what is really the first autobiography, *The Life of Benvenuto Cellini*, dictated in old age. There is no need to believe it all, for Cellini was a liar and a boaster, but in the view of John Addington Symonds, one of the greatest nineteenth-century writers on the Renaissance, in the person of Cellini so many sides of the age can be seen:

From the pages of this book the Genius of the Renaissance, incarnate in a single personality, leans forth and speaks to us. Nowhere else, to my mind . . . do we find the full character of the epoch so authentically stamped. . . . He touched the life of the epoch at more points than any person who has left a record of his doings. He was the first goldsmith of his time, an adequate sculptor, a restless traveller, an indefatigable workman, a Bohemian of the purest water, a turbulent bravo, a courtier and companion of princes; finally a Florentine who used his native idiom with incomparable vivacity of style.

Left *Titian's painting of Bacchus and Ariadne. Artists have come a long way since Giotto painted his frescoes. The riot of colour and the pagan feeling are typical of the last stages of the Renaissance.*

Chapter 7
The Empire of Charles V

Three years after the death of his father Louis XI, King Charles VIII of France (1481-98) was presented to the States General by his Chancellor. 'Look with joy, then, upon his face. How radiantly it displays such beauty, such serenity! How clearly it reflects a noble and illustrious nature! What promise it offers to all of his sagacity in the future!' What in fact the States General saw was an immoral hunchback of very doubtful sanity. Some six years later the Venetian ambassador reported home in less glowing terms: 'His Majesty the King of France is twenty-two years old, small and ill-formed in person, with an ugly face, large lustreless eyes which seem to be short-sighted, an enormous aquiline nose, and thick lips which are continuously open; he stutters and has a nervous twitching of the hands which is unpleasant to watch. In my opinion—it may well be wrong—he is not of much account either physically or mentally.' The ambassador was quite correct.

Charles, who had come of age in 1492, had a rather doubtful claim to be the rightful king of Naples and, urged on by the wilder nobles anxious for excitement, he decided to start his reign by winning a new kingdom. To Charles's dim mind, because he had been invited by the ruler of Milan, Ludovico Sforza, to support him in his quarrel with Naples, it seemed that he would be welcomed as a deliverer, who might then unite Italy and lead a crusade against the Turks. Every sane person in Paris opposed this Italian adventure; but Charles was not sane. Philip de Commines, now his represent-ative in Venice, wrote in his Memoirs: 'The King was young, feeble, self-willed, and with few wise advisers or good leaders in his company. Money was scarce, and before starting they had to borrow a hundred thousand francs . . . there were no tents or pavilions, yet the winter was come when they began to advance into Lombardy. . . . Thus we must conclude that the expedition was conducted through-out by the hand of God, for the sense of its leaders was unequal to the conduct of it.' So with streaming banners inscribed, as for a crusade, with 'Voluntas Dei' ('The Will of God') and 'Missus a Deo' ('Sent by God'), Charles VIII set out for Italy in 1494 on an expedi-tion which was to prove only the first of a long and dreary series of wars against the Spanish possessions in southern Italy, from which nothing was gained and which were to last on and off until 1559. French invasions of Italy followed a constant pattern: early success turning quickly to total failure. Ariosto, the contemporary Italian poet, was entirely accurate when he wrote: 'All who hold the sceptre of France shall see their armies destroyed either by the sword, or by famine, or by pestilence. They will bring back from Italy short-lived rejoicing and enduring grief, small profit and infinite loss, for the lilies may not take root in that soil.'

Since Ludovico Sforza had invited Charles into Italy, Charles could begin his advance without difficulty. Florence, at that moment under the influence of a Dominican friar, Girolamo Savonarola, had temporarily become a republic and the Medici had been expelled. Savonarola hailed Charles as God's scourge for the evils of the times, but all the same managed to persuade him to bypass rather than sack the city. Pope Alexander VI was powerless to stop Charles from entering Rome, and all resistance crumbled away in Naples. Within five months Charles had apparently achieved his aims without striking a blow.

Unfortunately for Charles, his army, which was partly German and Swiss, was very far from being the flight of purifying angels described by Savonarola. The wars of this period were being fought with far larger armies than in the past and, as they straggled from camp to camp or battlefield to battlefield, they left behind them a trail of devastation and distress. In addition to the ordinary casualties from wounds or disease, the plunder of the village granaries by desperate provision clerks meant food scarcities and high prices for the Italians as the armies moved on. Ferdinand of Aragon, who had his own plans for regaining Naples, once an outpost of Aragon, had no intention of seeing the kingdom fall into French hands. He had no difficulty in using the hatred and indignation aroused by the French troops to form a league 'for the maintenance of peace', or, to be more accurate, to drive the French from Italy. Venice, the pope, and, with no shred of loyalty to the man he had invited into Italy, Ludovico Sforza readily joined. Charles had no alternative but to make a dash for home. At Fornovo, between Florence and Milan, the League's army barred his way. In a savage fifteen-minute battle Charles cut his way through and got home safely at the price of losing most of his baggage. Mercifully he died in 1498 before his plans for a new Italian adventure were complete.

Before continuing the story of the Italian Wars we must return to Florence and Savonarola. He had been born in 1452 and, after some years of torturing doubts and an experience of being crossed in love, he joined the Dominicans in Bologna. In 1482 he was sent to the convent of San Marco in Florence, of which he became prior a year before the death of Lorenzo de' Medici. Through his sermons, as one of his friars testifies, he gained a magnetic hold over the Florentines.

The people got up in the middle of the night to get places for the sermon, and came to the door of the cathedral, waiting outside till it should be opened, making no account of any inconvenience, neither of the cold, nor the wind, nor of standing in winter with their feet on the marble. . . . They waited three or four hours till the Padre entered the pulpit. And the attention of so great a mass of people, all with eyes and ears intent upon the preacher, was wonderful; they listened so that when the sermon reached its end it seemed to them that it had scarcely begun.

The avoidance of any danger from Charles VIII made the influence of Savonarola greater than ever and his help was welcomed in drawing up a new constitution for the republic. In his sermons Savonarola was often a terrifying prophet of future doom which, he said, would fall on the city unless the Florentines destroyed what he regarded as luxuries and 'vanities'. He can have had little eye for

An unknown artist's painting of the burning of Savonarola and his companions in Florence. The cathedral can just be seen on the left.

the beauty of Florentine crafts, and in the bonfires which he demanded many lovely things must have perished. But, as happened in Puritan England a century and a half later, the inevitable reaction followed. Savonarola came into conflict with the pope, was excommunicated but refused to take any notice. The rival and hostile Franciscans challenged him to prove the truth of his beliefs and prophecies in a trial of ordeal by fire. The result was inconclusive, for a violent thunderstorm literally washed out the ceremony. Eventually he was tried by the Florentine court, cruelly tortured, and in May 1498 was hanged and then burned. Savonarola is important not just in the history of Florence but because in his attacks on the pope and the Church he was, although unaware of it, a forerunner of the Reformation. 'The scandal begins in Rome and runs through the whole clergy. . . . It has come to pass that all are warned against Rome, and people say, "If you want to ruin your son make him a priest." ' Savonarola was all his life a loyal member of the Church, but words like these might have been uttered by Luther.

Charles VIII was succeeded by his cousin, Louis XII (1498–1515), perhaps a slightly abler and pleasanter man, but still a poor creature. Nothing illustrates better than Louis's two Italian expeditions that in these dreary wars today's friend will be tomorrow's enemy. At first, with the help of Venice and the pope, it was Milan to which Louis laid claim. It was easily overrun in 1499, lost, and then regained and Ludovico Sforza was sent to France as a prisoner. The next step was to make another attempt to conquer Naples. Just at this moment it suited Ferdinand of Aragon to make sure of half of the kingdom of Naples for himself and he made an alliance with Louis to go shares in the spoils. Pope Alexander VI, whose chief interest was to help his evil son, Cesare Borgia, carve a territory for himself out of the Romagna, agreed to the plan. There was little resistance and the king of Naples joined Ludovico as a prisoner in France. The inevitable quarrel between the victors soon arose and fighting broke out between them. The great Spanish general, Gonzalo de Corboda, famed for his victories against the Moors in Granada, routed the French at Cerignola, a battle which gave Spain control of Naples for centuries to come. The new pope, Julius II, formed the so-called Holy League in whose battles he himself took part, to drive the French out of Milan, a task eventually achieved in 1513 at the battle of Novara. Once again the French armies went home having achieved nothing and having learned nothing, for the temptation of Italy remained; but it was even more the growing readiness of Italian rulers to call in foreign help to achieve their own selfish aims which ensured that Italy would for another forty years provide the battlefield for this struggle between France and Spain. No wonder that in 1514 Machiavelli made a passionate appeal for a national leader to end a foreign tyranny which 'stank in everyone's 'nostril'. No 'national' leader was to appear in Italy for over 300 years. With the death of Louis XII and the accession of his cousin, Francis I (1515–47), a new stage in the story opens.

The European scene is now to be dominated by three young rulers, born within eight years of each other, each proud of his humanist education, each keen to be a great patron of scholars and artists, each determined, though he could ill afford it, to outshine the other two in fame and power. Henry VIII, who inherited the English crown in 1509, was an attractive young man of 18, tall and handsome, bursting with animal life and vigour, a great performer in all manly sports, a passionate lover of hunting and of women, but also interested in the new learning and no mean musician. Of the three young men he had the least chance of becoming the leading prince in Europe and so he contented himself in the years when he and Wolsey played an active part in the European political game with promising his support to each of his rivals in turn and proving fickle to both. So the struggle for supremacy in Europe soon became a duel between Francis I and Charles V, who by 1519 had inherited a vast empire. Since their rivalry loomed so large in the history of their times it is important to see what each of these two very different men was like.

Francis, born in the year in which Charles VIII invaded Italy, was at the age of 21 determined to rule with authority, as he believed a true prince should rule. As a young man he was high-spirited and ambitious, but self-indulgent and lacking in the staying-power needed to deal with the two great problems of his reign—the rivalry with Charles V abroad and the religious crisis at home. He was impulsive and a poor judge of men; nor did he grow wiser with age. There is a flashy and superficial brilliance about Francis, so that he is remembered not as a great king of France but as the man under whose personal encouragement the Renaissance was at its height in France.

The closeness of Italy to France had ensured that the idea of the Italian Renaissance had begun to spread in France some years before French knights brought home artistic treasures as loot from the wars of Charles VIII and Louis XII. Some of the things sent home were not always artistic, as can be seen from the entry in the diary of a Paris citizen: 'In the year 1517 Monsieur de la Vernade, Knight, forwarded to the city of Paris a dead serpent boiled in oil, called a crocodile, which had been given to him at Venice by the city magistrate. . . . This serpent was captured near Cairo, when the Nile was in flood. It was found dead.' But Francis was a genuine lover of the arts, and set himself deliberately to hasten the acceptance in France of Italian art. He bought pictures by Leonardo, Raphael, and Titian; and he employed Italian architects and decorators like Rosso to transform his hunting lodge at Fontainebleau into a palace

Louis XII. He sent this portrait to Mary Tudor when he thought of marrying her.

Francis I. Portrait by Clouet.

Cellini's Salt-Cellar, made of chased gold and enamel on a base of ebony. It was made for Francis I in 1543.

for his treasures. Here he kept not only his pictures but also his collection of Greek manuscripts, and it was here that Cellini, the goldsmith, made such a magnificent salt-cellar that, as he boasted, 'the King cried aloud in astonishment and could not look at it long enough'. Attached to the palace was a workshop for making tapestries and Francis's love of music later led to the founding of a special school of singers.

During Francis's reign the country was becoming more prosperous and the wealthier people began to want to live in a more luxurious and refined way. They did this by building all those wonderful châteaux, especially in the Loire valley, which today can be visited with ease. The old medieval castle was turned as if by magic into a stately and gracious dwelling; water, once needed in the

197

moat for defence, was now used for ornamental lakes and fountains; the doorways of old guardrooms and the long passages were decorated with cupids and epigrams carved in the stone; many a château was provided with secret rooms for eavesdropping on private conversations or state secrets, and the way was made easy for courtiers to reach their ladies by means of exquisite, winding stairways on the outside of the building, purely French in design and owing nothing to Italy. To Francis's enthusiasm are due not only Fontainebleau but also Chambord and much of the palace at Blois; his wealthier subjects followed his example at Azay-le-Rideau, Chenonceaux, and many another lovely château.

The palace of Fontainebleau as it developed from the original hunting lodge.

One figure of this French Renaissance must be mentioned here because in his writings he sums up so much of the spirit of his times. François Rabelais (?1494–1553) was a monk who after thirteen years escaped from his monastery disgusted at the ignorance and immorality around him. He studied medicine and was the first man in France to dissect a corpse. It was at Lyons, where he practised as a doctor in the hospital, that in 1533 his book *Pantagruel* was printed, to be followed four years later by *Gargantua*. Rabelais believed that life should be lived to the full—'vivez joyeux' was his motto—and his heroes have gigantic appetites for tripe, sausages, hams, cheeses,

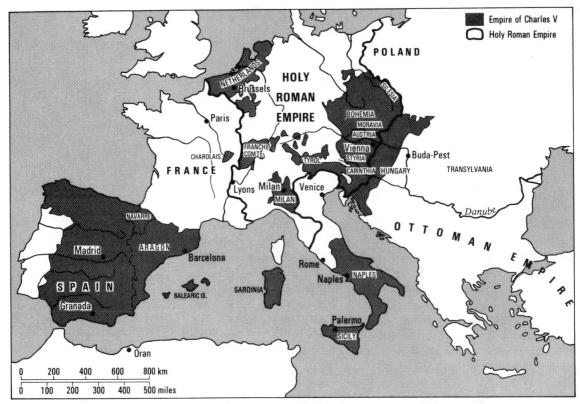

The Empire of Charles V.

sheep and cattle roasted whole, all washed down with torrents of wine. His Gargantua is born at an open-air festival calling lustily for drink, a symbol to Rabelais of a world athirst for knowledge and experience. Men roared with laughter at the cruel fun poked at priests and monks and at the grossly indecent passages in the books. But Rabelais made his reader think as well as laugh; he showed that God and goodness still mattered but might be found in new ways. 'If we would achieve a sure and satisfying knowledge of the divine two things are necessary—God's guidance and man's company'. In Rabelais's world life is good and the cloistered world of the medieval monastery is dead. 'At last we are out of the Gothic night,' he cried with joyful relief. In two months more copies of *Pantagruel* had been sold than copies of the Bible in nine years, and nobody delighted in his books more than Francis I.

Charles, the lifelong rival of Francis, was cast in a very different mould. He was born in 1500 and six years later his father, Philip, Duke of Burgundy, who was married to Juana, the mad daughter of Ferdinand and Isabella, died. Declared of age in 1515, Charles ruled the Netherlands, Luxembourg, and Franche-Comté. A year later his grandfather, Ferdinand of Aragon, died, bequeathing to him Castile and its New World possessions and Aragon with Naples and Sicily, thus making him the ruler of all Spain. As if this were not enough for one man, in 1519 his other grandfather, the emperor Maximilian I, died, and from him Charles inherited all the Hapsburg territory in Austria and around the upper Rhine. Much of the eastern part of his empire Charles wisely made over later to his brother Ferdinand, who added Bohemia and much of Hungary after 1526 to the family possessions. So, as you can see from the map, Charles, in close alliance with his younger brother, controlled a considerable part of Europe, in addition to the as yet hardly understood size and wealth of the New World.

What kind of man at the age of 19 carried such a burden? Charles was slight in build, with a pale face and rather staring eyes and, like so many Hapsburgs, with 'his lower jaw long and projecting, so that his teeth do not meet, and one cannot hear the ends of his words distinctly', as the Venetian ambassador later reported. He was blessed with no natural dignity and little charm of manner. Men aged then much more quickly than they do today, but Charles never really looked young. This was partly due to the cares of empire but also to gout, which his excessive eating and drinking did little to cure. Roger Ascham, an Englishman who saw Charles later in life, wrote home: 'I stood hard by the Emperor's table. He had four courses; he had sod [boiled] beef very good, roast mutton, baked hare . . . he fed well of a capon. . . . The Emperor drank the best that I ever saw; he had his head in the glass five times as long as any of us, and never drank less than a quart of Rhenish wine.' But this strangely unimpressive and rather dull little man was not to be despised, as he grew into the formidable ruler and the outstanding European figure whom Francis could never rival for long. His mind moved slowly but he never gave up. He was an intelligent plodder, who learned by experience and chose his ministers wisely. Above all, he took his responsibilities very seriously and had a high sense of duty, being firmly convinced that God had entrusted to him the welfare of Christendom. He saw himself as a new Charlemagne, destined, alongside the pope, to unite the Christian nations and to lead them against the Turks. He was not grasping but he was ambitious, and his motto was 'Plus Oultre' or 'Further still'.

On the face of it Francis had no chance against such a giant. In fact, at the start, the two rivals were more equally matched than might appear. Francis was in a much stronger position than Charles. He ruled a compact territory in which almost all opposition to the king had been crushed; his subjects were growing in numbers and in prosperity, and when it came to levying taxes to raise money for the wars Francis could count on meeting little trouble. Furthermore, right at the start of his reign Francis had invaded Italy and this time had secured a valuable base by capturing Milan after the two-day battle of Marignano in 1515. This victory enabled him to strike a bargain in 1516 with Pope Leo X, known as the Concordat of Bologna, whereby, despite the dislike of the bargain by the French clergy, Francis gained virtual control over all appointments to the Church in France.

Charles had no such advantages. As a child he had been brought up in the Netherlands, and although he spoke several languages badly, his homeland was the only part of his empire in which he felt at ease and did not appear to his subjects as a stranger. Nor was his empire in any sense united; its sole unity was the fact that the same man was ruler of each separate part of it. In Spain Charles was king of a nation which resented being part of a bigger empire; in Burgundy he was a duke; elsewhere he was count of various provinces. Despite all the efforts of his brilliant Chancellor, Gattinara, no scheme could be devised by which the Empire could be ruled centrally, and each separate territory continued to be governed on its own. To do this Charles appointed members of his family as regents —his brother looked after Germany, his wife was in Spain, and the Netherlands were in the care of first an aunt and then of his sister— but final decisions were his alone and he insisted on being kept informed of what was happening. He was thus forced to be always on the move, never able to give any problem his undivided attention for long because, wherever he might be, urgent messages were always reaching him requiring his presence in another part of the Empire.

With the death of Maximilian I in 1519 a new Holy Roman Emperor had to be elected. To be emperor meant great prestige as the official head of the German princes, but it did not bring with it any real power. As we have seen, since 1436 the emperor had been chosen from members of the house of Hapsburg, but this was not automatic, and Maximilian had worked hard before he died to secure for his grandson, Charles, the votes of the seven men in whose hands the choice lay. But in 1519 there were two other candidates in the field: Henry VIII of England, who had little chance of being elected, and Francis I. The Imperial Election of 1519 was the first round in the contest between Francis and Charles. For nearly a year each of them promised large bribes and future favours in return for an Elector's vote. In the end, at a cost of 850,000 florins, over half of which was lent to Charles by the great banking house of Fugger in Augsburg, Charles was elected unamimously. Three reasons gave Charles his victory. Francis's credit was not so good as Charles's; the Electors feared that if they chose Francis he would rule Germany with the authority which he held in France and they did not want this; in the end it was the mistaken belief that Charles would be more interested in Germany than in other parts of his empire that told in his favour.

Sooner or later war with Francis was inevitable, and war was to be the keynote of Charles's reign. Charles had not only to deal with Francis, whose interests clashed with his in Burgundy, in Milan, in Naples and Sicily; but it was his fate to have to use force against the Lutherans in Germany, to suppress risings in Spain and even in the Netherlands, and, above all, his armies were urgently needed to stem the tide of Turkish advance through Hungary towards Vienna. 'I was not invested with the imperial crown in order to rule over yet more territories, but to ensure the peace of Christendom and so unite all forces against the Turk for the greater glory of the Christian faith,' said the new emperor. Europe, alas for Charles's hopes, had no intention of being united under his rule; in fact, the very size of Charles's empire aroused jealousy and suspicion in the minds of more rulers than Francis. Charles's problems were so great as to be almost beyond solution, and only his courage, his dedication to never-ending work, and his high sense of duty enabled him to achieve as much as he did.

It was one thing to go to war, quite another thing to find the troops and to pay for them. The way that battles were fought was changing, and to a military historian the interest of the Italian Wars lies in the way that medieval methods of fighting were giving way to modern tactics, largely because of gunpowder. Many soldiers now had fire-arms, an arquebus or a horse-pistol. The arquebus, with a range at best of 200 yards, still took three minutes to load and another two minutes to fire, so that the long-bow and cross-bow could still be used against it; but this would not be for much longer. Guns in the Hundred Years War were only about three or four feet in length and had a range of up to 150 yards; now they could be ten feet long or more with a much greater range. When fighting a battle the infantry were still more important than the artillery, and it had become the practice to combine pikemen with arquebusiers: the pikemen kept off the enemy while the arquebus was laboriously re-loaded; the arquebusiers broke a cavalry charge before it could cut its way through the line of pikes. This needed much training, and so armies were becoming more professional, and most rulers going to war had to hire mercenaries from Switzerland or Germany to reinforce their own countrymen. Francis after Marignano had done a swift deal with the Swiss by which he managed to gain almost a monopoly of Swiss mercenaries. They later became the royal body-guard in Paris and their uniform can still be seen in Rome today, worn by the papal guard at the Vatican. Charles found that he could usually count on hiring the bulk of the German *landsknechte*, tough and unruly men, proud of their skill and likely to be loyal if paid regularly. As the sixteenth-century progressed, both Swiss and German mercenaries were gradually outclassed by the armies from Spain, widely regarded as the best fighters in Europe. These men

*The battle of Marignano
(1515). Part of a bas relief
from the tomb of Francis I.
Pikes and lances are much in
evidence as well as the cannon,
now an effective weapon.*

were usually not for hire but fought for Charles as their king. All these troops, Swiss, German, and Spanish, were mostly infantrymen; when it came to cavalry, the French were still the finest horsemen of the day.

In a long war it was the money that mattered most. As we have seen, French kings had won the right to tax without too many questions being asked, though the amount of money which could be raised was far from unlimited. Francis's entire revenue was rather less than the combined revenues of Spain and the Netherlands; but compared to Charles he was much freer to spend the money raised how he liked. On the other hand, systems of banking and credit had not been developed in any French city in the same way as at Augsburg, Genoa, or Antwerp, the great port on the Scheldt which had become the financial centre of Europe. Its wealth came in the first place from its own industries, the metal trades and the working-up and finishing of the rough cloth imported from England and Spain. Even greater wealth came from its busy docks and wharves, which daily handled all the goods coming down the Rhine and the sea-coast trade from the Baltic. So in the early years of his reign Charles relied on his homeland to provide the greater part of his wartime finances. Gradually this changed when religious quarrels

in the Netherlands became serious, and then Charles turned to Spain, into whose ports was beginning to flow the silver from the New World. By the end of his reign Spain had become the true heart of his empire.

Charles was sure that he must deal with Francis first and, if possible, knock out France once and for all so as to be free to turn against the enemies of the Faith, whether Lutherans or Turks. The trouble for Charles was that any considerable success in fighting was likely to be followed by an alliance against him by Christian rulers far more anxious to be independent than to go on a crusade. An

The battle of Pavia (1525), from a sixteenth-century tapestry. This shows the camp of Francis I inside a large park. The surrounding walls were not properly defended.

invasion of France by Charles and by English troops, coinciding with a rebellion inside France led by Charles of Bourbon, who had no hesitation in turning traitor, failed miserably. In Italy things went better for Charles, who was determined to be master of the whole country. To achieve this he needed to have the pope on his side and so, when Leo X died in 1521, Charles secured the election of his old tutor, Adrian of Utrecht (1522-3). Adrian VI was an austere man, determined both to reform the curia and not to be the tool of his former pupil; so there was relief among the cardinals and in Charles's mind when he died after a reign of little more than a year. His successor was Clement VII (1523-34), a nephew of Lorenzo de' Medici, a worthy but very weak man. Guicciardini, the Florentine historian, described him vividly: 'Both in discussion and in carrying out what had been discussed, every minute consideration that occurred to him again, every insignificant hindrance that might arise, seemed enough to throw him back into the original confusion from which he suffered before the discussion, so that after deciding on one course of action it always seemed to him that the rejected course would have been the best.' This was the man fated to deal with the Lutheran revolt and the problem of Henry VIII's divorce. On one thing, however, he was quite certain and that was his wish to be independent of Charles. He felt that this could be achieved by a rapid switch of alliance whenever Charles seemed to be too powerful. So, because in 1522 imperial troops had defeated the French near Milan, he decided in 1524 to ally with Francis.

Retribution followed swiftly. On 24 February 1525, Charles's twenty-fifth birthday, the French army, with Francis at its head, was utterly crushed at Pavia, one of the most famous battles of the century. Francis fought like a knight of romance, but as the old French chivalry went down for the last time before the imperial firearms, he was captured and sent as a prisoner to Madrid. Shattering as this defeat appeared to be for France, Pavia in fact decided very little. Within a year Francis had regained his freedom by signing away all his claims to Milan and Naples in the Treaty of Madrid (January 1526), a treaty which on the night before he signed Francis had secretly declared to be 'null and of none effect' because forced on him 'by constraint and long imprisonment and fear of the future'. The year 1526 illustrates well how impossible was Charles's task. Francis was free; a new league was formed by Charles's enemies against him; the Lutheran problem was becoming more and more urgent; and, to crown all, in the great battle of Mohacs the Turks destroyed the Hungarians and the way to Vienna was open. If ever there was a moment when Charles needed to lead the united armies of Christendom against the Turk it was now. Not only was there no hope of unity but Charles could not even lay hands on the ready money to pay his own troops, who were becoming mutinous.

The Empire of Charles V

To prevent a total breakdown of discipline, Charles of Bourbon, now at the head of a German and Spanish army, decided to march south through Italy and attack Rome, in the hope that this would teach the shifty pope Clement VII a lesson and also provide rich booty for his men. On 5 May they stormed the city in an attack led by Bourbon in person, who was shot and killed by a bullet fired, if we can believe him, by Benvenuto Cellini. Charles, no great soldier and seldom with his armies, received from his Chancellor, Gattinara, an account of the appalling horrors of the sack of Rome which followed its capture:

As the inhabitants in general relied on its being defended, none of them had fled, or removed their property, so that no one of whatever nation, rank, condition, age or sex escaped becoming prisoners—not even women in convents. They were treated without distinction according to the caprice of the soldiery; and after being plundered of all their effects, most of them were compelled by torture or otherwise to pay ransom. . . . Some women who had carried all their earthly possessions to Cardinal Colonna's house were left with but a single cloak or shift. . . . All the Church ornaments were stolen, the sacred utensils thrown about, the relics gone to destruction. . . . St. Peter's Church and the papal palace from top to bottom have been made into stables. . . . Most of the troops are enriched by the enormous booty, amounting to many millions of gold crowns.

Europe was aghast and Charles hastened to disclaim all responsibility, but he could not help agreeing with Gattinara that 'everyone is convinced that all this has happened as a judgement from God on the great tyranny and disorders of the papal court'.

As ever, Charles's enemies banded together in righteous anger against him and a French army marched south on Naples, only to be struck down by disease. For the moment both sides wanted peace, and in 1529 the Ladies' Peace of Cambrai, so called because the principal negotiators were the Queen Mother of France and Charles's sister, was signed. Charles had achieved his aim and was master of Italy, and in 1530 he went to Bologna to receive from a dutiful pope the iron crown of Lombardy and the golden crown of the Empire.

In the years after Charles's coronation the personal rivalry with Francis remained as bitter as ever, but there is no need to tell the story in detail. It is more important to understand the ways in which the struggle changed over the next fifteen years. Although there was to be some fighting in Italy, there were no more of the old style French expeditions. Instead, the interest shifts to Germany where, as we shall see in the next chapter, the Lutherans were strong enough to fight the Emperor in defence of their beliefs. To Francis all enemies of Charles were friends of France, even though they were Protestants. That religion played no part at all in the story is seen even more strikingly when Francis had no hesitation in allying

Titian's portrait of Charles V in middle age.

206

himself with Suleiman the Magnificent of Turkey, an alliance which shocked many people and which was destined to last for nearly two centuries. As the years went by, a change came over both rivals. Francis, often ill, began to lose heart and his efforts flagged. Charles, on the other hand, while also old before his time, grew steadily through experience and unremitting hard work into the man whom friend and foe alike regarded as the foremost ruler of his time.

In the Mediterranean the Turkish pirate admiral, Barbarossa, was a serious danger to Christian shipping from his bases at Algiers and Tunis, and in 1534 Francis saw fit to ally with him, thereby encouraging him to inflict great damage on the Adriatic coast of Italy. In the following year Charles, free from the moment from French wars, could at last appear as the champion of Christendom. At the head of a large force drawn from all his dominions he sailed for North Africa and in a brilliant campaign destroyed the pirate bases and captured Tunis. Nothing did more to increase Charles's reputation and he returned in triumph.

Twice more, in 1536 and 1544, war with Francis broke out afresh, but the fighting was indecisive. The Peace of Crespy in the autumn of 1544 was the last peace signed between the two men, though the agreement was no more lasting than earlier treaties. Three years later Francis was dead. As a contemporary wrote of him: 'He was magnanimous and generous and a lover of good literature, which, through his means, lit up the shades of ignorance which had reigned up to his time. He liked all men of learning and founded at Paris colleges for Latin, Greek and Hebrew studies. He died at the age of fifty-three after having had experience of much good and much evil fortune, though more of evil than of good.' Apart from his patronage of the arts, there was little to show for all his efforts.

The new king of France, Henry II (1547–59), was no improvement on his father. He was more determined than Francis had been to deal ruthlessly with the Protestants in France, but this in no way prevented him from making a full alliance with the Lutheran princes by the Treaty of Chambord (1552). In return for French military aid Henry was offered the title of Protector of the Holy Roman Empire and the Lutherans were prepared to put under his protection the three great fortress-bishoprics of Metz, Toul, and Verdun. No Emperor could ignore such an alliance and war again broke out. The French under the Duke of Guise captured Metz, which Charles, now old and ill, failed to regain. His sole consolation was that French ambitions in Italy were, as ever, held in check.

For some time now Charles's thoughts had been moving towards abdication and the handing over of his burden to his son, Philip. Throughout 1556 he divested himself of his many crowns, but the most moving scene of all came in the Great Hall of the Château of

Brussels when on 25 October Charles took his leave of the Netherlands and Philip became his successor both in the Netherlands and
in Spain. Dressed in mourning and surrounded by the Knights of
the Golden Fleece, Charles entered the Hall leaning on the arm of
William of Orange, destined before long to be the great enemy of
Philip and the hero of the Netherlands. The Venetian ambassador
described the scene which followed:

The Emperor, with a paper of notes in his hand, because he could not retain
firmly in his memory all he had to say, recounted in their order the various
actions of his life, the labours, hardships and dangers sustained in the course
of his journeys by sea and land . . . adding, that not feeling in himself the
vigour which the government of so many states required, and knowing that his
son was capable of supporting weighty duties, he wished to give the remainder
of his life to the service of God, and cede these states . . . to the King [Philip]. . . .
After which the emperor embraced him, with many tears on both sides, which
caused the Queen and many others to weep also.

*The abdication of Charles V.
This is an allegorical picture
showing Charles's greatness.
The emperor points with his
left hand to Philip II, his heir.
The riches of land and sea are
offered in tribute.*

Charles sank, exhausted and overcome with emotion, on his throne and it was Philip's turn to reply. Unable to speak French or Flemish but only Spanish, Philip was forced to ask the Bishop of Arras to speak for him. Nothing showed better than this that the great days of Charles's empire were over. Philip II, as he now became, was king of Spain, the New World possessions, and of the Netherlands, but he did not inherit the Hapsburg lands in Germany which passed to his uncle, and when the time came for another imperial election, no Elector would vote for a Spaniard. Charles, determined to spend his remaining years in peace, retired to Yuste, near Toledo, where he lived in a specially built set of rooms attached to a monastery. It was not a monastic life, but he refused to be drawn into affairs of state, preferring to devote himself to study, prayer, and the enjoyment of his enormous collection of watches.

Charles's abdication did not at once mean the end of the war. Philip II hoped for great things from his marriage to Mary Tudor, and a decisive victory in 1557 over the French at St. Quentin seemed to mark the final overthrow of France. But it was not to be. Mary died childless and the English alliance was at an end. Just before her death in 1558 she learned that Guise had captured Calais. Both sides were now exhausted and declared themselves bankrupt. Both Philip II and Henry II saw that no result would come from further fighting and that it was far more important to turn their attention to the religious divisions within their countries. So the long struggle which had begun with Charles VIII's frivolous expedition in 1494 ended in 1559 with the Peace of Cateau-Cambrésis. France, for over sixty years of fighting, had gained nothing at all in Italy and surrendered all her claims. As some compensation she kept Calais and, although not mentioned in the treaty, the bishoprics of Metz, Toul, and Verdun, still officially part of the Empire, remained under French control. It was a Spanish victory and there was much discontent in France. 'Three or four drops of ink and a stroke of the pen had abandoned everything and dishonoured all our fine victories.' To mark the start of a new friendship between France and Spain, Elizabeth, Henry II's daughter, was married to Philip II. The wedding festivities which followed were brought to a tragic end when Henry II, proud of his skill in tournament, died from a splinter which pierced his eye from his opponent's lance.

Charles did not live to hear of the peace; he had died in 1558 'the greatest man that ever was or will be' in the opinion of his confessor. Modern historians would not call him great and many writers have written him off as a failure. He certainly failed, as we shall see, in Germany; there was never any hope of his being accepted as the leader of Christendom against the Turk. On the other hand, he had ensured the Spanish hold over Italy, and Spanish greatness in the second half of the sixteenth century was due to him, not to his son.

Chapter 8
The Reformation:
the Church torn apart

(i) The background

To people living in Europe the sixteenth century was a time of violent upheaval and rapid change. So many changes seemed to be happening at the same time and to be happening so quickly. New forms of national government might bring unity to a country but not necessarily peace. There was, of course, nothing new in war; but bigger armies and the coming of firearms meant that the ravages of war grew worse. It was good that the power of the feudal nobles had been crushed in several countries, but to take their place came city men—lawyers and bankers, industrialists and merchants—eagerly thrusting forward to make the most of their new importance and to make money quickly. Wealth and power might be passing from the nobles to the new middle classes, but this did not much help the great bulk of men and women who still lived and worked on the land. The last decades of the fifteenth century had often seen years of bad harvests and prices had fluctuated wildly, which hit the peasants hard. In 1500, for example, there was a complete failure of all crops in Germany, at a time when the potato had not yet been brought from America to keep starvation at bay. Moreover, when there was money to spend it seemed no longer to buy as much as in the past, and nobody understood the inflation which was taking place.

The better educated people were excited by the ideas of the Renaissance, but they must also have found some of them disturbing. Printing enabled any new idea or discovery to be spread all over Europe with alarming speed. Undreamed of new worlds were being opened up by daring navigators and explorers at the same time as scientists were questioning the beliefs of the ancient Greeks—and, more significantly, of the Church—about the nature of the heavens. By the middle of the century Copernicus would declare that the sun and not the earth was the centre of the universe. It must have seemed at times as if the very ground were being cut from under one's feet.

For the uneducated, and that meant most people, there were other reasons, as we saw more fully in Chapter 5, which made their world an unsafe and frightening place. The shortness and insecurity of their lives, the effect of epidemics like the Black Death, the sudden and unexpected coming of death in a variety of ways affected them strangely. They could not believe that disease and disaster and death came without a cause, and so, in the hope of forecasting what was

The Church besieged by the forces of evil. Notice how the attackers are portrayed as blind and therefore as ignorant.

likely to happen and to be armed against it, some turned to astrology, the belief that men's lives were actually affected by the position of the stars in the sky. For example, one form of illness was said to occur when Saturn and Jupiter appeared to be close together. But far more people were sure that it was not only the stars which brought trouble but certain people on earth, and for these, especially the Jews and witches, nothing was too bad.

No part of Europe was free from social struggles; there were far too many underdogs determined to better their lot to make for

211

peace and quiet. In the countryside, landowners, with the help of their lawyers, worked hard to extend and often to reimpose their medieval rights at the expense of their tenants and serfs. To the aristocracy and to the lords of the manor the peasants were little different from beasts and could be treated as such. For the peasant life was harsh; not only did he work long hours but the rise in population all over western Europe meant that available land was becoming scarcer, and landowners, because of rising prices, were for ever demanding higher rents. Unable to share in the growing prosperity of the classes above them, it is small wonder that the peasants vented their fury in local rebellions and blind attacks on their oppressors. These riots and brief uprisings were more serious in Germany than in other parts of Europe because, as we have seen, there was no strong national ruler able to give the peasants some protection against their local lords, whether laymen or the even more hated princes of the Church and the monasteries. From about 1470 onwards there were constant risings in the Black Forest area and in parts of Austria, while in the lands around the upper Rhine and in Alsace a more ominous movement was starting. For here the peasants began to organize themselves and to band together, taking the *Bundschuh* (the peasant's laced boot) as their symbol. They threatened authority of every kind when they demanded that all men must be equal, and they found allies among discontented artisans and craftsmen of the small towns, often not much bigger than a village, who felt themselves oppressed by those in charge of town life.

In earlier times anxious, frightened, or merely discontened people would have turned for help and comfort to the Church. But for well over a century men's faith that the Church could put things right had been declining. There was a sense that a terrible catastrophe was about to fall on Christian Europe, and many people saw the steady westward advance of the Turks as a sign of this. In 1494 Sebastian Brant wrote a bitter satire on greedy and worldly clerics, which he called *The Ship of Fools* and in which he said that the Church no longer had any remedy against impending disaster:

> We have the archfoe [the Turks] close at hand,
> We perish sleeping one and all,
> The wolf has come into the stall
> And steals the Holy Church's sheep
> The while the shepherd lies asleep.

As the popes became more and more like any other Italian prince, so their power increasingly passed into the hands of national churches. Here the leading figures, with honourable exceptions like Cardinal Ximenes in Spain or John Fisher, Bishop of Rochester, were chosen for their knowledge of law or for their skill in diplomacy rather than for their saintliness. It is probable that most people were not so shocked, as we are today, at the way many leading churchmen behaved. Even those Frenchmen who knew of these things probably accepted the fact that the future Cardinal John of Lorraine had been made assistant bishop of Metz at the age of 3; or that Charles of Guise, Archbishop of Rheims at 14, also held two other bishoprics and ten abbeys. In Germany it was the financial demands of Albert of Brandenburg, Archbishop of Magdeburg, which roused people's anger rather than his habit of travelling around with his mistresses disguised in men's dress.

To people wanting help and comfort the Church seemed far removed from their everyday lives. Candidates awaiting Confirmation were lucky if they could waylay a bishop as he passed through their neighbourhood on some papal or diplomatic business. For the most part a bishop saw little of his diocese, and his habit of taking the stipend and paying somebody to do the work spread right down through the Church. Canons in cathedrals paid vicars choral to conduct the services, while even humble priests were happy enough to collect tithes from their village and leave an ill-paid, and often ignorant, chaplain to minister to the needs of the parish. Nor could people gain solace from reading the Bible, or hearing it read, for the Church insisted that the Bible must be in Latin and not in the native language. In fact most people only came into direct contact with the Church when it came to making payments, or in the Church courts. As one papal lawyer, speaking of these courts, said: "The Lord desireth not the death of a sinner but rather that he should pay and live.' None of all this was new: for far too long the Church had failed to provide the strength and comfort which men and women cried out for in an increasingly bewildering world.

This did not mean that people ceased to be religious—quite the reverse; they hated priests and monks who failed to live up to their calling, but they clung with even greater devotion to the Christian Faith as the only safeguard which they knew. At first they had little wish to listen to revolutionary sermons which demanded a drastic reform of the Church; they much preferred the security of old and familiar ways. This is why there was such a large increase in the number of pilgrimages and religious processions at the start of the sixteenth century. Great store was set upon the worship of saints and on prayers for their help. For those able to read there were many books of devotion aimed at teaching a Christian how to live well and, of greater importance, how to die well so as to avoid endless years in purgatory, the place to which it was believed that souls in need of further punishment before being fit for heaven were sent. There were various ways in which the length of time in purgatory might be lessened, the two most popular being a visit to some shrine where relics could be worshipped and the winning of an Indulgence. Relics probably appealed most to the humble and simple-minded and they certainly made Chaucer scoff when he wrote of the Pardoner who 'in a glas he hadde pigges bones', which he pretended were relics, and who made out of those who gazed on his relics 'more moneye Than that person gat in monthes tweye'. But it was not only poor folk who believed in relics. No less a person than Frederick the Wise, Elector of Saxony and shortly to become Luther's protector, had collected in his castle church at Wittenburg no less than 17,443 relics, and a strange assortment they were. Among the more important objects in the collection were a piece of Moses' burning bush, bits of the cradle in which Jesus lay and scraps from his swaddling clothes, some thirty-three fragments of the true Cross and, a gruesome sight, 204 portions of the bodies of the Holy Innocents, the children said to have been murdered at Herod's orders in his attempt to destroy Jesus. It was claimed that a reverent sight of the entire collection could reduce a person's time in purgatory by two million years.

Frederick the Wise, Elector of Saxony. A portrait by Dürer.

Since the sale of Indulgences was to spark off Luther's protest, it is important to understand what they were and to realize that they were nothing new. It was Boniface VIII who in proclaiming the Holy Year announced that the Church possessed an inexhaustible 'treasury of merit' from which the pope could grant to truly penitent sinners complete or partial remission of punishments imposed on them by the Church. What began as a reward for a long and dangerous pilgrimage or for risking one's life against the infidel, gradually came to be extended to those who gave money to good causes. It was a short step from this to the open sale of Indulgences and to maintaining that they could be bought on behalf of souls already in purgatory. Small wonder that ignorant people believed that pardon came from the Church rather than from God, and that the bigger the fee paid the shorter the period of punishment.

There had been, however, for over a century hopeful signs of renewed vigour in the religious life of many people. During the later part of the fourteenth century small communities of men and of women had been formed in the Low Countries and in northern Europe, intent on recovering the true spirit of Christianity through a life of prayer and service. The Brethren of the Common Life, as the members were called, were not monks or nuns, for they took no vows and were very much part of the life of their neighbourhood. The New Devotion was the name given to their teaching that simplicity and holiness were more important than quarrels about minute points of doctrine, and the Brethren strove through the study of the New Testament to recapture the zeal and spirit of the early Church. They earned their living principally by copying manuscripts and by teaching; their schools, to which poor boys were welcomed as boarders, became famous, especially that at Deventer in Holland. The movement was very much of a layman's protest against the way that the Church had become disastrously absorbed in worldly affairs, and its influence was far-reaching. The most famous product of the New Devotion was a book, the *Imitation of Christ*, which was probably compiled by Thomas à Kempis (1380-1471), a man who spent most of his life as a monk near Deventer. It was the most famous book of devotion of the age and it is still used as a guide by the individual Christian anxious to learn how to share something of the mystical life of Christ. 'Blessed are they', à Kempis wrote, 'who enter far into mystical things', and he was at pains to show that the truly religious man did not need a monastery to keep away temptation, for 'the wearing of a religious habit and shaving of the crown do little profit' compared with the life of the spirit. Nor to à Kempis was learning necessarily a passport to heaven. 'Lofty words do not make a man just or holy; but a good life makes him dear to God. I would rather feel contrition than be able to define it.'

If the Brethren's school at Deventer was the most famous school in northern Europe, its most famous pupil was undoubtedly Desiderius Erasmus (*c*.1466-1536). Erasmus was a Dutchman, the natural son of a priest and a doctor's daughter, whose parents could at least afford to send their brilliant son away to school. Probably thinking that a monastery would provide a library, time for study, and intelligent companions, Erasmus in due course took the monastic vows, only to find that he had no true vocation for the life. He quickly discovered that 'so hard a bed, so sparing and so cheap a diet, so much labour and such long vigils' upset his already poor health; at the same time he was bitterly disappointed at his fellow monks' lack of learning and way of life. Although he remained in Orders all his life, he was not forced to remain within the walls of a monastery and was free to travel all over western Europe in his 'passionate determination to educate himself as completely as possible'. Some of his happiest years were spent in England where he became a close friend of men like John Colet, Dean of St. Paul's, and Sir Thomas More, both great humanists, and for a while he was professor of Divinity at Cambridge. Before long Erasmus was recognized as the greatest scholar of the day, with an international reputation and influence but very little money. He might be a 'best seller', but the profits from his books in an age when copyright was unknown went to the publishers who had taken the financial risk in producing the lovely early folios, men like Froben of Basle or, greatest of all printers, Aldus Manutius of Venice.

We have seen how in Italy the humanists devoted themselves to recovering the accurate texts of Greek and Latin writers. As their influence spread northwards over the Alps, the same principles began to be applied to the study of the Bible. To Erasmus it was obvious that, if Christ's teaching were to be studied, it was essential to make sure that it was studied from an accurate text. Colet in his famous Oxford lectures on St. Paul's letters had the same purpose. It was his ambition, he told his hearers, to 'follow the mind of Paul', and this involved being quite sure of what Paul actually wrote and then explaining his meaning. So to Erasmus and his fellow humanists of the northern Renaissance, learning and piety went hand and hand. Erasmus may well have been a reluctant monk; he was certainly a deeply sincere and convinced Christian.

Erasmus's writings fall into two groups: his works of practical devotion and of Biblical scholarship, and his highly amusing satires on the Church and especially on monks. He happened to hear through a friend of a pious woman who was deeply distressed at her soldier husband's dissolute life, and so for them Erasmus in 1504 wrote a book which he called *Enchiridion Militis Christiani*. The title is important: *enchiridion* is a Greek word meaning both a handbook and a small dagger, and so Erasmus's book was a practical guide to the Christian warrior in his fight against evil. It was a good example of Erasmus's determination to make Christianity meaningful to ordinary men and women. Of far greater importance was his publication in 1516 of a revised Greek text of the New Testament, together with a new Latin translation and commentary. Never before had anyone suggested that the Vulgate, the officially approved Latin version of the Bible, could be inaccurate. Erasmus himself would have liked to have gone much further and to see translations of the Scriptures available to all in their mother tongue. 'I long', he wrote, 'that the husbandman should say them to himself as he follows the plough, that the weaver hum them to the tune of his shuttle, that the traveller should beguile with them the weariness of the journey.' The floodgates would soon be open.

When Erasmus and Colet walked together in London, the main topic of conversation, so Erasmus tells us, 'was Christ'. To Erasmus, steeped in the teaching of the New Devotion, the condition of the Church cried out for reform, and it came naturally to him, as a scholar, to use rapiers like wit and satire as his weapons rather than the more heavy-fisted methods of attack shortly to be used by Luther. As Erasmus put it: 'I laid a hen's egg; Luther hatched a bird of quite a different species.' Throughout his writings and his mass of letters the shortcomings of the Church were held up to ridicule. Perhaps the best example is his book *Moriae Encomium, The Praise of Folly*, written in 1509 and dedicated with its punning title to his friend Thomas More. Since it was to be Luther's attack on Indulgences which sparked off the conflagration it is interesting to see what Erasmus had to say about them in this book.

What shall I say of such as cry up and maintain the cheat of pardons and indulgences? that by these compute the time of each soul's residence in purgatory, and assign them a longer or a shorter continuance, according as they purchase more or fewer of these paltry pardons and saleable exemptions? Or

Erasmus. A portrait by Quentin Metsys.

what can be said bad enough of others, who pretend that by the force of such magical charms, or by the fumbling over their beads in the rehearsal of such and such petitions . . . they shall procure riches, honour, pleasure, health, long life, a lusty old age, nay after death a sitting at the right hand of our Saviour in His Kingdom; though as to this last part of their happiness, they care not how long it be deferred, having scarce any appetite towards a-tasting the joys of heaven, till they are surfeited, glutted with and can no longer relish their enjoyments on earth. By this easy way of purchasing pardons, any notorious highwayman, any plundering soldier, or any bribe-taking judge, shall disburse some part of their unjust gains, and so think all their grossest impieties sufficiently atoned for.

Educated men revelled in the gibes of Erasmus and of other humanists. There was a fine German scholar, Reuchlin, who, despite popular hatred of the Jews, insisted on the importance of studying Hebrew. When in 1514 he published *Letters of Famous Men*, a selection of letters written to him in support of his views, it suddenly occurred to others of his friends that it would be a telling joke to invent 'Letters of Obscure Men', in which imaginary defenders of dead traditions in the Church would give their views in appallingly bad Latin. The gale of laughter which greeted these two books showed that Germany was on the edge of revolt. The unrest and fears which have been described meant that an explosion might have happened in other countries and not necessarily because of religion. The storm broke in Germany because there the Church was particularly hated as the owner of one-third of the country; German peasants were the poorest in western Europe; the humanists had prepared the way but the up-and-coming men in the towns wanted more than scholarly jokes, they wanted action. All that was needed was someone to spark off the revolt, and it was at this moment that an obscure monk, Martin Luther, made his protest. The man is very important, but the state of Germany explains the astonishing speed with which his revolt spread.

(ii) Martin Luther

Martin Luther was born on 10 November 1483 and lived in the mining village of Mansfeld in Saxony where his father, once a peasant working on the land, had become sufficiently prosperous to lease three foundries and later to be elected to the town council. Nevertheless, Luther grew up in an atmosphere of poverty and knew at first hand the harshness of the German peasant's life. Being a good musician, he was able to join a choir school and get a free education in local schools, until in 1501 he went to the university of Erfurt where he proved to be a brilliant scholar. His parents had high hopes that their clever son would become a lawyer and be able to provide for them in their old age, but it was not to be. He had always been a religious young man, troubled like so many at this time by fears of hell and damnation. As a boy he would have gazed on the window in the parish church at Mansfeld which showed a frowning Christ with sword in hand coming to judge him in due time. He shared the fears and superstitions of the peasants and believed that 'many regions are inhabited by devils. Prussia is full of them and Lapland of witches.' His pious upbringing at home, in school, and at the university trained him to fear God and to obey the Church as the only road to salvation. The altar-piece in the church at Magdeburg, where for a short time he was at school, was a picture of a great ship sailing heavenwards, with nobody on board save priests and monks, who threw ropes to the laymen drowning in the sea around them. The one safe place for a man seemed to be a monastery, and in July 1505 Luther suddenly decided to enter the Augustinian monastery at Erfurt. Luther certainly feared death and it may be that he was influenced by the early death of his friend and his own near escape from a streak of lightning. But the main reason why Luther became a monk was to save his soul.

'I know from experience', Luther said, 'how peaceful and quiet Satan is accustomed to be in one's first years as a priest or monk.' He was completely happy, his days filled with prayer, study, and singing, and in 1507 he was ordained priest. But during the celebration of his first Mass he underwent an overwhelming religious experience, which left him appalled at his own sinfulness before the majesty and holiness of God. In despair he tried by every kind of discipline to drive away this sense of sin. 'I was a good monk,' he later wrote, 'and I kept the rule of my Order so strictly that I may say that if ever a monk got to heaven by his monkery it was I. . . . If I had kept on much longer, I should have killed myself with vigils, prayers, reading and other work.' But nothing brought peace of mind. In November 1510 he was sent on the business of his Order to Rome where he visited all the shrines and saw the relics. He climbed on hands and knees up the *Scala Sancta,* kissing the twenty-eight stairs which were said to lead to the site of Pilate's palace; but at the top doubts overcame him and he walked down, unhappy at the frivolity and worldliness of the Italian priests whom he saw everywhere and even more disturbed that all the devotions of a pilgrim could bring no relief to his troubled spirit. So despairing did he become on his return to Erfurt that one of the leading members of his Order, perceiving Luther's brilliance and sincerity, decided to see if he might cure Luther's anguish by setting him the task of curing others. Despite all his protests of his own unworthiness, Luther was sent in 1511 to the new university of Wittenburg, recently founded by Frederick the Wise, Elector of Saxony, to become professor of theology, a position which demanded much lecturing and preaching.

It was in preparation for a lecture on St. Paul's Epistle to the Romans that he pondered on the phrase 'the just shall live by faith'. Suddenly he realized that the God before whose holiness he had been afraid to stand was a God of love. Forgiveness for sins and unworthiness could not be earned by good works or hours of prayer and fasting. Forgiveness was the free gift of God to those who had unquestioning faith in the salvation of the world through Christ. 'I felt myself reborn and to have gone through open doors into paradise. The whole of Scripture took on a new meaning and whereas before "the justice of God" had filled me with hate, now it became inexpressibly sweet in greater love. This passage of Paul became to me a gate of heaven,' What Luther was to call 'justification [acquittal] by faith' was to become the battle cry of the Reformation.

For some four years Luther continued his lectures and sermons at Wittenberg, caring, as a priest, for the townsfolk. It was his belief that these people were being deluded into buying worthless Indulgences which provided the great outburst of 1517 and ultimately led to Luther's break with Rome. In this year Albert of Brandenburg was allowed by Pope Leo X to dispense an Indulgence, the proceeds of which were to go towards the completion of St. Peter's in Rome. While this was partly true, it was not stated that Albert, too young to be a bishop at all and already holding two sees, was determined to become archbishop of Mainz as well and that for this he would have to pay a large fee to the pope. The money was borrowed by Albert from the Fuggers and he was allowed to reimburse himself through the Indugence. Forbidden in the territory of Frederick the Wise, the Indulgences were being sold at no distance from Wittenberg by a peculiarly worthless Dominican monk, John Tetzel. An eyewitness describes the sermon which preceded the announcement that the gate of heaven was open:

> It is incredible what this ignorant and impudent friar gave out. He said that if a Christian had slept with his mother, and placed the sum of money in the pope's indulgence chest, the pope had the power in heaven and earth to forgive the sin, and if he forgave it, God must do so also . . .
>   As soon as gold in the basin rings,
>   Right then the soul to heaven springs.

On All Saints' Day, 1 November, 1517 Luther nailed to the door of the cathedral church, the normal place for university notices, 95 theses, or arguments, against Indulgences, offering to debate with any who cared to answer him. What followed was not what Luther intended. There was no debate, but the printing presses spread Luther's arguments far and wide. Luther was a monk little known outside his university; he rapidly became a figure of European importance whose challenge the pope could not lightly dismiss.

Between 1517 and 1521 Luther was made to defend his opinions before one authority after another. Perhaps if Leo X had been prepared to condemn the worst abuses of his Indulgence sellers Luther would have been satisfied, for he had no wish to become the leader of a revolt. Leo, however, appointed a new head of the Augustinians with orders 'to quench a monk of his Order, Martin Luther by name, and thus smother the fire before it should become a conflagration'. Little came from this, for when Luther appeared before the Chapter of his Order at Heidelberg he succeeded in making a deep impression on his superiors. So in August 1518 Luther was summoned to Rome. To obey would almost certainly mean life imprisonment, possibly death, as a heretic. In this extremity Luther appealed to the Elector, Frederick the Wise, who agreed to get the case transferred to Germany from Rome. The Elector's protection now and later was vital to Luther's cause and largely explains his survival, despite the growing number of his enemies. Frederick, who curiously never actually spoke to Luther in his life, was anxious to help the man who had brought fame to his new university. Moreover, he knew that he was safe in thus far opposing the pope, for an imperial

Martin Luther preaching. This is part of an altar piece painted by Cranach the Elder for the Town Church at Wittenberg.

election was impending, and Leo hoped that the Elector would not vote for Charles of Spain, whose growing power was a threat to papal ambitions in Italy. The elegant and indolent Leo, so much addicted to sport that he cared little that his long hunting boots stopped the faithful from kissing his toe, preferred to meet the Elector's wishes if thereby his Italian policy was furthered.

So in October 1518 Luther three times appeared before Cardinal Cajetan, the papal legate, at Augsburg. He refused to recant; Cajetan lost his temper but was uneasy at Luther's power. 'I am not going to talk to him any more. His eyes are as deep as a lake, and there are amazing speculations in his head.' Luther was not impressed by the cardinal, who, he said in a letter home, was no more fitted to handle the case than an ass to play on the harp—a remark which came to delight the cartoonists. Cajetan was determined that Luther should stand trial in Rome, and so Luther, fearing arrest, fled back to Wittenberg, where Frederick once again protected him. Every effort was made to win Frederick's vote in the imperial election; the Golden Rose, a papal honour awarded annually to the ruler who best aided the Church, was presented to Frederick, but Luther remained unmolested. Leo achieved nothing, for, as we saw in the last chapter, Charles V was unanimously elected.

The day before the votes were cast, the third round of Luther's case began at Leipzig where, in the presence of Frederick's cousin, Duke George of Saxony, Luther was made to defend his opinions in open debate before Dr. John Eck, one of the most skilful debaters of the day. We have an eyewitness's description of Luther at Leipzig: 'Martin is a man of middle height, emaciated from care and study, so that you can almost count the bones through his skin. He is in the vigour of manhood and has a clear, penetrating voice. He is learned and has the Scripture at his fingers' ends. . . . He is affable and friendly . . . equal to anything. In company he is vivacious, jocose, always cheerful and gay no matter how hard his adversaries press him.' Of his opponent the same eyewitness wrote: 'Eck is a heavy, square-set fellow with a full German voice, supported by a hefty chest. He would make a tragedian or town crier, but his voice is rather rough than clear. His eyes and mouth and his whole face remind one more of a butcher than a theologian.' In the course of debate Eck manoeuvred Luther into saying that much for which Huss had been condemned a century earlier was 'truly Christian'. The pope could not much longer remain inactive.

Luther spent much of the year 1520 writing three great treatises. If he had written nothing else in his life other than his 'Appeal to the Christian Nobility of the German Nation' he would still be famous. Written in German so that all could understand, it is a violent attack upon the scandals of the Church and a call to lay people, especially to the princes, to undertake the reforms which the Church had neglected. There was another reason why the work was addressed to laymen. By 1520 Luther had come to believe that there was no essential difference between a priest and a layman; they simply performed different duties within the Church. 'Our baptism', he wrote, 'consecrates us all without exception and makes us all priests.' Luther also suggested changes in the Communion Service, in the way that the Bible was studied—to Luther everything depended on the Word of God as revealed in the Bible—and he ended with an attack upon the power of the wealthy in Germany and the terrible hardships endured by the peasants. When we remember the unrest in Germany at this time, this was an explosive document. Of the other two treatises, one was addressed to the clergy and argued the need for fewer sacraments; the other was a work of devotion. Copies of all three poured from the presses and Luther became a national figure.

In May the pope had issued his bull against Luther, condemning his views as heresy. Leo X had been shown the draft of the bull while boar hunting near Rome and he appropriately added the opening words himself: 'Arise, O Lord, and judge thy cause. A wild boar has invaded the vineyard.' Luther was given sixty days after personally receiving a copy of the bull in which to recant or be excommunicated. On the sixtieth day, 10 December, Luther publicly burned the bull on the Wittenberg rubbish dump. Would the new emperor enforce the verdict of the Church against the monk who had now openly challenged the pope's authority?

'For three years', wrote Luther to Charles V, 'I have sought peace in vain. I have now but one recourse. I appeal to Caesar.' Charles was in a difficult position. He hated heresy, but saw that reform of the Church was needed; it was his first visit to Germany and he needed to leave the country peaceful and settled so as in safety to turn to his war against Francis I; he had promised at his election that no man should be condemned unheard. So with reluctance he agreed that Luther should appear before the forthcoming meeting of the Diet at Worms. Alexander, the papal nuncio, was furious that a condemned heretic should be allowed to plead his cause, and even more angry that Luther had become a popular hero. 'The whole of Germany', he wrote, 'is in full revolt. Nine-tenths raise the war cry "Luther", while the watchword of the other tenth who are indifferent to him is "Death to the Roman Curia".'

On 16 April Luther arrived in Worms to be greeted by a crowd of 2,000 people. Two days later the moving scene took place in which Luther, standing before the Diet, declared: 'Unless I am convicted by Scripture and plain reason—I do not accept the authority of popes and councils for they have contradicted each other—my conscience is captive to the Word of God. I cannot and will not recant anything, for to go against conscience is neither right nor safe. God help me. Amen.' Tradition has it, and may very well be correct, that Luther added the famous words: 'Here I stand, I cannot do otherwise.' Despite the courage of Luther and the powerful impression which he made, Charles V's verdict was inevitable: 'A single friar who goes counter to Christianity for a thousand years must be wrong. Therefore I am resolved to stake my lands, my friends, my body, my blood, my life and my soul . . . I will have no more to do with him . . . I will proceed against him as a notorious heretic.' By the Edict of Worms, Luther was given twenty-one days' grace, after which he could be caught and put to death as a heretic. Shortly after signing the Edict, Charles left Germany and it was to be nine years before he returned.

Once again Luther owed his safety to Frederick the Wise. On his way back from Worms Luther suddenly disappeared; nobody knew if he were dead or alive. As the artist Dürer wrote in his diary: 'O God, if Luther be dead, who will henceforth expound to us the holy Gospel with such clearness? What, O God, might he not still have written for us in the ten or twenty years!' But Luther was not dead; he had been taken, on the Elector's orders, to his castle of the Wartburg, where he remained hidden for nearly a year, dressed as a knight and heavily bearded. It was a particularly frustrating time for Luther, who was forced to remain inactive while his cause became more and more entangled in the rival ambitions of the German princes, who supported or opposed reform often for purely political reasons. Yet the time was far from wasted. The months in the Wartburg enabled Luther to produce with incredible speed the first draft of his German translation of the New Testament. He was to revise this constantly over the next twenty-five years and to translate the Old Testament as well. 'I sweat blood and water in my efforts to render the prophets into the vulgar tongue. Good God! What a work it is! How difficult it is to make these Jew writers speak German.' It was a monumental achievement and so successful that the High German dialect in which it was written became the literary language of northern Europe.

Nevertheless, for Luther it was the worst possible time to be removed from the scene of action. None of his colleagues or supporters was capable of wisely directing the next step—the building of a reformed church. There were men like Andrew Carlstadt, violent and revolutionary in the changes which he began to make at Wittenberg. Pictures and images were torn down from the church walls; the Communion Service was celebrated by Carlstadt wearing, instead of vestments, his ordinary clothes and a hat with feathers; he also announced, although a priest, his forthcoming marriage. Everything in the service must be simple. 'Relegate organs, trumpets and flutes to the theatre,' he cried. 'When we should be meditating on the sufferings of Christ, we are reminded of Pyramus and Thisbe.' Men like the brilliant but gentle and scholarly Philip Melanchthon could do little to introduce changes more slowly. 'The dam has broken,' he wrote, 'and I cannot stem the waters.' Realizing that his whole cause was endangered, Luther decided at the risk of his life to come out of hiding and return to Wittenberg. It was the turning-point in his career.

From 1523 onwards the future of the Lutheran movement depended less upon what Luther did than upon events too big for him to control. It is true that he introduced his own less violent reforms at Wittenberg, where the services were in German instead of Latin and where hymn singing was important, many of the hymns being written by Luther himself. Furthermore, in 1525 Luther married. It was not a romantic occasion, for his wife,

A wedding portrait of Catherine von Bora, Luther's wife, by Cranach.

Katherine von Bora, a former nun, could find no other husband in spite of Luther's efforts on her behalf. In the end their married life was happy and Luther was proud of his six children. But the spread of Lutheranism now turned on the use which the princes, the knights, and the peasants made of his teaching.

225

The German knights led the way by claiming that some of Luther's ideas justified their private wars against the powerful princes, and their example encouraged new and much more serious peasant revolts. Two nights after Luther's great speech at Worms placards had appeared all over the town stamped with the ominous sign of the *Bundschuh*, showing that the peasants saw in Luther their champion. At first Luther was sympathetic, for he well knew their plight; but when in May 1524 revolts in many parts of Germany, especially in the south and west, broke out and many castles and cloisters were attacked, Luther feared that violence, which he had always hated, would ruin his cause. So in May 1525 he wrote a pamphlet 'Against the Murdering Hordes of Peasants', which contained the famous sentence: 'Therefore, let everyone who can, smite, slay and stab, secretly or openly, remembering that nothing can be more poisonous, hurtful or devilish than a rebel.' The peasants were crushed and never forgave Luther for apparently turning against them. Luther certainly saw the justice in the peasants' hatred of heavy taxes and feudal labour service, but, to save his Church from extinction, he felt it necessary to rely upon the princes as the one strong political force in Germany. This meant that Lutheranism would now never become the religion of all Germany. How far it would spread depended upon the complicated political situation, which it is necessary to understand.

To the Emperor, Charles V, 'the common enemy of the Christian name' was the Turks not the Lutherans. While devotedly loyal to the Church and determined to have no dealings with Luther, Charles fondly hoped that a peace could be patched up so that both sides could unite against the Turks. But he did not understand the princes. He underestimated the strength of Luther's hold on many of them and he did not at first realize how determined all the princes were to run their own affairs at all costs. In practice this meant that no Catholic prince would support the Emperor against a prince who chose to be a Lutheran. Thus no decision of the Diet was ever likely to be effective, nor could Charles ever be in Germany long enough to have any hope of success. This is why the Edict of Worms against Luther was a dead letter even after his protector, Frederick the Wise, had died in 1525, and why for over a quarter of a century no final solution was reached.

So in 1526 at the Diet of Speier it was agreed, as a temporary measure, to allow each prince to decide the religious faith in his own lands—a foreshadowing of what was eventually to be the agreed settlement. Three years later the Diet, again meeting at Speier, revoked the temporary decision. On 19 April 1529 the Lutherans in the Diet took up the challenge. 'Our great and urgent needs require us openly to protest against the said resolution.' This was the origin of the word 'Protestant'. In 1530 the Peace of

Philip Melancthon. A portrait painted by Cranach in 1523.

Cambrai enabled Charles to return to Germany bent on conciliation. The Lutheran case was in the hands of Philip Melanchthon, for Luther could not, as an outlaw, appear before the Diet. He it was who had been largely responsible for drawing up what was called the Confession of Augsburg, the statement of Lutheran doctrine. Believing that talk of peace was all 'smoke and lies', Luther was in agony lest Melanchthon should yield too much ground in debate. He need not have worried. As Luther had prophesied: 'Agreement on doctrine is plainly impossible, unless the pope will abolish his popedom.' The Confession was condemned and the Lutherans were given a year in which to make their peace and return to the Church. It was an idle threat. Thanks to the wars with Francis I, the danger from the Turks, and the independence of the princes, Lutheranism flourished steadily for the next fifteen years.

In 1546 Luther died. Although no longer in control of events, his personal reputation remained high and the fame of the university of Wittenberg grew steadily. Between 1520 and 1560 some 16,000 students, about one-third of whom were foreigners, came to the university. Many of them must have listened to Luther and returned to their own lands to spread his teaching. He was one of those great but complex characters about whom historians will always argue. He could be crude and rash and, like other great religious leaders, perhaps sometimes given to believing that his own ideas must be the voice of God. But by any standard of judgement he was a giant force in his day; he managed in his life and teaching to give effect to the deep-seated hatred of the abuses within the Church and at the same time to meet the longing for a simple spiritual life. Two days before he died he had written a text from St. John's Gospel in a friend's book—'If anyone obeys my teaching, he shall never know what it is to die.' As he wrote, he said: 'How incredible is such a text, and yet it is the truth. If a man takes God's word in full earnest and believes in it and then falls asleep, he slips away without noticing death and is safe on the other side.'

We saw in the last chapter that the warfare which Luther so hated could not be avoided, and with his death the future of the Reformation in Germany rested more than ever with the princes. Between 1546 and 1552 Charles V, with the help of foreign troops, tried to crush the Lutherans, who, in their turn, sought help from France against the Emperor. Neither side won, and in 1552 negotiations for peace began. By the Religious Peace of Augsburg in 1555 Lutheranism was officially recognized within the Empire. Each prince was to decide for himself whether he and his state should be Catholic or Lutheran. Those subjects who disliked their prince's decision were to be allowed to move to another state. It was no victory for toleration, for Lutherans disliked the idea of two religions within the country as much as the Catholics. The Peace really recognized the fact that the agreement was the only alternative to useless fighting and that neither Emperor nor Diet was of much account any longer. What, on looking back, we can now see is that the Peace marked the moment when Germany, the boiling pot of Europe at the start of the century, began to become the backwater which it remained for 300 years.

But long before the Peace was signed, the Reformation had spread far beyond the borders of Germany and to this we next turn.

(iii) The Reformation spreads

Although the Reformation had begun in Germany, it was not to remain a purely German movement. The kind of things which had angered Luther were to be found in many other European countries, where the influence of the writings of scholars like Erasmus had prepared the way for reform. As it happened, Erasmus usually disapproved of the amount of change which took place, though he was not by temperament a man to get involved in politics. Quite apart from disagreeing about matters of doctrine, he and Luther disliked each other intensely. The shy and retiring scholar, who only wanted reform of abuses not a break with the pope, had little in common with the forthright Luther, who revelled in a fight. But once the explosion had occurred in Germany, thanks to the printing press, Luther's ideas travelled as far afield as those of Erasmus. Furthermore, the spread of the Reformation was also greatly helped by having started in the middle of Europe. The stone hurled into the centre of the pond sent out ripples in ever widening circles; for Germany was at the heart of European trade, and many a German merchant carried Luther's ideas and writings with his merchandise along the main trade routes.

From the ancient Hansa ports on the Baltic Lutheranism spread into Scandinavia. Since 1397 all Scandinavia was supposed to be united under the Danish Crown; in fact, while Denmark had some measure of control over Norway and Iceland, it had less and less over Sweden, which finally became independent in 1523. In both Denmark and Sweden, thanks to the active support of their kings, a Lutheran State Church was firmly established by 1560. In Sweden reform and independence went hand in hand, and under the royal house of Vasa the foundations were laid which enabled her to become the champion of Protestantism in the next century. Further to the east, in Poland, Bohemia, and Hungary, lived communities of German merchants, who were very ready to speak of Luther, but who found conditions for reform far less favourable than in Scandinavia, in spite of the unpopularity of the Church, especially in Poland. For the advance of the Turks into Hungary and the threat to all these eastern kingdoms overshadowed everything else, and fear tended to make people cling to the Catholic Church rather than embark upon new and uncertain ways. On the other hand, Luther's ideas spread over the Alps to Venice and down through Italy; his books were well known in France; and Dutch Lutheran merchants spread the new gospel in London.

But it was not only Lutheran beliefs which came out of Germany. We have seen how at the time of the Peasants' War wild preachers stirred up the peasants, and how Luther was forced to leave the safety of the Wartburg to prevent his movement from being wrecked by extremists. Such people came to be known as Anabaptists from the only belief which they held in common—that baptism should be for grown-ups and not for children. Apart from this they were only linked by the certainty of each Anabaptist that he had been specially chosen by God and that in anything to do with religion he could not possibly be wrong. Anarchy nearly always resulted when they came together in any number: churches were despoiled of statues, pictures, images, and relics; organs were destroyed and much damage done. No wonder that they were heartily disliked and opposed by all the great reformers. At best they were harmless and deluded folk, but many of their leaders were at times lunatic and dangerous revolutionaries. In the sixteenth century they were chiefly important for their nuisance value; but in the next century they were to have a short spell of power in Cromwell's England and in the New England colonies in America.

Lutheranism was never destined to take firm hold, save in northern Germany and Scandinavia. This was largely because here the cause of the Reformation was supported by the rulers and those in authority: where it failed to win this support it petered out. However, this did not mean that everywhere else in Europe the Catholic Church triumphed. For in the year after Luther made his protest against Indulgences a similar protest was made in Zürich. From Switzerland and, above all, from the city of Geneva a far more powerful attack on the authority of the Church than ever Luther made was to be launched.

The success of the Reformation in Switzerland is partly explained by the state of the country at the start of the sixteenth century. Although officially part of the Empire until 1648, the Swiss had virtually won their independence by 1500 and their country was now a very loose Confederation of thirteen largely self-governing cantons. There was, however, no real unity in Switzerland: the Alps had always made communications particularly difficult; there was no love lost between the poor peasant cantons and the richer and more powerful city cantons like Zürich, Berne, or Basle; there were differences of language between the cantons; and five Swiss bishoprics were under the control of foreign archbishops; more than this, there was no capital city, no head of state, no common law, no common coinage. There was a great deal of peasant unrest, as there was in the near-by Black Forest area of Germany, and most of the towns were not as wealthy as they once had been. Switzerland was in fact a poor country, forced to import both corn and salt, which were paid for by its chief export—soldiers. So by 1520 Switzerland was neither a very contented nor a well governed country and some kind of revolution could easily occur. As in Germany, it was not these conditions which caused the Reformation but they did enable it to succeed.

Two men dominated the Swiss Reformation: Huldreich Zwingli (1484–1531), a citizen of Zürich, who brought what came to be called the 'Reformed' Church into existence; and a Frenchman, John Calvin (1509–64), who settled in Geneva and gave the Reformed Church its organization and fighting spirit.

Zwingli was much the most attractive personality among the Reformers. Although he was born only fifty-two days after Luther, he always seems much younger than his German contemporary. This may partly be due to his comparatively short life, but more probably to his happy and carefree outlook. For Zwingli never seems to have been troubled by the sense of personal wickedness which caused Luther such agonies of mind; in fact he made no secret of having lived a far from blameless life in his earlier days. He was born in the hamlet of Wildhaus, high up in the mountains of eastern Switzerland, where the family farm-house can still be seen. It has been said that Wildhaus lay so exactly on the central watershed of Europe that the rain which fell on one side of the red-tiled roof of the village church ran into a streamlet which fed the Rhône, while the rain falling on the other side eventually reached the Rhine. This could be taken as a pleasant symbol of Zwingli's position as a reformer, midway between Luther and Calvin, prepared to make more drastic changes than Luther but not to go as far as Calvin. His family was closely connected with the political and religious life of the canton, and Zwingli himself, after studying at the universities of Vienna and Basle, where he developed a great admiration for Erasmus, became parish priest in the neighbouring canton of Glarus in 1506. His duties twice took him to Italy as an army chaplain to the mercenaries recruited in his district and he was present at the battle of Marignano in 1515. On returning home he denounced the whole mercenary system as likely to destroy the simple life of the Swiss peasant.

In 1518 Zwingli was appointed common preacher, a minor post, in the cathedral at Zürich and it was then that his real importance began. In a long series of powerful sermons he started the Swiss Reformation and guided its development. He became such a popular preacher that in order to reach the country folk with his message he used every Friday to preach in the market-place. That some reform of the Swiss Church was needed can be seen from an account of the

Ulrich Zwingli. A portrait painted by Hans Asper in 1531.

times written by Zwingli's son-in-law and successor, Henry Bullinger, though perhaps he may have been over eager to paint too black a picture. 'At one time during these years, when all the deacons of the Confederation were assembled together, there were found not over three who were well read in the Bible. The others acknowledged that none of them had read even the New Testament. . . . For among the clergy there was almost no studying, but their exercise was in feeding and in the practice of all luxuries.' There was more indifference than hatred shown by the Swiss people towards the Church, and opposition to the papacy was less marked than in some other countries, largely because the popes were the most regular customers when it came to hiring Swiss troops. But the canton of Zürich was certainly ready to listen to the Reformation teaching.

Zürich was a city of some 6,000 inhabitants and there were about another 50,000 persons in the rest of the canton. Working in close alliance with the powerful city council, Zwingli set out to reform the life of both city and canton. His earlier reforms were more political than religious, for he was always a great patriot, and to him the good citizen and the good Christian were one and the same. As a child in the long evenings in the farm-house he had heard not only Bible stories but also tales of Swiss heroes and with his musical family he learned to sing all the patriotic folk songs. 'When I was a child,' he said, 'if anyone said a word against my Fatherland, it put my back up at once.' So he continued to argue against the use of Swiss mercenaries and to protest against the loss of much-needed Swiss money when the Indulgence against which Luther had protested was sold in Zürich. As it happened, the pope was so afraid that the Swiss might stop hiring out their troops to him that he stopped the sale of the Indulgence in Switzerland himself.

It was between 1522 and 1525 that the most sweeping religious changes were steadily made. Zwingli always claimed that he was not influenced by Luther. 'I have not learned the teaching of Christ from Luther but from the very Word of God,' he said; but he probably owed more to Luther and to events in Germany than he realized. Everything had to pass the searching test of being allowed in Scripture; if not, it must go. Images and pictures and music in the service were soon denounced, though he had no intention of letting the Anabaptists take charge. Indeed, he approved of the drowning of one of their wilder leaders. He attacked fasting in Lent but did not join his friends in openly eating smoked sausage on a special occasion. One of the features of the Reformation in Switzerland was the use of public debate in order to decide on the course to be followed. In January 1523 Zwingli submitted 67 Articles for discussion, and their acceptance by the city council meant that changes came more quickly. The authority first of the Bishop of

Constance and then of the pope was denied; monasteries and nunneries were closed down and the work of poor relief taken over by the council; clerical marriage was allowed and Zwingli found himself a widow to be his wife. Since everything turned on knowledge of the Scriptures, 'prophesyings', or popular debates and tests of understanding the Bible took place in churches. By 1525 the Mass gave place to a simple service devised by Zwingli in which the bread was 'carried round by appointed ministers on large wooden trenchers from one seat to the next' and the wine in wooden beakers, so that 'no pomp come back again'.

But it was not enough to 'purify' worship. The 'Reformed' Church set great store on the need to ensure that its members lived virtuous lives. When a new lawcourt to deal with the marriage disputes, hitherto heard before the bishop, was set up, it soon became a watchdog over public morals. Spies discovered and then reported to the court lovers who stood in doorways or who hid behind barns. A watch was kept on women who received male visitors, and even innkeepers were expected to keep an eye out for bad behaviour in their taverns. This was to go much farther in Geneva under Calvin but it began in Zürich.

Of course the reforms made by Zwingli and the city council could only apply to the canton of Zürich, but before long Berne and Basle followed Zürich's example. There was, however, no possibility that Zwingli's ideas would be accepted all over Switzerland. He soon began to find that, while he was certain that his actions were justified in Scripture, there were always a large number of people who interpreted Scripture very differently. Moreover, Zwingli began to be unpopular both with those who unfairly said his reforms were as wild as those of the Anabaptists and also with those who did not wish to lose financially by the abolition of mercenaries. Most important of all was the fear of any kind of central control; like the German princes, the cantons were determined to remain independent. So, as in Germany, the cantons on both sides began to look for allies. Zwingli saw the urgent need of help from the German Protestants but this could not happen unless he and Luther could see eye to eye. They were deeply divided over the nature of the Communion Service, and a formal discussion at Marburg in 1529 failed to heal the breach. In 1531 war broke out, and the Catholics marched against Zürich and completely defeated the Zwinglians at the battle of Kappel. In this battle Zwingli, with twenty-four other pastors, fell in action—a Christian and patriotic warrior to the end. At the Peace of Kappel, which followed the battle, it was agreed, as at Augsburg a quarter of a century later, that each canton should have the same control over its religious life as it had over its political affairs.

France was a country which at first seemed likely to welcome the teaching of the Reformers. The Gallican Church (the name used for the Catholic Church in France) had long enjoyed considerable independence of Rome and had never been particularly eager to do just what the pope wanted. In fact the idea that the Church should be reformed by a General Council had been popular among leading Frenchmen. Furthermore, in the early days of his reign Francis I encouraged the humanist preachers, who found themselves even more enthusiastically welcomed at the court of his devout and intelligent sister, Margaret of Angoulême. Thus it was that the monk, Jacques Lefèvre (*c.* 1455–1536), a distinguished teacher of mathematics and physics before turning at the age of over 50 to a scholarly study of the Scriptures, was able to put forward ideas very similar to, though less revolutionary than, those of Luther ten years or so before Luther made his protest. In 1520 Lefèvre and his followers joined Briçonnet, Bishop of Meaux, in his attempt to reform his diocese and the bishop's court quickly became another centre for new ideas in religion. Before very long Luther's books were circulating freely in France.

Unfortunately for the Reformers, this happy state was not to last. Opposition to the new ideas had for some time come principally from two sources: the Sorbonne, which was the theological faculty of the university of Paris, and from the Parlement of Paris, the powerful judicial branch of the Royal Council (totally different from the English parliament), which existed to defend and extend the royal power. So long as the Reformers were protected by Francis, these two bodies could do little. But after the battle of Pavia in 1525, Francis was a prisoner in Madrid and a start was made in stamping out anything which seemed like heresy. Once released from Madrid, Francis himself began to change his attitude. The Concordat with the pope in 1516 had given him all the power that he wanted over the Gallican Church, and he did not need the Reformers as allies. Besides, they began to go much further than he liked, and so he did nothing to stop men like Lefèvre from being driven into exile. Serious persecution began in 1534. When people awoke on the morning of 18 October they saw on the walls of several French towns *placards*, or posters, denouncing the Mass. One was even fixed to the door of Francis's bedroom. Francis was genuinely shocked at an attack on the Mass and horrified to discover the extent to which heresy had taken root among his subjects. He had no hesitation in supporting the Sorbonne and the Parlement in their determination to stop the evil of heresy by a campaign of burning at the stake and exile. Among those who fled before this persecution was John Calvin.

Calvin was born in July 1509 at Noyon in Picardy. His father was a not very prosperous lawyer who was determined that his clever son should have the best possible education. Since he hoped that the boy would one day become a priest, he was able to get financial help from the cathedral authorities to meet the cost of school and university. In 1523 Calvin entered the university of Paris where, according to Erasmus, students were mobbed and hunted in the streets, lived in lodgings of ill-repute, used or heard foul language, and were expected to live indecent lives—a forbidding experience for a 'timid and fearful' theological student of only 14, as he described himself. 'Ever since I was a child,' Calvin later wrote, 'my father intended me for theology; but . . . as he considered that the study of the law commonly enriched those who followed it, this expectation made him incontinently change his mind. That is why I was withdrawn from the study of philosophy and put to the study of the law, to which I strove to devote myself faithfully in obedience to my father.' So Calvin dutifully left Paris for Orleans, where, in addition to his legal studies, he learned Greek and won fame as a rising humanist scholar. 'God, however, in his hidden providence, at last made me turn in another direction.' In 1531 Calvin's father died and Calvin felt free to return to Paris to renew his classical and Biblical studies and in 1532 to publish a brilliant commentary on a work of the Latin writer, Seneca.

Somewhere about 1533 Calvin underwent some kind of religious experience, which led him to abandon the Catholicism in which he had been brought up and join the Reformers. It seems to have been an intellectual conversion, very different from the agonies of mind experienced by Luther.

The more closely I considered myself, the more my conscience was pricked by sharp goadings; so much that no other relief or comfort remained to me except to deceive myself by forgetting. But since nothing better offered itself, I went on still in the way I had begun: then, however, there arose quite another form of teaching, not to turn away from the profession of Christianity but to reduce it to its own source, and to restore it, as it were, cleansed from all filthiness to its own purity. But I, offended by this novelty, could hardly listen to it willingly; and must confess that at first I valiantly and bravely resisted. For since men are naturally obstinate and opinionated to maintain the institutions they have once received, it irked me much to confess that I had been fed upon error and ignorance all my life.

However, the influence of Calvin's humanist friends, who were mostly Protestants, and the effect of studying the writings of Erasmus and Luther, combined to force Calvin to throw in his lot wholeheartedly with the cause of the Reformation. He became completely convinced of the overwhelming power and majesty of God and of himself as a man under orders, chosen by God to proclaim the truth. Thus, from the moment of the affair of the *placards*, Calvin's life was in danger and he fled from France to settle in 1535 at Basle.

1536 was to prove the critical year of Calvin's life. It was at Basle in this year that he published the first edition of his great work, the *Institutes of the Christian Religion*, a book written in Latin and originally in six chapters, but expanded over the years until by 1559 there were eighty chapters. For a young man of twenty-seven to write a book setting out the first reasoned statement of the Protestant faith was an astonishing feat. Calvin's name became famous throughout Europe and he was quickly recognized as the intellectual leader of the Reformers. No longer was the Protestant cause dependent upon the personality of any one man, such as Luther or Zwingli. If men wanted to know what Protestantism was they could read for themselves an account written with the clarity and precision of a lawyer but warmed with the passionate sincerity of a Reformer. It is impossible to exaggerate the importance of this book; its influence grew even greater after 1541 when Calvin produced the first version in French, a landmark in the history of French prose writing.

There was another reason why 1536 was so important in Calvin's life: it is the year when he first came to Geneva. He had intended to spend only a night in the city on his way to Strasbourg but, except for a brief period of three years, he was destined to remain there for the rest of his life and to make it the capital of western Protestantism. What Rome was for the Catholic Church, Geneva was, for a while, for the Reformed Church. Geneva in 1536 was a turbulent city of some 16,000 inhabitants, which had recently become a free city after a thirty-year struggle to get rid of its two overlords, the Duke of Savoy and its own Prince Bishop. In this struggle it had been greatly helped by the powerful canton of Berne, eager both to extend Protestant territory and to add to its own influence. Geneva was very ready for the Reformation—not only had it driven out its bishop but economic decline and lessening importance had led to a growing recklessness. Sober business habits gave way to the taking of wild risks in trade, while the citizens of Geneva had gained a reputation for excessive drinking, gambling, and immorality. The victorious party in the city, known as the Eidgenossen or sworn companions, a name soon to become famous in its French form of Huguenot, had encouraged visits from travelling Protestant preachers, the most effective being the French firebrand, Guillaume Farel, who had once belonged to the group of Meaux (see p. 233). Farel, a powerful preacher but a bad organizer, had found the task of reforming Geneva more than he could manage by himself. Learning that the author of the *Institutes* was actually in the city, Farel sought out Calvin's lodgings, overbore all Calvin's protestations that he was only fitted for a life of quiet scholarship, and threatening him with God's curse if he failed to help with the cause of reform, forced Calvin to abandon his journey and stay in Geneva.

John Calvin. A portrait by an unknown artist.

So for two years Calvin and Farel, with no official position in the city, guided the Reformation in Geneva. They set out to do this in two ways: by establishing a fully reformed Church and at the same time by transforming the behaviour and morals of all the citizens. At first they went too fast for the liking of the city council, and in September 1538 they were expelled. With great relief Calvin went to Strasbourg, where he was supremely happy as a scholar and teacher. It was only with the utmost reluctance that in September 1541, after months of debate, Calvin agreed to the earnest entreaties of the council that he should return to Geneva. Knowing what lay ahead of him 'in that place of torment', his naturally timid nature shrank from becoming involved in political affairs; but, once convinced that this was God's will for him, 'I submit my mind bound and fettered to obedience to God'. Calvin had not exaggerated the strife and bitterness which he would have to face among this 'perverse and illnatured people'. Officially he was nothing more than the leading minister to a quarrelsome community; his authority came from his iron will-power, which subdued his instinctive fears, his integrity, and his complete certainty of what had to be done. Yet it was fourteen years before his position was fully secure and he did not become a citizen of Geneva until 1556. At no time was he free from the danger that his plans would be overridden by the city council, not even when he had become the acknowledged leader of the Reformed Church and was maintaining a vast correspondence all over western Europe.

By the time that Calvin's *Institutes* appeared in its final edition in 1559, it contained all that he believed about God and about man's place and duty in this world and the next. The book is our main source for understanding what may seem to be the rather grim and forbidding doctrine which he taught and the austere and joyless life which he imposed on the citizens of Geneva. He had always revered Luther as his chief teacher and he set out to create a Church and a community which, he believed, would be the only way to put Luther's teachings into practice. But since his legal mind took everything to its logical conclusion, his own doctrines were much more rigid and uncompromising than Luther's. For the same reason they were also much more effective and lasting. What did he believe?

To Calvin God was majestic, overwhelming, and remote. He had created the world simply so that man could know of his existence. Man is hopelessly evil and can do nothing by his own efforts to win salvation in the next world. 'Our nature is not merely bereft of good, but is so productive of every kind of evil that it cannot be inactive.' Christ came into the world not primarily to save men from their sins but to prove that God exists. From the very first moment of creation God had decided that some men would ultimately be saved, while others would be damned. 'In conformity to the clear teaching of Scripture we assert by an eternal and immutable counsel God hath once for all determined both whom He would admit to salvation and whom He would condemn to destruction.' Since all men are evil, those who are saved illustrate the mercy of God and those who are condemned cannot complain of God's justice. Nobody but God knows who are the elect (the saved) and who the condemned. 'The Lord will have mercy upon whom He will have mercy.'

This is the doctrine known as predestination, a doctrine which Calvin certainly taught, but which was developed far more remorselessly by his followers. It might seem that if each man's fate was already predestined there was not much point in trying to live a blameless life. But 'the eyes of God alone see who will endure to the end' and so it was essential for everyone to try to live as one of the

elect. In practice the true Calvinist came to believe that 'by confession of faith, by exemplary life and participation in the sacraments'
there was a good chance that all would be well and there was a
comforting feeling that God was on his side. As William Tyndale,
working in Cologne and Worms in 1525 on his English version of the
Bible, which had later to be smuggled into England, translated a
verse from the book of Genesis: 'The Lorde was with Joseph, and
he was a luckie felowe' (Genesis 39:2).

Within two months of his return to Geneva, Calvin put forward
his plan for organizing the religious life of the city, for he was
adamant 'that no Church could exist unless a fixed rule of life were
established, such as is made known to us by the Word of God'. His
model was the early Christian community described in the Acts of
the Apostles. All citizens were assumed to be faithful members of
the Church, but to remain faithful they needed order and discipline.
There were to be four groups of officials to direct the life of this
Church: pastors to preach and administer the sacraments; doctors
to instruct people in doctrine and the Scriptures—for Calvin
passionately believed in the importance of education; elders 'to have
oversight of the life of everyone, to admonish amicably those whom
they see to be erring or to be living a disordered life'; and deacons
to care for the poor. Calvin was determined to make everyone
conform to his ideas but, as has been said, the city council did not
invariably support him. In fact, he had often to rely on numbers of
immigrants, mostly Frenchmen, whom he encouraged to settle in
Geneva, as his helpers and allies.

It was not so much the organization of the Church which aroused
opposition as the minute control of peoples' daily lives. Not many
of us today would enjoy living in Calvin's Geneva. In the first place,
attendance at a number of sermons was compulsory, and there came
to be seventeen official sermons each week, five on Sundays, with
the first at dawn, and two on each week-day, all carefully timed to
make it possible to listen to the lot. We must not imagine that our
views on this would necessarily have been shared by the citizens, for
there is not much evidence that this spate of sermons was resented.
On the other hand, many must have disliked the rigid control of the
moral life of the city. Every Thursday a body called the Consistory
met to make and enforce laws affecting every side of peoples' lives,
and from the minutes of its meetings we can gain a clear picture of
the ways by which Calvin sought to drive the devil out of Geneva.

The dress of men and women, their hair styles, the food served at
their tables, the jokes which they made in the street, the entertain-
ment in their houses, were strictly controlled, while dancing and
lewd songs were completely prohibited. In the business life of the
city high prices or any form of sharp practice were punished. It

must have been like living in a glasshouse, for everyone was enjoined to watch his neighbour and to report to the authorities the least fall from grace. At times Calvin could go too far, as when in 1546 he persuaded the city council to close all taverns and replace them with godly houses of refreshment, where there was grace before eating and a Bible close at hand for consultation. Not surprisingly they failed to pay their way and the taverns were reopened. Punishments were savage. Wrong-doers were invariably excluded from the Communion Service and thus shown up before their neighbours; whipping and banishment were frequent; for adultery death was the usual penalty. One young man was actually beheaded for striking his parents. For the blasphemer or the atheist there could be no mercy. In 1547 Jacques Gruet, the Secretary of State and an opponent of Calvin, was executed as an atheist. More famous was the case of Servetus, a noted Spanish free-thinker already denounced by Calvin, who unwisely decided to come to Geneva, hoping to dispute with Calvin. His presence in the city was reported by Calvin, who implacably approved of his being burned at the stake in 1553.

To us Geneva must have been a grim and often a frightening place to live in, but it was not so to everyone at the time. For example, John Knox, the reformer who was to bring Calvinism to Scotland, was ecstatic in praise of what he found: 'Geneva, where I neither fear man nor am ashamed to say that this is the most perfect school of Christ that ever was in the earth since the days of the apostles. In other places, I confess Christ to be truly preached; but manners and religion to be so sincerely reformed, I have not seen in any other place.' And to many a Genevan citizen it seemed that at long last there was a city in which men and women worshipped God 'not only with their lips but with their lives'.

Despite his incessant labours for Geneva, Calvin was also greatly concerned to ensure that his ideas spread and took root in his native France. In due course they were to penetrate the Netherlands and take firm hold in Scotland. There were two main reasons why Calvinism spread more rapidly and put down deeper roots than Lutheranism. First, the Calvinist church organization could be set up anywhere with ease; it provided for small tightly-knit communities of believers running their own affairs, difficult for the authorities to destroy and often difficult even to discover. More important was the effect of the doctrine of predestination, for this gave assurance to ardent Calvinists that, as the elect of God, it mattered little what men might do to them, for ultimately they could not fail. Calvinism was a stark faith, forged by a man easy to admire but difficult to like, a faith well suited to war. And war it was soon to be.

Chapter 9
'Turks, Infidels and Hereticks'

'O merciful God, who hast made all men . . . have mercy upon all
. . . Turks, Infidels and Hereticks, and take from them all ignorance,
hardness of heart, and contempt of thy Word . . .' These words will
be found in one of the collects which Cranmer's Prayer Book
appointed to be read on Good Friday, though it is seldom used
today. It is a heartfelt prayer for the speedy conversion of the Turks
and other infidels to Christianity, not least so that they should cease
to be a danger to Europe. Few of the great movements of peoples in
history are more important than the outpouring of Turkish and
Mongolian peoples from central Asia into the Middle East, a movement which affected almost the whole of the then civilized world and
which lasted for some five hundred years from about A.D. 1000.
Europe had already had experience of infidel attacks from the east
before this. Ever since the death of Muhammad in the seventh
century his Muslim followers had fought their way over much of
the Middle East, along the North African shore, up through Spain
and over the Pyrenees, until checked at Tours in France and driven
back into Spain where, as we have seen, many settled permanently.
But the Turkish advance was something quite new.

From about A.D. 1000 Turkish tribes living in Turkestan began
to move westward in search of new pastures, because their own had
started to dry up. On they came, over the river Oxus, through
Persia and into Asia Minor, until they found themselves up against
the eastern outposts of the Byzantine empire or in lands which had
for long been part of the Muslim world. Nomadic warriors from the
steppe lands found no difficulty in accepting much of the Muslim
faith, particularly when it meant fighting a Holy War against all
unbelievers. But they never became submerged in the Muslim
world, for they kept their own language and traditions, and from the
eleventh century onwards the Turks steadily became the chief
power in Asia Minor, except for the years 1206-27 when the armies
of the Mongol chief, Genghis Khan, swept all before them and
destroyed the great Arab civilization in the Middle East. In the case
of the Turks there was not just one invasion, as with the Mongols;
the Turkish attack was much more like an incoming tide with each
wave marking the irresistible forward march of yet another warrior
band.

One such band, destined to play the decisive part in the coming
centuries, was dominated by the Osmanli, or Ottoman, family. The

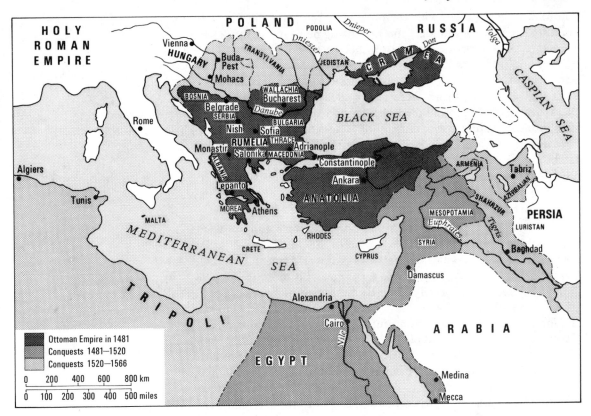

The Growth of the Ottoman Empire.

fame of this family dated from a leader called Ertughul, who died in 1281, and who, so his successors claimed, had been descended through twenty-one ancestors from Noah; later still another thirty-one ancestors were conveniently discovered, to make the family tree look even more impressive. The leaders of these bands were known as Ghazis, warriors of the Faith. They were very roughly the Muslim equivalent of the Christian knight; they were first and foremost fighters and largely uninterested in any form of settled government. Although these Turkish invaders came to dominate the Muslim world in the Middle East, they actually strengthened Islam by providing an endless supply of fierce and seasoned soldiers to fight against the Christians, with the result that by 1300 all that remained of the Byzantine empire in Asia Minor, apart from a few isolated cities, were the plains overlooking the Sea of Marmora and the Black Sea coastline for about a hundred miles to the eastward.

The rapid rise of the Ottoman state was due partly to geography and partly to the skill of its rulers. The main line of the Mongol invasions had not touched it, and ahead lay Byzantine lands ready to be conquered. Ertughul's son, Osman (1281–1326), proved to be a leader of genius. He attracted other Ghazis and their followers to

241

join him, dazzling them with the prospect of ceaseless fighting and unlimited chances of plunder, and promising new land to those who wanted it. Moreover, he was clever enough to keep control of the fighters and settlers who began to pour into his comparatively small state. By 1301 he had fought his way to within sight of Constantinople itself and Ottoman Turks were also quickly spreading along the Black Sea coast. Before he died Osman had turned a small border state into the leading power among the Turks and the Ghazi spearhead against Christendom. His son, Orhan (1326–62), continued his father's work, gave himself the title of Sultan, and gained control of most of the lands up to the Bosphorus. Europe now beckoned.

*   *   *

Ever since the time when Rome and the Western Empire went down into darkness before the barbarian invaders, the Eastern Empire had kept alive Constantine's vision of world rule. His capital, Byzantium or Constantinople, was far larger and more impressive than any other European city. The Byzantine emperors had a paid army and a paid civil service, they controlled the Orthodox Church, and for over six centuries Constantinople itself was both the centre of Greek learning and the heart of Christian civilization. However, from about the start of the twelfth century the power of the Byzantine empire had begun to decline. Crusaders and Seljuk Turks had fought each other and had seized parts of the empire of Asia Minor. In 1204 Constantinople was besieged and sacked in the horror and scandal of the Fourth Crusade, when so-called crusaders from the west, urged on by Venice, preferred to regard Orthodox Christians as their enemies rather than the Muslims in Palestine. The Greek emperor was removed, and for over fifty years a Latin empire existed. From 1261, although a new line of Greek emperors ruled in Constantinople, it was soon clear that the great days of the Eastern Empire were over. In the final 200 years of its history the empire gradually dwindled and broke up. On the eastern flank the Ottoman Turks, as we have just seen, had by 1300 overrun Asia Minor, while in the Balkans differences of race and language, inflamed by national feelings, led to the setting-up of a series of separate Greek kingdoms in place of a united Greek empire—Albania, Serbia, Bulgaria, and Rumania.

*   *   *

For a long while the Byzantine emperors feared the Turks less than they feared the troubles facing them much nearer home. Powerful nobles were now refusing to pay taxes or to provide their quota of soldiers. There was no money to pay for a mercenary army, for Venice and Genoa were busily engaged in diverting the empire's commerce to themselves. There was frequent civil war within the empire; the rich were attacked by the poor; the aggressive Serbs under their national hero, Stephen Dushan, were a more immediate menace than the Turks. This is why the emperors did not try to prevent their generals from making their own arrangements to hire Turkish troops. In 1344 the chief Byzantine minister, John Cantacuzenus, even married his daughter to Orhan himself. The Sultan in return kindly gave his father-in-law a present of 6,000 men to help him in his successful bid to become emperor; but when eleven years later Cantacuzenus in his turn fell from power, Orhan decided to invade Europe on his own account. Turks returning from the Greek wars to Asia Minor had no doubt where their future expansion should lie. Within six years Orhan had overrun Thrace.

Orhan was more than a great soldier. He skilfully built up an organized state without destroying the Ghazi spirit of endless adventure. This growing state now inevitably included an increasing number of Christians, who found that if they accepted his rule they would be allowed to keep their churches and their customs; but that, if they resisted, it was likely that one-fifth of a town's population would be enslaved, others from the surrounding countryside sent to forced labour, and boys made to join the Turkish armies for life. These armies Orhan reorganized into two distinct parts: a locally based militia, whose members were given land in return for their service, and a paid army, often hired for a single campaign, but including the famous corps of Janissaries, of whom more will be said later.

Murad I (1362–89), after putting a half-brother to death to remove a possible rival, took brilliant advantage of this army. He set up his own European capital at Adrianople and isolated Constantinople except by sea. As the Turks advanced they recruited Greek soldiers and administrators in the conquered territory. Hordes of Turks with their wives and families poured into Thrace unchecked and there was nothing to stop Murad from overrunning Macedonia and much of Bulgaria. By 1386 his European empire stretched from Monastir, near the border of Albania, to as far north as Nish.

In face of this growing danger the Serbs at long last organized a Balkan alliance against the Turks and in 1387 won their sole victory against the invaders. Vengeance was swift. In June 1389 on the plain of Kossovo (the Plain of the Blackbirds) Murad's forces faced those of the alliance. Early in the morning, before the battle started, a Serbian deserter, who promised to betray the Christian battle positions, was allowed to enter Murad's tent. Leaning forward, he suddenly stabbed the Sultan to the heart before he himself could be struck down. Murad's eldest son, Bayezit, at once took command, carefully suppressing all news of his father's death until the Turkish victory was complete. Then to make quite sure that he had no rivals, Bayezit gave orders that his younger brother should immediately be strangled. From his father, Bayezit had inherited the strongest military power in south-east Europe. By now the Greek emperor was little more than a Turkish vassal; indeed in 1373 the emperor John V had actually fought alongside Murad in Asia Minor.

Bayezit (1389–1403) was a hot-tempered man, more self-indulgent and a less able soldier than his father, but his reign opened brilliantly. By the end of the century he was master of the lands along the Danube frontier and in 1402 he appeared before Constantinople, haughtily ordering the emperor, who had for some time been forced to pay tribute in money and soldiers to the Sultan, to surrender. To Bayezit's envoys the emperor replied: 'Tell your master that we are weak, but that we trust in God, who can make us strong and can put down the mightiest from their seats.' Brave words which sprang partly from religious faith, perhaps even more from exciting news coming out of the East. Anatolia itself was now threatened by a Turk descended on the female line from Genghis Khan—Timur the Tartar, the man who figures in English plays as Tamberlane, or Timur the Lame. Timur, with an empire stretching from the borders of China and the Bay of Bengal to the Mediterranean, was as ruthless as his Mongol ancestor and had for some time been threatening Ottoman lands in Asia Minor. Timur's arrival in Anatolia forced Bayezit to abandon the siege of Constantinople and to bring his forces quickly back from Europe in order to face the vast Tartar army, with its corps of Indian elephants, at Ankara. The Sultan was no match for Timur; he was completely defeated and taken into captivity, where he died, probably by his own hand, in 1403. Having sacked the main Anatolian cities, Timur returned to Samarkand, only to die two years later while intent on plans for the conquest of China.

This might appear to have been the heaven-sent opportunity for the Western nations to unite and remove for ever the Turkish menace. It is true that the Ottomans had been humiliated by Timur, but they had not been destroyed and Timur was now dead. Far more important is the fact that by now hundreds of thousands of Turks were firmly settled in the Balkans, their numbers having been recently increased by those families, and even tribes, who had fled to escape the Tartar hordes. We know that the Genoese at this time made a small fortune out of ferrying Turkish families from Asia to Europe, and it has been calculated that by 1410 more Turks were living in Europe than in Anatolia. So even the strongest and most united Christian coalition, had it ever been formed, would have been powerless to drive the Turks out of Europe. Nor was there any chance of such a coalition. Eastern Orthodox Christians, who never forgave the events of the Fourth Crusade, hated Rome and Western Christianity almost more than they hated the Turk. Not long before Constantinople fell to the Turks an imperial official could say: 'I would rather see the Muslim turban in the midst of the city than

Part of the walls of Constantinople. This is an Ottoman tower called Yedi Kule.

the Latin mitre.' Even the formal reuniting of the two Churches in 1439 did little to heal the breach and no help came to the eastern emperor in his troubles. Despite ten years of fighting among Bayezit's sons and the reign of Muhammad I (1413–21), who kept on good terms with the emperor while he healed the wounds of civil war, there was no sign of any serious decline in the Ottoman power.

Under Sultan Muhammad II, 'the Conqueror' (1451–81), who was by far the ablest and most formidable ruler of the Ottoman dynasty up to this time, the Turks became a greater danger than ever before. While his father's widow was formally offering her congratulations on the start of the new reign, her young child was being smothered in his bath on Muhammad's orders. European ambassadors reported that the West had little to fear from the Sultan, whose amiability and peaceful protestations they unwisely took at their face value. But at the age of 19 Muhammad was already a dangerous man, intelligent, ruthless, and determined to achieve

245

his ambitions. He was striking in appearance and, especially as he grew older, his piercing eyes, hooked nose, and full red lips reminded contemporaries of a parrot about to eat ripe cherries. An unhappy childhood had made him secretive and unwilling to trust anyone, but drink could make him cordial, and he enjoyed the friendship of scholars and artists.

Two years earlier Constantine XI had become what proved to be the last Byzantine emperor. He was a competent soldier, a good administrator, and, above all, a man of great integrity, who inspired affectionate loyalty among all who served him. Poor man! he had need of every possible friend in a city that had been torn with religious dissensions ever since 1439, when an unpopular reunion between the Roman and the Greek Orthodox Churches had been negotiated. Nor, despite words of encouragement, could he expect any real help from the western European powers if an attack were to be launched on Constantinople. They preferred to believe that Muhammad II was a peaceful Sultan rather than send armed help to Constantine. In 1452 a solitary cardinal arrived from Rome and celebrated Mass in the church of Sancta Sophia.

Muhammad lost little time. In the winter of 1451 he began to build a large castle on the European side of the Bosphorus, which cut off supplies of corn to Constantinople. Protesting ambassadors were imprisoned and decapitated. About 80,000 troops and perhaps a further 20,000 irregulars and camp-followers were asembled to attack the fourteen miles of city walls, defended by less than 7,000 men. In addition, Muhammad had engaged the services of a Hungarian engineer to make a monster cannon nearly twenty-seven feet in length and other smaller cannon. On 5 April 1453 the Turkish army appeared before the walls of the city from the Golden Horn to the Sea of Marmora and a strong Turkish fleet was at sea. The sole help sent to Constantine from the West came in the form of supplies in three Genoese ships, which fought their way into harbour. The first Turkish attack was launched on 18 April and was beaten off, as was the naval attack next day. On 20 April four more Christian ships tried to get into harbour in a terrific battle, which Muhammad watched on horseback, often riding into the sea to encourage or to curse his sailors as the Christian ships were suddenly blown into harbour in a strong wind. Muhammad now realized that to capture the city he must attack by sea as well as by land and that a successful attack by sea meant getting his ships into the Golden Horn, which was protected by a great chain thrown across the entrance. He had already employed thousands of workmen to make a road from the shore of the Bosphorus over the intervening ridge to the edge of the Golden Horn; on each side of this road lengths of timber were placed to make a kind of slipway, carefully greased with oil and fat. The ships were then hoisted on to the slipway and hauled uphill by the

Muhammad II. A fifteenth-century miniature.

246

workmen. Nicolo Barbaro, who was in Constantinople during the siege, described vividly what he saw:

> The crews which followed each ship, overjoyed by what was going on and by the thought of what was to come next, boarded their craft, when at the top of the hill, as though they were at sea, and quickly travelled downhill towards the Golden Horn. Some of the sailors unfurled the sails . . . and the wind got into the sails and filled them. Others, sitting on the rowing benches, held their oars in their hands and pretended to row, while the overseers ran up and down the high wooden track spurring on their men with whistles, shouts and lashes from the whip. Thus the Turkish vessels, strange voyagers, slid across the country as if sailing the sea.

On 23 April seventy-two Turkish ships lay at anchor within the Golden Horn. The Christians defended the city with great courage but, with no help from Western allies, the outcome was certain. By the evening of 29 May all was over and, in accordance with Muslim custom, a city which had refused to surrender was given over to three days of hideous massacre and pillage. The emperor, fighting to the last, had been killed in the final onslaught.

To contemporaries the fall of Constantinople was a stunning disaster; to us it is a wonder how the city survived for so long. The Turks were now permanently settled in Europe and, sworn enemies as they were of all Christians, they believed that their growing empire was in accordance with the will of God quite as much as any pope or eastern emperor had believed that Christendom must triumph. Muhammad II believed, like Sultans before and after him, that God wanted all true Muslims to spread the faith of Islam throughout the world by force of arms. Had not the Prophet said in the Koran that good Muslims must not 'think that those who were slain in the cause of Allah are dead. They are alive and well provided for by Allah'? In fact, the fall of Constantinople was not quite so terrible as it appeared at the time. For long it had been a decaying and depopulated city: under Muhammad II and his successors the number of inhabitants grew from 100,000 or less in 1453 to nearly 800,000 in 1600—far larger and wealthier than any Christian or Muslim city of the time. A Turkish historian wrote after the death of Muhammad:

'Nothing greater or more magnificent could be imagined than the mosque which he caused to be built in the city of Stamboul . . . and the eight colleges destined to teach the sciences, which surround it . . . there is also a soup kitchen where morning and evening abundant meals are cooked for the poor of both sexes, as also for the students who eat in a large refectory built for the purpose. In the same place may be seen a hostel for foreign travellers, equipped with a separate kitchen, stables both for their mounts and for beasts of burden; there is also an infirmary for the poor with a separate bath and everything else necessary to take care of them. There is even a school to teach the children how to read.'

Nor was Byzantine art destroyed by the Turks, although they could not appreciate it. Byzantine art had been dying for a long while but not before it could influence the earliest Italian painters. Fortunately Greek scholarship survived, for a generation or more before 1453 Byzantine scholars, carrying with them their precious Greek manuscripts, had found new homes in Italy.

For Muhammad the Conqueror the capture of Constantinople was not the end but a beginning. When he died in 1481, Asia Minor, Greece, and the rest of the Balkans were unquestionably part of his empire. By his capture of the Ionian Islands he threatened Italy and by the capture of the Genoese outpost of Caffa on the Black Sea a base was secured from which in the next decade vast slave raids into the Ukraine and Poland were organized in order to meet the never-ending demand for manpower throughout the Ottoman empire.

★   ★   ★

The great success of the Ottoman Turks was due first and foremost to the unlimited power of the Sultan. No Christian monarch wielded such power, for the Sultan was warrior, lawgiver, and priest in one, a position which he claimed to inherit from Muhammad the Prophet himself, who had led his armies into battle and who had also given his followers both their laws and their Faith. The Sultans were active commanders in the field and usually spent all the summer fighting with their troops on the frontiers; only in the winter did they return to the problems of their ever-growing empire. After 1453 they had to deal with the new problem of somehow combining the idea of ceaseless fighting and conquest, hitherto the invariable rule of Turkish society, with the settled and peaceful life of a great capital city.

However successful they were at fighting, the Turks knew that in the lands which they conquered they were bound to be in a minority. They therefore did not upset existing ways of life more than they thought essential. After the fall of Constantinople the Orthodox Church continued to exist, though, as we shall see in the next chapter, Moscow became its headquarters. Christian communities in conquered territories kept their bishops and clergy as before, provided that they paid a heavy tax in return. Contrary to popular belief, the Turks were very much more tolerant of Christians and Jews than Catholics and Protestants were of each other, or both were of the Jews. Often the Turks found that Orthodox Christians did not mind joining them in fighting against the hated Latin Christians in Hungary and other parts of central Europe. When Muhammad II came to rule from Constantinople he found much to help him in his task. Much of the machinery of government, the elaborate court ceremonial, even the eunuchs in the harem he took over from the Byzantines.

Fortunately for the Sultan, his position was made even stronger by the Muslim tradition which insisted that a Sultan must always be obeyed whether he ruled well or badly. 'The apostle of God said: After me will come rulers; render them your obedience. . . . If they are righteous and rule you well, they shall have their reward; but if they do evil and rule you ill, then punishment will fall on them and you will be quit of it.' The Sultans had yet another advantage over European rulers. Even the most powerful of Western kings were often challenged by great nobles owning vast family estates. Not so the Sultan: Ghazi life meant continuous movement, perpetual campaigning, and a heavy toll of life, which made it difficult to put down roots and challenge the Sultan effectively.

The Sultans exercised their almost unlimited power through a system which had been largely devised by Muhammad the Conqueror. Since four was the mystic Muslim number, there were four great offices of state, of which the post of Grand Vizier was much the most important. These high officials were all personally appointed by the Sultan, as were the pashas, who governed provinces and large cities, and who were regularly moved around by the Sultan to new posts lest they became too popular, and therefore too powerful, in their districts. The throne was hereditary, though it was not always the eldest son who succeeded his father. Since a Sultan had many wives, and therefore many sons, it became the accepted practice for a new Sultan to execute his brothers and all their male children.

An empire always growing in size needed an unlimited supply of soldiers and administrators. Ghazi warriors were invaluable for frontier warfare, but were usually too unruly and unreliable for much else. So the need for manpower was met by wholesale slavery, the institution on which the entire Ottoman empire was based. The fear and hatred which the Turks aroused in Europe, together with the horrors experienced by galley slaves, have created the legend that slavery imposed by the Turks was much the same as that endured by Negroes in the New World. This was far from the truth. Because slaves were chiefly valued as personal bodyguards and for purposes of prestige, they were usually treated with consideration, once they had survived the undeniable terrors and misery of the raids along the fringes of the empire where they had been captured. When the Grand Vizier Rustem Pasha died in 1561 he had 1,700 slaves in his household, while Sultans in the sixteenth century might have had between 20,000 and 25,000 in their service. Nor were slaves used mainly as a form of cheap labour. Since the need was for soldiers and administrators, boys snatched from Balkan villages were trained to defend, extend, and to govern the empire. Unlimited opportunities were open to them, especially to those in the royal household. Although they remained as slaves, some of them rose to command armies, govern provinces, or frame policy, which was some compensation for having been torn away from the narrow village life of south-eastern Europe. This total disregard for questions of birth and good family amazed western Europeans who, except in the Church, could never rise above their station in life.

The flower of the Ottoman army was the janissary corps of archers, first formed in 1438, and recruited from young boys seized in the west Balkans. They were trained in special schools, where the discipline was rigid and absolute loyalty to the Sultan was inculcated. As they grew to manhood they were forbidden to marry. Any European ruler must have envied these dedicated soldiers, all skilled bowmen, who later became equally expert with muskets. Under

Turkish janissaries with their distinctive head-dress. This is a seventeenth-century picture and the janissaries are now armed with muskets.

Suleiman the Magnificent there were about 12,000 janissaries; a century later there were more than 60,000 of them, but by then their efficiency was declining. The imperial ambassador to the court of Suleiman, De Busbecq, described them in these words: 'They wear robes reaching to their ankles, and on the head a covering consisting of the sleeve of a coat . . . part of which contains the head, while the rest hangs down behind and flaps against the neck. On their foreheads rises an oblong silver cone, gilded and studded with stones of no great value.'

No European ruler could call on unlimited manpower as could the Sultans. This is why for so long the Turks seemed invincible. But in the end the system was doomed to perish because it never broke free from its Ghazi origins. Ghazi loyalty depended upon ceaseless fighting and booty; this meant that the areas under Turkish rule must always increase; this meant that more soldiers and administrators were needed; this meant more raids and more fighting to get more slaves. It was a vicious circle. Turkish power was finally halted when the old spectacular conquests could no longer be won by armies operating so far from the capital. It was never possible to create a truly stable state. But this lay well in the future.

*   *   *

As Scanderbeg (1443–68), the undefeated Albanian leader and one of the very few janissaries known to have escaped back to his people, jeeringly pointed out to Muhammad the Conqueror, so long as the Ottoman empire was confined to Anatolia and the Balkans it hardly ranked as a world empire. But within the first twenty years of the sixteenth century the Ottoman empire had doubled in size.

In between the Ottoman lands in Anatolia and the territory of northern Syria lay a no-man's land, which Turks and Syrians both claimed and which was always an excuse for fighting. A far greater source of trouble lay within the Ottoman empire itself when the two main rival sects in the Muslim world, long tolerant of each other, broke into open warfare. Under a fanatical leader called Ismail, the Muslims living around the southern shores of the Caspian had overrun most of Persia by 1508, had captured Baghdad and had begun to entice away the most easterly subjects of the new Sultan, Selim I (1512–20). Even the most powerful Sultans sometimes found it difficult to control the Ghazis on distant frontiers and, if love of fighting were to be inflamed by religious zeal and a likely alliance were made between Ismail and the Mameluke rulers of Syria and Egypt, a serious situation could rapidly develop.

Suleiman the Magnificent, painted about 1560 by an unknown artist.

Fortunately for the future of the Ottoman empire, Selim was a brilliantly ruthless soldier, who well deserved his nickname 'the Grim'. He had studied the life of Alexander the Great from Persian books and saw himself as equally great. He decided to act swiftly and by 1514 had crushed Ismail and prevented further trouble on his eastern frontier. Next came the turn of the Mamelukes. In 1515 Selim gained control of the no-man's land and he then went on to invade Syria and Egypt, capturing Cairo early in 1517. Syria was swallowed up in the Ottoman empire, and Egypt became a tributary state. Selim now found himself protector of Mecca and Medina, the two most sacred Muslim cities, and therefore the virtual head of the whole Muslim world. Not content with this, he led his armies westward along the North African coast, protecting them on their sea flank by his galleys. From Algeria he planned an attack on the island of Rhodes, where the Knights of St. John, whose ships were the terror of the Aegean for Christian and heretic alike, had long been a danger to Turkey. But before he could launch the attack, Selim died.

Under Suleiman I (1520–66), whom his subjects called 'the Law-Giver' and whom his enemies called 'the Magnificent', the Ottoman empire reached the summit of its power and glory. Suleiman was a remarkably gifted man. 'He is twenty-five years old,' wrote a Venetian, 'tall, but wiry, and of a delicate complexion. His neck is a little too long, his face thin and his nose aquiline. He has a faint moustache and a small beard: nevertheless, his expression is pleasant, although his skin has rather a pallor. His reputation is that of a wise lord, he is said to be studious, and everybody hopes that his rule will be good.' He had all his father's skill and energy as a soldier but without Selim's grim delight in butchery. He was an able administrator, anxious to rule justly, a genuine lover of the arts and himself a poet. To prove himself a worthy successor to his father, Suleiman planned a two-pronged attack against the West by land and by sea.

Even in times of official peace there had been constant border fighting between the Turks and Hungary. Only the capture of Belgrade could end this, and, once captured, the city would be an excellent base for further advances. Hungary in the sixteenth century desperately needed to be strong and united when forced to act as a buffer against Turkish attacks on central Europe; but, as we saw in Chapter 3, Hungary was hopelessly unfitted to ward off the coming onslaught. To King Lewis II of Hungary Suleiman sent envoys demanding tribute; the envoys were murdered by way of reply. Therefore, in 1521, Suleiman advanced against Belgrade and by its capture opened the line of the middle Danube to his troops. However, for the moment it was more important to remove the danger from the Knights of St. John on the island of Rhodes, which lay across the middle of the route from Constantinople to Egypt. The Christian Knights could expect little help from any quarter, for, as has been said, their ships had for years preyed upon any vessels which came their way; but they fiercely defended the island and only capitulated when, after a siege of 145 days, their ammunition ran out. The terms which Suleiman imposed were not excessively harsh and the Knights were allowed to depart to Crete, whence they later sailed to their new home in Malta. By Suleiman's capture of the two bulwarks of Christendom, Belgrade and Rhodes, as Pope Adrian VI wrote at the time, 'the passages to Hungary, Sicily and Italy lie open to him'.

It was not only the weakness of Hungary but also the long-standing quarrel between Charles V and Francis I which greatly aided Suleiman's advance. In 1525 Francis was a prisoner in Spain but had no scruples in entering into negotiations with the infidel if he could regain his liberty in this way. Suleiman's reply was couched in splendid language and may have brought some comfort to Francis, despite the careful lack of any definite promise:

I who am Sultan of Sultans, the Sovereign of Sovereigns, the distributor of crowns to the monarchs of the surface of the globe, the shadow of God on earth, the Sultan and Padishah of the White Sea, the Black Sea, Rumelia, Anatolia, Caramania, Rum, Sulkadr, Diabekr, Kurdistan, Azerbaijan, Persia, Damascus, Aleppo, Cairo, Mecca, Medina, Jerusalem, all Arabia, Yemen, and other countries, which my noble ancestors (may God brighten their tombs) conquered and which my august majesty has likewise conquered with my flaming sword, Sultan Suleiman Khan, son of Sultan Selim, son of Sultan Bayazid; you who are Francis, King of France, you have sent a letter to my Porte [government], the refuge of sovereigns . . .

Suleiman assured Francis that 'night and day our horse is saddled and our sword girt on'. But before anything could happen, Francis had been set free in return for a promise to help Charles V against Suleiman. However, not even the emperor could organize his army so that it arrived in time to save Hungary.

We know a great deal about Suleiman's campaigns from the diaries which he kept; in his diary he made no secret of his anxiety about the wet summer of 1526, which seriously delayed his advance. It is possible that had the Hungarians avoided a pitched battle, Suleiman might have been forced to return home before the winter set in; but, full of wild ideas of chivalry and crusading zeal, they chose to hazard everything in the open field. On 29 August Suleiman's army of 100,000 men and 300 guns annihilated the Hungarians at Mohacs, just east of the Danube. Lewis II escaped from the battle only to be drowned in a stream when his horse's feet

A Turkish painting of the battle of Mohacs (1526), showing the rout of the Hungarians. The janissaries can easily be distinguished.

slipped on the muddy bank. Buda and Pest were entered and duly plundered before the Turks returned to their base at Belgrade.

The defeated Hungarians had now to elect a new king. They rejected the Archduke Ferdinand, brother of Charles V, in favour of John Zapolyai, a leading Hungarian noble. Suleiman backed Zapolyai, thinking that he would be a convenient puppet who would have no intention of helping the Hapsburgs to bar his further advance. War broke out between the rival candidates, and this brought Suleiman back again in 1529. For eighteen days he encamped around Vienna, but he never captured the city. Over-long lines of communication and further troubles at the eastern end of his empire made it impossible for Suleiman to press further west, but by the time of his death in 1566 most of Hungary had become part of the Ottoman empire.

The second prong of the Turkish attack on the West, the naval war in the Mediterranean, began in earnest after Suleiman's check at Vienna. The naval power of Turkey had grown greatly after the capture of Constantinople with its arsenals and easy access to the timber forests of Greece and the Black Sea coast. Then Selim I's conquest of Syria and Egypt not only meant a great increase in the length of coastline in Ottoman hands, but it also gave Turkey famous ports and, even more important, new subjects used to the sea. Once in Egypt, the Turks joined forces with the Muslim pirate states along the North African coast, where they were able to enlist famous corsair admirals and skilled naval craftsmen, for in naval warfare, as in so many other activities, the Turks relied to a remarkable extent on foreigners. The designers and builders of their galleys were mostly Italians; while the galley crews were wretched slaves who had been captured in battle. The Turks themselves supplied the money and the driving force; and by sea as on land Suleiman found that almost his greatest aid was the quarrels among his enemies.

However, at first it looked as if the Christian forces might well have held their own in the Mediterranean, for during the long struggle between France and Spain there had been as much development of naval strength as was taking place in the Ottoman empire. The *condottieri*, the soldiers of fortune, seemed to find no difficulty in taking to the water, either to cover the passage of their armies through coastal areas or to safeguard bullion and supplies. The best example of such men was Andrea Doria, a mercenary soldier who did not turn to the sea until the age of 46. Untroubled by any sense of loyalty, Doria was in turn Admiral of France, the Papacy, and Spain. When in 1512 he first offered his services to France, he owned a mere couple of galleys; when he deserted to Spain in 1528, he possessed twelve. The scale of naval warfare was growing rapidly, for in 1537 Doria commanded a fleet of 45 Spanish, 80 Venetian, and 26 papal galleys.

'Turks, Infidels and Hereticks'

Suleiman took no personal part in naval warfare but relied on
North African corsairs, of whom the most famous was Khaireddin,
or Barbarossa, the 'King' of Algiers. Barbarossa came from a pirate
family of Greek origin, who had seized land for themselves around
Algiers and Tunis. Under pressure from both Turks and Spaniards,
he decided to throw in his lot with the Turks and offered himself and
his captains to Suleiman in return for possession of his 'Kingdom'.
Eventually Barbarossa went to live at Constantinople where he
directed Turkish naval strategy until his death in 1546. His work
was carried on by his chief captain, Dragut, whose forces overran
Malta in 1565, though they failed to capture the fortress, which held
out until Spanish help saved it.

*This portrait of Barbarossa
was painted by Nigari, who
was not only an artist but also
a well-known seaman.*

The final phase of the naval war in the sixteenth century came after Suleiman's death, when the Ottoman empire was ruled by his successor Selim II (1566-74), the Sultan under whom Turkish power began its decline and who was accurately nicknamed 'the Sot' because, as people said, he loved bottles more than battles. In 1570 the Turks seized Cyprus from Venice, but a year later it looked as if their days as a naval power were numbered. At Lepanto in the Gulf of Corinth in 1571 the last great battle between galleys was fought. Don John of Austria, half brother of Philip II of Spain, at the head of 208 vessels, totally defeated a Turkish fleet of 230, of which 80 galleys were sunk and 130 were captured. Well might Pope Pius V exclaim, perhaps a little blasphemously, 'There was a man sent from God, whose name was John.' Among those fighting against the Turks was Cervantes, author of *Don Quixote*, who refers to the battle in some chapters called 'The Captive's Tale', which also give a vivid account of the piracy which went on in the Mediterranean at this time. Yet, while Christian Europe celebrated Don John's victory, it is important to notice that the Turks retained Cyprus and within a year had made good the losses in ships. 'The infidel has only singed my beard: it will grow again,' was the Sultan's accurate boast. That there were to be no more battles on the scale of Lepanto did not mean that the Turks had been finally checked—the truth is that both sides had reached a point when large scale galley warfare no longer produced results which made the huge cost worthwhile.

The astounding success of the Turks was due to a combination of causes. First, the brilliant efficiency of the Turkish armies was more than a match for armies in which ideas of chivalry were still powerful. Next, the Turks were always aided by the hopeless divisions not only among Christian rulers but within their own lands. On the eve of Mohacs the papal nuncio wrote from Hungary: 'Among the Estates reign hate and need. And the subjects would, if the Sultan promises them freedom, raise an even more gruesome revolt against the nobles.' It was a sad but true fact that the peasants of eastern Europe enjoyed greater freedom under the Sultan than they would have received, especially if they were Protestants, at the hands of Catholic rulers. Finally, as we have seen, unlimited manpower gave the Turks a tremendous advantage.

But their success could not last for ever. However brilliant the Turkish armies were, it was impossible in the sixteength century to overcome the problem of distance. Hungary was about 100 days' march from Constantinople, and the further away from the capital the fighting, the harder it became to provide food and fodder for the men and their horses. Much the same was true at sea where the sheer size of the Mediterranean made decisive warfare almost impossible. The average sea journey from Constantinople to Alexandria took fifteen days, and from Constantinople to Venice thirty-four days. As campaigns on land were restricted to the summer months, so winter storms severed all contact between Constantinople and Algiers. But even had the problems of distance been overcome, the Turks would probably have failed to conquer further west. Germany would have proved a far stronger and more determined foe than Hungary or the Balkan states; while under Philip II the Spanish navy had been reformed and strengthened until it was more than a match for an enemy whose resources had been stretched to the limit.

Since the Ottoman empire rested largely on the power and ability of the Sultan, its decline was due more than anything else to the long line of bad or mad Sultans which began with Selim II and which continued for much of the next 200 years. It was towards the end of the sixteenth century that the Turks became hated for their corruption and cruelty. Where the Turkish horse sets foot, ran a saying, there no grass will grow again. As we have seen, in earlier days the Turks had often been preferred as rulers in the Balkans to Christian nobles. This was no longer true. The dream of a universal Muslim empire was coming to an end as frontiers became fixed and no more expansion was possible. With weak Sultans, the janissaries began to get out of hand and to interfere in politics. At the end of the century they demanded and obtained the head of any minister they disliked. By the start of the seventeenth century they showed their new power by murdering the Sultan. Those who had once been slaves were now to be the masters.

Chapter 10
Russia, 'signories unknowne'

In the year 1555 a group of merchant adventurers in London set up a new trading company and received from the queen, Mary Tudor, a royal charter granting them the monopoly of English trade wherever they might go. It was stated in the charter that they would voyage and traffic in 'landes, territories, isles, and signories unknowne'. This new venture was called the Muscovy Company; Russia—or Muscovy—was the chief objective, and Russia still presented adventurous merchants with 'signories unknowne'. Information about the land and its people was scanty and generally reached western Europe by travellers' tales or by contact with the unpopular Germans of the Hanseatic League who had had a trading post in the town of Novgorod, on and off, since 1269. Agents of the Muscovy Company soon began to report back to London that there was great scope for commerce and many areas which were specially tempting because they were untouched by other merchants. One of them wrote, 'The countrie of Russia stretchethe to the North Sea where the sea coaste extendethe eastwards . . . more than towe thousand myles in lengthe, all in a free open course by sea from England, *out of danger of all other prences.*'

To understand the reasons for ignorance about Russia and for its long isolation from the countries of western Europe it is necessary to go far back in history. Because it was so remote it had never formed part of the Roman empire nor been linked with Roman civilization through the legions and the roads, the buildings, laws, and organization on which that civilization was built. It was through the remains of the Roman world that the German barbarians, even after they had so nearly destroyed it, were able slowly and painfully to rebuild Western civilization. The Russians had no such advantages and no such patterns to build on as they developed into a nation. There were also the physical facts of the enormous size of the country and the harsh extremes of its climate: blistering heat in summer followed by five months of cold so fierce that according to Giles Fletcher, an agent for the Muscovy Company who travelled much in Russia, 'men are mortally pinched and killed withall so you see manie drop downe dede'. Russia is a vast plain through which great rivers coil slowly and tortuously on their way to the sea, rivers like the Neva flowing north to the Baltic, the Dnieper and the Volga southward to the Black Sea and the Caspian. In places there

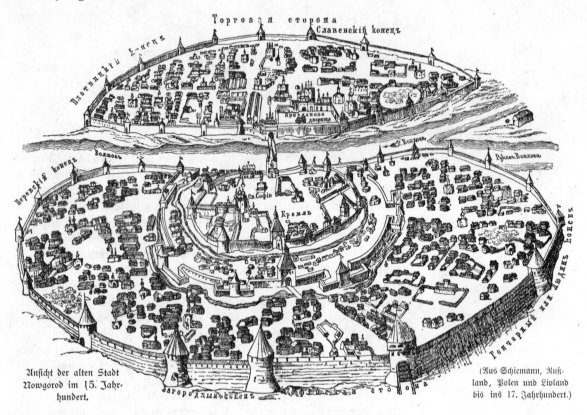

Ansicht der alten Stadt Nowgorod im 15. Jahrhundert.

(Aus Schiemann, Rußland, Polen und Livland bis ins 17. Jahrhundert.)

were, and still are, impassable marshes, and miles of uninhabited steppe-land; in places 'the land was ful of desert woodes', as Giles Fletcher reported to Elizabeth I. It was a country daunting to travellers and traders alike. For centuries roads were non-existent, or appallingly bad and very dangerous, and only along the great waterways could traffic move with any ease. These were vital to the life of Russia, so it is not surprising that three cities which at different periods have been the capitals of Russia all lie on these broad waterways: Novgorod on the Neva, Kiev on the Dnieper, Moscow on the Volga.

Two other factors much increased Russia's isolation from the West. The first was that when Christianity was adopted in the tenth century it came through the Greek Orthodox Church at Constantinople and not from Rome. The second, and perhaps the most important of all, was that in the thirteenth century Russia was conquered and held in subjection by Asiatic invaders who dominated the land and its people, forcing them to look eastward to exacting masters for 200 years.

Throughout the three centuries covered by this book, the people of Russia were thinly scattered over a small fraction of the vast area

Novgorod in the fifteenth century, the city said to have been founded by Rurik the Northman in the ninth century.

The Inguri valley, Georgia. One of the great waterways of Russia winds its way through the land.

of their land. By race they belonged to the great Slavonic group of peoples which included Czechs, Poles, Serbs, and Bulgarians. All these sections have intermingled, not only with each other, but also with various foreign invaders and infiltrators, much as the people of the British Isles have done in the course of their history. The first important invaders were Northmen from Scandinavia who came in small war bands across the Baltic Sea in the same way and at the same time as their kinsmen the Danes raided England. In the manner of Northmen, some of them simply raided and returned home laden with plunder and full of strange tales. Others, for example Thorstein the Swede, whose name we know because his two sons put up a fine carved stone in his memory, did not return but 'fell in battle eastward in Russia'. Others, again, survived and settled in the north of Russia, first subduing the native Slavs but later being absorbed by them. Novgorod on the river Neva was the first place where they settled in any number, and there according to tradition a Northman, Rurik, made himself prince in the middle of the ninth century.

The Slav name for the Norse invaders was *Rus*, meaning rowers, and true to that name they steadily penetrated by the water-roads

Left *The Cathedral of St. Sophia in Kiev. A few magnificent buildings like this dominated the wooden houses of Russian cities.*

into the heart of Russia, reaching the Black Sea and the Caspian and coming at last to the great city of Constantinople with the marvellous dome of Sancta Sophia towering above its walls. An old Russian Chronicle says of the Northmen, 'They began to build them towns and to wage war everywhere'. In A.D. 879 one of them, Oleg son of Rurik, established himself as an independent ruler in Kiev on the Dnieper, just a year after Alfred the Great had emerged from the Somerset marshes and defeated Guthrum the Dane.

Kiev, known by the proud if inaccurate title of 'the mother of Russian towns'—for others were founded earlier—grew in importance under Oleg and his successors. Their power depended on force and they warred incessantly against all and sundry: their own family, their immediate neighbours, and other distant tribes like the Bulgars who lived on the middle Danube. Four times in seventy years they boldly attacked Constantinople itself, and when in 971 a peace treaty was made, they had won the right to enter the imperial capital. Soon trade between Kiev and Constantinople was well established. It was agreed that 'every year it shall be lawful for the Great Prince [of Kiev] to send to the Greek Tsar as many ships as

Right *Detail from a door in the Cathedral of St. Sophia.*

the Prince shall desire'. The Russians had to go unarmed into Constantinople and were lodged in a special quarter of the city. They were given free bread, fish, fruit, wine, and baths for as long as they were there on lawful business. Money hardly changed hands at all in these transactions, for the Russians were accustomed to barter, and Byzantine silks, gold, wine, and fruit were easily exchanged for Russian furs, wax, honey, and slaves.

Even more important than these exchanges of merchandise was the impression made on the Russians by the imperial city, the eastern capital of the Roman empire, Constantinople's 'New Rome'. There they came into direct contact for the first time with the remains of Graeco-Roman civilization, were awed and astonished by the elaborate splendour of the imperial court, the magnificent buildings, and, most of all, by the solemn and mysterious ceremonies of the Greek Orthodox Church which they saw in the church of Sancta Sophia—the Holy Wisdom. As one result of this a small Christian church was built in Kiev in 955 and the mother of the Great Prince was baptized. Thirty years later her grandson, Vladimir, followed suit. He was a man of great ability and dynamic energy. After his death a chronicler wrote a 'Eulogy of Prince Vladimir' in which he was described in very complimentary terms: 'This celebrated ruler grew strong from childhood and was filled with energy and power; he excelled in valour and intelligence . . . and shepherded his land with justice.' On the other hand, he had not hesitated to murder his brother to become Great Prince; he could be absolutely brutal, particularly to women, and he had several wives and many concubines. However, 'there came God's visitation upon' the pagan prince and he was baptized into the Greek Orthodox Church. Before doing so he received religious missions of various faiths, Jewish, Muslim, and Roman Catholic, and heard what they had to say and then sent envoys to make close inquiries about the church in Constantinople. They reported to him, 'We were led to the edifices where they worship their God . . . and we knew not whether we were in heaven or on earth, for on earth there is no such splendour or such beauty and we are at a loss how to describe it.' Evidently Justinian's church even after 400 years was still so splendid that 'it reduced men to speechless wonder' just as it did when it was finished in A.D. 597. 'We only know', said the Russians simply to the Great Prince, 'that God dwells there among men.' So in 988 Prince Vladimir accepted baptism for himself and his family and organized a general christening of his subjects. Later the new faith was also forced on the reluctant people of Novgorod whose elected prince was Vladimir's son.

Of course Christianity only slowly affected the everyday lives of Russians; for a long time it remained a thin veneer over paganism and superstition, but the fact that the Greek Church was the one to

266

become firmly established in Russia had a profound influence on the future of the country, as, from warring tribes and cities and conflicting princely families, a nation slowly developed. The links with Constantinople became close and often strong even though they were frequently broken by bouts of fierce enmity and war. In A.D. 990 Prince Vladimir married Anna, sister of the emperor. As a fair exchange for this princess 'born in the purple', Vladimir supplied his brother-in-law with 6,000 fighting men of Norse ancestry. Gradually the influence of the Byzantine civilization showed itself in the art, architecture, and education of Russia and gave them an Eastern rather than a Western slant. Above all, the acceptance of Christianity from Constantinople rather than from Rome meant that Russia turned her back on the Western Church, and so on Western civilization in general.

Throughout the eleventh and twelfth centuries Kiev remained the chief of Russian towns, the prize for which the most powerful among the princes plotted and fought. It could not have been a particularly impressive place, being built almost entirely of wood (though often the houses were painted in bright colours), with unpaved streets and no dignified buildings. The Great Prince, even when his prestige was high among his friends and foes alike, was not the tsar of all Russia and was not often regarded as anything more than a barbarian chieftain by the ruling houses of Europe. His authority was local rather than national, confined to territories he inherited or seized for just as long as he could hold them and dominate his rivals. He was one among the other princes who formed the highest rank in Russian society. Just below them, but constantly intermingling, came the land-owning aristocracy, the *boyars*. The greatest of these were members of the prince's *druzhina* or household, trained and armed as his bodyguard and able to mix and intermarry with the princely class. The lesser *boyars* varied in wealth and land, down to humble men not much different from peasants. The peasants themselves were of two sorts. There were free men who, though they did not own the land they worked, and had to pay heavy dues in kind to the *boyars* who did, were nevertheless different from the villeins in other parts of Europe because they were not tied to the land but were free to move about and change their masters if they chose. There were other peasants who were simply slaves, the chattels of their lords with no rights of any kind. A wide gulf, which in time was to become wider, lay between the princes and *boyars* and the peasants, for a middle class of merchants and lawyers hardly existed except in the larger towns. The craftsmen and small traders were sometimes free men but sometimes slaves.

The peasants, sparsely scattered over the plains and the steppes, grew crops of rye, barley, oats, and flax. Although in some areas the soil was exceedingly rich, the harsh climate and the primitive

methods of farming meant that, by extreme labour, they produced only enough for a bare living and for a little bartering at the local market after the dues had gone to the *boyars*. They were almost entirely ignorant about the use of fertilizers, and long after other European farmers had harnessed oxen or horses to their iron ploughs, the Russian peasants still turned the soil with forked sticks. When they had exhausted the land in one place, they moved in a semi-nomadic way to another. It was therefore not from farming that the main merchandise for trade came but from the great wealth of natural products that lay in the steppes and forests: furs, timber, honey, wax, and salt.

A plough used in Russia in the sixteenth century. It has two wooden teeth tipped with iron but no ploughshare and is much more primitive than the one shown on page 130, which was contemporary with it.

268

The greatest of the princes of Kiev was Yaroslav (1016–54), whose reign was a golden age of increasing trade and expansion. He dominated the Russian scene, recovered land from Poland, and colonized the coasts of the Baltic Sea eastwards. For the first time the laws were collected and written down. In Kiev some fine buildings of stone appeared, including a library, a school of divinity, and the church of Sancta Sophia, all built by architects brought by the prince from Constantinople. Yaroslav was recognized in western Europe as the greatest ruler in Russia. His sister was married to the king of Poland, one of his daughters to Harold Hardrada of Norway and another to John I of Hungary. But he did not succeed in making a united Russia, and when he died a long period of disruptive turmoil set in. This was largely because, according to ancient custom, his lands were divided at his death among his sons, and the power and authority which he had built up crumbled away in the strife between them and other princes. One of them stormed Kiev, massacred the inhabitants, and burnt everything that would burn, and 'the mother of Russian towns' never quite recovered its supremacy after this disaster.

For the next 170 years no prince and no town succeeded in dominating Russia as Kiev and her princes had temporarily done. Strife was incessant, and matters were not helped by occasional interference from foreign powers, like Poland and Hungary, who fished in the troubled waters hoping for expansion and profit at Russian expense. Then in 1223 a menace even more terrible than civil war appeared, this time from the East in the shape of a 'great horde' of savage warriors, sweeping westward with incredible force. The suddenness of their arrival shocked and mystified the Russians. 'For our sins', wrote a chronicler of Novgorod, 'came unknown tribes. No one knows who they are, nor whence they came, nor what their faith is . . . God alone knoweth whence he fetched them against us for our sins. Very wise men who understand books know but we do not.' But the 'very wise men' would probably not have found the answer in books, though they may have realized that the mysterious hordes were nomads from Outer Mongolia, who, under Genghis Khan, one of the greatest conquerors of history, had first overthrown China and then turned westward. A badly organized Russian army under the prince of Kiev met them on the river Volga, but it was totally destroyed and the prince was killed. Those European states nearest to the Russian borders held their breath in suspense, but this time the danger passed as suddenly as it had come; for this was only a first reconnaissance, and the Mongols, or Tartars as they are usually called, disappeared eastward again.

The relief did not last long. In 1240 'the pagan and godless Tartars, a host of shedders of Christian blood', sometimes known as the 'great Horde', came again in even greater strength. This time they conquered Russia, and for nearly 200 years held the Russian people in thrall.

The havoc they wrought at first was terrible, even though in time the outward signs of it disappeared. 'They slew all, from the male sex even to the female, all priests and monks, and all stripped and reviled gave up their souls to the Lord in a bitter and a wretched death.' Towns were their special targets, and they went out of their way to destroy them completely so that there should be no dangerous centres of resistance. Only a few survived and these almost by accident. Novgorod, for instance, was not sacked. It was saved because in a summer of extraordinary wetness the marshes round the town 'stood with wet' and the Tartars gave up the attempt to reach it. After a time the main horde withdrew, leaving only small and mobile bands for purposes of discipline, and life in Russia went on apparently much the same, but in truth the Tartar yoke was a very heavy one with far-reaching effects. The conquerors demanded poll-tax from all except the clergy—an example of the unexpected religious tolerance from these unpredictable people who were either pagans or Muslims—and the princes were responsible for collecting the money and delivering it in person to the camp of the Great Khan of the Tartars wherever that might be, perhaps Saray on the Volga, perhaps even at Karakorum in Outer Mongolia. Only by doing this could they receive a charter confirming their own titles and authority, and if they failed to turn up with the tribute, the most savage punishment was inflicted on their subjects. One prince of Novgorod—for that city, though not actually conquered, was compelled to pay up like all others—spent most of his twenty-year reign on continual journeys to the Great Khan, hoping to improve the lot of his subjects by his own constant and humiliating submission. It was a useful method of keeping the princes out of dangerous mischief.

The Tartars drained not only money from the Russians but men as well, conscripts by the thousand for their armies, craftsmen of every kind for their towns. Russian industry shrivelled for lack of workers and trade was strictly controlled by the Tartars; only agriculture increased. In addition to this draining of material wealth the 'Tartar yoke' had two less tangible results. First, it increased the tendency—now from bitter necessity—of the Russian people to look east rather than westward towards Europe, so that they became even more isolated from their western neighbours, from Western ideas, art, and education. Only the Russians out of all European nations had this prolonged experience of close contact with the Asiatic nomads. And secondly they learned through these 200 years to take orders and obey them swiftly; to pay tribute in money and in men without delay or argument, lessons which later allowed the authority of the state, whether in the hands of tsar or soviet, to suppress individual freedom and exact iron conformity.

270

The main Tartar conquest had begun in 1240 and it ended, except for spasmodic raids, by 1480. Resistance in Russia never completely ceased, even though for the first twenty-five years of Tartar rule the Russians were too stunned and divided to revolt, and when they did, their punishment was swift and sharp, as the people of Novgorod found in 1257 when they rebelled against conscription of their menfolk for the armies of the Khan. The gradual end of domination came partly because the Tartars themselves lost their unity and broke up into sections which conducted raids against each other as well as against the Russians for the purpose of capturing booty and slaves; partly because the khans were no longer men of such tremendous force as Genghis Khan or Kublai Khan; and partly because there developed in Russia a line of princes who gradually were able to unite the Russians as none had ever done before. This was the princely family of Moscow. Moscow had been sacked only once by the Tartars and as a result had drawn to it settlers from more exposed places who brought increased prosperity and a revival of trade on the Volga. The princes claimed to be descended from Rurik the Northman, and among them were some remarkable rulers exactly suited to cope with the problems they faced. Only a few were pleasant characters; they were generally ruthlessly ambitious, some cool and calculating, some unbalanced to the verge of insanity; all quite willing to grovel before the khans, equally ready to rob or kill unwanted rivals or relations. They were firmly settled in Moscow when the Tartars came, having by wars, treaties, and picturesque methods such as asking wealthy princes to dinner and throwing them into dungeons, increased their territories from 5,000 square miles to 15,000. They also broke with the destructive custom whereby on the death of the prince his lands were parcelled out among his sons, so that Moscow and the Muscovite territories were able to develop a unity and not be perpetually rearranged under different rulers.

But even their characters and their concentration of power would not have allowed the Muscovite princes to rise so high as they did, and to become in the end nothing less than the tsars of all Russia, if they had not had, and managed for 150 years to keep, three exceedingly powerful allies. The first of these were the khans of the great horde, before whom for as long as it suited them they bowed themselves with pleasing humility. The second was the Russian Church and its highest officials, the metropolitans, who had moved their residence and treasury from Kiev to Moscow and put all their influence and wealth behind the princes. The third was the powerful but cantankerous city of Novgorod. The friendship between Moscow and Novgorod was not an easy one. The northern city was a republic, proud and independent, which had never accepted a hereditary prince, only one elected by the common council, and was bitterly jealous of Kiev, Moscow, and all other large Russian towns. Although it had escaped devastation by the Tartars, it was dangerously dependent for bread supplies on distant grain-growing areas which were very vulnerable to Tartar raids. These Moscow was in a position to protect, and it was therefore convenient to Novgorod to keep on reasonably good terms with the Muscovite princes.

In 1462 Ivan III, the Great, became prince of Moscow. His reign lasted for forty-three years, and at the end of it Russia had emerged at last as a distinct state of European importance. Ivan was at last independent of the Tartars, and he had assumed the title of tsar of Russia. His cautious but persistent work had built up his authority and dominions, but he had been helped by the crumbling of the Tartar menace and, more important still, by the fall of Constantinople to the Turks in 1453. After this the Orthodox Church was no longer thought of as centred in Greece but in Russia, 'in the blessed city of Moscow'. 'Two Romes have fallen for their sins', declared the Russian Church, 'but the third stands.' Moscow was the true centre of the Christian world and its importance and the authority of its rulers were greatly enhanced. Ivan III married the niece of the last emperor of the Eastern Roman Empire and took as his standard the double-headed eagle of the imperial family. No wonder that he was able to think of himself as the heir to that emperor and felt fully justified in calling himself tsar—the Russian word for Caesar! No wonder that in 1489 when Frederick III, the German emperor, offered him the title of king he replied with dignity to this patronizing suggestion, 'By God's grace we have been sovereigns in our own land since the beginning, since our earliest ancestors, our appointment comes from God as did that of our ancestors . . . and as beforehand we did not desire to be appointed [sovereign] by anyone, so now we do not desire it.'

Ivan III had a very clear idea of his aims: to shake off the last shred of Tartar control, to reconquer lands that had been snatched by other powers such as Poland, to unite all Russia under the leadership of the prince of Moscow; and he moved steadily and relentlessly towards their achievement. He did everything cautiously and after cool and careful planning. But although he did remarkable things for Russia, he remains, as so many Russian princes do, an indistinct figure to most of us, very different from his contemporaries on the thrones of Europe, and this in itself is a sign of the isolation of Russia from the West. It is not until his grandson Ivan IV (1533–84) became tsar that the ruler of Russia seems to emerge from 'signories unknowne' as an individual personality, though he was the most fantastic of them all.

It was in his reign that the contact between Russia and England really began, with the voyage of Willoughby and Chancellor to

A Moscow street of nothing but simple wooden houses, c. 1500. The covered sledge probably contains a woman of high rank.

search for the North-West Passage to India in 1553. It was sanctioned by Queen Mary I, and it was after the disastrous loss of Willoughby's ship with all on board, when Richard Chancellor returned alone with a personal message from the tsar to the queen, that the Muscovy Company was formed.

The Company had some intrepid servants and fortunately a few of them wrote vivid reports of their doings. Anthony Jenkinson, for instance, who arrived on company business in Moscow in 1557, spent the next year in travelling by river to the Caspian Sea and back. Another, Michael Lock, sent home reports which are full of practical details. He carefully listed the 'natural commodities' of Russia:

Fysshe of divers kindes	Pitche
Salte	Tarre
Buffe hydes	Timber
Cow hydes	Cables for shippes
Furres of all kyndes	Other marchandise

(and included a rather puzzling item called 'trayne oylle'). Michael goes on to say that 'the colde and rytche countries of Russia and

273

Russia, 'signories unknowne'

Muscovy had greate neade of the warm wollen commodities of Englande' and that, in spite of their 'furres', the Russians eagerly buy 'wollen clothes and carseys'.

Besides being agents for the Company, some of these men acted as official ambassadors to the Russian court. One of them, Giles Fletcher who was knighted by Elizabeth for his services, vividly described the country, the climate, and the houses, which he said were 'of wood, built very warm and close with firre trees. They were fastened with dentes or notches at the everye corner and so clasped faste. They [the Russians] thrust in mosse to keepe out the colde.' Another, Sir Jerome Horsey, who was in Russia in 1580, was dangerously frank about Ivan IV, saying he was 'verie puisante, prowd, cruell and bloudie'. It is not surprising that Horsey's dispatches had to be carried to the coast in the 'fals sieds of a wodden bottell fyld fulle with aqua-vitae to hang under my horse's maine, not worthe 3 pence.' When he reached London and presented them to the queen, he tried to remove the smell of the spirits, but Elizabeth was not deceived and asked for an explanation.

Horsey's judgement indeed was a true one. Ivan IV, though a very gifted man, thoroughly earned his nickname, the Terrible. He

A cap, made of gold, decorated with jewels and edged with fine sable fur, used in 1547 for crowning the Tsar, Ivan IV.

*Ivan IV the Terrible shown in
a stiff magnificent robe and a
cap very like the one shown on
page 274 if not the same one.
This portrait, by V. Vasnetsov,
reveals the unstable suspicious
personality of the Tsar.*

succeeded to the throne at the age of 3, and from then onwards, until at 16 he came of age and began to rule for himself, he lived in circumstances which seem, not surprisingly, to have distorted his whole personality. The court was a hot-bed of power-hungry *boyars*, his mother the regent was poisoned by one group, and those who had supported her were murdered. The young tsar was often terrified and half-starved, treated at one moment with contempt or cruelty, at another with a hypocritical respect when he was bundled hastily into rich robes and placed as a figure-head on the imperial throne to receive important visitors. He learned to suspect everyone, and he developed a persecution mania so strong that he lived 'in great feare and danger of treasons, and his mayking awaye'. Indeed he had plenty of natural enemies both abroad and at home who would gladly have made away with him. The king of Poland was one of these, and Ivan wrote to Elizabeth of England proposing that she should 'joyne hym as one agaynst the Pole . . . and suffer him to have out of England alle kyndes of artillerie and thynges necessarie for warre'. On the other hand the king of Poland also urged Elizabeth to join forces with him against 'the Muscovite puffed up in pryde', who would shortly 'make assault . . . on Christendome to slay or make bounde all that shal withstande hym'. Elizabeth, however, neatly avoided firm commitments to either. She refused the Polish request to forbid her merchants to trade with Russia; she also sent an evasive answer to the tsar's request that her cousin Lady Mary Hastings should be dispatched to Russia as his affianced bride. Even Elizabeth would not go so far as to make such a human sacrifice to a man described by her envoy as notorious for 'his most cruell slautherings, murtherings, and incessant massacring'.

Ivan the Terrible was far more than 'cruell and bloudie', he was highly intelligent and far-sighted in his sane moments and always a good soldier. He led his army against the now feeble Tartar tribes, seizing the towns of Kazan and Astrakhan, once their strongholds, so that the whole vast basin of the river Volga was at last in Russian hands with its possibilities of trade with Asia, Siberia, and even, in the far future, with the Pacific Ocean. To the west he was less successful, and the hostile neighbours who ringed him there—Poland, Hungary, and Sweden—remained hostile and unsubdued. At home he made himself supreme, but at a terrible cost. He had, of course, strong personal reasons for hating the *boyars*. The bitter memory of his childhood was always with him and he also realized that the great landowners alone had the wealth and power to challenge his own. Accordingly he never lost a chance of degrading and dividing them. Against the hereditary *boyars* he built up a strong class of service-*boyars* who performed military or other services for the tsar and were rewarded with estates held for their lifetime. Often these estates were removed from hereditary *boyars*, who were then deported to distant and impoverished districts. Their peasants were expected to work for the new service-*boyars* and, in order to force them to do this, were deprived of their freedom of movement. In this way the free peasants of Russia became serfs, tied to the land of the lord at a time when everywhere else in Europe the bondage of serfdom had all but disappeared. In 1565 Ivan gave his subjects a foretaste of a terrible weapon, one which has not in the twentieth century lost its terror. He set up an organization called the *oprichnina*, to which he recruited first 1,000, later 6,000, of his most loyal followers of all classes. They wore black garments and called each other 'brother', and took a special oath of allegiance to the tsar. Whole towns and districts were set aside for them as their estates, again confiscated from hereditary *boyars* and even from those service-*boyars* who did not please the tsar. The members of the *oprichnina* were ruthless and above the law—worse than that, they worked as a secret police, their evil deeds concealed as far as possible from all inquiries and certainly from foreign powers. Anthony Jenkinson had a taste of their methods when on one visit he was 'so straightlie kepte prisonere with such uncourtoyse usage . . . as worse coulde not have been showed to an enemie'.

It was tragic for Russia that Ivan grew more and more unbalanced as he grew older, till no one could safely cross him or disagree with him even in the smallest matters. In 1582 in a fit of mad fury he struck and killed his eldest son and heir, Ivan, and when he died two years later he left a feeble-minded and sickly successor Theodore, the last of the dynasty. He also left a country filled 'full of grudge and mortall hatred'.

Chapter 11

The Church strikes back:
the Counter-Reformation

Demands that the Church should put her house in order had been constantly made, as we have seen, for at least 150 years before Luther was born. A serious, though small-scale, start at reform had begun in Italy shortly before Luther made his protest against Indulgences; so that what are sometimes called the Catholic Reformation and the Protestant Reformation in fact began about the same time. Devout Catholics did not need Luther to point out abuses of which they were only too painfully aware. But the effect on the Church of the full blast of the Protestant challenge was great: reform from within the Church became a much more urgent matter and, more strikingly, the Church abandoned any attempt to conciliate the Protestants, as some people would have wished and which might have been successful, and went on to the attack. This twofold movement is known as the Counter-Reformation and was brilliantly successful. By the middle of the sixteenth century it looked as if most of western Europe might well become Protestant; a century later much of the land lost to the Protestants had been won back to the Church and it was the Protestants who were on the defensive.

Although the Protestant reformers had shattered the old unity of the Christian Church, the hope that this unity might be restored remained strong. Most people still believed that it was possible to reach absolute certainty on questions of religion. This is why learned debates, such as that between Luther and Eck, were popular and were preferred to the warnings of humanists like Erasmus that it was only asking for trouble to try to solve all religious problems. 'It would be better', he wrote, 'to postpone them to that further period when the glass shall be removed and the riddle solved, and we see God face to face.' But who was to say what the truth was? The Church had always insisted that she alone had the authority to do this, but respect for the papacy had declined steadily and a powerful monarch like Henry VIII of England was quite prepared to be Head of the Church in his own country and to lay down what his subjects should believe. This is what happened in Germany when by the Religious Peace of Augsburg in 1555 it was agreed that each prince should decide on the religion of his own state. Four years later Henry VIII's daughter, Elizabeth I, made her own settlement of religious affairs when she brought to an end her half-sister Mary's attempt to bring England back to the Catholic fold and by act of parliament defined what the faith of Englishmen should be, how they should worship, and her own position as Supreme Governor of the Church. Nothing was resisted by the papacy more strongly than a ruler's determination to dictate in matters of religion, but, as the Venetian ambassador reported: '. . . in many countries obedience to the pope has almost ceased, and matters are becoming so critical that, if God does not interfere, they will soon be desperate. . . . . Germany . . . leaves but little hope of being cured. Poland is in almost as hopeless a state. The disorders which have just lately taken place in France and Spain are too well known for me to speak of them, and the Kingdom of England . . . has again fallen into heresy. Thus the spiritual power of the pope is so straitened that the only remedy is a council summoned by common consent of all princes.' Memories of the Council of Constance did not encourage popes to busy themselves unduly with calling a General Council of the Church once again.

However, long before any Council was to meet there was a notable revival of religious feeling in Italy. Popes, cardinals, or even bishops did not come into contact with most men and women, who learned what they knew of Christianity from the teaching and example of their parish priest. So it seemed to a few leading churchmen, distinguished for their learning and piety, that any reform of the Church ought to begin with raising the standards, both in understanding of doctrine and in morals, of the ordinary priest. This is why the Oratory of Divine Love was formed in Rome about 1517; it consisted of some sixty members, whose aim was to show by means of prayer and strict discipline what the life of a good priest entailed—not least in how to conduct a service reverently. This example was soon followed in other cities. At much the same time there was a move to found new religious Orders and to bring new life into existing Orders, whose members had often grown slack and corrupt. For example, the Franciscans had frequently fallen far short of the life of poverty and service decreed by St. Francis; so in 1528 a reformed Franciscan Order, the Capuchins—so called from the capuce, or pointed hood which they wore—was founded, and these friars did much to keep peasants and poor townsfolk loyal to the Church. Orders for women grew up as well; the Ursulines, who looked after the sick, were the first teaching Order of women to be established. But when it came to winning back lands lost to the Protestants or working as missionaries all over the world, there was no Order to compare with the newly founded Society of Jesus, or the Jesuits, as its members were called.

$$\star \quad \star \quad \star$$

If the first steps towards a reform of the Church were taken in Italy, the story of the Jesuits bears the indelible stamp of Spain. There the long struggle against the Moors had kept alive the old crusading spirit, that mixture of fervent faith and romantic chivalry, which was to mark the foundation of the new Order. The distinctive characteristic of the Society of Jesus was that it was founded, given its constitution and its rule of life, and was commanded for the first twenty-five years of its existence by one man—the Spaniard, Don Inigo Lopez de Recalde de Loyola, more conveniently known as Ignatius Loyola (1491-1556). What the Society was to lose by being rigidly organized and controlled by one man it was to gain by being absolutely clear in its mission. Well have the Jesuits been described as the spearhead of the Counter-Reformation, the most powerful missionary organization which the world has ever seen.

Ignatius Loyola came from an aristocratic Basque family, which had long lived in the little mountainous province of Guipuzcoa at the corner of the Bay of Biscay. The family crest of two wolves in search of prey was well suited to a family of soldiers, whose younger sons had often been invited to the Spanish court as pages, and Ignatius had served Ferdinand of Aragon in this way before becoming a soldier himself. As a youth he had read every romance of chivalry on which he could lay his hands and he burned to excel in knightly deeds. His chance came in 1521 when he was put in charge of the garrison of Pampeluna in Navarre, with orders to resist a powerful French attack on the town. His men would have surrendered without a fight had not Loyola rallied them to attempt a desperate defence. In the course of the fighting his leg was shattered by a bullet and soon afterwards the town fell to the besiegers, who had been so impressed by the young officer's gallantry that they extricated him from the heap of dead under which he lay and took him to his family castle. Here his leg was so badly set that it had to be twice broken and twice reset. The agony which he endured was to no avail; with a permanently lame leg Loyola would never fight again.

As he lay in bed he wondered how he could still win fame. 'What', Loyola is reported to have said, 'if I were to do the deeds of a St. Dominic or a St. Francis?' Realizing that as yet his life had hardly been very saintly, he began to read lives of the great saints and a life of Christ. Determined to change his way of life, Loyola vowed that directly he could travel he would go on pilgrimage to Jerusalem. Soon he persuaded his servants to hoist him on to a donkey and he set out for Montserrat, the holy hill of Aragon. Here in the Church of Our Lady he dedicated himself to the service of the Virgin Mary in much the same way that a true knight vowed to be faithful to his lady love. At dawn he put on a hermit's dress, gave his clothes to the first beggar he met, and rode on to the nearby Dominican monastery of Manresa to prepare himself for the saintly life he had sworn to lead. A gruelling and testing ten years lay ahead.

At first Loyola at Manresa could gain no peace of spirit. Like Luther at Erfurt, he found that hours of prayer, severe fasting, and thrice daily scourging did not bring him apparently any nearer to God. 'Show me, O Lord, where I can find Thee;' he tells us that he used to shriek aloud, 'I will follow like a dog, if I can only learn the way of salvation.' As with Luther, peace only came when he threw himself helplessly on God's mercy; but unlike Luther he seems to have had no further spiritual difficulties and henceforward he believed that through visions granted to him he could find God and learn his will at any time. He was at Manresa for ten months and was then ready to fulfil his vow of a pilgrimage to Jerusalem, which he reached in 1523. It had been a ghastly journey for he had refused to take any money with him, determined to rely solely on charity. To his bitter disappointment his project for a mission to the Turks so alarmed the Franciscans in Jerusalem that they shipped him back to Spain. Once home again he realized that without a proper education he could never achieve his aims. To study theology at a university meant knowing Latin; so, quite undismayed, Loyola at the age of 30 sat alongside schoolboys on a bench in a Barcelona school. By 1528 he reached the university of Paris, where at this moment Calvin was a fellow student, though unfortunately there is no record of these two powerful religious enemies ever having met. Loyola was no scholar or theologian and he must have found the work hard. To him doctrines were like military commands, to be accepted without question; disbelief was mutiny. All the time that he was studying he was also watching his companions intently, getting to know them, testing their characters, deciding to which of them he would reveal his plans for the revival of the Church. Eventually on 15 August 1534 he and six companions met in a Paris church where they vowed to undertake missionary work in the Holy Land or, if this were impossible, to go wherever the pope sent them. War between Venice and the Turks made any journey to Palestine impossible and so, after dispersing for a time, the friends met again in Rome at the end of 1537. Here they offered themselves unconditionally to the service of Pope Paul III and on 27 September 1540 the Society of Jesus received the pope's confirmation.

It was at Manresa that Loyola had studied how best to control the weaknesses of his nature and how to surrender himself completely to God. He there began to write down his experiences and they later became the basis of one of the most remarkable books of the age, the *Spiritual Exercises*. Loyola's purpose was ·to write a manual of instruction which could be used in the training of every intending Jesuit; a kind of drill-book from which the raw recruit could be disciplined for God's service by following the pattern of meditation on Christ's life laid down by his drill-sergeant instructor. The Exercises were to extend over twenty-five days, during which time the pupil must live utterly alone, shut off from the world, wholly absorbed in meditation. He had to imagine himself actually present

Ignatius Loyola casting out devils. This highly emotional picture was painted by Rubens in 1620, a century after the Order of Jesuits was founded. The baroque architecture of the church is typical of the seventeenth but not of the sixteenth century. Notice the serene assurance of Loyola and those near him compared with the writhing forms of those in the grip of evil.

at the events of Christ's life and be able to 'taste the loaves and fishes with which Jesus feeds the multitude' or to see the drops of sweat falling from Jesus's forehead in Gethsemane, to be so near him as to feel the material of his clothes. When meditating on a future life the pupil is exhorted to smell the sulphur of hell's flames and to hear the shrieks of the damned as they burn. It probably seems a very strange kind of training to us, but there is plenty of evidence that for many a Jesuit it was remarkably successful, giving them a strength and a courage which they did not believe that they possessed.

The rule of life for a Jesuit, the long and rigorous course of training, the marked character and organization of the Order were all the work of Loyola. The purpose of the Order was to spread the Catholic faith by means of 'public preaching and ministry of the Word of God, spiritual exercises, works of charity, and especially by the training of boys and the uneducated in Christianity.' The Society of Jesus had a military quality about it, which is not surprising when we remember Loyola's upbringing. Rules for recruitment and promotion had a military strictness, and a military discipline was enforced on every member. The keynote of a Jesuit's life was obedience. All monastic Orders had always demanded a vow of obedience but never so strictly as that required of a Jesuit. 'They that live under obedience', wrote Loyola, 'ought to allow themselves to be borne and ruled by divine providence working through their superiors exactly as if they were a corpse which suffers itself to be borne and handled in any way whatsoever.' Not only must a Jesuit do as he was told, he must also learn to think as he was told to think. 'If the Church defines anything that seems to us white to be black, we must at once assert that it is black.' At the head of the Order stood the General to whom unquestioning obedience was due, though even he had always a special 'admonitor' at his side 'to call attention to faults in his behaviour or in the conduct of his office'. Well might Loyola declare: 'I have never left the army: I have only been seconded for the service of God.'

'Consult the schools of the Jesuits, for nothing better has been put in practice.' This was the tribute paid by Lord Chancellor Bacon, a man who did not like the Jesuits, to their educational work. Loyola had started by insisting on a good education for all members of his Order and he soon came to realize that good schools would be the best possible way of bringing boys up as faithful Christians. Before long the Jesuit schools became famous all over Europe. First and foremost the purpose of the Order was to convert men and women to the Catholic faith and this is why the Jesuits were always men of action living in the world and not in monasteries, wearing no distinctive habit as did other monks. The discipline which they had undergone made them able to endure every kind of hardship and they were strikingly successful both in converting the heathen and in

Jesuit missionaries in Japan. The painting is on a screen. The Jesuits are receiving a party of merchants, showing the connection between religion and trade.

winning back those who had become Protestants. Jesuit missionaries were soon at work all over Europe and later reached the Spanish colonies in the New World. Greatest of all Jesuit missionaries was Francis Xavier, one of Loyola's original companions, who went to India in 1542 and moved gradually eastwards to Malacca and on to China and Japan, dying in China in 1552.

Loyola was never a great scholar like Calvin, nor a great preacher like Luther, nor even a much-loved and cheerful companion like Zwingli: his greatness lay elsewhere. His terrific will-power and clear vision made it certain that he must succeed. His lameness and a lifetime of illness and racking pain were conquered by a remarkable self-control. Ribadeneira, one of his followers, wrote: 'And though his bodily condition had its ups and downs, for his health was inconstant, nevertheless his soul was invariably of an even temper.... With him there was no such thing as "feeling his pulse", no "taking a reckoning by the North star, no steering by a sea chart" as is the usual way of dealing with men in authority, for he was always in a

283

state of calm self-mastery.' Added to all this he had an astonishing understanding of men, which enabled him both to choose the right men for his Order and to use each man to the best advantage. In his apparent coldness and singleness of purpose he was curiously like Calvin; yet each man could win the devotion of those closest to him, who could see at moments a warmness of heart beneath the discipline and self-control. 'I have seen him', added Ribadeneira, 'in his old age, standing out on the balcony, or on some place of vantage where he could look at the sky, fix his gaze upwards and remain motionless, lost in thought, for a long time, and then, overcome by emotion, shed tears of joy. And I have often heard him say: "How contemptible the world seems when I look up at the sky".'

★　　★　　★

In the last resort the Jesuits were only a weapon. By placing themselves unconditionally in the hands of the pope, they were powerless unless the pope decided to use them, as he might or might not use other weapons of the Counter-Reformation to which we shall shortly come. The religious revival in Italy had been important but it had achieved less than was hoped, largely because little encouragement came from popes like Leo X or Clement VII. So the chance of any serious reform of the Church turned on what the new pope, Paul III (1534-49), might choose to do. Historians disagree about him and what he tried to achieve. Some praise him highly for his genuine wish to set about the work of reform; others point out how little he actually accomplished. Some extol his diplomatic ability, his intelligence, and his shrewd judgement; others, while admitting these qualities, describe his private life as being as much in need of reform as the Church. The truth would seem to be that he was a man whose weaknesses in the end choked the good intentions with which he began his reign.

At first Paul III showed his support for reform by making several leading Catholic reformers cardinals. Then in 1536 he appointed a commission to report on exactly what needed reforming, though the abuses in the Church were plain for all to see. When the report was completed, it was so damaging to the papacy that it was never allowed to be officially published. The source of all the trouble, so the report said, was the popes themselves and their love of riches. 'From that spring, Holy Father, as from the Trojan horse, have erupted into the Church so many abuses and such grave diseases . . . that because of us—us ourselves, we say, Christ's name is blasphemed among the nations.' Somehow a copy of the report got to Germany, where it was printed with scoffing comments suggesting that nothing would be done about it.

A bust of Contarini.

What, in fact, should Paul III do? Two men, both made cardinals by him, stand out as leaders of rival courses of action: Contarini, who wanted reconciliation with the Protestants and believed that, if only the Church could really reform herself, differences of doctrine could be amicably settled and the old unity of the Church restored; Caraffa, who looked on all heretics with implacable hatred and was determined that both heretics and abuses should be mercilessly rooted out.

Paul III at first inclined towards Contarini; even though it meant starting to put his own house in order. At once he ran into money troubles. The Sack of Rome in 1527 had almost wiped out one of his most valuable sources of income, the Roman customs revenues, and if he were to take serious notice of the report of his commission many other ways of raising money would have to go. Not surprisingly, Paul began to be less enthusiastic about reform. He did, however, send Contarini to an important meeting with the Protestants at Regensburg in 1541, a meeting to which Luther sent Melanchthon and Calvin himself came. But here again Paul was in a quandary. The emperor Charles V was very anxious to come to an agreement with the Protestants so as to turn his attention to his wars against France and the Turk. But if Charles were relieved of trouble in Germany, he would then have more time to control Italy and this Paul III most certainly did not want. However, in spite of Contarini's hopes, there was never much chance of reconciliation with the Protestants, certainly not with Calvin. Protestants would not have been content with a cleaning-up of the papacy, for they had happily thrown off their allegiance to the pope. Contarini never really understood the strength of men who were determined to set up their own churches and who saw little need for priests to ensure their own salvation. So reconciliation had failed and nothing had come of Paul's half-hearted attempts at reform. The way was clear for Caraffa.

Caraffa was a man of extraordinary contrasts. Always austere and simple in his private life—as a boy he had hoped to be a monk and later he became a member of the Oratory of Divine Love—he nevertheless revelled in the pomp and power which came to him as bishop, archbishop, cardinal, and, finally, as pope. The character of the man was first clearly seen when, as bishop of Chieti, a wild and mountainous diocese to the east of Rome, he used the sternest measures, such as excommunication, to bring both priests and people to a better way of living. The most important influence in his life was the years spent in Spain as papal nuncio. Coming from an ancient Neapolitan family, he had a well-nigh insane hatred of Spaniards because they ruled in Naples, yet he could not help being deeply impressed by the methods used by Ferdinand of Aragon to root out heresy, not least the Spanish Inquisition. In 1542 Caraffa persuaded Paul III to revive the Inquisition, which had existed since the thirteenth century but had largely fallen into disuse. His purpose was to extend the methods used in Spain to the whole Church, and he became at once one of the Chief Inquisitors. 'Heresy is to be suppressed as vigorously and as sharply as the physical plague, because it is the plague of the soul. If rags and clothes infected with the plague are removed and burnt, why should we not with the same severity extirpate, annihilate and remove heresy which is a disease of the mind, incomparably more precious than the body.' These are Caraffa's words, and it is not surprising that when he became pope as Paul IV in 1555 he reintroduced the use of torture. The Inquisition proved to be the least effective weapon in the armoury of the Counter-Reformation. It was too obviously a hangover from the Middle Ages to persuade Protestants that submission to it was the way to save one's soul. It succeeded, in fact, in stiffening resistance to the Church, especially north of the Alps, and was only efficient in those countries which needed it least, Italy and Spain, where there was very little heresy.

If the Church were to stamp out heresy and to prevent any backsliding by Catholics it was necessary to try to control the books that were read. There was nothing new in this. During the Middle Ages it had been easy enough to burn the few handwritten copies of any heretical book along with its author. By the sixteenth century, printing had made this an almost hopeless task. At first no book was supposed to be printed without a licence but it later became clear to Caraffa that what was needed was an official list of books which no faithful Catholic must read. Informal lists had existed long before the Counter-Reformation, and Protestants were often no less ready than Catholics to keep their followers from reading books which might change their minds. As Pope Paul IV, Caraffa decided in 1559 to issue an authoritative list in the name of the Church, the *Index Librorum Prohibitorum*, and to entrust the supervision of this task to the Inquisition. For a time, especially in Italy, it was an effective weapon and must have done much to suppress Renaissance freedom of thought. As we shall see in a later chapter, it did something to curb the new spirit of scientific inquiry. But in the long run it could not be the success which Caraffa intended.

*   *   *

The breakdown of the attempt at Regensburg to come to some agreement with the Protestants and the failure to bring about any noticeable reform forced Paul III to the reluctant conclusion that he could no longer avoid the call, made most strongly by the emperor Charles V, to summon a General Council of the Church. He had no wish whatever to do this, for he feared that a General Council might be declared to be superior to a pope and thus lead to a considerable lessening of his power. The Curia equally disliked the idea of a Council; many members of the Curia held posts of considerable value, which could be sold to the highest bidder, and the very suggestion of a Council sent values tumbling down. But Paul III was under too much pressure from the Emperor to resist much longer. If he did nothing there was a grave risk that Charles V might copy Henry VIII and create a national church for Germany with himself at its head. So pope and emperor agreed on a plan of action. Charles was to defeat the Lutherans in battle while the pope set about reforming the papacy. Then the defeated Lutherans would be brought to the Council for a discussion on their beliefs and, so Charles fondly hoped, would be won back to the Church by the proof that reforms really were taking place and peace would come once again in Germany.

Once a Council had been summoned there would be two main topics for discussion: reform of the Church and the drawing up of an exact statement about the Catholic faith. If Caraffa's plans for the destruction of heresy were to be pursued with the vigour which he wished, it was obviously important to decide precisely which opinions were heretical and which were not. The papal bull summoning the Council made it clear that both topics were to be discussed, but it mattered greatly to both pope and emperor which topic was to be considered the more important, and on this they violently disagreed. Charles V was mainly anxious to see reforms brought about quickly so as to help him solve his German problems; Paul III had no personal wish for sweeping reform and, as an Italian prince, he had even less wish to help Charles out of his German difficulties.

The immediate question was where the Council should meet. The pope would have an enormous advantage if it were held in Italy, for, since voting was to be by heads and not by nations, he could easily make sure of securing a majority vote for his plans as Italian bishops would have no difficulty in attending the Council at critical moments. Charles naturally hoped that it would be held in imperial territory. Eventually it was decided that the Council should meet at Trent, a city which was just inside the borders of the Empire but was strongly Italian in sympathy. Paul III decided not to attend in person but to send three Legates to represent him and to guide the deliberations. On 13 March 1545 the Papal Legates made their solemn entry into Trent. It was not such an auspicious occasion as was hoped, for the rain fell in torrents and the rapturous welcome accorded to the Legates by the local clergy could not disguise the total lack of interest shown by the townsfolk. Moreover, most of the delegates had not yet arrived. The representatives of the Emperor came fairly soon, but bishops straggled in from all over Europe throughout the summer and the Council did not finally get going until December. This slowness was to be typical of the whole history of the Council.

Titian's painting of one of the last sessions of the Council of Trent.

Its proceedings were to spread over a period of eighteen years, but in only about six of these years—1545-7, 1551-2, and 1562-3—were the delegates actively at work. Yet when one remembers the reluctance of popes to summon a Council at all, the lack of agreement between Paul III and Charles V, and the virtual impossibility of getting any work done in years when the Empire and France were at war, the wonder is not that the Council lasted so long but that it ever managed to meet at all. In fact its proceedings were to be of the greatest importance, for the Council marks the moment when the old medieval Church came to an end and the modern Roman Catholic Church began to emerge.

In the end the pope won hands down. There were several reasons for this. As has been said, a pope could always ensure a full attendance of Italian bishops pledged to support his policy, whereas other bishops often had long distances to travel as well as the expense and inconvenience of living far from home at Trent. Surprisingly few delegates actually arrived at the Council, not much more than 200 at any one time, and the Italians were always in a majority. The French bishops, for instance, never appeared in any strength until the final session. Moreover, the pope had the added advantage of being able to decide when to prorogue and when to resummon the Council. Caraffa, as Paul IV, never summoned the Council at all, partly from fear that it would attack his power, partly from his insane hatred of all things Spanish (and the Spanish bishops were pressing for thorough reform). In the end, by skilful guiding of the Council, reform featured very little in the final decrees of the Council of Trent. Considerable importance was, however, given to the proper education and training of priests; bishops were to be required to reside in their dioceses and have only one diocese; benefices were not to be bestowed on children or laymen; monks were to remain in their monasteries. How all this was to be enforced was not stated. The pope himself emerged from the Council with his authority upheld. This mattered less than might appear, for from the mid-sixteenth century the personal character of the popes was steadily changing for the better. Gone were the spectacular days of the Renaissance papacy; reforms were promised in the papal machinery and were gradually carried out.

On the other hand there was a host of decrees dealing with doctrine and all aimed at laying down a clearly defined statement of the Catholic faith, a task in which the Jesuits played a notable part. In the past the Church had seldom needed to issue rigid and binding definitions in matters of belief, for the choice before most people was quite clear: Christianity or paganism. The Protestant challenge had altered all this and Christians now found themselves faced with a choice between rival brands of Christianity. Although the Protestants appeared at the second session of the Council, they gained nothing from the debates. On every issue the decision went against them and in the final decrees their beliefs were condemned and all hope of compromise extinguished. The spirit of Caraffa, the belief that the Church could only be saved by imposing uniformity at whatever cost, prevailed. It was to be war between Catholic and Protestant: the Council of Trent cleared the decks for action and strengthened all Catholics against the coming day of battle.

Chapter 12
The Age of Philip II

Two compelling reasons forced Philip II of Spain and Henry II of France to bring the long drawn-out struggle between Hapsburg and Valois to an end, even though no decisive result had been achieved—bankruptcy and heresy. Neither side could raise any more money either from taxes or from the bankers to keep the war going; and both rulers were seriously alarmed at the spread of Calvinism. So in a disused château, with hastily improvised paper windows in wooden frames, the Peace of Cateau-Cambrésis was signed in 1559, in the hope that in a peaceful Europe Catholic rulers could turn their undivided attention to stamping out heresy. Any hopes of peace were to be quickly disappointed: Europe was about to be plunged into a series of religious struggles, wars of Catholic against Protestant, in which both sides sought help from men of the same faith in other lands. In the very year in which peace was signed, John Knox returned from Geneva to Scotland bent on making his country Calvinist and, within a year, on organizing resistance to the attempt of the Catholic Mary Queen of Scots to rule the land with French help. In 1562 France was torn by the first of seven wars between Catholic and Huguenot, which made her largely powerless in Europe for thirty years. In 1566 the Dutch rose in revolt against their Spanish rulers and a long and heroic struggle began which was to win for the Dutch their freedom by 1609. In 1568, in a much shorter but no less desperate war, the Moors in Granada rebelled in an attempt to end the oppressive treatment which they received at the hands of the Spaniards. And, as if this catalogue of wars were not long enough, there was the continuing danger from the Turks, especially in the Mediterranean.

'This war', wrote a French Protestant pastor about the Civil War in France, 'is not like other wars, for even the very poorest man has an interest in it, since we are fighting for freedom of conscience.' 'You may assure His Holiness', wrote Philip II to his ambassador in Rome, 'that rather than suffer the least damage to religion and the service of God, I would lose all my states and a hundred lives, if I had them; for I do not propose nor desire to be the ruler of heretics.' What Philip did not add was that he had no intention of losing a single one of his possessions if he could help it, and the pastor said nothing about Calvin's brilliantly organized attempt to make France a Protestant country, which was bound to affect the position of any king of France. Wars of religion they certainly were, but politics played as big a part in them as in any previous war.

Preaching at the funeral service of Mary Tudor in 1558, the Bishop of Winchester warned the congregation of the dangers of Calvinism: 'The wolves be coming out of Geneva and other places of Germany, and have sent their books before, full of pestilent doctrines, blasphemy and heresy to infect the people.' Books are easy things to smuggle into a country and for several years translations of the Bible, pamphlets about Calvinism, and copies of Calvin's *Institutes* had travelled safely in pedlars' packs, in the holds of ships, or had been secretly passed from hand to hand, bought, perhaps originally at the great book fair at Frankfurt. The number of printing presses in Geneva increased rapidly and some 30,000 volumes a year poured out from them. Frontiers became easier for missionaries to cross after the peace of Cateau-Cambrésis had been signed and Calvinist pastors were eagerly welcomed, especially in France, Holland, and Scotland. The way that the Calvinist churches were organized and disciplined made them excellent centres for religious rebellion. For the little communities were linked together all over the country to make sure that Calvinists were not isolated but could feel themselves to be every bit as much of an international church, run from Geneva, as the Catholics with their headquarters at Rome.

Because Calvinism depended so much upon study of the Bible and of Calvin's writings, it was bound to appeal to the educated classes— the skilled artisans, merchants, lawyers, and other professional men in the towns—rather than to the peasants in the countryside. In fact the peasants were usually hostile to missionaries who told them that the saints' days and festivals, which made such a welcome break in the endless work on the farms, should be abolished, along with the colour and mystery of the Mass, which had brought comfort to them and their forebears over the centuries. The big development in the second half of the century, however, was the success of Calvinism in winning over members of the nobility and gentry. This was due to a number of causes: genuine contempt for the corrupt and ignorant state of so many of the French clergy; the influence of wives who found time to study the new doctrines and then to convert their husbands; sometimes it was a means of opposing the king who upheld the old ways. As more and more Calvinist communities were formed, so, especially in France, did they place themselves under the protection of the nearest Huguenot nobleman. On top of a religious organization devised to overthrow the Catholic faith in a country was added a military organization. A very dangerous situation was being created, which rulers were often powerless to control. In France alone there were said to be 2,150 Huguenot churches in 1561. Kings had long been accustomed to dealing with rebellious nobles or with heretics; never before had they had to face an alliance between the two.

Although in Chapter 3 we saw something of the growth of strong monarchies, yet for a long time even the strongest was very much at the mercy of the accidents of birth and death. France is a striking example of this. When Henry II was killed in 1559, his widow, Catherine de Medici, was left with a large family including four sickly sons, hopelessly unfit by reason of age, health, or character to govern firmly. Until 1598 France had no king strong and able enough to stop the civil wars or to play a leading part in European affairs. In England the power of the Tudors declined for a while after Henry VIII's death, for that much-married monarch left only an ailing boy and two girls to succeed him. Moreover, it was an age when a queen was thought to be at a grave disadvantage compared to a king. It was not until she had reigned successfully for thirty years that Elizabeth I could proudly say to her troops at Tilbury, 'I know I have the body of a weak and feeble woman, but I have the heart and stomach of a King, and of a King of England too.' Even a powerful king like Philip II of Spain was haunted by the problem of making sure that he was succeeded by a worthy son.

This chapter is called 'The Age of Philip II' but it might almost as well have been called 'The Age of Catherine de Medici' or 'The Age of Elizabeth I', for these three rulers dominated the second half of the century and their rival policies to a great extent made up the complicated pattern of events. They came to power within the space of three years—Philip in 1556, Elizabeth in 1558, and Catherine in 1559—and they were all long-lived; Catherine, who died in 1588, and Elizabeth, who died in 1603, were both 69 years old at their deaths, while Philip was 71 when he died in 1598. Since a contemporary in 1559 would have said that Spain was undoubtedly the leading nation in Europe and since Philip was to play a central part in the tangled affairs of France, England, and also Holland, it is right to accord him pride of place.

* * *

Philip had been born on 21 May 1527 at Valladolid in Spain. All the festivities to celebrate the birth of an emperor's son and heir had to be hastily cancelled because a fortnight previously Charles V's mutinous troops had scandalized Europe by sacking Rome and holding the pope prisoner in his own castle—an omen, perhaps, of the strained relations between the pope and Spain, which were to be a marked feature of Philip's reign. Philip grew up in Spain, unsure of himself and desperately anxious to live up to his father's high hopes for him. Before he was 17 he had married a Portuguese princess, who died a year later in giving birth to a son, the ill-fated

Titian's portrait of Philip II. The armour which he is wearing does not mean that Philip himself was a great soldier.

Don Carlos. Charles, as we have seen, was always on the move in his efforts to govern his scattered empire, and in 1549 Philip joined him in Brussels to learn at first hand something of the task that lay not so very far ahead, for Charles's thoughts were already turning towards retirement. The journey to Brussels had not been a great success. As the Venetian ambassador was later to report: 'His Majesty, when he first quitted Spain, passed through Italy and Germany to Flanders, and conveyed a universal impression that he was of a severe and intractable disposition and therefore was not much liked by the Italians, thoroughly disliked by the Flemings and hated by the Germans.' Although Charles tried to teach his son to be more affable, Philip never learned the secret of getting on well with people. After two years with his father, Philip returned to Spain as regent, where he remained until the death of Edward VI of England opened up visions to Charles of a brilliant stroke of policy. Mary Tudor, a passionately devout Catholic, was now on the throne, determined to bring her country back to the Roman fold. She was 38 and Philip only 26; but what did this matter compared to the advantages which the Hapsburgs would gain from an alliance of Spain and England? Philip was nothing if not dutiful: 'As a son ever obedient,' he wrote to his father, 'it is not for me to have any other will.' Charles made the proposal and even wrote the love letters; for Philip dreaded the seasickness of the voyage to England, hated the beer which he expected to have to drink, and had no affection for his new bride. It proved a joyless and barren marriage, which ended in 1558 with Mary's death and the return of England to the Protestant cause under Elizabeth I.

But before Mary's sad life ended, Charles had handed over most of his empire to his son in that moving scene in Brussels, which was described on p. 208. It was not the whole inheritance which passed to Philip, for the Hapsburg lands in Germany were to be governed by Charles's brother, Ferdinand. Philip never became an emperor like his father, but to be king of Spain gave him land enough to rule. After the acquisition of Portugal in 1580, the whole Iberian peninsula was at last under one king; in addition, the Netherlands, Milan, Naples, Sicily, and all of the Spanish possessions in the New World were his. Charles V had always been on the move, but once Philip returned to Spain after Cateau-Cambrésis he never left the peninsula and, to emphasize this change, in 1561 Madrid became his permanent capital.

Philip II had the misfortune to become during his reign the enemy of three national heroes—Elizabeth I of England, William the Silent in Holland, and Henry of Navarre in France. The man who sent the Armada against England, who tried to crush the Dutch, and who wanted to keep France weak and to prevent a powerful man from becoming king, is not likely to be popular with English,

Dutch, or French writers. Yet the Spanish think of him as one of their greatest kings; the people of Castile among whom he spent most of his life adored him; and in his reign learning, literature, and painting flourished. Spain had twenty-nine universities, crowded with students. From the fourteenth to the seventeenth centuries Spain had one of the great literatures of the world; great plays were being written, and five years after Philip's death Cervantes (1547–1616) published his immortal story of *Don Quixote*. He was the son of a poor doctor and after receiving some kind of education became a regular soldier at the age of 21. He fought at Lepanto and in other battles against the Turks, was taken prisoner by pirates, became a slave in Algiers and was finally ransomed in 1580. On returning to Spain he earned a precarious living by writing plays and by getting various small government posts, including one in which he was employed in provisioning the Armada. The first part of *Don Quixote* was published in 1604, and the adventures of the mad knight of La Mancha and his faithful servant, Sancho Panza, quickly became famous. Cervantes does not seem to have made his fortune from the book, for he was described by a French visitor shortly before his death as 'old, a soldier, a gentleman and poor'. At the same time the religious spirit of the Spanish people was being expressed on canvas in the violent colours and writhing shapes of a painter from Crete, who made Toledo his home, Domeniko Theotokopoulos (1541–1614), whom the Spanish not surprisingly found it easier just to call El Greco, the Greek.

Philip himself was a strange, outwardly cold person, untouched by the warmth of Spain. 'In face he was the living image of his father, having the same skin and features with that mouth and the one pendulous lip overhanging the other, and all the other characteristics of the Emperor, except for his smaller stature,' reported the Venetian ambassador to England. 'He wears his beard short and pointed and his hair is light and yellow,' wrote another contemporary. 'He looks like a Fleming but his loftiness is that of a Spaniard'. Others speak of a voice so soft that he was difficult to hear, of a piercing eye, and of a smile which 'cut like a sword'. He was shy and diffident with people, mistrustful of his advisers, and determined that every decision must be his alone. His self-control was phenomenal: the news of a great victory over the Turk like Lepanto or the disastrous defeat and loss of the Armada was received with sign of neither joy nor grief. But he was by no means inhuman under the icy exterior, as we can tell from the charming letters which he wrote to his daughters from Portugal, letters in which he scolds himself for eating too many melons or says wistfully how much he misses the song of the nightingales at home.

Philip's capacity for work was terrifying. Insistent that every important document from all his dominions was passed to him by his secretaries, he toiled all day and far into the night, ruling Spain from his desk. 'No secretary in the world uses more paper than his Majesty,' was the acid comment of one of the governors in the Netherlands. Philip was essentially a weak man who found it hard to make up his mind and who probably only felt completely sure of himself behind the ever-growing mountains of documents. 'Your Majesty spends so long considering your undertakings', wrote Pope Pius V to him, 'that when the moment to perform them comes, the occasion has passed and the money has all been spent.' As he grew older and more weary, he seemed unable to distinguish between what was important and what did not matter. At the time that he was working on the preparations for the Armada he was also wasting long hours writing angrily to the pope about details of the dress which Spanish priests ought to wear. He was capable of returning a vital document, which urgently needed an answer, with a note in the margin pointing out a spelling mistake. No wonder that in the end both king and government ground to a halt. 'I have a lot to send you from yesterday, but it is not possible now. I will do it tomorrow,' wrote the exhausted king to his secretary. There is no better monument to this deeply religious, aloof, and all-powerful ruler than the Escorial, a building originally intended as a tomb for the body of Charles V but which became as well a palace, a monastery, and a church. Here, among the lonely grey hills, twenty miles north-west of Madrid, Philip could escape from the capital, pursue his own religious devotions, work in quiet, and enjoy the little relaxation that he ever allowed himself among his paintings, manuscripts, and rare books, which he collected with a scholar's devotion from all over Europe.

(i) Spain on the defensive

The Peace of Cateau-Cambrésis ended for a time the wars between the Hapsburgs and Valois, but Spain and France remained national enemies. France had no more intention of helping Philip II to crush the Dutch Protestants than Philip had of giving French Catholics any worthwhile support against the Huguenots. Each nation delighted in its rival's difficulties. France had no wish whatever to see Philip's hold over the Netherlands strengthened, for she felt herself to be a nut in Spanish nutcrackers. On three sides she was hemmed in by Spanish possessions—in the north lay the Netherlands, on her eastern frontier Luxembourg and Franche-Comté, further south came Milan, while, as a final warning, the little district of Roussillon in south-west France was like a Spanish finger stretching over on to the French side of the Pyrenees. But if France longed to break the ring around her, it was vital to Spain to maintain her hold, for, apart from the sea, her only line of communication with the Netherlands ran northwards from Milan. In their continuing struggle both Spain and France were concerned with the extraordinary position of England, which, in their view, ought to be begging for protection from one or other of them. But Elizabeth I, that brilliant, patriotic, and, when necessary, unscrupulous states-woman, knew that England's salvation lay in joining neither side. She realized that France was no great danger so long as civil wars wasted her strength and Philip with his hands full in the Mediterranean and the Netherlands dared not provoke her too far. In fact, as time went on, it became France and Spain who angled for an English alliance, though Elizabeth proved too shrewd for them. She played the marriage comedy with zest and, until quite an old woman, shamelessly flirted with rival suitors but gave her hand to none. One day accounts would have to be settled between England and Spain but not until Elizabeth felt sure that England was powerful enough to win.

★   ★   ★

For the first twenty-five years of his reign Philip was forced to be on the defensive. Although this suited his cautious temperament, two factors prevented him from taking the initiative. Spain had to bear the brunt of the Turkish attacks in the Mediterranean at the very time when the peoples of the Netherlands were trying to become independent and when events in France added to Philip's troubles. An even greater deterrent to an all-out offensive on her enemies by Spain was Philip's chronic lack of money. So, before seeing what part Spain played in the affairs of Europe, it is important to understand the financial background.

Throughout the fifteenth and early sixteenth centuries every European ruler discovered that war was much the heaviest part of his expenses—far more costly than the building of palaces, the upkeep of a brilliant court, and the payment of the growing number of officials. In England the Tudors quickly learned that if they wanted to be financially independent of nobles and parliament they could not afford the luxury of wars across the Channel. Between 1557 and 1559 first Spain and then France went bankrupt and announced that they could not pay their debts to the bankers who had helped to finance their wars. Many of the smaller banking houses collapsed and even a great house like that of the Fuggers was badly shaken.

Although kings were usually hopelessly short of money, Europe as a whole was becoming more prosperous. Up to about the middle of the sixteenth century the nations of western Europe had largely traded among themselves. In the second half of the century two new trading areas became important—eastern Europe and the Spanish colonies in the New World. We have seen how Poland and Bohemia and Hungary had become the great grain-producing area of the Continent. In the 1560s almost one quarter of the grain consumed in the Netherlands arrived from Baltic ports. As the population of Europe was steadily increasing, this new supply of grain often made all the difference between starvation and survival for those living in the rapidly growing towns. From the east also came wood, fibres, and metals, shipped from Danzig and other ports to Amsterdam, which soon outstripped Antwerp in wealth and importance. But of far greater effect on the economy of Europe and on Philip II's finances was the New World, or the 'Indies', as the Spaniards always called their American possessions.

It took time to develop the new colonies and not until the 1550s were they beginning to be a valuable asset to Castile. Castilians fiercely maintained that the profits were theirs alone because their soldiers had conquered the lands and they had met the cost. They insisted that the pope had awarded the New World to the Crown of Castile and so no other part of Spain, and certainly no other European nation, must be allowed to share in the wealth. In time Drake and Hawkins were to take little notice of this, but for the moment a great trading system between Spain and America was built up on which the power of Philip II in the last resort rested. By about 1570 there must have been some 118,000 Spaniards living in Mexico and Peru and these settlers needed the foodstuffs, clothing, metal goods, wine, corn, and oil which would have been theirs in Castile. In return they sent home pearls and dye-stuffs, some gold, but above all silver, which, when turned into coinage, was sent to pay Philip's troops, helped to meet his debts to the new Genoese banking houses, and found its way into the hands of superb Italian silversmiths like Benvenuto Cellini. It was in 1545 that the great Potosi silver mines in modern Bolivia had been discovered, and three years later another big mine was found in Mexico. Round about 1560 a new way of getting the silver out of the ore by using an amalgam of mercury was discovered, and what had been a stream became a river of silver flowing into Spain. It was this fact which made it possible for Philip II in the last twenty years of his life to take the offensive against the Portuguese, the Dutch, and the English.

Seville, a thriving port with 100,000 inhabitants, a fine cathedral, great trading houses, and streets thronged with merchants, sailors, and dockers from many lands, was the heart of the new trade. Every spring a fleet of some sixty or seventy vessels would be assembled here and in May would sail for Vera Cruz in Mexico. Three months later another fleet would leave for Nombre de Dios (later called Portobello) on the isthmus of Panama. The fleets would winter in America and then, laden with silver laboriously transported by sea from Peru and then by land across Panama and Mexico, would meet

The port of Seville. This is part of a large sixteenth-century painting by Sanchez Coello.

in Havana and, closely guarded, sail for home, reaching Seville about September. It was not only Spaniards who anxiously awaited the safe arrival of the treasure fleets each autumn; most of Europe depended on this annual supply of new silver. Merchants clamoured to be paid for the goods which they had exported to the Indies; shipbuilders and provisioners equally needed quick repayment; bankers had risked much and expected high profits; the ordinary business of buying and selling in towns or at the great international fairs depended on a supply of ready money.

In spite of this apparent wealth pouring into Seville and finding its way into most countries of Europe, all was not well. Prices, which had been fairly stable at the end of the Middle Ages, were rising alarmingly, particularly in Spain, where by the 1550s the cost of most things was double what it had been in 1500. People were baffled by a frightening rise in the cost of living; there was more money about, but it bought less and less. This is something with which the modern world is all too familiar, but then only a few men understood the reasons. It was a Frenchman, Jean Bodin, who in 1568 wrote a book suggesting that there must be a close connection

299

between the bullion coming from the Indies and the rise in prices. He was right in this and even wiser when he suggested that there was more than one cause. Prices of food, especially of grain, were rising faster than other prices, and this we would expect to happen in an age when the population was increasing more rapidly than the amount of food which could be produced. If too many people want something in short supply its price is likely to rise sharply. Bodin also pointed to a rise in the general standard of living of the nobility and of the wealthy townsfolk. They became discontented with meagre furnishings for their homes, with all but the richest clothes; they wanted to live in some luxury and were prepared to pay for it. So for this reason also prices rose. The effect on rulers was striking. Philip II, with the wealth of the Indies at his door, could not pay his debts in 1575 or in 1596. In the next century the Stuarts in England were more and more in the hands of parliament as they failed to make ends meet. So in studying the story of Europe in the second half of the sixteenth century, the financial background is all important.

★   ★   ★

At the start of his reign Philip regarded the Turkish threat to his Italian possessions as easily the most pressing danger to be overcome. Italy lay right across the path of Suleiman the Magnificent's attack by sea, and if the Italian defences were once to crumble, then not only might Spain lose a valuable source of grain but her own coasts would be threatened. If any part of Philip's dominions had to be sacrificed, in the last resort the north mattered far less than the Mediterranean. Philip's immediate problem was that his fleet was not yet up to the task. In 1561 the Turks were sighted west of Majorca, and three years later Philip saw with his own eyes a Turkish pirate ship from Algiers come into the harbour of Valencia. So, regardless of cost, the building of galleys began with feverish haste which, as we have seen, brought Philip his reward at the battle of Lepanto.

The Turks were not only a danger at sea. In the south of Spain were the Moriscos, the so-called New Christians, descendants of those who had been forcibly converted in the days of Ferdinand and Isabella, but who had never become loyal citizens. Some were known to be in touch with their countrymen in North Africa and few paid more than lip-service to Christian beliefs and customs. They might be compelled to have their children baptized, but the holy oil was quickly washed off the moment that they got home. They had to wear Castilian clothes when being married, but the wedding feast was celebrated in Moorish dress with traditional singing and dancing. The Spaniards despised them for being effeminate in their liking for hot baths, but much more for their hard work and the money which they made from trade. In Spanish eyes no real gentleman made money by working for it. Unfortunately Philip was not the kind of man to turn a blind eye to all this. He was advised to expel them from the country but could only make up his mind to pass severer laws against the use of Moorish language and customs. Eventually, driven to desperation by constant harrying, the Moriscos rose in revolt on Christmas night 1568. Hideous cruelties were perpetrated, especially against priests and monks and nuns, whose eyes and tongues were torn out. For two years the Moriscos defied Philip's soldiers in the mountains of Granada, but the outcome was inevitable. Philip's solution was to move them from Granada and to spread them in new homes all over Spain. It did not work. It was left to Philip's son to expel them from the country in 1609, and thereby to strike a deadly blow at the Spanish economy.

1568 was a terrible year for Philip: the Moriscos in revolt, religious turmoil in France, a dangerous situation developing in the Netherlands, the immediate need to face the tragic problem of his only son, Don Carlos, and the death of his third wife. At the age of 23, with a head too big for his body, one shoulder too high, and one leg too short, of doubtful sanity as his ungovernable rages and his savage delight in whipping horses and even small girls shows, Don Carlos was clearly hopelessly incapable of one day ruling the Spanish dominions. His dangerous hatred of his father, who believed, though wrongly, that he was intriguing with Spain's enemies, made Philip decide that his son could no longer be allowed to go free. On the night of 18 January 1568 Philip led a small and grim procession to the prince's room. Terrified, the young man begged his father not to kill him, but Philip had no intention of this. It was enough to seal up the windows, lock the doors, and place a guard outside. Philip never saw his son again, and six months later Don Carlos was dead. Wild rumours quickly spread that the prince had been killed on his father's orders; there was no need for this. Don Carlos's excesses had already undermined his feeble health and while under guard he either went on hunger strike or gorged like a glutton. Once an enormous pie containing three partridges was wolfed down with the aid of quantities of iced water. Dysentery set in and this was the cause of death. Philip's cold reserve and proud dislike of telling the world what his son was really like seemed to confirm the rumours; but they were not true. An heir to the throne was essential, and so in 1570 Philip was married for the fourth time to an Austrian princess who was to bear him four sons. Of these only one, the future Philip III, survived.

★   ★   ★

When Henry II was accidentally killed in the tournament in 1559, France desperately needed three things, none of which she was to get: a long period of peace, firm government, and strict economy. Henry's wars and his own extravagance had made France bankrupt, and the precarious future of the house of Valois passed to his four sons, the eldest of whom, the new King Francis II, was only 15 and in poor health. Although Francis was officially old enough to rule, there was bound to be a struggle between those anxious to advise and ultimately control him. Chief of these was Henry II's widow, Catherine de Medici, who at the age of 40 was determined to rule France through her sons. This very remarkable woman, a niece of Pope Clement VII, came from the great Florentine banking family, though her mother was French. As part of his Italian schemes Francis I had married Henry to Catherine, then only 14, never expecting this son to succeed to the throne. When this happened, Catherine was made to feel that by birth she was not worthy to be a queen and, although she dutifully presented her husband with ten children, her married life was never very happy, for Henry's affections were squandered on his powerful mistress, Diane de Poitiers. On Henry's death Catherine saw her chance of making up for years of contempt and neglect by becoming the real ruler of France.

Catherine was an able and courageous woman of incredible vitality and strength of purpose; a schemer who, by twists and turns of policy, clung to the power in which she revelled. The mainspring of her ambition was her devotion to her children, and she set out to secure a crown for each of her sons—the French crown for the eldest, and any crown that happened to be going begging, like that of Poland, for her younger boys. Her Italian blood made her a politician to her fingertips, but being almost entirely without principle she fell short of true statesmanship. For example, in an age in which religious passions ran as high as in modern Ireland, she found it difficult to understand what all the fuss was about, and she always hopefully believed that her skill would persuade hated rivals to discuss their differences round a table and shake hands at the end. Like a true Renaissance figure she loved to be surrounded by beautiful things and she greatly enjoyed splashing her private fortune around, especially on splendid new buildings. She was plain in appearance, intensely disliked by many who came her way, and, with good reason, mistrusted by most of them; but for thirty years neither friend nor foe could afford to ignore her. Perhaps the kindest verdict on her was pronounced some years after her death by Henry IV, the man who became the first Bourbon king of France after the deaths of all her sons: 'But I ask you, I ask you what a poor woman could do, left by the death of her husband, with five little children on her arms, and two families in France who were thinking to grasp the crown—

A drawing by Clouet of Catherine de Medici.

ours and the Guises. Was she not compelled to play strange parts to deceive first one and then the other, in order to guard, as she has done, her sons, who have successfully reigned through the wise conduct of that shrewd woman? I am surprised that she never did worse.'

There were, in fact, three rival families, each intent on controlling the young king. Catherine's policy was to play off one against another and thus to keep the control herself. The chief of these families was the Bourbons, heirs to the throne if and when the Valois line should die out. Two members of this family matter. There was Louis, Prince of Condé, a brilliant soldier, marvellously gay despite being deformed and always in financial straits, and Henry of Navarre, destined to reunite France as Henry IV. Next in importance, though of first importance in their own eyes, were the Guises. They were immensely wealthy and powerful and already related to the French monarchy through their master stroke in marrying Mary Stuart, their niece and later Mary Queen of Scots, to Francis II. At the head of this family was the Duke of Guise, who had won fame as a soldier when he captured Calais from the English. The third great family was the Montmorencys, of whom the head was Anne (a man's name here), Constable of France, the chief military official in the land. Close to him was his nephew, Coligny, Admiral of France, and the one man in the whole sordid and dreary story whose integrity was beyond question.

Rival political ambitions were dangerous enough, but what made their feud deadly beyond Catherine's understanding was religion. For the Bourbons were Huguenots, the Guises Roman Catholics, while the Constable was a Catholic and the Admiral a Huguenot. Civil war was inevitable when neither side in the sixteenth century believed that toleration was possible. If peace were patched up it was known to be temporary and only a sign that at the moment neither side was strong enough to destroy the other.

Catherine's great chance to achieve her ambition came at the end of 1560 when the ailing Francis II died, to be succeeded by his brother, a boy not quite 10 years old, as Charles IX. There had to be a regency this time, and Catherine, standing beside her son as he received the homage of the nobility, showed that she had every intention of being the regent. As further proof that she alone was in charge of her son, she ordered her bed to be moved into his bedroom. Passions were running dangerously high and needed to be cooled. As ever, Catherine believed that soft words would be enough but events rapidly moved beyond her control. Three times between 1562 and 1570 the country slipped into civil war. 'We fought the first war like angels,' said a Huguenot leader, 'the second like men and the third like devils.' There was nothing very angelic or manly about the first two wars, but the remark does reflect the steady slide

A drawing by Clouet of Coligny.

into barbarism and anarchy on both sides. Huguenots slaughtered women and children and compelled the monks in a captured abbey to hang each other. In Orleans Catholics burned Huguenots to death in locked prisons; elsewhere a sick marquis was dragged from bed and roasted alive in his own oven.

By 1570 Guise had been assassinated and Condé killed in battle. Although outnumbered, the Huguenots had held their own, and Catherine felt that the time for a truce had come. The Huguenots were officially given the right to worship as they wished—a right which they seldom accorded to Catholics in areas under their control—and, as guarantee of good faith, the right to garrison four towns in the south of France. Coligny, now their undisputed leader, came to Court where he fascinated the young king by the charm of his personality. To make the peace more lasting Catherine arranged

for her daughter, Margaret, to marry the young Huguenot, Henry of Navarre, while Coligny began to persuade the king that France could best be united by a new war against Spain. In Catherine's eyes he was becoming too powerful an influence over her son and must be eliminated. A plot to murder him miscarried and he was only wounded. Huguenots, in Paris in great numbers for the wedding of Henry of Navarre, breathed vengeance and at this critical moment Catherine lost her head. She persuaded her son that the Huguenots were planning to overthrow his government. 'Then kill them all,' he is said to have shrieked. Catherine probably only intended to get rid of the leading figures, but the situation was utterly beyond control. In the early hours of Saint Bartholomew's Day, 24 August 1572, a general massacre of Huguenots began in Paris, in which Coligny did not this time escape, and spread to the provinces. The thirteen-year-old Duke of Sully, later to become a famous minister under Henry IV, wrote:

I put on my student's gown and, taking a large breviary [a book of Catholic services] under my arm, went downstairs. As I walked out into the street I was horrified; there were madmen running to and fro, smashing down doors and shouting, 'Kill, Kill, massacre the Huguenots.' Blood spattered before my eyes and doubled my fear. I ran into a clump of soldiers who stopped me. They plied me with questions and began to jostle me about when luckily they saw my breviary. That served as my safe conduct. Twice again the same thing happened and twice again I escaped.

Estimates differ about the numbers killed, perhaps 4,000 in Paris and as many more in the provinces. One Parisian butcher boasted that he himself had slaughtered 400. Philip II wrote to congratulate Catherine on 'the best and most cheerful news which at present could come to me'. The pope attended a service of thanksgiving and had a medal struck in honour of the massacre.

Catherine's black deed brought her no victory. The Huguenots remained strong in the country south of the Loire where before long they defied the government by setting up a rival republic. The Catholics were more divided amongst themselves than ever before, especially as a number of them, to be known as *Politiques*, began to ask themselves whether religious unity was worth the horror of St. Bartholomew's Day. The civil wars began again, and it seemed as if war had become a normal part of French life. The great nobles fought to control the country, the lesser nobles, ruined by inflation and the devastation of their estates, tried to recoup their losses by hiring themselves out to the rival armies. Young men with no other way of earning a living found it better to join a plundering band than to do much else. Two years after the massacre Charles IX died and his abler but idle and very unpleasant brother, for whom in the previous year Catherine had secured the vacant Polish crown, came home again as Henry III. He was the last man to bring unity and strong government. Years later Sully in his Memoirs wrote: 'I shall never forget the fantastic and extravagant equipage and attitude in which I found this prince in his cabinet: he had a sword at his side, a Spanish hood hung down upon his shoulders, a little cap, such as collegians wear, upon his head and a basket full of little dogs hung to a broad ribbon about his neck.' His life varied between long bursts of dissolute gaiety and periods of repentance when he and his courtiers would roam the streets in disguise, chanting psalms and scourging each other. These courtiers, nicknamed the *mignons* ('daintily small'), became notorious. They were fantastically dressed, with long hair 'crimped and re-crimped in the most artificial way', their heads sitting on their ruffs 'like the head of John the Baptist on a platter'. Their days and nights were passed in a riot of gambling, swearing, fighting, dancing, and loose living. Catherine was tireless in her desperate efforts to prevent France from falling apart, and by 1580 her long talks with party leaders all over the country brought some sort of calm, which made it possible for general support of the Duke of Anjou's expedition to help the Dutch against Philip II.

At this point it is necessary to see what had been happening in the Spanish Netherlands.

★　　★　　★

The Netherlands over which Philip ruled had no national unity and today are split up between four countries: Holland, Belgium, Luxembourg, and France. They were divided into seventeen provinces, each having its own local government, lawcourts, trade guilds, and ancient privileges. In addition there were some 300 walled towns, whose inhabitants showed great local patriotism and were fiercely determined to uphold their rights and liberties. Charles V had tried to bring some kind of unity, but the only real power which the central government at Brussels possessed was the right to appoint the chief official in each province, the Stadtholder, and the chief magistrate, the Grand Pensionary, in each town. The three million inhabitants of the Netherlands spoke Dutch in the ten northern provinces, French in the six southern provinces, and in the remaining province, both languages. At the time of Philip's accession the overwhelming majority of the population were officially Roman Catholics, but more in the spirit of Erasmus than of their new king. There were already signs that Calvinism was spreading among the middle classes, but, in contrast with France, it was a long time before the nobility took up the Protestant cause. Most of these nobles were jovial, carefree men, eating and drinking to excess—none of the banquets which they so frequently gave each other was a success unless the guests had drunk themselves stupid and had

The United Provinces.

0 20 40 60 80 100 120 140 km
0   20   40   60   80 miles

slipped off their chairs to sleep peacefully under the table—often deeply in debt from the state which they kept. (Once when he decided to make a real effort to economize, William of Orange dismissed twenty-eight head cooks.) Like all the Netherlanders they prized their independence above all else and regarded their civilization as far richer, finer, and more ancient than anything which the upstart Spaniards, whom they detested, could produce. They were intensely proud of the splendours of Brussels, of their land famous

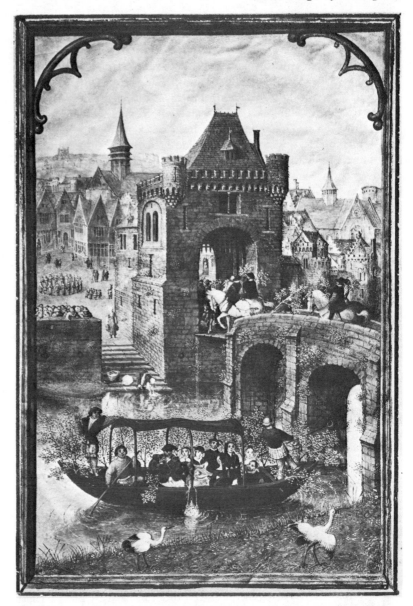

for its painting, its exquisite miniatures, its rich stained glass, for its tapestries from Arras, the fine linen which came from Cambrai, and the lace of Malines. In music it was to the Netherlands that even musical nations like England and Italy looked for inspiration.

Economically the Netherlands were extremely prosperous. Much of the northern part of the country remained rural, relying on its dairy produce, with the big cheeses from Edam and Gouda, still famous, and on the breeding of fat cattle and sheep. In the south, however, changes had begun, for the coal and iron mines of Liège and Namur were helping to make the Netherlands a newly industrialized country. After the New World colonies, the Netherlands were the wealthiest part of Philip's dominions and they were the chief market for Spanish wool and the supplier of Spain's needs for metal products, cereal, and the naval stores which originally came from the Baltic lands. The sea was both a danger and another source of wealth. Unless careful watch was kept on the dykes, the low-lying countryside could quickly be drowned. At the same time the wharves of great ports like Amsterdam and Middleburg were ceaselessly busy with a thriving coastal trade and fishermen grew rich on vast catches of herrings. At the heart of all this economic activity stood Antwerp, the most important financial centre for the whole of Europe in the second half of the sixteenth century.

Although he had taxed the Netherlands heavily and had persecuted the Protestants there by means of his own brand of inquisition, Charles V had always been popular. Philip did not inherit his father's love of the Netherlands, and many a leading nobleman saw in his withdrawal to Spain an ominous sign of future trouble. From being an important and cherished part of a great empire, the Netherlands suddenly found themselves part of Spain's possessions, under the rule of a foreign king who neither understood them nor showed much likelihood of trying to get to know them. Inflexible government from Madrid had replaced the old easy-going ways. Philip, as much as his father, urgently needed all the money that he could extract from the Netherlands, but he was not the kind of man to allow any of his subjects freedom to run their own affairs in return for prompt payment of taxes. As his deputy, Philip appointed his half-sister, Margaret of Parma, daughter of Charles V by a Flemish woman. She was a commanding manly figure, with a deep bass voice and a famous moustache, a homely person who meant well but who had little influence over Philip. Real power lay in the hands of Cardinal Granvelle, Primate of the Netherlands from 1561, a diplomat trained under Charles V, a collector of classical statues and modern paintings, a man for whom the Church had provided the avenue to a successful career which his humble birth might otherwise have prevented. He did not share Philip's rigid views but was completely loyal to his master.

The new method of government hit the nobles hard. Not only did they watch their valued independence being steadily destroyed, but they had always counted on well-paid posts in the government to help them pay for their extravagant ways of living and to meet rising prices. These were largely at an end, and flattering membership of the Order of the Golden Fleece did not make up for hard cash. At this time there were three nobles who mattered more than the rest—

Count Egmont, the popular victor of the battle of Saint Quentin, his friend the gruff and rather forbidding Admiral of the Netherlands, Count Hoorne, and, above all, William of Nassau, Prince of Orange.

William had been born in 1533 into a German Rhineland family of limited means. At the age of 11 he suddenly found himself inheritor of vast estates in Brabant, Flanders, and Luxembourg, as well as of the Principality of Orange on the Rhône. Overnight he had become the biggest landowner in the Netherlands and the possessor of considerable wealth. To prepare him for his great responsibilities young William was packed off to Brussels by his father, where he received a French education at Court, changed from the family Lutheranism to being a Roman Catholic, and was soon a firm favourite of the emperor. It was on William's arm that Charles V had leant as he entered the hall for the famous abdication scene. He grew up to be immensely popular, a man of great charm and courtesy, whose nickname 'The Silent' gives no impression of his gaiety. The nickname came from his enemies who used a Dutch word meaning 'sly' and this, when translated into Latin, totally obscured the original description of a man of great diplomatic skill, who knew how to keep his mouth shut when it suited him. But as yet only the extent of his estates and the mountain of his debts singled him out from his fellow nobles. Time was to show his quality as a statesman and national leader.

Serious trouble began in 1561 when Philip, in the spirit of the Council of Trent, persuaded the pope to create fourteen new bishoprics in the Netherlands. The Church here was undoubtedly corrupt and lazy and the new bishops would be expected to discipline the faithful and to wage implacable war on the heretics. William and his friends protested vigorously against yet another sign of Spanish interference. Some of them may have feared that it was going to be harder for younger sons of noble families to gain an easy living in the Church, but their far less selfish fears were that bitter persecution, which they detested, would be unleashed and the Spanish Inquisition introduced. On the last score their fear was groundless, for, as Philip cynically explained in a letter to Margaret of Parma, there was no need to take this step: 'The story they invent that we wish to introduce the Spanish Inquisition there is false and without foundation, because the Inquisition of the Netherlands is more merciless than the one here.' Philip had no intention either of stopping persecution or of allowing his subjects to control their own religious affairs; but he was prepared to remove Granvelle, whom the nobles hated. But Granvelle's departure from the Netherlands did nothing to halt the rapidly deteriorating situation.

With the example of the Huguenots close at hand, Calvinism spread rapidly and there was open talk of armed resistance. A bad harvest in 1565 and rising unemployment made things worse. This was the moment when power passed for a brief while to the lesser nobles, who were far more headstrong than Orange, Egmont, and Hoorne. Margaret feared an attack on Brussels. One of her councillors tried to comfort her. 'What, Madame!' he said, 'are you afraid of these beggars?' With remarkable speed the contemptuous remark became known everywhere and at a drunken banquet in April 1566 the toast 'Vivent les Gueux!', 'Long live the Beggars!', was cheered to the echo. Wilder spirits adopted the beggar's wooden bowl as their symbol, and before long knick-knack makers were doing a roaring trade in little model bowls, which ladies could wear as earrings and men dangle from their caps. It was the first sign of a national spirit being aroused in the Netherlands. In August Calvinist mobs attacked churches in Antwerp, Ghent, and other cities and the violence culminated in an attack on Antwerp Cathedral. An Englishman, Richard Clough, wrote an account of what he saw on 20 August: 'I, with about ten thousand more, went into the churches to see what stir was there; and coming into our Lady Church, it looked like a hell; where were above 1,000 torches burning and such a noise! as if Heaven and Earth had gone down together, with falling of images and beating down of costly works; in such sort that the spoil was so great that a man could not well pass through the church.'

Calvinist excesses led many to support the government for the moment. Those Calvinist leaders who avoided capture escaped to Germany, where they were joined by William of Orange, who had fruitlessly urged both sides to be moderate and who knew that Philip planned vengeance. In June 1567 the Duke of Alva, the finest Spanish soldier of the day, set out for the Netherlands at the head of an army of Spanish and Italian troops with orders to crush the revolt ruthlessly.

On 22 August Alva entered Brussels, confident that he would quickly bring the rebels to heel. 'I have tamed men of iron,' he boasted, 'and shall soon have done with men of butter.' Margaret of Parma, angry at being displaced by Alva, left the country, and Alva set about teaching the Netherlanders that 'Kings are born to give orders, subjects to obey them.' He set up the Council of Troubles, which rapidly earned for itself the name of the 'Council of Blood', and in the course of his six-year reign of terror, over 1,000 people were executed and some 9,000 others severely punished. To avoid falling into the hands of the Council about 60,000 people are believed to have fled abroad. William of Orange and his brother, Louis of Nassau, strove to organize some kind of resistance from Germany and France, but for the moment Alva had so cowed the populace that none rose to help and all attempts at invasion failed ignominiously. Using the invasion as an excuse for yet more repression, Alva brought Egmont and Hoorne out of prison, where they

The Duke of Alba. The Order of the Golden Fleece hangs round his shoulders. The crucifix on his right side shows that he regarded himself as a champion of the true faith.

had been for some months, and had them executed in June 1568 in the market-place in Brussels. Despite all William's warnings, they had pathetically trusted that personal loyalty to Philip would save them. For Alva it was merely a matter of time before William followed them to the scaffold. 'We may regard the Prince of Orange as a dead man,' he wrote triumphantly. He did not know his enemy. At the depth of his fortunes William could still write in hope: 'With God's help I shall go on.'

313

Alva now proceeded to put the second part of his plan into operation—the taxation of the Netherlands to such an extent that they would no longer be a burden on the Spanish treasury. His proposed taxes, especially the Tenth Penny, a 10 per cent tax on all exports and on the sale of goods, could only have been levied by a man unable to understand that trade was the life-blood of the people. 'It is far better', said Alva, 'to preserve by war for God and the King a kingdom that is impoverished and even ruined than, without a war, preserve it entire for the benefit of the devil and his disciples, the heretics.' A nation of merchants and traders protested so violently that the Tenth Penny was never levied and before long Alva found himself in a rising tide of revolt which, as he later wrote to Philip, engulfed him 'not only up to my neck but over my head'.

'Tide' was the right word, for it was the sea which saved the Netherlands and defeated Spain. The Spaniards never fully understood that to control the Netherlands they must be as supreme at sea as they were on land. The sea was the lifeline by which the revolt could be sustained and, in the last resort, the dykes could be cut and Alva's soldiers held at bay by the waters as they rose over the submerged fields. As Alva prepared to levy his new taxes, the struggle was kept going by French, English, and Dutch privateers. From their base at La Rochelle, Huguenot ships attacked the passing Spanish vessels. When in November 1568 four Spanish treasure ships with a cargo of £85,000 urgently needed to pay Alva's army were storm-bound in Plymouth, Elizabeth I blandly ordered them to be seized. On the other side of the Atlantic her seamen were happily attacking Spanish harbours in the New World. Most important of all were the battered ships with their patched sails and second-hand cannon belonging to those patriotic ruffians, Dutchmen, Flemings, Frenchmen, even Englishmen, who, proudly calling themselves the Sea Beggars, flew William of Orange's flag at their mast-heads and sent him the prize money which they captured to replenish his empty coffers. William tried vainly to control their worst excesses, when they put into home or foreign ports to revictual, but by March 1572 Elizabeth, partly under pressure from the Spanish ambassador, had had enough of them and ordered 'all freebooters of any nation' to leave her harbours. Twenty-five ships sailed towards Holland with no clear plan of action. On 1 April they were blown towards the little port of Brill which they found temporarily without a Spanish garrison. They sacked the port and, almost as an afterthought, decided to stay. That evening William of Orange's flag flew for the first time on land in the Netherlands.

Events moved fast. Flushing, Rotterdam, and other towns declared for William, and in a short while practically the whole of the provinces of Holland and Zeeland were in open revolt against Spain. Two reasons account for the quick success of the Sea Beggars and their growing number of followers. Fearing an attack from France, Alva had withdrawn most of his troops from the north. The Sea Beggars, although Calvinists when most Dutchmen were still Roman Catholics, were welcomed as preferable to Spanish soldiers, and the small number of Calvinists in each town could usually open the town gates as the Sea Beggars warned them of their approach. But they were a disorderly crowd, and it was time for William to take control. On 8 July 1572 he returned to the Netherlands determined to drive out the Spaniards or die in the attempt. 'I have come', he wrote, 'to make my grave in this land.'

William's avowed aim was 'to restore the entire fatherland in its old liberty and prosperity out of the clutches of the Spanish vultures and wolves'. He was no great general; his strength lay in his integrity, his determination never to give up, his skill in diplomacy, and his ability to rally people to his cause. Sooner or later, as he knew well, two things would be essential: foreign help and religious toleration. At present hopes of help from abroad were slight. Elizabeth I had bluntly refused to intervene, and the massacre of St. Bartholomew ended all chance of immediate Huguenot support. In 1573 William officially became a Calvinist, but he had never had any use for fanatics and he knew the terrible dangers of religious strife. As a contemporary Roman Catholic wrote: 'He used to say that in all matters of religion, punishment should be reserved to God alone . . . in short the Prince would have liked to see established a fancy kind of religion of his own, half Catholic, half Lutheran, which would satisfy both sides.' Catholics and Calvinists would have to learn to live together if William's dream of an independent united Netherlands were ever to be realized.

From 1572 to 1576 the revolt was concentrated in Holland and Zeeland. The Spaniards were invincible in the open field, but the rivers and canals of the north made it possible for the most part to avoid pitched battles and to defy the enemy from behind town walls, sometimes unsuccessfully, sometimes triumphantly, always heroically. Throughout the icy winter of 1572–3 Haarlem had been closely besieged by troops under the command of Alva's son. The hopes of the defenders had been kept alive by canal-skating messengers to and from William's headquarters, but a relieving army was destroyed and the town forced to surrender in July 1573. Alva had urged his son to show mercy and believed that he had been obeyed when only 2,000 of the townsfolk were executed. Such horrors only stiffened Dutch resistance. Greatest of all sieges was that of Leyden, which held out for eleven months from November 1573. By September 1574 the defenders faced starvation. The dykes had been breached so that the great barges piled high with food in Rotterdam might float across the flooded fields to the city gates. But the waters would not rise sufficiently to let Admiral Boisot's men push and pole the ungainly fleet forwards under Spanish fire. On 1 October the miracle happened for which men and women in crowded churches had prayed. Strong winds came with a high tide. The barges, shoved by swimming and wading men, moved slowly forwards, while the Spaniards, in danger of being drowned in the rising waters, abandoned their guns and marched away. When discussions took place about how best to commemorate Leyden's deliverance, it was William who suggested the foundation of the great university which still flourishes.

Meanwhile Alva, 'a decrepit old bird', as he described himself, his policy in ruins, asked to be recalled. His successor, Don Luis de Requesens, ended the terror but failed to win back the north or to persuade the nation to return to its allegiance. With no money coming from the Netherlands in taxes, Spain went bankrupt once again in 1575, and a year later unpaid Spanish troops mutinied and sacked Antwerp. 'They neither spared age nor sex; time nor place; person nor country; young nor old; rich nor poor . . . they slew great numbers of young children . . . and as great respect they had to the church and churchyard as the butcher hath to his shambles . . . within three days Antwerp, which was one of the richest towns in Europe, had now no money nor treasure to be found therein, but only in the hands of murderers.' This 'Spanish Fury' gave William his chance. In face of such horrors all enmity between Catholic and Protestant was forgotten as the seventeen provinces joined together on 8 November 1576 in the Pacification of Ghent to expel the Spanish troops and to regain their ancient liberties, even though they were still prepared to acknowledge Philip II as their king.

Requesens had died at his post and the Governor-General, Don John of Austria, the victor of Lepanto, could do little save accept the Pacification for the time being. Moreover, he was glad enough to be on friendly terms with the Netherlanders, whose help he needed if he were ever to succeed in his wild scheme of going to England where he planned to set Mary Queen of Scots free and then marry her. Together they would reign in Elizabeth's place. The States General, the central government, was unimpressed and, like the soldier that he was, he believed that he should rely once again upon the sword. William's hopes that 'the entire fatherland' would remain united against Spain began to fade. The jealous independence of each province made the task of creating an effective central government unbelievably difficult. Then, when war began again early in 1578, the Spanish army was as invincible as ever. Above all, Calvinist determination to control town governments and to indulge in destruction of images and pictures in Catholic churches made their name feared 'worse than the Spanish tyranny and insolence'. In January 1579 the ten southern provinces formed the Union of Arras to defend their faith and by May they had made their separate peace with Philip II. In this act lay the first step towards the creation of the modern kingdom of Belgium. To William's bitter disappointment the seven northern provinces followed suit and in the Union of Utrecht set up a federation of independent states, the United Provinces, which would grow into the future kingdom of Holland.

From now on it was a religious struggle for independence. In June 1580 Philip published his Ban against William. 'On the word of a king and as a minister of God, we promise to any one who has the heart to free us of this pest, and who will deliver him dead or live, or take his life, the sum of 25,000 crowns in gold or in estates for himself and his heirs.' William at once defied Philip in his 'Apology', an open letter addressed to all the people of the Netherlands. 'I take it as a signal honour that I am the mark of the cruel and barbarous proscription hurled at me by the Spaniard for undertaking your cause and that of freedom and independence . . . I was bred up a Catholic and a worldling, but the horrible persecution that I witnessed by fire, sword and water . . . made me resolve in my soul to rest not till I have chased from the land these locusts of Spain.' A year later the United Provinces renounced all allegiance to Philip.

Foreign help was essential if the new state were to survive. Don John had died, and in his place Philip sent in 1578 the finest soldier of the century, handsome, clever, and no lover of Alva's cruelty, Alexander Farnese, Duke of Parma, son of Margaret of Parma. Nothing shows better the desperate straits to which William was reduced than his negotiations with the Duke of Anjou, Catherine de Medici's fourth son, now heir to the French throne. He was to become Prince of the Low Countries, but his help was of little account. For most of the time he preferred to be in England carrying on the hilarious courtship of Elizabeth, and his death in June 1584 was no loss. William, however, insisted that help must still be sought in France. Ever since Philip's offer of a reward to William's murderer, William's life had been in constant danger. On 10 July 1584 a Burgundian fanatic, Balthasar Gérard, made his way into William's house at Delft and shot him dead as he came out of his dining-room. It was a terrible moment for the United Provinces. No words better sum up what William had meant to the whole story of the revolt than the wonderfully simple and moving tribute in a state document: 'As long as he lived he was the guiding star of a whole nation, and when he died the little children cried in the streets.'

(ii) Spain takes the offensive

In spite of having had to repudiate his debts to his bankers in 1575, Philip, thanks to the increasing flow of silver coming to him from the New World, was able to listen more sympathetically by 1580 to those who urged him that the time was now ripe to launch an offensive against the enemies of Spain and of the Catholic Church. Cardinal Granvelle, once Philip's viceroy in the Netherlands, had been summoned back from Rome in 1579 to help his master again and he argued in favour of going on to the attack. Not only was there now more money available to pay the troops and to equip the fleets but there were also other facts which overcame the king's natural caution. All immediate danger from the Turks had been removed by a truce signed between Philip and the Sultan in 1580. Both enemies realized that neither was likely to win an all-out victory in the Mediterranean and each wished to turn his attention in a different direction: the Turks to the East and Spain towards the Atlantic. Drake's voyage round the world in 1577–80 was an unpleasant shock and showed Philip that, if Spain were to continue to enjoy the riches of the Indies alone, foreign pirates must be driven from the seas. Furthermore, the Portuguese throne fell vacant in 1580, an opportunity for action which could not be missed.

In 1578 the young King Sebastian of Portugal had rashly embarked on a pointless crusade against the Moors in Morocco which ended not only in his death, which mattered little, but in the destruction of the Portuguese army. The new king was an old man, Sebastian's great-uncle, who only survived for two years. Philip had a good claim to the throne through his mother, but the Portuguese heartily disliked Castilians and had no wish to become yet another part of the Spanish empire. However, a recently defeated nation with many of its soldiers still prisoners in Moorish hands saw that an alliance with Spain might bring the silver needed to ransom them. On Granvelle's advice, Alva was recalled from retirement and led an army into Portugal to support Philip's claim. There was practically no fighting and in April 1581 Philip was formally recognized as king of Portugal on condition that Castilians held no positions of authority in the country or in the Portuguese empire. Philip wisely accepted the terms, and for the first time since Roman days the peninsula was united under one king. Castile, Aragon, and Portugal had the same man as their king, but Aragon and Portugal still enjoyed considerable independence of Castile. It was an uneasy partnership which only lasted until 1640, but Philip gained greatly from it. A million new subjects, a long and valuable coastline with fine harbours and dockyards, a fleet of some 100,000 tons, and an empire in India, Africa, the Moluccas, and Brazil fell to him almost without a battle.

At once it became alarmingly clear to France and England that Philip had become ruler of a world empire which threatened their very existence. In the Netherlands the situation was immediately even more serious for, as we have seen, from the arrival of Alexander Farnese, Duke of Parma, in 1578 the tide had begun to turn in favour of Spain. William of Orange had always maintained that the

United Provinces could never remain independent of Spain without foreign help. Coligny, the other great Protestant leader, just before the massacre of St. Bartholomew told the English agent in Paris that Philip intended 'to make himself monarch of Christendom or at the least to rule the same'. Here once again was the threat of a universal empire in conflict with the new nation states. Could the Dutch survive as long as France was torn by civil war and Elizabeth I of England shrank from openly challenging Spain? Both Philip and Elizabeth were strangely reluctant to give orders for the inevitable conflict. In England Sir Thomas Walsingham and the Earl of Leicester had for long been urging the queen and the more cautious Burghley to send full help to the Dutch and to take the lead as champion of Protestantism. Philip was also being urged to undertake what came to be known as the Enterprise of England. The death of William of Orange and events in France drew both rulers into the struggle from 1584 onwards.

*   *   *

In France, as in Portugal, a death in the royal house brought about a crisis. Henry III, who both feared and hated his younger brother and heir, the Duke of Anjou, had been glad enough to encourage him to keep out of his way with his adventures in the Netherlands and in England and it was no sorrow to him when Anjou died of a fever in August 1584. The country, however, was suddenly brought face to face with the fact that since Henry III was certain to die childless, the Valois line was ending and the heir to the throne was a Huguenot, Henry of Navarre. To oppose this and to further their own ambitions, the Guise family formed the Catholic League, which quickly gained supporters everywhere and not least in Paris where, quite independently, Catholic preachers and mob orators had been whipping up a dangerous hatred against the Huguenots and also against a king whose way of life was steadily becoming stranger and more degenerate. The leader of the League had no scruples about entering into an alliance with the national enemy, Spain; and with the money which they got from Philip they set about raising an army. Henry III and the sick and ageing Catherine de Medici were between two fires—the Huguenots on one side and the Catholic League, clearly bent on toppling Henry from his throne, on the other. Catherine's days of peace-making were over, and the desperately weak position of her son can be seen from the fact that nobody would lend him any money at less than 50 per cent interest. Henry could only submit completely to the Guises, who demanded that he should cancel all the concessions ever made to the Huguenots. When Henry of Navarre heard this, he said that one half of his moustache turned white. Once again it was civil war.

Loyalty to the king was almost at an end. In May 1588 in the famous Day of Barricades, the Paris mob took control and Henry III

fled from his capital, never to return to it. He could see only one way
to free himself from his humiliating dependence on the Guises and
that was assassination. Early on the morning of 23 December 1588
Guise was summoned to the royal Council at Blois. As he reached
the top of the famous outside staircase of the château, he was
murdered. Next day his brother suffered the same fate. Henry
gleefully gave the news to his dying mother: 'I intend to be a king
now and no longer a prisoner and slave.' Catherine was too ill to
help her favourite son and ten days later she was dead. Henry's
triumph was short lived and the end inevitable. In August 1589 the
king went the way of the Guises when he was stabbed to death by a
young Dominican friar, Jacques Clément. When the Parisians heard
the news, they dragged tables into the streets and celebrated the
ending of the Valois line with feasting, singing, and dancing. Henry
of Navarre was now king of France as Henry IV, provided that he
could defeat the League. The age of Catherine de Medici was over.

★   ★   ★

France's tragedy was welcome to both Philip and Elizabeth. With
France out of action, Philip was free to concentrate on settling his
account with England, after which the United Provinces could be
destroyed at leisure. For Elizabeth both France and Spain had long
been a danger to her country, but there was now little chance that
France would come to dominate the southern provinces in the
Netherlands; and if Spain were also to be kept out of this part of
Europe, then it was essential to give some open help to the Dutch.
In August 1585 Elizabeth agreed to take the United Provinces under
her protection, though she had refused to become their ruler.
Leicester was sent off to the Netherlands at the head of an army and
quickly found that he had arrived at a moment when Dutch fortunes
were at their lowest ebb. Not only was Alexander Farnese, Duke of
Parma, steadily regaining lost ground but the seven provinces were
finding it hard to work together even in the face of a common
danger. Leicester himself was no soldier and no politician. He
quarrelled with the leading statesman of the province of Holland,
Jan van Oldenbarnevelt, and his failure at Zutphen, where Sir
Philip Sidney died bravely, was part of a mismanaged campaign.
Something had been achieved to help the Dutch, but it was costing
Elizabeth more than she liked.

Thus it is understandable that Elizabeth still tried hard to avoid
an open conflict with Spain. She was happy enough to send Drake
to attack Vigo and to prey on Spanish treasure ships, but she was not

*The so-called 'Armada' portrait of Queen Elizabeth I, which hangs at Woburn
Abbey, attributed to Marc Gheeraerts. The Spanish fleet is advancing in the
top left corner but is battered by storms on the opposite side. The Queen's hand
proudly rests on the globe.*

prepared to declare war. Philip equally held back on the brink of war. He wanted to be able to say that he was fighting in a righteous cause and not just to extend his empire. Mary Queen of Scots gave him what he wanted. In 1587, after a time of agonized indecision, Elizabeth signed Mary's death warrant and she was executed in Fotheringay Castle. Before she died she had disinherited her son and named Philip as her heir to her claims to the throne of England. With papal blessing and papal money the cause of Spain and the Church seemed at last to be the same.

'The Enterprise of England' was in Parma's view doomed to failure from the start as being a hopelessly unsound scheme. Philip's laboriously slow preparations, the alarming cost, the death of the man chosen to take command, Drake's 'singeing of the King of Spain's beard' in Cadiz harbour, were bad enough. But the Armada, with no deep-water port in the Netherlands for shelter, was expected to cover in safety Parma's embarkation of his invading army and to hold the Channel while his barges sailed across. Parma knew that this was impossible, for he knew that the Dutch fleet could destroy his barges before he had even started for England. Philip, convinced that he was doing God's will, kept to his plan. The running fight up Channel was the biggest sea battle fought up till then; it was also the first to be fought entirely by artillery. In the end forty-four of the sixty-eight ships struggled back to Spain—no mean achievement by the Spanish commander, Medina Sidonia, who had been unjustly derided as quite incompetent. To the English it seemed a miracle. 'Deus flavit et dissipati sunt' was the motto, 'God blew with his winds and they were scattered.' Winds and tides played a vital part, but victory lay with the seamen whom Elizabeth needed no longer to disavow. England was now irrevocably ranged alongside all enemies of Spain.

Philip of Spain was by no means defeated and Spanish trade with the Indies was still under his control, but the failure of the Armada was a terrible blow to Spanish pride and confidence. The English victory was heralded as the saving of Protestant Europe, while the Spanish could not understand how God had forsaken them. As a Huguenot leader wrote to Walsingham: 'The prince of Parma has been frustrated in his design, and has seen beneath his very nose the chariots of Egypt submerged beneath the waves . . . the Spaniard wanted to take Flanders by way of England, but it is now for you to take Spain by way of the Indies. . . . In saving yourselves you will save all the rest.' The troubles in France were by no means over and the United Provinces were not yet safe, but the story of the Armada had given Protestants a new confidence.

★　　★　　★

Help from England and the fight between Henry IV and the League in France were invaluable to the Dutch, but their final victory was equally due to their own heroic efforts. For a long while the United Provinces were little more than a very loose federation of independent states, and so it was lucky that the lead in their affairs was taken by Holland, the wealthiest and most important province. For thirty-two years, from 1586 to 1618, the affairs of Holland and, to an increasing extent, those of the United Provinces, were in the hands of Jan van Oldenbarnevelt, an outstandingly wise statesman, who by tact and skilful handling of the representatives of the other provinces became the voice of the new republic. Closely allied with him was Maurice of Nassau, William's second son, a boy of 16 at the time of his father's death, who made himself into a magnificent soldier. He set himself to forge an army capable of defeating Spanish troops in the open field and by the closing years of the century he had triumphantly succeeded.

In the last years of his life Philip concentrated his efforts increasingly on France. War with England continued, but he knew that he had failed to defeat the heretic queen. He was making less and less headway against the Dutch heretics. At all costs he must save France from being ruled by a heretic. Henry IV faced a long, uphill task before he could claim to be king of a united France. The fortunes of war fluctuated and he had to contend not only with the forces of the League but with Parma's veterans out of the Netherlands, who twice came to the aid of Paris, and thereby gave the Dutch invaluable relief. Gradually it became clear that in the end Henry was going to win. He had much in his favour, not least his own strength of character, his leadership, and his charm, qualities which France always hoped for in her kings and had so seldom found. The alliance of the League with Spain proved to be an embarrassment; nor had its leaders any alternative to Henry as king. One step was essential, and Henry had long foreseen it. In July 1593 he allowed himself to be converted to Roman Catholicism and a year later he entered Paris to the cheers of his people. 'Paris', as he rather cynically remarked, 'is worth a Mass.' Fighting continued for another four years against those who refused to recognize him but before long had dwindled into a war to drive out the Spanish.

In April 1598 Henry issued the Edict of Nantes by which the Huguenots were once again allowed freedom to worship where they had worshipped in the past and, as proof of good faith, they were given a hundred small towns which they were allowed to garrison at royal expense. A month later Henry concluded the Peace of Vervins with Philip, which more or less confirmed the terms made forty years earlier at Cateau-Cambrésis.

Was it all worth it? Certainly not, in the opinion of a remarkable man, Michel de Montaigne (1533–92), friend of Henry IV, who had no use at all for wars of religion. 'In trying to make themselves angels,' he said, 'men transform themselves into beasts.' He preferred to live in his castle, shut away in a tower, where he could observe the follies of men and comment on them in a new form of writing which he invented—the essay. 'I would willingly carry a candle in one hand for St. Michael and a candle for his Dragon in the other.' In his refusal to accept Christianity and in his detachment from the things which stirred men's hearts in the fifteenth and sixteenth centuries he belongs to an age which he did not live to see. What is certain is that, had France had the good fortune to have a king like Henry IV in 1559, her history would have been very different and far happier.

As for the Dutch, although the United Provinces were not officially recognized until 1648, their independence had been gained by 1609 when a truce was made with Spain. Philip did not live to see their triumph, for in September 1598 he died. He had achieved much for Spain: he had beaten off the Turk, won the crown of Portugal, and by his intervention in France had probably made Henry IV see the need to become a Catholic. But he had paid a higher price than he knew, for Spain was on the road to economic ruin and the days of her greatness were over. Five years later his lifelong rival, Elizabeth, turned her face to the wall and on 24 March 1603 yielded to Death whom she had faced standing for fifteen hours. It was the end of an era.

Chapter 13
New Horizons

We take it for granted nowadays that the sum of human knowledge will always increase. Such an attitude of mind would have been very uncommon even among educated people in the fifteenth and sixteenth centuries, for it was an age which was usually very respectful of authority. This respect for the wisdom and achievements of the ancients, which was so marked a feature of the early Renaissance, broke down as a result of the voyages of discovery and the rise of modern science. The scientific spirit and a readiness to apply the result of scientific discovery in practical ways became the new hallmarks of western civilization.

(i) The voyages of discovery

The century between 1450 and 1550 witnessed the transformation of the way in which Europeans regarded the world around them. A few dates are the most striking illustration of the speed of this change: in 1488 the Cape of Good Hope was rounded; in 1492 the West Indies were discovered; by 1498 India had been reached by sea; in 1500 Brazil had been described; in 1513 Balboa had first seen the Pacific. It clearly took much longer to assimilate all the new information about distant lands which came back to Europe, but by 1600, with the exception of Australia, the Antarctic, and the northern coastlines of America and Asia, the outlines of the world map had been established.

To speak of voyages of 'discovery' can mean two very different things. It can refer to the work of an expedition happening upon largely uninhabited territory and thereby 'discovering' lands able to be developed by future settlers. It can also, as in the case of the 'discovery' of India, mean becoming aware of a fabulously wealthy and highly advanced civilization, with rulers like the Emperor Babur at Agra, who easily outshone his contemporary Renaissance princes in Europe.

The motives which drove Europeans to undertake these extremely hazardous voyages were complex. First would come the desire to lay hands on goods which Europe increasingly desired and which were difficult to acquire since by their capture of Constantinople in 1453 the Turks had set up a road-block across the old land trade routes. There was an insatiable European appetite for what are

called 'spices'. This was a term used in the later Middle Ages to cover four quite different things: condiments, which were essential for the preserving and seasoning of food; medical drugs; certain dyes, perfumes, ointments, and cosmetics; and various exotic and expensive articles of food. In a fourteenth-century merchant's handbook 288 different 'spices' are listed, the most valuable being pepper (the best coming from Sumatra), cinnamon from Ceylon, and cloves from the Moluccas. Since precious metals were in short supply in Europe, envious eyes were cast upon the gold coming from beyond the Sahara. Standards of living were rising in Europe and this encouraged men to amass wealth, not least to be able to afford the silks and damasks from the East. Nor should a desire for land itself be forgotten. Land and the labour of those working on it were then one of the chief sources of wealth and the New World was later to open up far more land than could be immediately worked.

When Vasco da Gama arrived in India in search of 'spices and Christians', he may have got his ambitions in the right order, but it would be quite wrong to disregard the religious motive. The old crusading zeal was by no means dead. For the Spaniards entering the New World the fighting was very much a continuation of the crusades within Spain against the Moors. Moreover, the majority of explorers and settlers were genuinely devout men, moved by a

The need of European countries for spices. Marco Polo's voyages had shown how rich China and the Indies were in spices. Marco Polo is shown visiting the pepper-growing district of Malabar in southern India.

desire to convert to Christianity the natives who met and often opposed them. Later settlers would be more likely to live peaceably if the original inhabitants of the conquered territory had abandoned their old gods. At the same time, conversion, however desirable, did not pay for the expenses of an expedition, and more obvious profits were demanded by the great merchant bankers of north Italy and south Germany, who played such a big part in financing the voyages.

Two other motives also were at work. A leader of an expedition would certainly be influenced, however unconsciously, by a curiously Renaissance attitude of mind—a passion for his personal reputation, both in what he successfully achieved and, if need be, by the way in which he met his death. Cortes, for example, when urging his men on the beach at Vera Cruz to burn the boats which had brought them from Cuba, encouraged them, so we are told, by reciting 'many comparisons with brave deeds done by heroes among the Romans'. The familiar story of Sir Humphrey Gilbert on board the *Squirrel*, serenely facing death as he cried: 'We are as near to Heaven by sea as by land', makes one wonder whether his death might perhaps have been avoided. Add finally another typically Renaissance motive—curiosity. There was a natural wish to discover what really lay beyond the horizon; whether the scholars who argued that the East must be able to be reached by sailing west were right. This spirit of disinterested curiosity had been whetted by the invention of printing, for the rising demand for books to read was met by the printing of travellers' tales. The popularity of travel books and the constant references to remote lands in plays and poems became a marked feature of the sixteenth century.

The wealth, splendour, and antiquity of the civilizations of India, China, and Japan may make it seem strange that the East never came in search of the West, that it was Europeans and not Orientals who took the initiative in the voyages of discovery. The reasons are clear. Eastern nations on the whole were inward-looking, content with their achievements, and shrank from any contact with foreigners. A brash and over-confident European explorer was out of place at an Eastern court. Nor were the motives impelling Europeans to break out of Europe of any force in the East. Apart from a lack of desire to seek for new lands, Eastern nations had not the organized economic resources to carry out a sustained programme of exploration as had the West. Above all, the West possessed the one essential for a voyage of discovery, suitably designed and equipped ships. Chinese junks, Indian dhows, the lateen-rigged Arab vessels, were all designed for a particular purpose, to sail in known waters. The long-oared galley or the Mediterranean coaster were equally useless for a dangerous and uncertain voyage. A ship bent on a voyage of discovery must rely on wind and not on oars; it needed to be tough and able to stand up to storm and tempest; it should be able to be sailed close to the wind and thus to go as far as possible in the required direction. Trade between northern and southern Europe resulted in the building of the right kind of vessel, a lucky combination of the Atlantic coast traders and the most easily manoeuvrable Mediterranean craft. This was evolved over the years, aided by the use of ports through which guns could be fired, thus eliminating the need for soldiers on board. It was the task of the sailors to fight, if need be, as well as to sail the ship.

It was one thing to have the urge to go in search of spices and gold or new lands; the problem which first had to be solved was how to reach the East. The old land routes were increasingly dangerous, very slow and extremely costly. Even in the days of Marco Polo, when it was politically safe to travel, the journey to China by land was thirty-five times more expensive than the comparable sea voyage, if the route could be discovered. Three types of map existed, none of them offering a solution. There was, first, the old *mappa mundi*, such as can be seen in Hereford Cathedral, with Jerusalem in the centre of the world and, usually, three equal-sized continents surrounding it. This was an expression of Christian belief, not a piece of practical information. Of greater accuracy was the Ptolemaic map, which dated from the second century A.D. Ptolemy lived and worked in his native city of Alexandria and his fame rests on two works: the *Geography* and an *Astronomy*, usually known by its Arabic title of *Almagest* ('the Greatest'). Of the latter book more will be said later in this chapter. Here it is sufficient to state that it was widely known and did much to ensure that educated people in the fifteenth century thought of the earth as round. The *Geography* did not appear in its Latin translation in Europe until about 1406 but was quickly accorded the respect with which any classical writings were then hailed. It consists mostly of a list of places arranged by regions and with a latitude and longitude assigned to each place-name. In addition there are a series of maps, probably not drawn by Ptolemy himself. What was depressing about the maps for those anxious to reach the East is that the Indian Ocean is shown as a land-locked sea. One other fact that was later of momentous importance to Columbus was that Ptolemy popularized in his book a considerable underestimate of the circumference of the earth and consequently of the length of a degree, which he estimated at a figure too small by about a quarter. The third type of map, the *portolani*, were essentially records of what was already known, accurate drawings of landfalls, harbours, capes, and inlets. They are very beautiful to look at and the totally imaginative drawings of the hinterland are attractive to us, but of no help to any explorer.

What was needed was a combined effort of scholars interested in maps and geography, sailors ready to verify their theories, rulers

Mappa Mundi in Hereford Cathedral. Jerusalem is in the very middle of the map, at the centre of the three known continents, Europe, Africa and Asia. Asia is at the top. A great gulf, the Mediterranean, which stretches downwards towards the bottom of the map, separates Europe on the left from Africa on the right; two smaller inlets at the top right, the Red Sea and the Persian Gulf, separate Africa from Asia. The world is round and the Ocean surrounds the whole land mass.

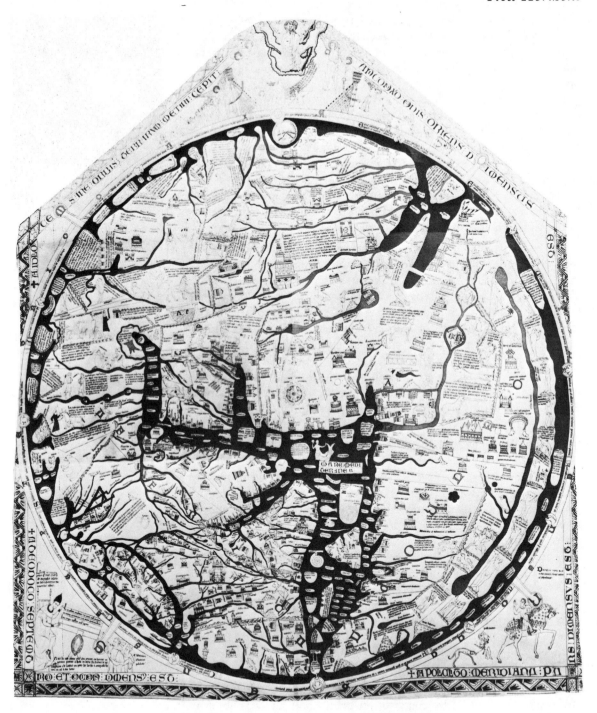

and educated men of wealth prepared to put up the money. This was first provided by the Portuguese. By the end of the fourteenth century Portugal had become a united nation, containing a prosperous merchant class which, unlike the neighbouring Spaniards, did not despise commerce. Geographically Portugal was the ideal exploring base and Portuguese sailors had become accustomed to long voyages out into the Atlantic. The necessary leadership was provided by the royal family. King John I had five sons whom he was anxious should show their zeal in crusades against the Moors. It was his third son, Prince Henry, known as 'the Navigator' who, on becoming governor of the Algarve in 1419, set up his observatory at Sagres, where scholars, map-makers, and sailors were welcomed, and their ideas and information shared. Henry was the first man to put into effect a planned programme of discovery.

Prince Henry the Navigator; part of a large altar-piece.

Prince Henry was a man of rigid piety, with a medieval obsession for a crusade. He firmly believed in his horoscope, which predicted that he was bound 'to engage in great and noble conquests and above all . . . to attempt discovery of things which were hidden from other men'. In 1415 Ceuta, in North Africa, had been captured from the Moors, and the ease of this success led the Portuguese into believing that they might set up their own empire where the heathen were ruling. Since it was widely believed that the Nile might flow into the Atlantic, Henry planned his expeditions down the west African coast as part of a pincer movement, which would destroy the Moors by joining up with other Portuguese forces moving along the North African shore.

During the fourteenth century the Azores, Madeira, and the Canaries had been discovered and an Atlantic triangle formed by Lisbon, the Azores, and Cape Bojador in west Africa had provided a training ground for Portuguese sailors. But to sail further south along the African coast demanded great courage in men led to believe that since tides raced ever faster to the south a return journey might prove impossible; that there was a magnetic power which ruined the compass and pulled the nails from the ship's timbers; that the heat of the sun not only melted the pitch between the planks of a ship's sides but turned men black. Thus it was that the early expeditions felt their way cautiously along the coast, growing bolder as their worst fears were proved groundless, and urged on by the financial possibilities of a slave trade which began in west Africa in 1441.

Prince Henry the Navigator died in 1460, but his work was continued and greatly developed twenty years later by King John II (1481-95). Spurred on by competition from Spain, he was able to give greater financial backing than was possible for Prince Henry. Under his patronage Bartholomew Diaz was blown round the Cape of Good Hope in a storm in 1488, the Cape being so named by

John II because it proved Ptolemy wrong in his belief that the Indian Ocean was land-locked. In the same year a two-man expedition began to work down the east coast of Africa: Alfonso de Paiva went into Ethiopia, Pero de Covilan went south, then crossed to Calicut and came back to Mozambique. The work of Diaz and de Covilan established most of the African coastline, a considerable feat when it is remembered that there was no help from the experience of coastal shipping once south of Cape Verde; the native language difficulty was greater in Africa in spite of Arabic being taught in parts of west Africa, whereas Arabic interpreters abounded when Asia was reached; the Indian Ocean was well known to Arab traders and this presented fewer navigational obstacles. Thus, once safely around the Cape, Vasco da Gama could reach India without exceptional difficulty in 1498. Two years later a Portuguese ship, blown off course, discovered Madagascar. By 1500 the exploration of the African coastline was virtually complete; the interior of the continent was not opened up to Europeans until the nineteenth century.

The Portuguese were not concerned to found a far-eastern empire but rather to control the lucrative trade which was largely carried in Arab or Chinese vessels. The first half of the sixteenth century was devoted to this, and perhaps the greatest figure in the story was the experienced soldier and administrator, Alfonso d'Albuquerque. He saw that success depended upon sea-power, together with the possession of fortresses at key points in the Indian Ocean. To this end he worked out a system of convoys to protect his fleets and was responsible for the capture of Goa (1510), Malacca (1511), and Ormuz (1515). By the time of his death in 1515 he had forced the Arabs to pay for trade licences in the Indian Ocean and his ships dominated the chief Chinese trade routes.

Spain came into the story nearly a century later than Portugal. Before any voyages of discovery or the settlement of new lands could be undertaken, the country had to be united. Not until the marriage of Ferdinand of Aragon with Isabella of Castile in 1469 was there any firm promise of such unity and, even then, as we have seen, thirty years of warfare lay ahead. It was, in fact, the Moorish wars which prevented Columbus from obtaining any help from Queen Isabella until 1491, when Granada was on the point of falling. There was neither time nor money available for new schemes until the Moors had been defeated. Nevertheless, in fighting the Moors both for their faith and for personal profit, Spanish soldiers had learned to endure extremes of climate and prolonged campaigns. With the fighting in Spain over, many a soldier was eager for new lands to conquer. Furthermore, the techniques of occupying a conquered country, of building cities to hold down newly won lands, and of administering a subject population had been mastered. The

Crown also had learned the danger of being too generous in grants of land to successful soldiers and relied increasingly upon strictly drawn-up contracts with each individual explorer.

When the Portuguese worked their way down Africa, they were exploring a land mass which had always been known to exist, although its size and shape were the subject of guesswork. The existence of an American continent, on the other hand, was entirely unsuspected. The general belief by the second half of the fifteenth century was that the Atlantic was, as Cardinal Pierre d'Ailly wrote at that time, 'navigable in a few days if the wind is favourable'. This wildly optimistic statement sprang from Ptolemy's miscalculations. Maps had long exaggerated the east-to-west length of Asia, and Toscanelli, the best authority of Columbus's day, estimated the distance between the Atlantic seaboard and the eastern shores of Asia at 5,000 miles, which was, in fact, 7,000 miles too short. Thus to the geographers and theorists of the day there could be no room for America. The interest of Ferdinand and Isabella lay in the discovery of islands in the Atlantic, which would serve as stepping-stones to Cathay [China] or Cipangu [Japan]. Such islands, although entirely mythical, like the island of 'Brazil', of Atlantis, the Fortunate Isles, or St. Brendan's Isle, owed their position on contemporary maps probably to some fisherman's sighting of a fog bank or clouds on a distant horizon when blown far west from known waters.

By the end of the fifteenth century the belief that Cathay could be reached by sailing across the western ocean was so firmly held that earlier unrecorded voyages may have led to this conviction. However, Columbus needed all his persuasive oratory and patience to win the ears of Ferdinand and Isabella after his rejection by John II of Portugal. The son of a poor Genoese weaver, he had little but his faith in 'The Enterprise of the Indies' and his experience as a navigator and chart-maker to commend him. The money required was not great and, indeed, did not come at first from government sources. What Columbus asked and gained was a contract which, had it ever been fully honoured, would have ennobled him and his descendants for ever and made him the richest and most powerful man in Europe, with one-tenth of all the gold and spices coming from the new lands.

The first of his four voyages, in 1492, was remarkably plain sailing. His little fleet of three ships sighted San Salvador after thirty-three days. He moved southwards through the Bahamas, believing that gold, the colour of the sun, was likeliest to be found where the sun shone most fiercely. On reaching Cuba he was convinced that he had at last come to an outpost of the territory of the Great Khan, and the subsequent discovery of Haiti confirmed the likelihood of the existence of off-shore islands. He recorded tales of nearby territories, one ruled by a breed of warlike Amazons, another 'where there were

A portrait of Christopher Columbus by a sixteenth-century Italian artist.

one-eyed people and others with dog faces, who ate people', and yet another where men were born with tails. Since Spain hoped to found an overseas empire, some of Columbus's men were left behind on Hispaniola under orders to build houses and to seek for gold. Columbus himself had a dangerous passage home but eventually arrived before Ferdinand and Isabella with some poor specimens of gold, a few wretched 'Indians', and the certainty that he had proved his theory right that Cathay could be reached by sailing across the western ocean. The increasing disappointments of his remaining three voyages never led him to doubt the nature of the lands which he had reached.

In the meantime the Portuguese were becoming alarmed at the threat to their commercial supremacy raised by Spanish enterprises. In 1454 Portugal had been granted by the pope a trade monopoly 'in the Ocean Sea towards the region lying southwards and eastwards', that is, trade to the south of the Canaries and east to the Indies. In 1492 a new pope, Alexander VI, was elected, who was conveniently a Spaniard. A year later Alexander, by the bull *Inter caetera*, excluded all other nations from territories discovered by Spaniards lying westward of a line drawn north and south 300 miles out from the Azores, thus unwittingly making Spain a present of the Americas. The Portuguese protested and entered into direct negotiation with Spain. The result was the Compromise of Tordesillas in 1494, which moved Alexander's line 370 leagues further west to secure the Portuguese route to India and, as quickly appeared, gave Brazil to Portugal. This extraordinary division of the world between two powers—much as if outer space were to be divided between the Americans and the Russians—kept Spain and Portugal apart in the western hemisphere, was useless on the other side of the globe where the line ran right through the Spice Islands, and was totally ignored by the English and the Dutch when they later came on the scene. It also produced a masterly comment in the name of the French king: 'We fail to find this clause in Adam's will.'

Columbus's second voyage, in 1493, was a colonizing expedition, for with him went 1,200 people, agricultural tools, animals, and seeds intended for the settlement of Hispaniola. Later voyages in 1498 and 1502 were increasingly disappointing, for no route to the Spice Islands had been found and gold was not available in any quantity. But Columbus, though he died as a largely discredited figure in 1506, was no failure. His discoveries of the Antilles, of Central America, and of the northern coast of South America, although misunderstood by him, were vital when more flexible minds pieced together the evidence. Even before Columbus's death it was quickly becoming apparent from his own voyages, from that of Cabot in 1497 to Newfoundland and Labrador, and Cabral's discovery of Brazil in 1500, that a vast land barrier lay between the

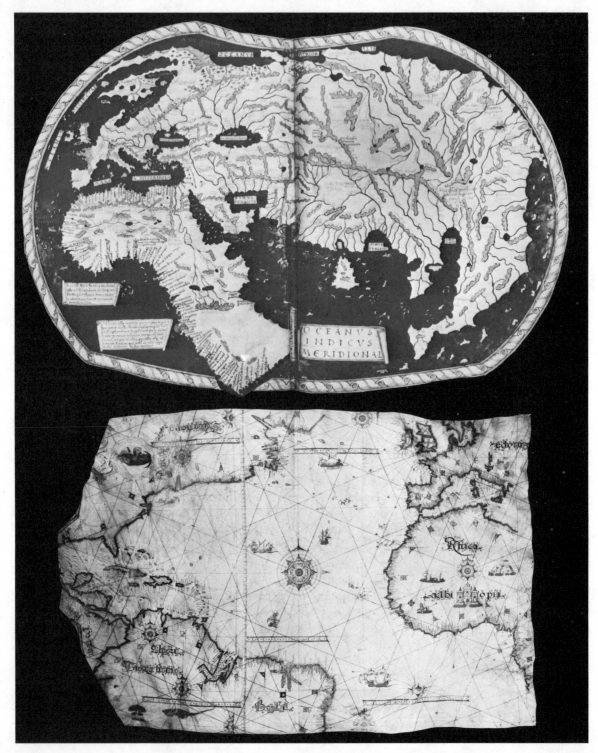

Left *Two examples of early
maps.*
Top *Map of the world made
by Henry Martellus in 1489.
Diaz had rounded the Cape of
Good Hope in 1487 but had
been forced to turn back. Note
how the names on the map stop
abruptly. The shape of Asia is
largely guesswork.*
Bottom *A Portuguese ·
portolano made about 1550.*

Right *A contemporary woodcut of Magellan's ship
'Vittoria'.*

western ocean and the Spice Islands. Brazil had probably been
reached a year earlier by Amerigo Vespucci, an Italian ship-chandler
sent by the Medici to Spain. He is a strange figure in the story, for
he never commanded an expedition and the exploits in which he
claimed a part are occasionally suspect. He was, however, a popular
writer and sound geographer, whose Christian name was bestowed
on the New World by a fellow geographer, Martin Waldseemuller,
in 1507, the year after Columbus died. In 1501 Vespucci took part
in the exploration of much of the eastern coast of South America,
but it was not until 1513 that the final confirmation came that a new
continent had been found when Balboa and his men crossed the
isthmus of Panama, to gaze for the first time on the Pacific.

Thus a hitherto totally unsuspected barrier still had to be surmounted before men could reach the East by sailing west. It was a
Portuguese, sailing in Spanish employ, Magellan, who found the way

round Cape Horn into the Pacific in a three-year voyage (1519–21) in which Magellan himself was killed and only thirty-five of the original 280 men survived. It is small wonder that no one again attempted such a journey till Drake in 1573. In the meantime the New World, although a barrier, was proving that it might yield compensating riches. Cabot had found no spices but he discovered a teeming fishing industry. Pearls fished on the coast of Venezuela, the valuable brazil-wood, and, before long, the immense wealth of gold and silver from Central and southern America poured into Spain and Europe.

Because the Moluccas lay on the equator, exploring activity had tended to be directed towards a broad belt of the world, lying roughly between 40° north and 40° south. The Spice Islands remained the goal of all voyages throughout the sixteenth century and well into the seventeenth. How could they be reached by English seamen without trespassing on Portuguese and Spanish preserves? 'There is but one way to discover, which is to the North. . . . For out of Spain they have discovered all the Indies and seas occidental, and out of Portugal all the Indies and seas oriental, so that by this part of the orient and occident they have compassed the world.' So wrote an English merchant, Robert Thorne, to Henry VIII in about 1527. It was this reasoning which drove Englishmen to the dangerous and fruitless task of seeking for a north-east or a north-west passage, an impossibility until the days of modern ice-breakers. Explorers like Willoughby and Chancellor, who set out for the north-east in 1553, had not only to contend with ice and snow but also with the ravages of scurvy, no less a danger in northern latitudes, and the wide variations of compass readings as ships approached the magnetic pole. Willoughby and his crew were trapped in the ice and never returned. Chancellor succeeded in reaching Archangel and from there he opened up an overland route to Moscow, shortly to be exploited by the new Muscovy Company of London (see p. 261).

The determination to share in the wealth of the Far East accounts for the refusal to abandon the search for a new route. 'The voyage to Cathay by the east', wrote Thorne, 'is doubtless very easy and short', once the slight obstacle of the northern capes had been overcome. Thus it was that in 1580 Arthur Pet and Richard Jackman were dispatched with sublime optimism to discover a market for English cloth, if the northern parts of China proved to be cold; to present letters from Queen Elizabeth in Latin (though with a Chinese translation) to all Chinese princes; to give gifts of marmalade and maps of London to all who dined on board; and even to estimate the chances of selling anti-dust spectacles to those living on the Chinese plains. All that they could do was to reach the Kara Sea before being turned back by pack-ice. Pet struggled home; Jackman went down with all hands off the coast of Norway.

The Dutch tried their luck to the north-east but similarly failed. To the north-west the story was the same: great heroism, heavy loss of life, little progress. Following in the wake of Humphrey Gilbert, men like Frobisher, Davis, Hudson, Baffin, and Foxe have given their names to places on the map. Perhaps their most important achievement was to prove the impossibility of the task with existing equipment. Both English and Dutch soon found it safer and infinitely more rewarding to challenge Spain and Portugal in the New World and the East Indies.

(ii) The beginnings of science

While European seamen were revolutionizing men's ideas about the map of the world, men of equal, if different, courage were doing the same to ideas about the nature of the world and its place in the universe. Science had begun with the ancient Greeks, but the Greek spirit of inquiry had largely died out when the barbarians overran western Europe. It was the Arabs, whose civilization flourished from the eighth to the eleventh centuries, who developed Greek scientific ideas and it was through contact with Arab scholars that these ideas returned to western Europe and were once again taught in the lecture rooms of the rising universities of Bologna, Paris, Oxford, and Cambridge. As far as science is concerned, it was the achievement of the Middle Ages to recover and preserve for the use of later ages the ideas of classical times. This was good in so far as it enabled men to see how far Greek thinking had reached; it was a fatal blow to any further progress when Greek ideas on the laws governing earth and the heavens were given by the Church almost the same authority as was accorded to the Scriptures. Both were placed above criticism. In the history of science the Renaissance is the period when a few thinkers and experimenters broke through these fetters of the past and in so doing made possible the rise of modern science in the mid-seventeenth century. To break with ideas which had been accepted for centuries and which were backed by the authority of a Church in which most of the new scientists firmly believed was no easy task, and it is thus not surprising to find that many of the great Renaissance figures in science were often still partly medieval in outlook.

However, one giant had little of the past about him. We have already seen (pp. 183ff) the position occupied by Leonardo da Vinci in the world of art; he was, if possible, an even greater figure in the world of scientific thought. It was probably his painting which first drew Leonardo to science, for he needed to make accurate studies of human anatomy for his figures and of plant life or strange rock formations for the background. Throughout his life he was driven by a passionate desire to observe exactly in order to understand fully. For example, the most tangled forms of blackberry brambles became in Leonardo's drawing not only a thing of beauty but a scientifically accurate picture of growth.

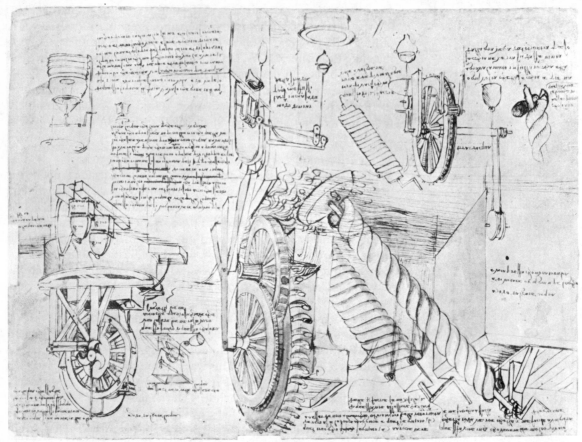

A page from one of Leonardo's Notebooks. The drawings show his design for a machine which would raise water.

Leonardo became increasingly concerned with observation and experiment as ends in themselves and not just as an aid to his painting. It would seem that there was nothing which did not excite his curiosity, and the immense range of his thought was staggering. As a painter he felt the need to study the laws of optics and from this to study the structure of the eye. His considerable knowledge of anatomy was gained from the secret dissection of at least ten human corpses, a strictly forbidden practice at the time, and he foreshadowed by a century Harvey's discovery of the circulation of the blood. A man of great physical beauty himself, his researches led him to make studies of the failings of old age and of human deformities. When he went to Milan as a civil engineer he was greatly concerned with water, then much used in pageants and formal gardens and also needed for purposes of defence. Aristotle had written learnedly about hydrostatics but Leonardo had little use for other men's theories compared with his own experimental studies of things as they really are. Water came, in fact, to exercise an increasing fascination over him, both its power and the fantastically complicated patterns to be found in a whirlpool or a torrential rainstorm. He even sketched designs of ships which might travel under water. He rejected the ancient belief in perpetual motion as being scientifically impossible; he experimented with the lever, regarding it as the primary machine from which all other machines were ultimately developed; he clearly understood the principle of inertia, which Galileo and Newton were to expound more than a century after his death. His interest in fossils and their discovery on mountains made literal acceptance of the Creation story in Genesis impossible, and he realized something of the vast changes which must have occurred in the earth's crust. From minute observation of the flight of birds and the structure of a bird's wing he sketched ways in which perhaps one day man himself might fly.

As can be seen, Leonardo was at least a century ahead of his contemporaries, but only in comparatively recent times has the full extent of his genius become recognized. There is some evidence that he intended to publish his discoveries and his speculations, but this he never did. Instead he left behind him a wonderful series of notebooks in which he confided his thoughts and the details of his experiences. Unfortunately the extreme difficulty of deciphering them prevented his ideas from spreading. From the shading on his drawings and paintings it has been deduced that he was almost certainly left-handed. With his left hand he not only decided to write his notes from right to left but each letter was inverted in 'mirror' style. Add to this an absence of punctuation and a constant use of abbreviations and it becomes clear why little attention was paid to the notebooks on his death. In fact no serious study of them took place until the mid-nineteenth century. This explains why a man who might have advanced science at one step to the point which it only reached early in the seventeenth century apparently contributed little to Renaissance science. Yet by any standards of judgement Leonardo must be regarded as one of the greatest intellects in the history of mankind.

The most profoundly upsetting changes in traditional thinking came as a result of the work of astronomers and mathematicians, but before turning to this, some note must be taken of preliminary work in other branches of science.

Medieval knowledge of medicine was a strange and dangerous mixture, consisting of the writings of the Roman physician, Galen (*c*.A.D. 130–200), Arabic theories, and a deep-seated belief in the efficacy of charms and amulets. For the sake of the patient no branch of knowledge was in more urgent need of scientific approach, and it is here that we come across the highly coloured and extraordinary personality of a Swiss doctor, Theophrastus Bombast von Hohenheim (*c.* 1490–1541)—later, to his dislike, known in Basle as Paracelsus. His career began among the mineworkers of the Tyrol whose conditions of work and the consequent accidents and diseases he studied.

Then between 1514 and 1526 he wandered through many European countries noting the common diseases and the rival national remedies. In 1526 he settled in Basle as a teaching physician, but his arrogance and vitriolic tongue caused him to leave the city after about a year. This was not surprising when it is recalled that at his first public lecture he placed the works of Galen and other classical physicians in a brass pan with some sulphur and burned them as a sign of his superiority over all past doctors of physic. Nevertheless, his work in some directions was valuable. His writings were largely incomprehensible nonsense, but he did introduce or popularize a number of drugs, such as opium and some mineral drugs—compounds of mercury, antimony, lead, and copper. He stumbled upon what he called 'extract of vitriol', which was obviously ether, for, as he said, it 'possesses an agreeable taste; even chickens will eat it, whereupon they sleep for a moderately long time, and rewake without having been injured'. It is luckily unknown how many of his patients died from the prescriptions which he tried out upon them, but he did at least turn chemists away from the hopeless search for an *elixir vitae*, or cure for all ills, and from trying to transmute base metals into gold. Instead, thanks to Paracelsus, they began the serious study of medical drugs. As can be seen, Paracelsus was no scientist, and nothing shows his essentially medieval outlook better than his scorn for anatomy, the first scientific study of which was made by a Flemish doctor, Andreas Versalius (1515-1564), whose thinking laid the foundations of modern medicine.

The use of vegetable drugs in medicine encouraged a new interest in botany. In the Middle Ages the monasteries had been centres for the cultivation of certain plants, but the doctrine of 'signatures', the belief that the Creator had conveniently shown the use to which plants might be put by the shape of the leaf and the colour of the flower, prevented any serious study. Greater wealth and security, combined with a generally developing artistic sense, led at the Renaissance to the laying out of private parks and gardens and also to the creation of special botanic gardens. The first was at Padua in 1545 and the example was followed at Leyden and Pisa. To these gardens explorers sent the rare plants brought home from their travels and here they were carefully tended. The medieval knowledge of plant life had been virtually forgotten and there was a need for new writing on the subject. Accordingly in the sixteenth century herbals, books containing descriptions of plants with notes on their use in medicine and cookery, began to be written. Two famous ones were written by Englishmen, William Turner and John Gerard.

One of the signs of a modern approach to science is the importance accorded to experiment. The science which a boy learned in a sixteenth-century grammar school consisted solely in learning by heart the principles handed down unchanged from the days of the ancient Greeks; there was no such thing as laboratory work. This may not be so very surprising, but it is remarkable for how long Greek theories were accepted without question by learned men. No man was more insistent on the essential need for experiment than William Gilbert of Colchester (1540–1603). He had studied mathematics at Cambridge and then changed to medicine, ultimately becoming physician to Queen Elizabeth I. His London house became a centre for meetings of men interested in scientific discussion and experiment. Gilbert's interest lay chiefly in electricity and magnetism, and in 1600 he published his important book *De Magnete*, which contained all that had been previously known on the subject and an account of his own work. Sailors had used a magnetic needle ever since the thirteenth century, but nobody knew why a compass pointed in one direction or why the needle dipped downwards at various angles to the horizontal. Gilbert became convinced that the explanation was that the earth itself must be a magnet. He was also interested in static electricity and in fact invented the word electricity from the Greek word for amber, *elektron*, because he found that certain forces developed when bodies, such as amber, are rubbed.

Ever since Ptolemy (*c*.A.D. 90–168) wrote the *Almagest*, which was his summary of Greek astronomical theories, there had been virtually no change in men's ideas about the earth and its relation to the heaven above it. Most people believed and the Church firmly taught that the earth was fixed at the centre of a universe of spheres which revolved around it with perfect regularity. These spheres were unfortunately invisible but their paths could be followed by studying the movements of the various heavenly bodies attached to them— sun, moon, stars, and planets. Since the Creator's work must be perfect and since it was held that the perfect form of movement was a circle, medieval astronomers were forced to claim that there were as many as eighty of these invisible spheres so as to account for all the movements which became observable as their skill in astronomy increased. As Alphonso the Wise of Castile remarked after studying the Ptolemaic system: 'If the Almighty had consulted me before the Creation I should have recommended something simple.'

So thought a very remarkable Polish mathematician, statesman, and churchman, Nicolaus Kopernik, or Copernicus, to give him his Latin name. Born in 1473, educated in both Poland and Italy, Copernicus for a short while was professor of mathematics in the university of Rome before returning to Poland, where he was soon appointed a canon of Frauenburg Cathedral, a post which he held until his death in 1543. The extreme complexity of the Ptolemaic system offended his mathematical mind and was not, he felt, what was to be expected of the Creator. Despite the assertion of the Psalmist 'He hath made the round world so sure that it cannot be moved', one or two men before Copernicus had already wondered if the earth rather than the sun was fixed, but no proof of such wild ideas had been forthcoming. Copernicus's greatness consisted in making a leap in the dark by assuming a dual motion of the earth, both round the sun and on its own axis, and then spending over a quarter of a century of brilliant mathematical calculations to prove his theory.

Copernicus.

It is sometimes said that Copernicus feared to publish his great book *De Revolutionibus Orbium Caelestium* until 1543, the year of his death, because of the danger of religious attack. It is far more likely that he feared ridicule. He was an intensely shy man, whose work in its early stages was well known in Rome and moreover the Counter-Reformation had not yet begun. He shrank from publishing what most men would have regarded as an utterly fantastic idea, and he only received the first copy of his book on his death-bed. The title of his book *On the Revolutions of the Heavenly Spheres* shows that Copernicus had still not fully broken with the Ptolemaic system in that he continued to believe in the existence of the spheres, though he reduced their number to thirty-four. In this he was, of course, wrong, but his book had delivered the first major blow against popular beliefs, and the calculations of subsequent astronomers only proved his fundamental correctness and his right to his life's work being known as the Copernican system.

The work of three men completed the destruction of the Ptolemaic system—Tycho Brahe (1546-1601), a Dane; Johann Kepler (1571-1630), a German; and Galileo Galilei (1564-1642), an Italian.

In 1576 Tycho Brahe was offered the island of Hven by his friend and patron King Frederick II of Denmark. Here he built an observatory surrounded by attractive gardens with a library, a printing-shop, a chemical laboratory, and an instrument workshop, christened by Tycho Brahe Uraniborg, the tower of Heaven. For twenty years he nightly made the most brilliant observations, having set himself the task of correcting through observation the mathematical errors in the calculations of Ptolemy and Copernicus. In the course of his observations two discoveries still further upset traditional ideas. In November 1572 a new star appeared in the constellation Cassiopeia, though according to Greek teaching no change was possible among the heavenly bodies. His calculations convinced him that a new star existed and therefore that the stars were subject to change. In 1577 a comet appeared. Hitherto comets had been explained as exhalations of the earth's atmosphere. Tycho Brahe proved that it must be more distant from the earth than was the moon and so ranked as a heavenly body. In 1597 Tycho Brahe, an ill-tempered man who readily attacked enemies, was forced to leave Uraniborg and in place of it to accept the emperor of Bohemia's offer of a new observatory in a castle near Prague. Here for the few remaining years of his life he was joined by Kepler.

The years that Kepler worked as Tycho Brahe's assistant were the only years in his life that he was not in acute financial worry. His father had lost what money he possessed, and at the age of 9 Kepler had to leave school and become a pot-boy in his father's tavern. Thanks to the help of friends, his schooling began again after three years and at the age of 17 he entered the university of Tübingen. Here his mathematical genius was recognized and in 1594 he became professor of mathematics at the university of Graz in Styria. This was not a well-paid post and his difficulties increased as a result of an unhappy marriage and the cares of a family. Furthermore, from early youth he had been dogged with poor health which had affected his eyesight. The value of the brief partnership between Tycho Brahe and Kepler lay in the fact that a brilliant observer and an outstanding mathematician joined forces.

Kepler is historically interesting as a man whose discoveries about how planets moved prepared the way for Newton, but who at the same time believed in astrology. When in 1612 he became professor at Linz he used to supplement his income by telling fortunes and by publishing a kind of *Old Moore's Almanack* predicting the future. Nevertheless, his first wife having died, Kepler preferred statistics to astrology when it came to solving the problem of choosing a new wife from eleven possible candidates.

Kepler's work was vitally important in two directions. In 1627 he discharged his promise to Tycho Brahe to complete the calculation which Tycho Brahe left unfinished at his death, and a new and far more accurate set of tables was published, which were a great help to navigators. Secondly, he continued his astronomical work in the Copernican tradition. Although reluctant to abandon his old beliefs, he was forced to conclude from his mathematics that heavenly bodies did not move in a perfect circle but in an ellipse. 'If you find this work difficult or wearisome to follow,' he wrote, 'take pity on me, for I have repeated these calculations seventy times, nor be surprised that I have spent five years on this theory of Mars.' Kepler's three laws of planetary motion belong to a full history of science and need not be stated here. In all he published some twenty volumes, much of his writing being useless nonsense. For example, he wrote that 'the heavenly motions are nothing but a continuous song for several voices'—Saturn was, apparently, a basso profundo, Jupiter a bass, Mars a tenor, Earth a contralto, Venus a soprano, and Mercury a counter-tenor! In view of this, as a modern writer has said: 'Not the least achievement of Newton was to spot the three laws in Kepler's writings, hidden away as they were like forget-me-nots in a tropical flowerbed.'

With the career of Galileo Galilei we are, scientifically, on the threshold of the modern world. He was born at Pisa in the same year as Shakespeare, went to the university there, and after nine years became professor of mathematics. Galileo quickly showed his characteristic qualities—a genius for experiment, a forceful pen when recording the facts which he discovered, and an intellectual integrity which prevented him from ever accepting long-held beliefs if his laboratory proved them to be fiction. It was therefore probable that before long he might be in trouble from Church authorities, since the old tolerance once extended to scholars had given place to the intolerance of the Counter-Reformation. When it is remembered that in all universities the doctrines of Aristotle were still being taught and accepted without question it was highly likely that an avowed Copernican and an experimenter who actually put Aristotle's statements about motion to the test would become the centre of controversy.

Several picturesque but probably untrue stories of Galileo's early days exist. It may be that a lamp swinging above his head in the cathedral at Pisa disturbed his devotions when a young man of 18 and led him to time the swings of the lamp by the beat of his own pulse, for no watch had yet been invented. At any rate then, or more likely later, he discovered the properties of the pendulum, finding that the time of a single swing remained the same whether the pendulum swung through a wider arc or a narrower one. Unfortunately there is no contemporary record of a legend which only appears some time after Galileo's death to the effect that he disproved Aristotle's contention that heavier bodies fall to the ground more quickly than lighter ones by dropping two different weights from the Leaning Tower of Pisa and showing that they reach the ground simultaneously. This experiment had in fact been carried out a few years earlier by Stevinus of Bruges, although Galileo, who took nothing on trust, probably repeated it for his own satisfaction. His experiments were mainly aimed at discovering not *why* bodies fall but *how* and they led him to an understanding of the principle of inertia, that is the tendency of a body to continue in uniform motion in a straight line and to resist a change of motion. In this way he destroyed the old belief that every motion on earth needed a continual force to maintain it. Other experiments proved that the path of a projectile was a parabola, a discovery of considerable practical importance in gunnery.

Although his work in mathematics and physics did not arouse religious controversy, Galileo's outspoken comments on the unscientific attitudes of his colleagues in the university made him very unpopular and in 1592 he moved to Padua, in the republic of Venice, where he was again professor of mathematics. Here he invented a thermometer, but his work in physics was soon overshadowed by his increasing interest in astronomy. So long as he remained in Venetian territory he was safe from attack as Venetian tolerance and support of its scholars was well known. Nevertheless, he probably exercised some caution at the start in view of the fate of Giordano Bruno, a noted philosopher, who had taught that the universe was infinitely vast and without any centre and that the innumerable stars were suns. Bruno had left the safety of Venice in 1593, was arrested and tried as a heretic in the following year, and in 1600 was burned to death by the Inquisition for refusing to recant his religious or scientific views.

However, in 1604 another brilliant new star appeared, making it impossible for those not blinded by prejudice to believe in Aristotle's unchanging heavens. Five years later the whole Ptolemaic system was destroyed, not by a continuation of the mathematical labours of Copernicus and Kepler, but by the accidental invention of the telescope. There is still some dispute as to the name of the inventor. Experiments with lenses had begun in the Middle Ages and in the sixteenth century spectacles were increasingly used. The most likely inventor was an apprentice, working for Hans Lippershey, a Dutch spectacle-maker from Middelburg, who chanced to arrange a combination of lenses which formed a primitive telescope. News of this reached Galileo, who, using his own vague knowledge of lenses and books on the structure of the eye, puzzled out how it could be made. Writing soon afterwards to a relative he said:

> . . . I set about contriving how to make it, and at length I found out, and have succeeded so well that the one I have made is far superior to the Dutch telescope. It was reported in Venice that I had made one, and a week since I was commanded to show it to his Serenity [the Doge] and to all the members of the Senate to their infinite amazement. Many gentlemen and senators, even the oldest, have ascended at various times the highest bell-towers in Venice to spy out ships at sea making sail for the mouth of the harbour, and have seen them clearly, though without my telescope they would have been invisible for more than two hours. The effect of this instrument is to show an object at a distance of say fifty miles, as if it were but five miles.

Galileo's salary was doubled.

It was one thing to look at ships, quite another thing to turn the telescope on to the night sky. Galileo was amazed at the number of new stars suddenly made visible and he realized that the Milky Way 'is nothing else but a mass of innumerable stars planted together in clusters'. The irregularity of the moon both in surface and in brilliance was revealed, as were sun-spots—an unacceptable blemish on the perfection of Creation. Perhaps most exciting of all was his study of Jupiter, an account of which he gave in his *Siderius Nuncius* ('The Starry Messenger'). An hour after sunset on the night of 7 January 1610 Galileo was looking through his telescope from the top of the campanile of St. Mark's in Venice, and happened to

A replica of Galileo's telescope.

notice three fixed stars near the planet Jupiter, two on one side and one on the other. By now he was so accustomed to discovering new stars that he thought little of it. By pure chance next night he again looked at Jupiter to find all three stars on the same side, to the west. Impatiently he waited for the next evening, only to be prevented from observation by thick cloud. Eventually on 11 January he saw only two stars; this time both were east of the planet. Two nights later he saw all four satellites of Jupiter and realized that like the earth Jupiter had a moon, or rather, four moons. What in fact he was looking at was the Copernican system in miniature.

Such exciting discoveries could not be kept to himself. All that Galileo asked of his critics was that they should look through his telescope and respect the evidence of their own eyes. His scorn for

A seventeenth-century Flemish painting in the National Gallery which shows the interest taken in voyages of discovery and scientific instruments to help navigators. Beautifully illustrated travel books, maps and a globe are shown as well as a compass, near the globe, and to his left an astrolabe. This was an instrument to enable a navigator to determine his position by taking a bearing on certain fixed stars.

their refusal even to look comes out in a letter which he wrote to Kepler: 'Oh, my dear Kepler, how I wish that we could have one hearty laugh together. Here at Padua is the principal professor of philosophy whom I have repeatedly and urgently requested to look at the moon and planets through my glass, which he pertinaciously refuses to do. Why are you not here? What shouts of laughter we should have at this glorious folly!' If some professors refused to look through a telescope, at least one monk did and confirmed Galileo's observation of sun-spots, which he reported to the superior of his Order. The reply which he received was: 'I have searched through Aristotle and can find nothing of the kind mentioned. Be assured, therefore, that it is a deception of your senses, or of your glasses.'

Later in 1610 Galileo, to the anger of the Venetians who had supported him and had doubled his salary, returned to his native Tuscany and settled in Florence where the Grand Duke made it possible for him to devote his entire time to research. Here he discovered the 'rings' of Saturn, began to study hydrostatistics, and wrote on how longitude might be determined. At the same time he never ceased to attack the ideas of Aristotle and Ptolemy, with the result that, no longer protected by Venice, he found himself in 1616 on pain of torture and imprisonment ordered 'to abandon and cease to teach his false, impious and heretical opinions'.

The years which followed his reluctant acceptance of this order were comparatively quiet and when in 1623 an old friend and supporter became Pope Urban VIII Galileo had good reason for thinking that, devout Christian as he was, his work could continue in safety. So he came to write the great book of his life *The Dialogues concerning the Two Chief Systems of the World*, which he got published in 1630. The book is in the form of a debate between Salviati, a supporter of Copernicus, and Simplicio, who upheld the views of Aristotle; a vague and benevolent chairman, Sagredo, held the ring. There was, however, little doubt that Salviati won all the arguments, and the situation for Galileo suddenly became dangerous when his enemies persuaded the pope that Simplicio was meant as a caricature of himself. All copies of the book were seized and Galileo was summoned to Rome to appear before the Inquisition. What followed is tragic but understandable. Galileo was now an old man whose health was beginning to fail; his friends urged him to yield and he probably needed little reminding of the fate of Bruno. In face of the power of the Inquisition his spirit broke and he made the famous recantation of all that he had taught and written about the nature of the heavens. The recantation was ordered to be read from every pulpit and in every university.

Galileo had nearly ten more years to live. He escaped imprisonment and was permitted to live in strict retirement near Florence.

As the years went by, friends and admirers were allowed to visit him and among them was Milton, who makes clear reference to him in *Paradise Lost*:

> . . . the moon, whose orb
> Through optic glass the Tuscan artist views
> At evening from the top of Fesole,
> Or in Valdarno to descry new lands,
> Rivers or mountains in her spotty globe.

His intellect remained clear, and it was in this last phase of his life that he wrote his *Dialogues on Motion*, which was printed in 1636 in Amsterdam. However, before long the deterioration in his health became more rapid and he lost both sight and hearing. In January 1642 death came to him as a friend. On the following Christmas Day Isaac Newton, the man who dominated the scientific revolution of the seventeenth century and who owed so much to Galileo, was born.

As can be seen, the Renaissance in science was a period of preparation for the great developments which were to come within the next half century. What matters is that, as in other spheres, the authority of the Church over men's minds had been decisively challenged. Bruno might be burned to death and Galileo be beaten to his knees, but no Inquisition could ultimately defeat the spirit of free inquiry. Medieval man had believed in a fixed universe with human beings at the heart and centre of the cosmic scheme of things. From the time of Copernicus onwards the idea of heaven as a 'place' above the skies to which the souls of faithful Christians went was no longer tenable. More important, man's own place in an increasingly vast universe became no longer a certainty but the subject of endless speculation.

Epilogue:
Authority and Challenge

In every period of history the old ways are challenged by new ideas and new discoveries. If this did not happen there would be no progress. The 300 years covered by this book saw the authority of long-accepted beliefs challenged as violently as at any other time. The idea of a united Christendom was shattered by the Reformation; lands which in the mid-sixteenth century adopted some form of Protestant faith remained Protestant and never returned to the Catholic Church. The very idea of any form of universal empire, whether ruled over by pope, emperor, or king of Spain, had been rejected in the course of savage fighting by the new nation states which, whether Catholic or Protestant, bowed to no superior authority. In a remarkably short period of time the whole world picture had been changed out of all recognition; while the discoveries of the astronomers were altering, rather frighteningly, man's idea of his own place in the universe.

Yet in spite of the deep divisions caused by religion and politics, Europe in 1600 remained a united continent, especially when facing the challenge of the Eastern form of civilization brought by the Turks. There was, however, a growing shift of importance from the south to the north; from the Mediterranean to the Atlantic. By the end of our period a new life and spirit seemed to be stirring in northern lands. The struggle for political liberty and the development of parliamentary government, the high importance attached to business and commerce and the rapid progress in scientific discovery were to mark northern Europe off from the southern countries in the coming century.

By no means everyone believed that all these changes were necessarily for the better. Rapid and violent change, the challenge to the authority of known and tried ways, do not make for comfort and ease. It is interesting to note how many of the great writers of the sixteenth century longed wistfully for a world of good order and harmony in place of the bitter divisions and discords which they saw around them. This sometimes led them to yearn for a return to a golden age of happiness and good government, a country life in which shepherds and shepherdesses looked after their flocks and at the same time managed to write poetry, sing love-songs, and play the flute. Such an age never existed except in their imagination, but the search for harmony whether in the ways that men were governed or in the movements of the planets absorbed much of their time and thoughts. Don Quixote was crack-brained, but Cervantes obviously wishes that the simple world in which his hero believed might exist. Montaigne hated the folly and savagery of the France in which he lived, but all that he could do, as we saw, was to retire to his tower and comment on the follies of men who did not realize the overriding need for order and good government. Greatest of all was Shakespeare with whom we end this book, a man typical of his age and yet one who belongs to all ages.

Shakespeare (1564–1616) was as true a patriot and as devoted a subject of the queen as any nation state could have wanted; he was also a marvellous poet whose theme was man's passions—love, hatred, jealousy, revenge, ambition. He knew that unless these passions were controlled, tragedy must follow. So, early in his career he wrote that series of historical plays spanning the reigns of English kings from Richard II to Richard III, plays full of superb poetry and insight into why men behave as they do, but also intended to point a moral. Peace and harmony, he is saying, can only come when the monarch holds unquestioned authority and every man knows his place in an ordered society. As he puts into the mouth of the pathetically weak Henry VI:

> Civil dissension is a viperous worm
> That gnaws the bowels of the commonwealth.

At times it almost seems that Shakespeare feared the new ideas which not only challenged the state but looked like upsetting the heavens. New notions must not be allowed to disturb the stars in their courses or chaos will come again. When he writes of these things his references are always to astrology, never to the new astronomy.

Yet it is not this reluctance to break with the past, nor his use of history to teach the lessons of good order that matter most. In the splendour of the great tragedies which he wrote in the first decade of the new century Shakespeare scaled the heights and plumbed the depths of human passion, of triumph and disaster. He was the first supremely great European poet to face the mystery of man's destiny without the consolation of any formal religious belief.

His plays show us to what heights the human spirit can rise and what man at his noblest can endure. No such writing would have been possible in 1300, for man was of little account and could only with luck find his way to heaven if he accepted the authority of the Church. Three centuries later, in unsurpassed poetry, Shakespeare proclaimed to the world the grandeur of man as he faced the challenge of the future.

Bibliography

I. GENERAL WORKS

There are the three series of massive books published by the Cambridge University Press:

1. *The Cambridge Medieval History*
   Vol. IV *The Byzantine Empire* (edited by J. M. Hussey) 2nd ed. 1967
   Vol. VII *The Decline of the Empire and Papacy* (edited by J. R. Tanner, C. W. Previté-Orton, and Z. N. Brooke) 1932
   Vol. VIII *The Close of the Middle Ages* (edited by J. R. Tanner, C. W. Previté-Orton, and Z. N. Brooke) 1936
2. *The New Cambridge Modern History*
   Vol. I *The Renaissance 1493-1520* (edited by G. R. Potter) 1957
   Vol. II *The Reformation 1520-1559* (edited by G. R. Elton) 1958
   Vol. III *Counter-Reformation and Price Revolution 1559-1610* (edited by R. B. Wernham) 1968
3. *The Cambridge Economic History of Europe*
   Vol. I *The Agrarian Life of the Middle Ages* (edited by M. M. Postan) 1966
   Vol. II *Trade and Industry in the Middle Ages* (edited by M. M. Postan and E. E. Rich) 1966
   Vol. III *Economic Organization and Policies in the Middle Ages* (edited by M. M. Postan, E. E. Rich, and E. Miller) 1963
   Vol. IV *The Economy of Expanding Europe in the Sixteenth and Seventeenth Centuries* (edited by E. E. Rich and C. H. Wilson) 1967

The Shorter Cambridge Medieval History, Vol. II *The Twelfth Century to the Renaissance* (edited by C. W. Previté-Orton) 1952

These volumes, though not always easy to read, provide a fund of information. Other and rather more digestible books can be found in the following series:

(i) *A History of Medieval and Modern Europe*, published by Methuen
   C. W. Previté-Orton, *A History of Europe 1198-1378* (1937)
   W. T. Waugh, *A History of Europe 1378-1494* (1932)
   A. J. Grant, *A History of Europe 1494-1610* (1931)
(ii) *A General History of Europe*, published by Longmans
   Denys Hay, *Europe in the Fourteenth and Fifteenth Centuries* (1966)
   H. G. Koenigsberger and George L. Mosse, *Europe in the Sixteenth Century* (1968)
(iii) *The Fontana History of Europe*, published by Collins. This starts at 1480.
   J. R. Hale, *Renaissance Europe 1480-1520* (1971)
   G. R. Elton, *Reformation Europe 1517-1559* (1963)
   J. H. Elliott, *Europe Divided 1559-1598* (1968)

H. A. L. Fisher's *A History of Europe* (Eyre and Spottiswoode, 1935) remains very readable, as does J. M. Thompson's *Lectures in Foreign History* (republished by Blackwell in 1959). C. N. Routh, *They Saw it Happen in Europe 1450-1600* (Blackwell, 1965) is an excellent collection of documents for the second half of the period.

II. NATIONAL HISTORIES

These vary greatly in length and interest, but they are all valuable additions to the list of General Works.

(1) *France*

The monumental *Histoire de France* by Ernest Lavisse, published by Hachette in many volumes during the first decade of this century, must be given pride of place.

Simpler works are:

The National History of France, published, in translation, by Heinemann

F. Funck-Brentano: *The Middle Ages* (1922)

L. Batifol: *The Century of the Renaissance* (1916)

André Maurois: *A History of France* (Cape, 1949)

Charles Seignobos: *A History of the French People* (Cape, 1933)

J. A. R. Marriott: *A Short History of France* (Methuen, 1942)

(2) *England*

By far the best series of volumes are those contained in the *Oxford History of England* published by the Clarendon Press. The relevant volumes are:

May McKisack: *The Fourteenth Century 1307–1399* (1959)

E. F. Jacob: *The Fifteenth Century 1399–1485* (1961)

J. D. Mackie: *The Earlier Tudors 1485–1558* (1952)

J. B. Black: *The Reign of Elizabeth 1558–1603* (1959)

(3) *Spain*

W. H. Prescott's *History of the Reign of Ferdinand and Isabella* though published by George Routledge as long ago as 1837 is still a valuable work with much interesting material in it.

The two most up-to-date general histories of Spain are:

J. H. Elliott: *Imperial Spain 1469–1716* (Edward Arnold, 1963)

J. Lynch: *Spain under the Hapsburgs* Vol. I (Blackwell, 1964)

For works dealing with the history of Italy, the Netherlands, Germany, and the Ottoman empire reference should be made to the book lists which now follow for each chapter.

III. ADDITIONAL READING TO EACH CHAPTER

Prologue: The Holy Year

T. S. R. Boase: *Boniface VIII* (Constable, 1933)

Alan Kendall: *Medieval Pilgrims* (Wayland Documentary Histories, 1970)

Dante: *The Divine Comedy* (the translation used is that by Dorothy L. Sayers, Penguin, 1949)

1. *The Church under Attack 1300–1450*

Geoffrey Barraclough: *The Medieval Papacy* (Thames and Hudson, 1968)

Yves Renouard: *The Avignon Papacy 1305–1403* (Faber, 1970)

Friedrich Goutard: *The Popes* (Barrie and Rockcliff, 1959)

2. *A Hundred Years of Fighting*

(i) *How men fought*

C. W. C. Oman: *A History of the Art of War in the Middle Ages* (Methuen, 1924)

Richard Barber: *The Knight and Chivalry* (Longmans, 1970)

Geoffrey Hindley: *Medieval Warfare* (Wayland, 1971)

Dudley Pope: *Guns* (Weidenfeld and Nicolson, 1965)

(ii) *French and English 1328–1380*

A. H. Burne: *The Crecy War* (Eyre and Spottiswoode, 1955)

(iii) *French, English, and Burgundians 1380–1461*

E. F. Jacob: *Henry V and the Invasion of France* (Hodder and Stoughton, 1947)

A. H. Burne: *The Agincourt War* (Eyre and Spottiswoode, 1956)

Christopher Hibbert: *Agincourt* (Batsford, 1964)

Alice Buchan: *Joan of Arc and the Recovery of France* (Hodder and Stoughton, 1948)

A. L. Rowse: *Bosworth Field* (Macmillan, 1966)

3. *The King's Majesty*

For the story of the Italian *condottieri* there is an excellent, recent book:

Geoffrey Trease: *The Condottieri: Soldiers of Fortune* (Thames and Hudson, 1970)

4. *Living and Working*

A. R. Myres: *England in the Late Middle Ages* (Pelican, 1952)

D. Waley: *Later Medieval Europe* (Longmans Green, 1964)

M. Block: *Feudal Society* (Routledge and Kegal Paul, 1962), particularly the last section.

E. Power: *Medieval People* (C.U.P., 1970; also Pelican series)

E. R. Chamberlain: *Life in Medieval France* (Batsford, 1967)

Joan Evans (ed.): *The Flowering of the Middle Ages* (Thames and Hudson, 1967)

R. S. Lopez and I. W. Raymond: *Medieval Trade in the Mediterranean World* (Columbia University Press, 1955)

E. R. Chamberlain: *Everyday Life in Renaissance Times* (Batsford, 1965)

Shakespeare's England (O.U.P., 1916)

A. Fremantle: *The Age of Faith*

E. Simon: *The Reformation*

(both in the 'Great Ages of Man Series', Times Inc., 1970, with excellent illustrations)

Horizon Book of the Elizabethan World (Paul Hamlyn, 1967)

C. Wienen: *Trades and Crafts* (Wayland, 1972)

G. Duby: *Rural Economy and Country Life in the Medieval West* (Edward Arnold, 1968), particularly the last section.

Maurice Beresford: *New Towns of the Middle Ages* (Lutterworth, 1967)

P. Lindsay and R. Groves: *The Peasants' Revolt of 1381* (Hutchinson, 1950)

G. Deaux: *The Black Death* (Hamish Hamilton, 1969)

P. Weigler: *The Black Death* (Collins, 1969)

William Anderson: *European Castles* (Elek, 1970), sound text and excellent illustrations.

A. T. P. Byles (ed.): *The Boke of the Order of Chyvalry* (Early Eng. Text Society, 1926)

G. W. Anderson (ed.): *The Chronicles of Froissart* (Centaur, 1963)

H. S. Bennett: *The Pastons and their England* (C.U.P., 1970)

The Paston Letters, ed. N. Davis (O.U.P., 1958; also in Everyman edition)

5. *'Timor mortis conturbat me'*

Roger Hart: *Witchcraft* (Wayland, 1971)

Christina Hole: *A Mirror of Witchcraft* (Chatto and Windus, 1957)

H. Trevor-Roper: *The European Witch Craze of the Sixteenth and Seventeenth Centuries* (Pelican, 1969)

6. *Renaissance in Italy*

With the excellence of modern photographic reproduction the number of books on the Renaissance is vast. In addition to volumes on individual artists produced by the Phaidon Press there are:

E. Gombrich: *The Story of Art* (Phaidon Press, 1950)

Kenneth Clark: *Civilisation* (BBC and John Murray, 1969)

Denys Hay (ed.): *The Age of the Renaissance* (Thames and Hudson, 1967)

Kenneth Clark: *Leonardo da Vinci* (Pelican edn., 1959)

Christine Price: *Made in the Renaissance* (Bodley Head, 1963)

E. R. Chamberlin: *Everyday Life in Renaissance Times* (Batsford, 1965)

J. H. Plumb: *The Penguin Book of the Renaissance* (Penguin Books, 1964)

Vincent Cronin: *The Florentine Renaissance* (Collins, 1967)

Vincent Cronin: *The Flowering of the Renaissance* (Collins, 1969)

Marcel Brion: *The Medici* (Elek Books, 1969)

7. *The Empire of Charles V*

Karl Brandi: *The Emperor Charles V* (translated C. V. Wedgwood) (Cape, 1939)

Anne Denieul-Cormier: *The Renaissance in France 1488–1559* (translated A. and C. Fremantle) (Allen and Unwin, 1969)

8. *The Reformation: the Church torn apart*

Norman Sykes: *The Crisis of the Reformation* (Unicorn Press, 1938)

R. D. Jones: *Erasmus and Luther*, Clarendon Biographies (O.U.P., 1968)

M. M. Phillips: *Erasmus and the Northern Renaissance* (English Universities Press, 1949)

Margaret Aston: *The Fifteenth Century: The Prospect of Europe* (Thames and Hudson, 1968)

R. Bainton: *Here I Stand* (Hodder and Stoughton, 1951)

V. H. H. Green: *Luther and the Reformation* (Batsford, 1964)

A. G. Dickens: *Reformation and Society in Sixteenth Century Europe* (Thames and Hudson, 1966)

L. W. Cowie: *The Reformation in the Sixteenth Century* (Wayland, 1970)

9. *'Turks, Infidels and Hereticks'*

Paul Coles: *The Ottoman Impact on Europe* (Thames and Hudson, 1968)

Steven Runciman: *The Fall of Constantinople: 1453* (C.U.P., 1965)

10. *Russia, 'signories unknowne'*

Georg Vernadsky: *History of Russia* (Yale University Press, 1929; also paperback edition, Bantam Matrix, 1961)

J. D. Clarkson: *History of Russia from the Ninth Century* (Longmans, 1962)

J. L. I. Fennell: *Russia 1462–1583*, Vol. II *New Cambridge Modern History* (C.U.P., 1961)

B. Pares: *History of Russia* (Jonathan Cape, 1947)

★S. H. Cross (ed.): *The Russian Primary Chronicle* (O.U.P., 1932)

★R. Hakluyt: *Early Voyages and Travels to Russia and Persia* (Everyman edition)

★E. A. Bond (ed.): *Russia at Close of the Sixteenth Century* (Hakluyt Society, 1856)

11. *The Church strikes back: the Counter-Reformation* (as for Chapter 8)

B. J. Kidd: *The Counter Reformation* (S.P.C.K., 1933)

A. S. Turberville: *The Spanish Inquisition* (Thornton Butterworth, 1932)

12. *The Age of Philip II*

Trevor Davies: *The Golden Century of Spain* (Macmillan, 1937)

R. Altamira: *A History of Spanish Civilisation* (Constable, 1930)

J. E. Neale: *The Age of Catherine de Medici* (Cape, 1943)

J. L. Motley: *The Rise of the Dutch Republic* (Routledge, 1871)

P. Geyl: *The Revolt of the Netherlands* (Benn, 1958)

W. Wedgwood: *William the Silent* (Cape, 1944)

G. Mattingly: *The Defeat of the Spanish Armada* (Cape, 1959)

13. *New Horizons*

(i) *Voyages of Discovery*

J. H. Parry: *The Age of Reconnaissance* (Weidenfeld and Nicolson, 1963)

P. Richardson: *The Expansion of Europe 1400-1660* (Wymans, 1966)

(ii) *Science*

A. E. E. McKenzie: *The Major Achievements of Science*, Vol. I (C.U.P., 1960)

A. Butterfield: *The Origins of Modern Science* (Bell, 1962)

Shorter books suitable for individual work on topics

W. O. Hassall (ed.): *They Saw it Happen, 55 B.C.–1485* (Blackwell, 1963)

C. R. N. Routh (ed.): *They Saw it Happen, 1485-1688* (Blackwell, 1956)

——: *They Saw it Happen in Europe, 1450-1600* (Blackwell, 1965)

M. Harrison and M. Royston: *How They Lived, 1485-1700* (Blackwell, 1963)

People of the Past Series (O.U.P.):

C. Harnett: *A Fifteenth Century Wool Merchant* (1962)

F. Makower: *A Fifteenth Century London Housewife* (1965)

——: *A Sixteenth Century Clothworker* (1962)

B. Richmond: *A Band of Beggars and Rogues* (1966)

H. Richardson: *An Elizabethan Lady of the Manor* (1963)

E. J. Boog-Watson: *An Elizabethan Sailor* (1964)

Index

Index